Microsoft® Official Academic Course

Microsoft Outlook 2010, EXAM 77-884

WILEY

EDITOR	Bryan Gambrel
DIRECTOR OF SALES	Mitchell Beaton
EXECUTIVE MARKETING MANAGER	Chris Ruel
ASSISTANT MARKETING MANAGER	Debbie Martin
MICROSOFT STRATEGIC RELATIONSHIPS MANAGER	Merrick Van Dongen of Microsoft Learning
EDITORIAL PROGRAM ASSISTANT	Jennifer Lartz
CONTENT MANAGERS	Micheline Frederick, Kevin Holm
PRODUCTION EDITOR	Amy Weintraub
CREATIVE DIRECTOR	Harry Nolan
COVER DESIGNER	Jim O'Shea
INTERIOR DESIGNER	Amy Rosen
PHOTO EDITORS	Sheena Goldstein, Jennifer MacMillan
EXECUTIVE MEDIA EDITOR	Tom Kulesa
MEDIA EDITOR	Wendy Ashenberg

This book was set in Garamond by Aptara, Inc. and printed and bound by Courier/Kendallville. The covers were printed by Lehigh Phoenix.

Founded in 1807, John Wiley & Sons, Inc. has been a valued source of knowledge and understanding for more than 200 years, helping people around the world meet their needs and fulfill their aspirations. Our company is built on a foundation of principles that include responsibility to the communities we serve and where we live and work. In 2008, we launched a Corporate Citizenship Initiative, a global effort to address the environmental, social, economic, and ethical challenges we face in our business. Among the issues we are addressing are carbon impact, paper specifications and procurement, ethical conduct within our business and among our vendors, and community and charitable support. For more information, please visit our website: www.wiley.com/go/citizenship.

ISBN 978-0-470-90851-8

Printed in the United States of America

10 9 8 7 6 5 4 3 2

Wiley's publishing vision for the Microsoft Official Academic Course series is to provide students and instructors with the skills and knowledge they need to use Microsoft technology effectively in all aspects of their personal and professional lives. Quality instruction is required to help both educators and students get the most from Microsoft's software tools and to become more productive. Thus our mission is to make our instructional programs trusted educational companions for life.

To accomplish this mission, Wiley and Microsoft have partnered to develop the highest quality educational programs for information workers, IT professionals, and developers. Materials created by this partnership carry the brand name "Microsoft Official Academic Course," assuring instructors and students alike that the content of these textbooks is fully endorsed by Microsoft, and that they provide the highest quality information and instruction on Microsoft products. The Microsoft Official Academic Course textbooks are "Official" in still one more way—they are the officially sanctioned courseware for Microsoft IT Academy members.

The Microsoft Official Academic Course series focuses on *workforce development*. These programs are aimed at those students seeking to enter the workforce, change jobs, or embark on new careers as information workers, IT professionals, and developers. Microsoft Official Academic Course programs address their needs by emphasizing authentic workplace scenarios with an abundance of projects, exercises, cases, and assessments.

The Microsoft Official Academic Courses are mapped to Microsoft's extensive research and job-task analysis, the same research and analysis used to create the Microsoft Office Specialist (MOS) exams. The textbooks focus on real skills for real jobs. As students work through the projects and exercises in the textbooks, they enhance their level of knowledge and their ability to apply the latest Microsoft technology to everyday tasks. These students also gain resume-building credentials that can assist them in finding a job, keeping their current job, or furthering their education.

The concept of lifelong learning is today an utmost necessity. Job roles and even whole job categories are changing so quickly that none of us can stay competitive and productive without continuously updating our skills and capabilities. The Microsoft Official Academic Course offerings, and their focus on Microsoft certification exam preparation, provide a means for people to acquire and effectively update their skills and knowledge. Wiley supports students in this endeavor through the development and distribution of these courses as Microsoft's official academic publisher.

Today educational publishing requires attention to providing quality print and robust electronic content. By integrating Microsoft Official Academic Course products, *WileyPLUS*, and Microsoft certifications, we are better able to deliver efficient learning solutions for students and teachers alike.

Joseph Heider
General Manager and Senior Vice President

Welcome to the Microsoft Official Academic Course (MOAC) program for Microsoft Office 2010. MOAC is the collaboration between Microsoft Learning and John Wiley & Sons, Inc. publishing company. Microsoft and Wiley teamed up to produce a series of textbooks that deliver compelling and innovative teaching solutions to instructors and superior learning experiences for students. Infused and informed by in-depth knowledge from the creators of Microsoft Office and Windows, and crafted by a publisher known worldwide for the pedagogical quality of its products, these textbooks maximize skills transfer in minimum time. Students are challenged to reach their potential by using their new technical skills as highly productive members of the workforce.

Because this knowledge base comes directly from Microsoft, architect of Office 2010 and creator of the Microsoft Office Specialist (MOS) exams (www.microsoft.com/learning/mcp/msbc), you are sure to receive the topical coverage that is most relevant to students' personal and professional success. Microsoft's direct participation not only assures you that MOAC textbook content is accurate and current; it also means that students will receive the best instruction possible to make them successful on certification exams and in the workplace.

THE MICROSOFT OFFICIAL ACADEMIC COURSE PROGRAM

The Microsoft Official Academic Course series is a complete program for instructors and institutions to prepare and deliver great courses on Microsoft software technologies. With MOAC, we recognize that, because of the rapid pace of change in the technology and curriculum developed by Microsoft, there is an ongoing set of needs beyond classroom instruction tools for an instructor to be ready to teach the course. The MOAC program endeavors to provide solutions for all these needs in a systematic manner in order to ensure a successful and rewarding course experience for both instructor and student—technical and curriculum training for instructor readiness with new software releases; the software itself for student use at home for building hands-on skills, assessment, and validation of skill development; and a great set of tools for delivering instruction in the classroom and lab. All are important to the smooth delivery of an interesting course on Microsoft software, and all are provided with the MOAC program. We think about the model below as a gauge for ensuring that we completely support you in your goal of teaching a great course. As you evaluate your instructional materials options, you may wish to use the model for comparison purposes with available products.

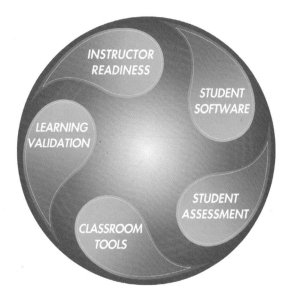

www.wiley.com/college/microsoft
or call the MOAC Toll-Free Number: 1+(888) 764-7001 (U.S. & Canada only)

PEDAGOGICAL FEATURES

The MOAC textbooks for Microsoft Office 2010 are designed to cover all the learning objectives for the MOS exam, which is referred to as its exam objective. The Microsoft Office Specialist (MOS) exam objectives are highlighted throughout the textbooks. Many pedagogical features have been developed specifically for Microsoft Official Academic Course programs. Unique features of our task-based approach include a Lesson Skill Matrix that correlates skills taught in each lesson to the MOS objectives; Certification, Workplace, and Internet Ready exercises; and three levels of increasingly rigorous lesson-ending activities, Competency, Proficiency, and Mastery Assessment.

Presenting the extensive procedural information and technical concepts woven throughout the textbook raises challenges for the student and instructor alike. The Illustrated Book Tour that follows provides a guide to the rich features contributing to the Microsoft Official Academic Course program's pedagogical plan. Following is a list of key features in each lesson designed to prepare students for success on the certification exams and in the workplace:

- Each lesson begins with a **Lesson Skill Matrix.** More than a standard list of learning objectives, the skill matrix correlates each software skill covered in the lesson to the specific MOS exam objective domain.

- Each lesson features a real-world **Business Case** scenario that places the software skills and knowledge to be acquired in a real-world setting.

- Every lesson opens with a **Software Orientation.** This feature provides an overview of the software features students will be working with in the lesson. The orientation details the general properties of the software or specific features, such as a ribbon or dialog box; and it includes a large, labeled screen image.

- Concise and frequent **Step-by-Step** instructions teach students new features and provide an opportunity for hands-on practice. Numbered steps give detailed instructions to help students learn software skills. The steps also show results and screen images to match what students should see on their computer screens.

- **Illustrations** provide visual feedback as students work through the exercises. The images reinforce key concepts, provide visual clues about the steps, and allow students to check their progress.

- When the text instructs a student to click a particular button, **button images** are shown in the margin or in the text.

- Important technical vocabulary is listed in the **Key Terms** section at the beginning of the lesson. When these terms are used later in the lesson, they appear in bold italic type with yellow highlighter and are defined. The Glossary contains all of the key terms and their definitions.

- Engaging point-of-use **Reader aids**, located throughout the lessons, tell students why this topic is relevant (*The Bottom Line*), provide students with helpful hints (*Take Note*), show alternate ways to accomplish tasks (*Another Way*), or point out things to watch out for or avoid (*Troubleshooting*). Reader aids also provide additional relevant or background information that adds value to the lesson.

- **Certification Ready** features throughout the text signal students where a specific certification objective is covered. They provide students with a chance to check their understanding of that particular MOS exam objective and, if necessary, review the section of the lesson where it is covered. MOAC provides complete preparation for MOS certification.

- The **New Feature** icon appears near any software feature that is new in Office 2010.

- Each lesson ends with a **Skill Summary** recapping the MOS exam skills covered in the lesson.

- The **Knowledge Assessment** section provides a total of 20 questions from a mix of True/False, Fill-in-the-Blank, Matching or Multiple Choice testing students on concepts learned in the lesson.

- **Competency, Proficiency, and Mastery Assessment** sections provide progressively more challenging lesson-ending activities.

- **Internet Ready** projects combine the knowledge that students acquire in a lesson with Web-based task research.

- Integrated **Circling Back** projects provide students with an opportunity to renew and practice skills learned in previous lessons.

- **Workplace Ready** features preview how Microsoft Office 2010 applications are used in real-world situations.

- The student companion website contains the **online files** needed for each lesson. These data files are indicated by the @ icon in the margin of the textbook.

LESSON FEATURES

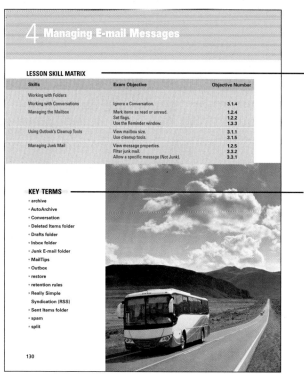

Lesson Skill Matrix

Key Terms

Software Orientation

Business Scenario

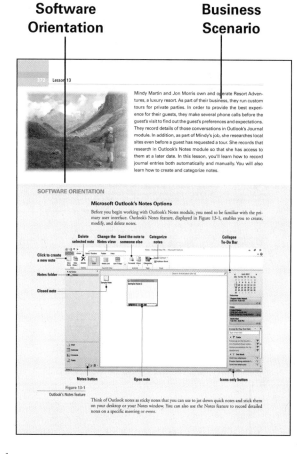

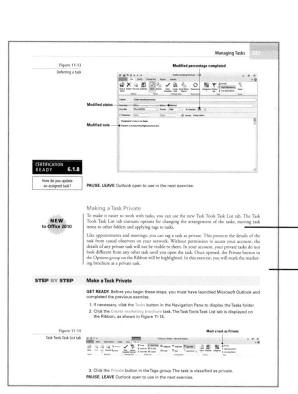

New Features

Step-by-step Exercises

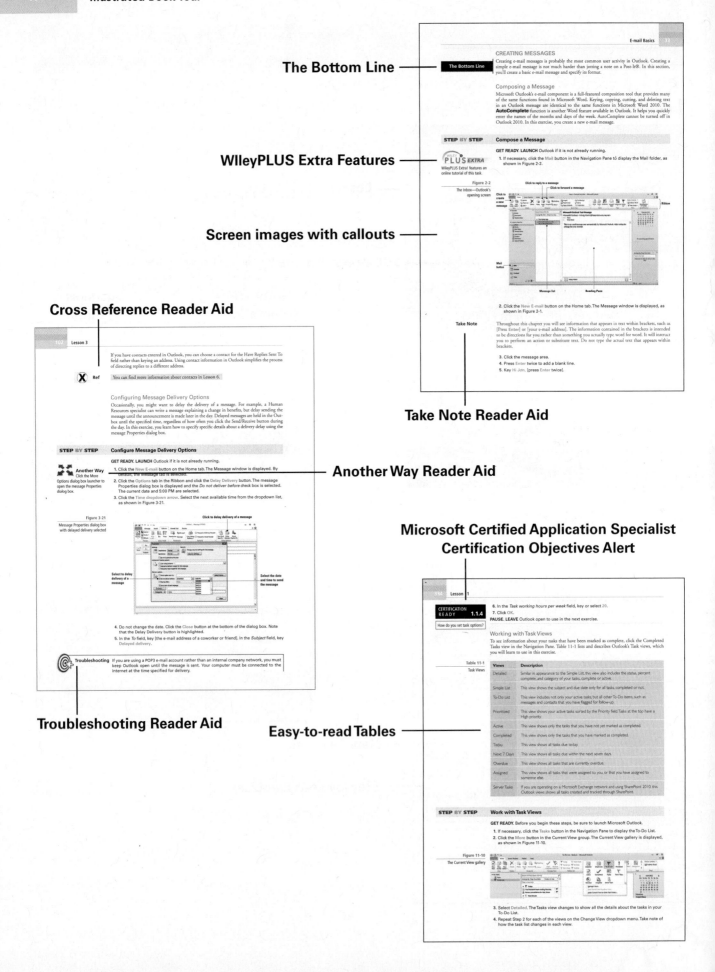

The Bottom Line

WlleyPLUS Extra Features

Screen images with callouts

Cross Reference Reader Aid

Take Note Reader Aid

Another Way Reader Aid

Microsoft Certified Application Specialist
Certification Objectives Alert

Troubleshooting Reader Aid

Easy-to-read Tables

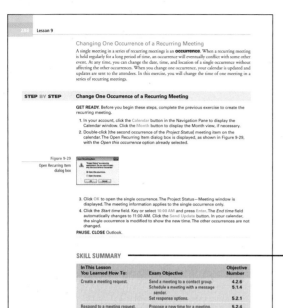

Changing One Occurrence of a Recurring Meeting

A single meeting in a series of recurring meetings is an **occurrence**. When a recurring meeting is held regularly for a long period of time, an occurrence will eventually conflict with some other event. At any time, you can change the date, time, and location of a single occurrence without affecting the other occurrences. When you change one occurrence, your calendar is updated and updates are sent to the attendees. In this exercise, you will change the time of one meeting in a series of recurring meetings.

STEP BY STEP   Change One Occurrence of a Recurring Meeting

GET READY. Before you begin these steps, complete the previous exercise to create the recurring meeting.

1. In your account, click the Calendar button in the Navigation Pane to display the Calendar window. Click the Month button to display the Month view, if necessary.
2. Double-click [the second occurrence of the Project Status] meeting item on the calendar. The Open Recurring Item dialog box is displayed, as shown in Figure 9-29, with the Open this occurrence option already selected.

Figure 9-29
Open Recurring Item dialog box

3. Click OK to open the single occurrence. The Project Status—Meeting window is displayed. The meeting information applies to the single occurrence only.
4. Click the Start time field. Key or select 10:00 AM and press Enter. The End time field automatically changes to 11:00 AM. Click the Send Update button. In your calendar, the single occurrence is modified to show the new time. The other occurrences are not changed.
PAUSE. CLOSE Outlook.

SKILL SUMMARY ───────────────────────── **Summary Skill Matrix**

In This Lesson You Learned How To:	Exam Objective	Objective Number
Create a meeting request.	Send a meeting to a contact group.	4.2.6
	Schedule a meeting with a message sender.	5.1.4
	Set response options.	5.2.1
Respond to a meeting request.	Propose a new time for a meeting.	5.2.4
Managing a meeting.		
Updating a meeting request.	Update a meeting request.	5.2.2
	Cancel a meeting or invitation.	5.2.3
Managing a recurring meeting.		

Knowledge Assessment

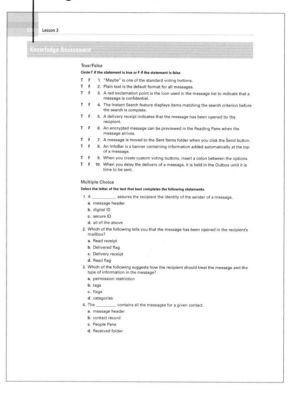

Knowledge Assessment

True/False

Circle T if the statement is true or F if the statement is false.

T F 1. "Maybe" is one of the standard voting buttons.
T F 2. Plain text is the default format for all messages.
T F 3. A red exclamation point is the icon used in the message list to indicate that a message is confidential.
T F 4. The Instant Search feature displays items matching the search criterion before the search is complete.
T F 5. A delivery receipt indicates that the message has been opened by the recipient.
T F 6. An encrypted message can be previewed in the Reading Pane when the message arrives.
T F 7. A message is moved to the Sent Items folder when you click the Send button.
T F 8. An InfoBar is a banner containing information added automatically at the top of a message.
T F 9. When you create custom voting buttons, insert a colon between the options.
T F 10. When you delay the delivery of a message, it is held in the Outbox until it is time to be sent.

Multiple Choice

Select the letter of the text that best completes the following statements.

1. A _____ assures the recipient the identity of the sender of a message.
   a. message header
   b. digital ID
   c. secure ID
   d. all of the above
2. Which of the following tells you that the message has been opened in the recipient's mailbox?
   a. Read receipt
   b. Delivered flag
   c. Delivery receipt
   d. Read flag
3. Which of the following suggests how the recipient should treat the message and the type of information in the message?
   a. permission restriction
   b. tags
   c. flags
   d. categories
4. The _____ contains all the messages for a given contact.
   a. message header
   b. contact record
   c. People Pane
   d. Received folder

Competency Assessment

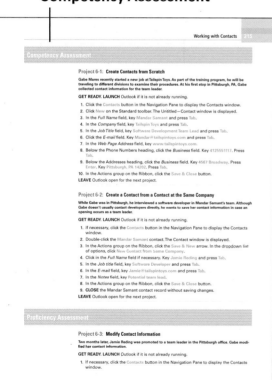

Competency Assessment

Project 6-1: Create Contacts from Scratch

Gabe Mares recently started a new job at Tailspin Toys. As part of the training program, he will be traveling to different divisions to examine their procedures. At his first stop in Pittsburgh, PA, Gabe collected contact information for the team leader.

GET READY. LAUNCH Outlook if it is not already running.

1. Click the Contacts button in the Navigation Pane to display the Contacts window.
2. Click New on the Standard toolbar. The Untitled—Contact window is displayed.
3. In the Full Name field, key Mandar Samant and press Tab.
4. In the Company field, key Tailspin Toys and press Tab.
5. In the Job Title field, key Software Development Team Lead and press Tab.
6. Click the E-mail field. Key Mandar@tailspintoys.com and press Tab.
7. In the Web Page Address field, key www.tailspintoys.com.
8. Below the Phone Numbers heading, click the Business field. Key 4125551117. Press Tab.
9. Below the Addresses heading, click the Business field. Key 4567 Broadway. Press Enter. Key Pittsburgh, PA 14202. Press Tab.
10. In the Actions group on the Ribbon, click the Save & Close button.
LEAVE Outlook open for the next project.

Project 6-2: Create a Contact from a Contact at the Same Company

While Gabe was in Pittsburgh, he interviewed a software developer in Mandar Samant's team. Although Gabe doesn't usually contact developers directly, he wants to save her contact information in case an opening occurs as a team leader.

GET READY. LAUNCH Outlook if it is not already running.

1. If necessary, click the Contacts button in the Navigation Pane to display the Contacts window.
2. Double-click the Mandar Samant contact. The Contact window is displayed.
3. In the Actions group on the Ribbon, click the Save & New arrow. In the dropdown list of options, click New Contact from Same Company.
4. Click in the Full Name field if necessary. Key Jamie Reding and press Tab.
5. In the Job title field, key Software Developer and press Tab.
6. In the E-mail field, key Jamie@tailspintoys.com and press Tab.
7. In the Notes field, key Potential team lead.
8. In the Actions group on the Ribbon, click the Save & Close button.
9. **CLOSE** the Mandar Samant contact record without saving changes.
LEAVE Outlook open for the next project.

Proficiency Assessment

Project 6-3: Modify Contact Information

Two months later, Jamie Reding was promoted to a team leader in the Pittsburgh office. Gabe modified her contact information.

GET READY. LAUNCH Outlook if it is not already running.

1. If necessary, click the Contacts button in the Navigation Pane to display the Contacts window.

Proficiency Assessment

Mastery Assessment

Online Files

Circling Back Excercises

Internet Ready

Workplace Ready

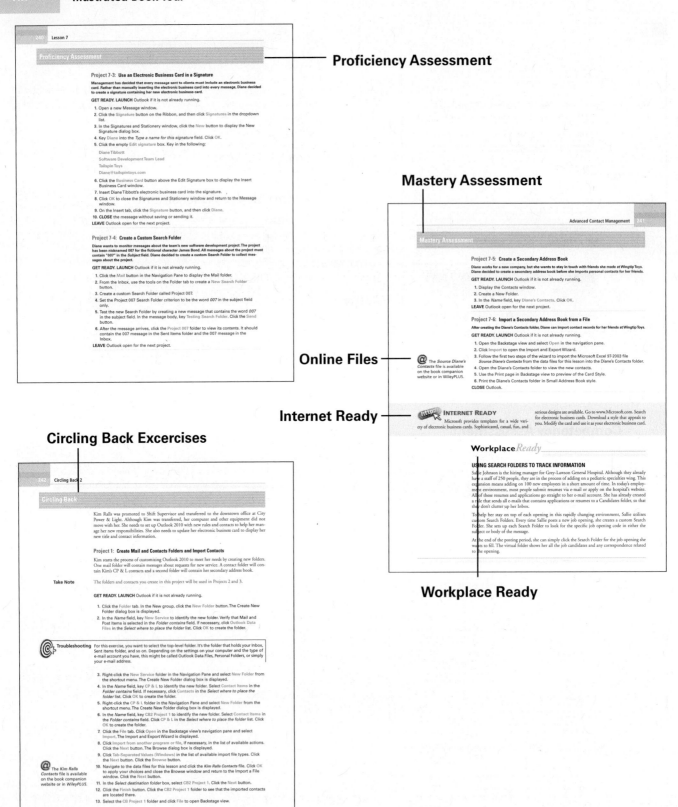

Conventions and Features Used in This Book

This book uses particular fonts, symbols, and heading conventions to highlight important information or to call your attention to special steps. For more information about the features in each lesson, refer to the Illustrated Book Tour section.

NEW to Office 2010

This icon indicates a new or greatly improved Windows feature in this version of the software.

The Bottom Line

This feature provides a brief summary of the material to be covered in the section that follows.

CLOSE

Words in all capital letters indicate instructions for opening, saving, or closing files or programs. They also point out items you should check or actions you should take.

CERTIFICATION READY

This feature signals the point in the text where a specific certification objective is covered. It provides you with a chance to check your understanding of that particular MOS objective and, if necessary, review the section of the lesson where it is covered.

Take Note

Take Note reader aids, set in red text, provide helpful hints related to particular tasks or topics.

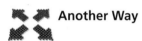 **Another Way**

Another Way provides an alternative procedure for accomplishing a particular task.

 Ref

These notes, set in gray shaded boxes, provide pointers to information discussed elsewhere in the textbook or describe interesting features that are not directly addressed in the current topic or exercise.

Alt + Tab

A plus sign (+) between two key names means that you must press both keys at the same time. Keys that you are instructed to press in an exercise will appear in the font shown here.

Key terms

Key terms appear in bold with highlighting.

Key My Name is

Any text you are asked to key appears in color.

Click OK

Any button on the screen you are supposed to click on or select will also appear in color.

Budget Worksheet 1

The names of data files will appear in red, bold, and italic, for easy identification.

The *Microsoft Official Academic Course* programs are accompanied by a rich array of resources that incorporate the extensive textbook visuals to form a pedagogically cohesive package. These resources provide all the materials instructors need to deploy and deliver their courses. The following resources are available online for download.

- The **Instructor's Guide** contains solutions to all the textbook exercises as well as chapter summaries and lecture notes. The Instructor's Guide and Syllabi for various term lengths are available from the Instructor's Book Companion site (www.wiley.com/college/microsoft).

- The **Solution Files** for all the projects in the book are available online from our Instructor's Book Companion site (www.wiley.com/college/microsoft).

- The **Test Bank** contains hundreds of questions organized by lesson in multiple-choice, true/false, short answer, and essay formats and is available to download from the Instructor's Book Companion site (www.wiley.com/college/microsoft). A complete answer key is provided.

    This title's test bank is available for use in easy-to-use Respondus software. You can download the test bank free using your Respondus, Respondus LE, or StudyMate Author software.

    Respondus is a powerful tool for creating and managing exams that can be printed to paper or published directly to Blackboard, WebCT, Desire2Learn, eCollege, ANGEL, and other eLearning systems.

- A complete set of **PowerPoint Presentations** is available on the Instructor's Book Companion site (www.wiley.com/college/microsoft) to enhance classroom presentations. Tailored to the text's topical coverage and Skills Matrix, these presentations are designed to convey key Microsoft Office 2010 concepts addressed in the text.

    All **images** from the text are on the Instructor's Book Companion site (www.wiley.com/college/microsoft). You can incorporate them into your PowerPoint presentations, or create your own overhead transparencies and handouts.

    By using these visuals in class discussions, you can help focus students' attention on key elements of Office 2010 and help them understand how to use it effectively in the workplace.

- The **MSDN Academic Alliance** is designed to provide the easiest and most inexpensive developer tools, products, and technologies available to faculty and students in labs and classrooms, and on student PCs. A free three-year membership is available to qualified MOAC adopters.

- **Office Grader** automated grading system allows you to easily grade student data files in Word, Excel, PowerPoint, or Access format, against solution files. Save tens or hundreds of hours each semester with automated grading. More information on Office Grader is available from the Instructor's Book Companion site (www.wiley.com/college/microsoft).

- The **Student Data Files** are available online on both the Instructor's Book Companion site and for students on the Student Book Companion site.

- Microsoft Official Academic Course books can be bundled with MOS exam vouchers from Certiport and MOS practice tests from GMetrix LLC or Certiport, available as a single bundle from Wiley, to create a **complete certification solution**. Instructors who use MOAC courseware in conjunction with a practice MOS exam find their students best-prepared for the MOS certification exam. Providing your students with the MOS exam voucher in addition, is the ultimate workforce preparation.

- When it comes to improving the classroom experience, there is no better source of ideas and inspiration than your colleagues. The **Wiley Faculty Network** connects teachers with technology, facilitates the exchange of best practices, and helps enhance instructional efficiency and effectiveness. Faculty Network activities include technology training and tutorials, virtual seminars, peer-to-peer exchanges of experiences and ideas, personal consulting, and sharing of resources. For details, visit www.WhereFacultyConnect.com.

WILEYPLUS

Broad developments in education over the past decade have influenced the instructional approach taken in the Microsoft Official Academic Course programs. The way that students learn, especially about new technologies, has changed dramatically in the Internet era. Electronic learning materials and Internet-based instruction are now as much a part of classroom instruction as printed textbooks. WileyPLUS provides the technology to create an environment where students reach their full potential and experience academic success that will last a lifetime.

WileyPLUS is a powerful and highly integrated suite of teaching and learning resources designed to bridge the gap between what happens in the classroom and what happens at home and on the job. WileyPLUS gives instructors the resources to teach their students new technologies and guide them towards their goals of acquiring the skills to become certified and advance in the workforce. For students, WileyPLUS provides tools for study and practice that are available to them 24/7, wherever and whenever they want to study. WileyPLUS includes a complete online version of the student textbook; PowerPoint presentations; homework and practice assignments and quizzes; image galleries; test bank questions; gradebook; and all the instructor resources in one easy-to-use website.

The following features are new to WileyPLUS for Office 2010.

- In addition to the hundreds of questions included in the WileyPLUS courses that do not appear in the testbank or textbook, we've added over a dozen projects that can be assigned to students.
- Many more animated tutorials, videos, and audio clips to support students as they learn the latest Office 2010 features.

MSDN ACADEMIC ALLIANCE

Free Three-Year Membership Available to Qualified Adopters!

The Microsoft Developer Network Academic Alliance (MSDN AA) is designed to provide the easiest and least expensive way for universities to make the latest Microsoft developer tools, products, and technologies available in labs and classrooms and on student PCs. MSDN AA is an annual membership program for departments teaching Science, Technology, Engineering, and Mathematics (STEM) courses. The membership provides a complete solution to keeping academic labs, faculty, and students on the leading edge of technology.

Software available in the MSDN AA program is provided at no charge to adopting departments through the Wiley and Microsoft publishing partnership.

As a bonus to this free offer, faculty will be introduced to Microsoft's Faculty Connection and Academic Resource Center. It takes time and preparation to keep students engaged while giving them a fundamental understanding of theory, and the Microsoft Faculty Connection is designed to help STEM professors in this preparation by providing articles, curriculum, and tools that professors can use to engage and inspire today's technology students.

Contact your Wiley rep for details.

For more information about the MSDN Academic Alliance program, go to **msdn.microsoft.com/academic/**

IMPORTANT WEB ADDRESSES AND PHONE NUMBERS

To locate the Wiley Higher Education Rep in your area go to www.wiley.com/college, select Instructors under Resources, and click on the Who's My Rep link, or call the MOAC toll-free number: 1 + (888) 764-7001 (U.S. and Canada only).

To learn more about becoming a Microsoft Certified Professional and exam availability, visit www.microsoft.com/learning/mcp.

WHY MOS CERTIFICATION?

Microsoft Office Specialist (MOS) 2010 is a valuable credential that recognizes the desktop computing skills needed to use the full features and functionality of the Microsoft Office 2010 suite.

In the worldwide job market, Microsoft Office Specialist is the primary tool companies use to validate the proficiency of their employees in the latest productivity tools and technology, helping them select job candidates based on globally recognized skills standards. An independent research study has shown that businesses with certified employees are more productive than non-certified employees and that certified employees bring immediate value to their jobs.

In academia, as in the business world, institutions upgrading to Office 2010 may seek ways to protect and maximize their technology investment. By offering certification, they validate that decision—because powerful Office 2010 applications such as Word, Excel, and PowerPoint can be effectively used to increase academic preparedness and workforce readiness.

Individuals seek certification to increase their own personal sense of accomplishment and to create advancement opportunities by establishing a leadership position in their school or department, thereby differentiating their skill sets in a competitive college admissions and job market.

BOOK COMPANION WEBSITE

The students' book companion site, www.wiley.com/college/microsoft, for the MOAC series includes any resources, exercise files, and Web links that will be used in conjunction with this course.

WILEY DESKTOP EDITIONS

Wiley MOAC Desktop Editions are innovative electronic versions of printed textbooks. Students buy the desktop version for 50% off the U.S. price of the printed text, and get the added value of permanence and portability. Wiley Desktop Editions provide students with numerous additional benefits that are not available with other e-text solutions.

Wiley Desktop Editions are NOT subscriptions; students download the Wiley Desktop Edition to their computer desktops. Students own the content they buy to keep for as long as they want. Once a Wiley Desktop Edition is downloaded to the computer desktop, students have instant access to all of the content without being online. Students can also print out the sections they prefer to read in hard copy. Students can also access fully integrated resources within their Wiley Desktop Edition. From highlighting their e-text to taking and sharing notes, students can easily personalize their Wiley Desktop Edition as they are reading or following along in class.

COURSESMART

CourseSmart is a lower-cost option that goes beyond traditional expectations in providing instant, online access to the textbooks and course materials you need. You can save time and hassle with a digital eTextbook that allows you to search for the most relevant content at the very moment you need it. To learn more, go to: www.coursesmart.com.

PREPARING TO TAKE THE MICROSOFT OFFICE SPECIALIST (MOS) EXAM

The Microsoft Office Specialist credential has been upgraded to validate skills with the Microsoft Office 2010 system. The MOS certifications target information workers and cover the most popular business applications such as Word 2010, PowerPoint 2010, Excel 2010, Access 2010, and Outlook 2010.

By becoming certified, you demonstrate to employers that you have achieved a predictable level of skill in the use of a particular Office application. Employers often require certification either as a condition of employment or as a condition of advancement within the company or other organization. The certification examinations are sponsored by Microsoft but administered through exam delivery partners like Certiport.

To learn more about becoming a Microsoft Office Application Specialist and exam availability, visit www.microsoft.com/learning/msbc.

Preparing to Take an Exam

Unless you are a very experienced user, you will need to use a test preparation course to prepare to complete the test correctly and within the time allowed. The Microsoft Official Academic Course series is designed to prepare you with a strong knowledge of all exam topics, and with some additional review and practice on your own and to give you confidence in your ability to pass the appropriate exam.

After you decide which exam to take, review the list of objectives for the exam. This list can be found in Appendix A at the back of this book. You can also easily identify tasks that are included in the objective list by locating the Lesson Skill Matrix at the start of each lesson and the Certification Ready sidebars in the margin of the lessons in this book.

To take the MOS test, visit http://www.miscrosoft.com/learning/msbc to locate your nearest testing center. Then call the testing center directly to schedule your test. The amount of advance notice you should provide will vary for different testing centers; it typically depends on the number of computers available at the testing center, the number of other testers who have already been scheduled for the day on which you want to take the test, and the number of times per week that the testing center offers MOS testing. In general, you should call to schedule your test at least two weeks prior to the date on which you want to take the test.

When you arrive at the testing center, you may be asked for proof of identity. A driver's license or passport is an acceptable form of identification. If you do not have either of these items of documentation, call your testing center and ask what alternative forms of identification will be accepted. If you are retaking a test, bring your MOS identification number, which will have been given to you when you previously took the test. If you have not prepaid or if your organization has not already arranged to make payment for you, you will need to pay the test-taking fee when you arrive.

Test Format

All MOS certification tests are live, performance-based tests. There are no multiple-choice, true/false, or short-answer questions. Instructions are general: you are told the basic tasks to perform on the computer, but you aren't given any help in figuring out how to perform them. You are not permitted to use reference material other than the application's Help system.

As you complete the tasks stated in a particular test question, the testing software monitors your actions. Following is an example question.

> Open the file named *Wiley Guests* and select the word *Welcome* in the first paragraph. Change the font to 12 point, and apply bold formatting. Select the words *at your convenience* in the second paragraph, move them to the end of the first paragraph using drag and drop, and then center the first paragraph.

When the test administrator seats you at a computer, you will see an online form that you use to enter information about yourself (name, address, and other information required to process your exam results). While you complete the form, the software will generate the test from a master test bank and then prompt you to continue. The first test question will appear in a window. Read the question carefully, and then perform all the tasks stated in the test question. When you have finished completing all tasks for a question, click the Next Question button.

You have 45 to 60 minutes to complete all questions, depending on the test that you are taking. The testing software assesses your results as soon as you complete the test, and the test administrator can print the results of the test so that you will have a record of any tasks that you performed incorrectly. A passing grade is 75 percent or higher. If you pass, you will receive a certificate in the mail within two to four weeks. If you do not pass, you can study and practice the skills that you missed and then make an appointment to retake the test at a later date.

Tips for Successfully Completing the Test

The following tips and suggestions are the result of feedback received from many individuals who have taken one or more MOS tests.

- **Make sure that you are thoroughly prepared.** If you have extensively used the application for which you are being tested, you may feel confident that you are prepared for the test. However, the test might include questions that involve tasks that you rarely or never perform in using the application at your place of business, at school, or at home. You must be knowledgeable in all the MOS objectives for the test that you will take.

- **Read each exam question carefully.** An exam question might include several tasks that you are to perform. A partially correct response to a test question is counted as an incorrect response. In the example question on the previous page, you might apply bold formatting and move the words *at your convenience* to the correct location, but forget to center the first paragraph. This would count as an incorrect response and would result in a lower test score.

- **Use the Help system only when necessary.** You are allowed to use the application's Help system, but relying on the Help system too much will slow you down and possibly prevent you from completing the test within the allotted time. Use the Help system only when necessary.

- **Keep track of your time.** The test does not display the amount of time that you have left, so you need to keep track of the time yourself by monitoring your start time and the required end time on your watch or a clock in the testing center (if there is one). The test program displays the number of items that you have completed along with the total number of test items (for example, "35 of 40 items have been completed"). Use this information to gauge your pace.

- **You cannot return to a question once you've skipped it.** If you skip a question, you cannot return to it later. You should skip a question only if you are certain that you cannot complete the tasks correctly.

- **Make sure you understand the instructions for each question.** As soon as you are finished reading a question and you click in the application window, a condensed version of the instruction is displayed in a corner of the screen. If you are unsure whether you have completed all tasks stated in the test question, click the Instructions button on the test information bar at the bottom of the screen and then reread the question. Close the instruction window when you are finished. Do this as often as necessary to ensure you have read the question correctly and that you have completed all the tasks stated in the question.

If You Do Not Pass the Test

If you do not pass, you can use the assessment printout as a guide to practice the items that you missed. There is no limit to the number of times that you can retake a test; however, you must pay the fee each time you take the test. When you retake the test, expect to see some of the same test items on the subsequent test; the test software randomly generates the test items from a master test bank before you begin the test. Also expect to see several questions that did not appear on the previous test.

Office 2010 Professional Six-Month Trial Software

Some editions of the MOAC Office 2010 series come with six-month trial editions of Office 2010 Professional. If your book includes a trial, there will be a CD glued into the front or back cover of your book. This section pertains only to those editions that came with an Office 2010 Professional trial:

STEP BY STEP   Installing the Microsoft Office System 2010 Six-Month Trial

1. Insert the trial software CD-ROM into the CD drive on your computer. The CD will be detected, and the Setup.exe file should automatically begin to run on your computer.
2. When prompted for the Office Product Key, enter the Product Key provided with the software, and then click Next.
3. Enter your name and organization user name, and then click Next.
4. Read the End-User License Agreement, select the *I Accept the Terms in the License Agreement* check box, and then click Next.
5. Select the install option, verify the installation location or click Browse to change the installation location, and then click Next.
6. Verify the program installation preferences, and then click Next.

Click Finish to complete the setup.

UPGRADING MICROSOFT OFFICE PROFESSIONAL 2010 SIX-MONTH TRIAL SOFTWARE TO THE FULL PRODUCT

You can convert the software into full use without removing or reinstalling software on your computer. When you complete your trial, you can purchase a product license from any Microsoft reseller and enter a valid Product Key when prompted during Setup.

UNINSTALLING THE TRIAL SOFTWARE AND RETURNING TO YOUR PREVIOUS OFFICE VERSION

If you want to return to your previous version of Office, you need to uninstall the trial software. This should be done through the Add or Remove Programs icon in Control Panel (or Uninstall a program in the Control Panel of Windows Vista).

STEP BY STEP   Uninstall Trial Software

1. Quit any programs that are running.
2. In Control Panel, click Programs and Features (Add or Remove Programs in Windows XP).
3. Click Microsoft Office Professional 2010, and then click Uninstall (Remove in Windows XP).

Take Note

If you selected the option to remove a previous version of Office during installation of the trial software, you need to reinstall your previous version of Office. If you did not remove your previous version of Office, you can start each of your Office programs either through the Start menu or by opening files for each program. In some cases, you may have to re-create some of your shortcuts and default settings.

STUDENT DATA FILES

All of the practice files that you will use as you perform the exercises in the book are available for download on our Student Companion site. By using the practice files, you will not waste time creating the samples used in the lessons, and you can concentrate on learning how to use Microsoft Office 2010. With the files and the step-by-step instructions in the lessons, you will learn by doing, which is an easy and effective way to acquire and remember new skills.

Copying the Practice Files

Your instructor may already have copied the practice files before you arrive in class. However, your instructor might ask you to copy the practice files on your own at the start of class. Also, if you want to work through any of the exercises in this book on your own at home or at your place of business after class, you may want to copy the practice files.

STEP BY STEP   **Copy the Practice Files**

OPEN Internet Explorer.

1. In Internet Explorer, go to the student companion site: www.wiley.com.
2. Search for your book title in the upper-right corner.
3. On the Search Results page, locate your book and click on the Visit the Companion Sites link.
4. Select Student Companion Site from the pop-up box.
5. In the left-hand column, under "Browse by Resource," select Student Data Files.
6. Now select Student Data Files from the center of the screen.
7. On the File Download dialog box, select Save to save the data files to your external drive (often called a ZIP drive, a USB drive, or a thumb drive) or a local drive.
8. In the Save As dialog box, select a local drive in the left-hand panel that you'd like to save your files to; again, this should be an external drive or a local drive. Remember the drive name that you saved it to.

Acknowledgments

We'd like to thank the many reviewers who pored over the manuscript, providing invaluable feedback in the service of quality instructional materials.

Access 2010

Tammie Bolling, *Tennessee Technology Center—Jacksboro*
Mary Corcoran, *Bellevue College*
Trish Culp, *triOS College—Business Technology Healthcare*
Jana Hambruch, *Lee County School District*
Aditi Mukherjee, *University of Florida—Gainesville*

Excel 2010

Tammie Bolling, *Tennessee Technology Center—Jacksboro*
Mary Corcoran, *Bellevue College*
Trish Culp, *triOS College—Business Technology Healthcare*
Dee Hobson, *Richland College*
Christie Hovey, *Lincoln Land Community College*
Ralph Phillips, *Central Oregon Community College*
Rajeev Sachdev, *triOS College—Business Technology Healthcare*

Outlook 2010

Mary Harnishfeger, *Ivy Tech State College—Bloomington*
Sandra Miller, *Wenatchee Valley College*
Bob Reeves, *Vincennes University*
Lourdes Sevilla, *Southwestern College—Chula Vista*
Phyllis E. Traylor, *St. Philips College*

PowerPoint 2010

Natasha Carter, *SUNY—ATTAIN*
Dr. Susan Evans Jennings, *Stephen F. Austin State University*
Sue Van Lanen, *Gwinnett Technical College*
Carol J. McPeek, *SUNY—ATTAIN*
Michelle Poertner, *Northwestern Michigan College*
Tim Sylvester, *Glendale Community College (AZ)*

Project 2010

Tatyana Pashnyak, *Bainbridge College*
Debi Griggs, *Bellevue College*

Word 2010

Portia Hatfield, *Tennessee Technology Center—Jacksboro*
Terri Holly, *Indian River State College*
Pat McMahon, *South Suburban College*
Barb Purvis, *Centura College*
Janet Sebesy, *Cuyahoga Community College*

We would also like to thank Lutz Ziob, Jason Bunge, Ben Watson, David Bramble, Merrick Van Dongen, Don Field, Pablo Bernal, and Wendy Johnson at Microsoft for their encouragement and support in making the Microsoft Official Academic Course program the finest instructional materials for mastering the newest Microsoft technologies for both students and instructors. Finally, we would like to thank Lorna Gentry of Content LLC for developmental editing and Jeff Riley and his team at Box Twelve Communications for technical editing.

About the Author

CHRISTY PARRISH

Christy Parrish has spent the last 20 years developing, designing, and delivering corporate training programs. She has written several books on Microsoft Office and other productivity software packages. As a freelance author, she has also written a magazine series and hundreds of online articles on a wide variety of topics. Christy is also a member of her community artists group and is recognized for her unique photographic skills that are on display at various galleries. She is married and has two sons who both share her love of writing and art.

Brief Contents

Contents

3 Advanced E-mail Tools 86

4 Managing E-mail Messages 130

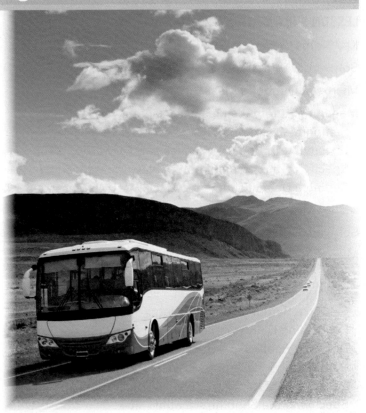

5 Automating Message Processing   159

6 Working with Contacts 190

7 Advanced Contact Management 218

8 Calendar Basics   247

9 Managing Meetings   265

10 Advanced Calendar Management 293

11 Managing Tasks 327

12 Categories and Outlook Data Files 354

13 Managing Notes and Journal Entries   371

LESSON SKILL MATRIX

Skills	Exam Objective	Objective Number
Starting Outlook		
Working in the Outlook Window		
Using Backstage View to Manage Outlook	Set General options.	1.1.1
	Set Advanced options.	1.1.6
	Set Language options.	1.1.7
Personalizing Outlook	Change the reading view.	1.3.2
	Show or hide fields in a List view.	1.3.1
	Use the People Pane.	1.3.4

KEY TERMS

- Backstage view
- desktop shortcut
- feature
- fields
- fly-out
- folders
- gallery
- group
- item
- Navigation Pane
- People Pane
- Quick Access Toolbar (QAT)
- Reading Pane
- Ribbon
- Screen Tip
- Status bar
- Title bar
- To-Do Bar

Resort Adventures is a luxury resort. During the summer, activities such as kayaking, canoeing, hiking, and horseback riding are available. In the winter months, visitors enjoy skiing, snowshoeing, and sleigh rides. Partners Mindy Martin and Jon Morris own and operate Resort Adventures. They work hard to ensure that guests enjoy their stay. Employees are well-trained and well-treated professionals. For one week every year, Mindy and Jon close the resort to guests and open the facilities to employees and their families.

Microsoft Outlook is an ideal tool for managing communication with their clients and their staff. Whether you need to send a message to a vendor making a late delivery, look up an old friend's phone number, or schedule a staff meeting, Outlook provides the tools that will save time and make your job easier. In this lesson, you will learn how to customize the Microsoft Outlook environment to suit your needs.

SOFTWARE ORIENTATION

Microsoft Outlook's Opening Screen

Before you begin working in Microsoft Outlook, you need to be familiar with the primary user interface. When you first launch Microsoft Outlook, you will see a screen similar to that in Figure 1-1.

Figure 1-1

The Inbox—Outlook 2010's opening screen

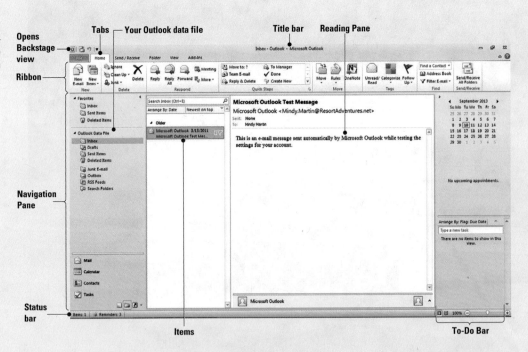

The elements and features of this screen are typical for Microsoft Outlook. Your screen may vary if default settings have been changed or if other preferences have been set. Use this figure as a reference throughout this lesson as well as the rest of this book.

STARTING OUTLOOK

Microsoft Outlook 2010 can be launched in two different ways. You can launch Outlook from the Start button on the Windows taskbar at the bottom of your screen. You can also launch Outlook by double-clicking a shortcut created on the Windows desktop.

Launching Outlook from the Start Menu

As in all Microsoft Office applications, using the Start button may be the most common method of launching Outlook. After Outlook is installed, click the Start button on the Windows taskbar, point to All Programs, point to Microsoft Office, and click Microsoft Office Outlook 2010. In this exercise, you will learn how to launch Outlook from the Start menu and familiarize yourself with the locations of many of Outlook's features.

STEP BY STEP   **Launch Outlook from the Start Menu**

Another Way
You can also locate the Microsoft Outlook link by typing the word Outlook in the Search programs and files box at the bottom of the Start menu.

GET READY. Before you begin these steps, be sure to turn on or log on to your computer.

1. Click the Start button.
2. Click All Programs, then click Microsoft Office. Click Microsoft Outlook 2010. Microsoft Outlook 2010 is launched.
3. Compare your screen to Figure 1-1 and locate each of the labeled elements.
4. Click the Close button in the upper-right corner.

PAUSE. You will launch Outlook again in the next exercise.

Launching Outlook from a Desktop Shortcut

As you saw in the previous exercise, you can launch Outlook from the Start menu. However, if you find that you open Outlook frequently, you might find it easier to create a desktop shortcut. A **desktop shortcut** is an icon placed on the Windows desktop that launches an application, opens a folder, or opens a file. Simply double-click the desktop shortcut to perform the specified action. In the next exercise, you will create an Outlook shortcut and use it to launch Outlook.

STEP BY STEP   **Launch Outlook from a Desktop Shortcut**

GET READY. Before you begin these steps, be sure that Microsoft Outlook is not running.

1. Click the Start button.
2. Click All Programs, then click Microsoft Office. Right-click Microsoft Outlook 2010. Point to Send To. Click the Desktop (create shortcut) option. The desktop shortcut shown in Figure 1-2 is created and appears on your desktop.

Figure 1-2

Desktop shortcut for Microsoft Outlook 2010

3. Minimize any applications so you can see the desktop.
4. Double-click the Microsoft Outlook 2010 desktop shortcut. Microsoft Outlook 2010 is launched.

PAUSE. LEAVE Outlook open to use in the next exercise.

As you have just seen, Outlook can be launched in two different ways. Use the method you prefer.

- Click the Start button on the Windows taskbar, point to All Programs, point to Microsoft Office, and click Microsoft Outlook 2010.
- Double-click the desktop shortcut.

Take Note   Once you've created a desktop shortcut for Outlook, you can right-click the shortcut and pin it to the taskbar for even more convenience, or click the shortcut and drag it down to your taskbar. Just click once on your new Outlook taskbar icon to launch Outlook and get to work.

In the previous exercise, you launched Microsoft Outlook. Outlook opens to your mailbox when launched, as shown in Figure 1-1. By default, the Outlook mailbox is divided into five main sections: the Ribbon, the Navigation Pane, the message list, the Reading Pane, and the To-Do Bar. You can use Outlook's onscreen tools to control the Outlook environment and access Outlook's features.

WORKING IN THE OUTLOOK WINDOW

The Bottom Line   Outlook has a variety of tools that help you organize your communication and manage your time. The Outlook 2010 window was designed to help you get your work done as quickly and efficiently as possible. In this section, you'll explore the Ribbon, which displays common commands in groups arranged by tabs. You will also learn about other onscreen tools to help you get your work done faster, such as the To-Do Bar and the Navigation Pane.

Using the Onscreen Tools

Outlook's onscreen tools enable you to access and control all of Outlook's features. To get the most out of Outlook, you'll want to familiarize yourself with each of the onscreen tools. The two tools that you'll be using most frequently are the Navigation Pane and the Ribbon. The **Navigation Pane** includes tools that help you navigate through Outlook's features, such as your mailbox, Calendar, notes, etc. When you hover your cursor over any command, a **ScreenTip** appears providing a brief description of the command's purpose in a small, pop-up text box. As you click buttons or select menu commands, the Outlook window changes to display the information you requested or to provide space to enter new information. The **Ribbon** contains the most commonly used commands and buttons you need for each of Outlook's features. These commands are sorted into **groups** of related commands. In this exercise, you'll use Outlook's onscreen tools to take a quick look at the Outlook features.

STEP BY STEP   **Use the Onscreen Tools**

GET READY. LAUNCH Outlook if it is not already running.

Take Note   We've added some content to the screens in this section so that you can see how your content will appear. Your screen will look different if default settings have been changed or other content has been added to your PC. Use these figures as a reference.

1. Locate the Navigation Pane. The Navigation Pane is located on the far left of the screen. The bottom third of this pane contains tools that help you access each of Outlook's primary functions, such as the Calendar and the Contacts list.
2. Click the Calendar button in the Navigation Pane. The Calendar is displayed showing today's date, as shown in Figure 1-3.

Figure 1-3

Outlook 2010 Calendar

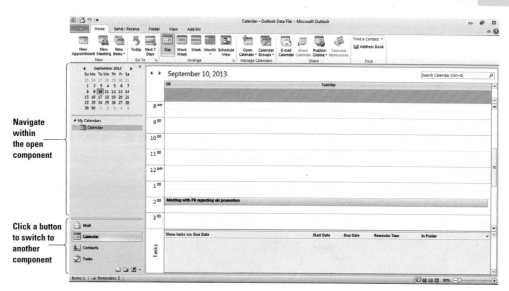

Navigate within the open component

Click a button to switch to another component

Take Note

Notice that the top two-thirds of the Navigation Pane have changed. This section updates automatically to provide you with tools for navigating with the selected Outlook component, which in this case is the Calendar.

Another Way
You can also access Outlook Calendar by using the keyboard shortcut Ctrl+2.

3. Point to the small left-facing arrow at the top of the Navigation Pane. A ScreenTip appears identifying the arrow as the Minimize the Navigation Pane button (Figure 1-4). These minimize buttons are often referred to as collapse buttons.

Figure 1-4

Using ScreenTips

Click to collapse the Navigation Pane

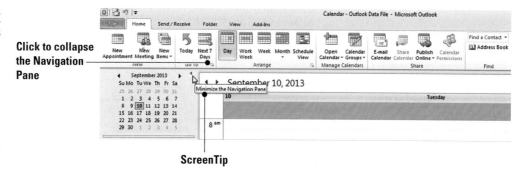

ScreenTip

4. Click the Minimize the Navigation button in the Navigation Pane. The Navigation Pane collapses to show more of the Calendar, as shown in Figure 1-5.

Figure 1-5

Collapsed navigation

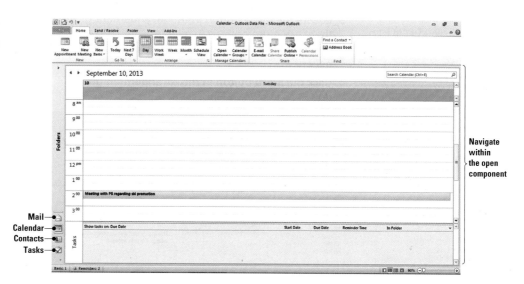

Mail
Calendar
Contacts
Tasks

Navigate within the open component

5. Click the word Folders on the collapsed Navigation Pane. A fly-out of the Navigation Pane is displayed showing you all the information in the Pane, as shown in Figure 1-6. A **fly-out** is a menu or pane that opens floating above the main window, instead of docked to a fixed place on the screen, which changes the way every other pane appears.

Figure 1-6

Fly-out Navigation Pane

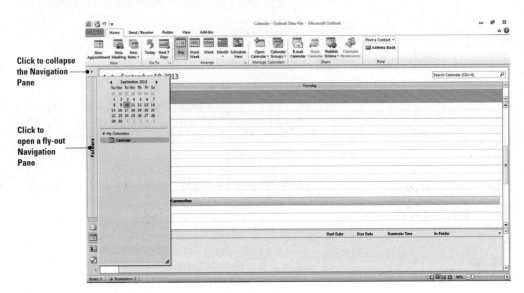

6. Click Folders again to remove the fly-out. Click the expand arrow on the Navigation Pane. The full Navigation Pane is restored.

7. Click the Mail button in the Navigation Pane and then click the View tab on the Ribbon, as shown in Figure 1-7.

Figure 1-7

The Ribbon features a variety of tools

Another Way
You can also access Outlook Mail by using the keyboard shortcut Ctrl+1.

8. Click the collapse arrow on the Ribbon. The Ribbon collapses into a single bar showing only the tab names. Click the expand arrow to restore the Ribbon.

9. Locate the More button in the Arrangement group. The More button tells you that there are more options available. When too many options are available to store neatly as buttons in a group, Outlook places the buttons in a dropdown window called a **gallery**.

10. Click the More button in the Arrangement group. A gallery of available views drops down, as shown in Figure 1-8.

Figure 1-8

The Arrangement gallery displayed

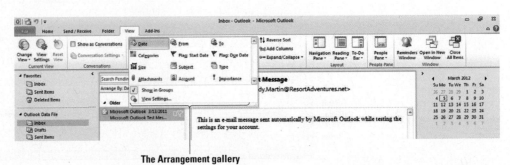

11. Click the Home tab. Click the New E-mail button in the New group. A window is displayed, as shown in Figure 1-9. Notice that it has its own Ribbon. The Ribbon is divided into tabs based on the type of options available. The options on each tab are organized into groups of similar commands.

Figure 1-9

The Untitled-Message window

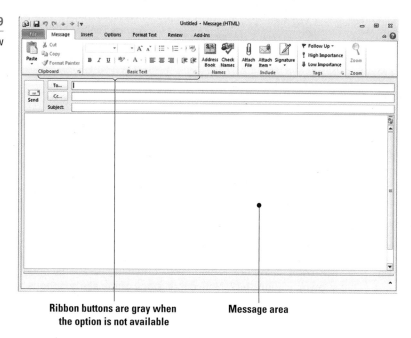

Ribbon buttons are gray when   Message area
the option is not available

12. Notice that most of the buttons in the Clipboard and Basic Text groups are gray. When buttons on the Ribbon are gray, it means that the option is not available. Since this message window contains no text, the options for formatting and working with text are not available.

 Ref   You'll learn more about working with e-mail messages in Lesson 2.

13. Click in the message area. Most of the buttons on the Ribbon are now available in preparation for entering text.

14. In the message area, key Hello World. The Ribbon fills with color as options become available. The Undo button also appears on the Quick Access Toolbar, as shown in Figure 1-10.

15. Click the Undo button. The last letter you typed is erased and the Redo button appears in the Quick Access Toolbar.

16. Click the Redo button to restore the *d*. The Redo button grays out again to let you know that there are no more actions that can be redone, as shown in Figure 1-10.

Figure 1-10

Accessing the Quick
Access Toolbar

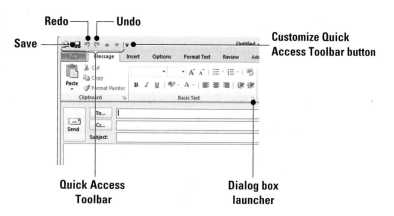

Redo ——— Undo

Save

Customize Quick
Access Toolbar button

Quick Access
Toolbar

Dialog box
launcher

17. Click the Customize Quick Access Toolbar button. A list of available buttons is displayed, as shown in Figure 1-11. To add or remove buttons from the Quick Access Toolbar simply select or deselect a function from the list.

Figure 1-11

Customizing the Quick
Access Toolbar

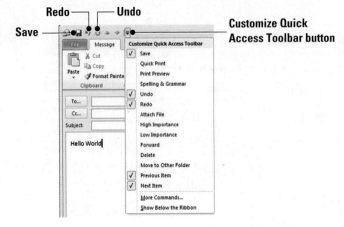

Another Way
The Customize Quick Access Toolbar offers a selection of commonly used buttons. If you want add a particular command that is not in the list, you can click More Commands to open the Customize Quick Access Toolbar window, where you can choose from every command in Outlook.

18. Drag the mouse over the word *Hello* in the message area to select it. In the Basic Text group on the Ribbon, click the dialog box launcher shown in Figure 1-10. A traditional Microsoft dialog box is displayed containing additional options for this command group, as shown in Figure 1-12. Notice that many of the same options are available in both locations.

Figure 1-12

Font dialog box

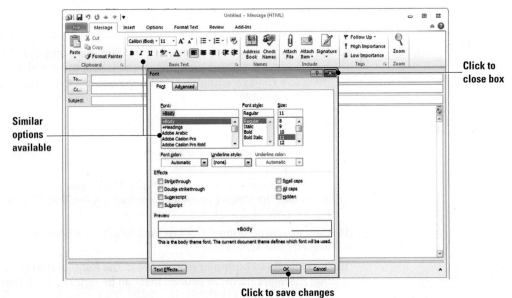

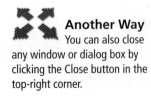
Another Way
You can also close any window or dialog box by clicking the Close button in the top-right corner.

19. In the Font Style box, click Bold Italic. Notice how the text *Hello* in the Preview area of the dialog box changes to reflect your choice. Click the Cancel button to close the dialog box without saving changes.

20. Locate the Title bar at the top of the window. It tells you that this window is named Untitled—Message. You can always identify windows and dialog boxes using the Title bar, as shown in Figure 1-12.

21. Click the Close button at the far right of the Title bar to close the message window. If Outlook prompts you to save your work, click No.

PAUSE. LEAVE Outlook open to use in the next exercise.

Table 1-1 describes the basic functions of onscreen tools used to access Outlook's features. More detailed information about using each of the features is available in the following sections of this lesson and the remaining lessons.

Table 1-1

Onscreen Tools

Onscreen Tool	Description
Backstage	The Backstage view is new in Outlook 2010. Backstage can be accessed by clicking on the File tab in the Outlook Ribbon. The commands in Outlook's Backstage can be used to customize most Outlook features.
Groups	The Outlook 2010 Ribbon is divided into groups that contain buttons for frequently used commands.
Item	An **item** is a record stored in Outlook. A message, appointment, contact, task, or note is an item in Outlook.
Navigation Pane	The Navigation Pane provides access to each of Outlook's features, such as the Calendar and To-Do List. The Navigation Pane can be minimized to enlarge the Reading Pane.
Reading Pane	The **Reading Pane** displays information about the selected Outlook item. For example, in the mailbox, it displays the text of a selected e-mail message.
Ribbon	The Ribbon contains the menus and commands available in Outlook 2010. The Ribbon contains tabs that replace the menus in the old Menu bar. Each tab is divided into groups of commands that replace the old toolbar options.
Status bar	The **Status bar** identifies the number of items in the active feature. For example, when the Contacts tool is active, the number of contacts stored is displayed in the Status bar.
Title bar	The **Title bar** identifies the application and the active feature. For example, when the Calendar is active, the Title bar says "Calendar—Microsoft Outlook."
To-Do Bar	The To-Do Bar summarizes information about appointments and tasks.
Quick Access Toolbar	The **Quick Access Toolbar (QAT)** appears on the left side of the Title bar, above the Ribbon. If you want the toolbar closer to your work area, you can move it to below the Ribbon. This toolbar should contain the commands you use most frequently.

Outlook stores and organizes many of the little pieces of information that form the core of your daily activities. In a single day, you might use Outlook's Calendar, Mail, and Contacts features to schedule the meetings, look up the phone numbers, send e-mail messages, and set up reminders that help you arrive on time for every meeting.

In the previous exercise, you took a quick look at the different Outlook onscreen tools. In this exercise, you will look at some of the ways you can change the viewing options available in Outlook. The features you use most frequently are covered in more detail in the following lessons.

Changing Outlook's View

Every Outlook **feature** stores specific information and offers you several options for viewing that information. For example, the Contacts feature provides the names, addresses, and phone numbers for the individuals and companies you contact. The Calendar tracks your appointments and meetings. Mail enables you to send and receive e-mail messages. You can use Ribbon commands to change the way that information is shown to suit your needs. In this exercise, you'll use the View tab and other Ribbon commands to explore some of Outlook's different views.

STEP BY STEP   Change Outlook's View

GET READY. LAUNCH Outlook if it is not already running and ensure that the Home tab is active.

1. If necessary, click the Mail button in the Navigation Pane and then click the Inbox folder to display your mailbox.
2. Click the View tab to display more options.
3. Click Change View in the Current View group to see the basic viewing options for the Mail feature. The currently selected view is highlighted.
4. Three views are available for the Mail window. The default view is Compact, which shows the items in your mailbox as simple two-line items containing the sender, the date, and the subject.
5. Click Single. The Single view flattens the mailbox items into a single line with all the e-mail information spread out in columns.
6. Click Preview. Notice how the screen changes to provide a single compressed line for each item similar to Single view, except that Preview view does not have the Reading Pane.

Take Note   We've added some content to the screens in this section so that you can see how your content will appear. Your screen will look different if default settings have been changed or other content has been added to your PC. Use these figures as a reference.

7. Click Change View in the Current View group, as shown in Figure 1-13.

Figure 1-13

The Outlook Mailbox in Preview view

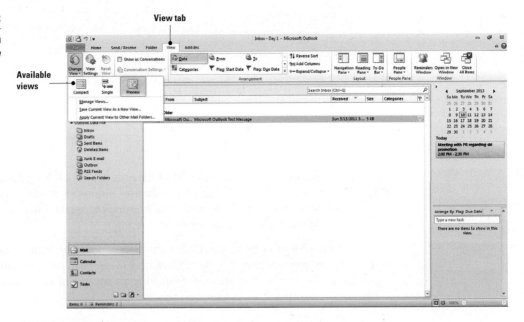

8. Select Compact to return to the default Mail view.
9. Click the Calendar button in the Navigation Pane to display the Calendar feature, and click the View tab to see the different Calendar viewing options.
10. You can change the arrangement of the onscreen Calendar in each view. Day is the default option. On the Home tab, click the Week button to show an entire week's schedule. Click the Month button to view an entire month. Click Work Week options. The Calendar view now displays the current workweek, as shown in Figure 1-14.

Figure 1-14

The Outlook Calendar in Work
Week arrangement

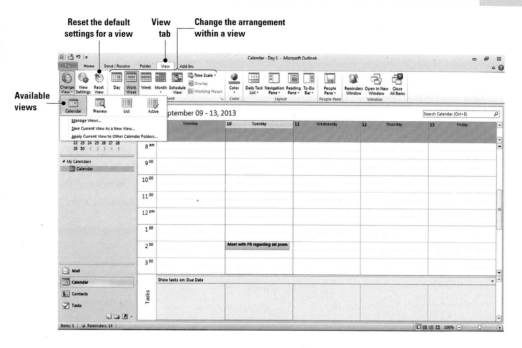

Take Note

The Work Week arrangement shows the workweek as Monday through Friday, by default. However, you can change the workweek to reflect your personal work schedule.

11. Click the View tab. Click Change View in the Current View group to see the available views. Make sure that the default Calendar is selected.

12. Click List. The Calendar changes to provide a simple list of calendar items. The Active view is similar, but only shows those events that have not already occurred.

13. Click Change View in the Current View group. Select Calendar. Click Reset View in the Current View group to change to the default Calendar view.

Take Note

Throughout this chapter you will see information that appears in black text within brackets, such as [Press Enter], or [your e-mail address]. The information contained in the brackets is intended to be directions for you rather than something you actually type word for word. It will instruct you to perform an action or substitute text. Do **not** type the actual text that appears within brackets.

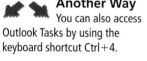

Another Way
You can also access
Outlook Tasks by using the
keyboard shortcut Ctrl+4.

14. Click the Tasks button in the Navigation Pane. Your To-Do List is displayed. Click the *Type a new task* field and key Sample. [Press Enter.] The new task drops to the Task List and a flag appears indicating that the task is for today.

Ⓧ Ref   You'll learn more about working with tasks in Lesson 11.

15. Click the Sample task. The Ribbon fills with color as options become available, as shown in Figure 1-15.

16. On the Home tab, click Change View in the Current View group to see the viewing options, as shown in Figure 1-15.

Figure 1-15

Available views in the Outlook To-Do List

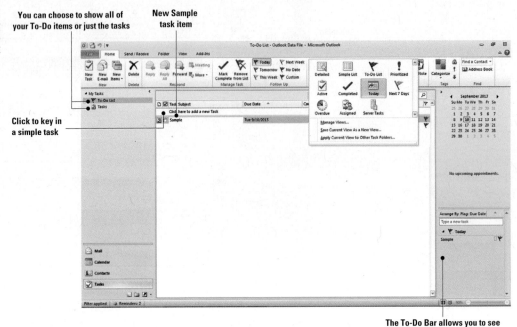

You can choose to show all of your To-Do items or just the tasks

New Sample task item

Click to key in a simple task

The To-Do Bar allows you to see the To-Do items that are due soon

17. Click on each option in the Change View gallery to see how the screen layout changes. You can choose from a number of different options—views that show all the details about a task item (Detailed) or views that let you filter your Task List to contain only items that fit the criteria you choose (Prioritized, Active, Completed, Today, Next 7 days, Overdue, Assigned).

18. On the View tab, click Change View and select Today. Select the Sample task and click Delete in the Delete group to remove your sample task.

19. Click the Folder List button in the Navigation Pane to display the Folder List in the upper area of the Navigation Pane, as shown in Figure 1-16.

Figure 1-16

The Folder List

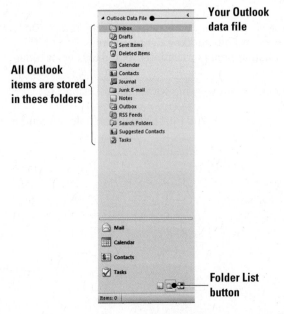

Your Outlook data file

All Outlook items are stored in these folders

Folder List button

20. Click the Inbox in the Folder List to return to the Inbox.

PAUSE. LEAVE Outlook open to use in the next exercise.

In the previous exercise, you changed the view displayed in each of the commonly used Outlook features (Calendar, Contacts, Mail, Tasks, Notes). When you display Outlook's Folder List, you can see that each Outlook feature has its own folder, as shown in Figure 1-16. Every Outlook item (message, meeting, task, etc.) is stored in one of the folders in the Folder List.

Take Note

Because each Outlook feature is stored in a folder, the features themselves are sometimes referred to as **folders**.

If you create folders to help organize your Outlook items, those folders will typically appear as subfolders. For example, if you create a folder to store e-mails relating to a specific project you are working on, the Project folder will appear in the Folder List under the Inbox folder by default.

Table 1-2 briefly describes how these Outlook features are typically used.

Table 1-2

Descriptions of Outlook Features

Feature	Description
Mail	The Mail feature contains your e-mail messages. The Mail feature includes the following folders: Inbox (messages received), Sent Items (messages sent), Outbox (messages waiting to be sent), and Junk E-mail (unwanted messages you received that were not directed to another folder).
Calendar	The Calendar feature contains a calendar and appointment book to help you keep track of your schedule.
Contacts	The Contacts feature stores contact information about individuals, groups, and companies.
Tasks	The Tasks feature displays tasks and To-Do items.
Notes	The Notes feature stores small pieces of information on electronic sticky notes. Notes can be forwarded as e-mail messages.
Journal	The Journal feature automatically tracks communications and attachments as they are sent back and forth to contacts. The Journal is a great tool for keeping you organized and seeing how the Outlook items in different folders relate to one another.
Folder List	The Folder List identifies all of your Outlook folders. If your company or organization uses Microsoft Exchange Server, public folders you can access are also listed.

USING BACKSTAGE VIEW

The Bottom Line

Microsoft Outlook 2010 is designed to adapt to you. Outlook now places all of the settings and controls in one easy-to-navigate place called Backstage. You can use the **Backstage view** options to control the way Outlook acts and looks. You can use Backstage to create and modify accounts and to clean up your Outlook file. You can also use the *Options* area of Backstage to change all the settings used for mail, calendars, tasks, journals, and contacts, or use the Advanced options to access settings that control the way Outlook handles your information.

Using the File Tab to Open Backstage View

The File tab in Microsoft Office 2010 has replaced the Office button. Clicking the File tab opens the Microsoft Office Backstage view. You'll notice a menu-like list running down the left side of the window; this list is called a navigation pane. You can click any of the commands in the navigation pane to open a new Backstage page that contains the options and settings that were scattered among many different dialog boxes in Outlook 2007. In this exercise, you learn to use the File tab to open Backstage view and look over the options available through some of its commands.

STEP BY STEP   **Use the File Tab to Open Backstage View**

GET READY. LAUNCH Outlook if it is not already running.

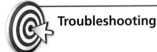

WileyPLUS Extra! features an online tutorial of this task.

1. In the Outlook window, click the Microsoft Outlook Test Message and then click the File tab. This opens the Backstage view with the Info page active, as shown in Figure 1-17. The Info page includes information about your account and tools for maintaining your mailbox.

Troubleshooting If you no longer have the Microsoft Outlook Test Message, you can still complete the remaining steps in this exercise. However, the preview images in Backstage view will be different from those shown here.

Figure 1-17

Microsoft Office Backstage view for Outlook

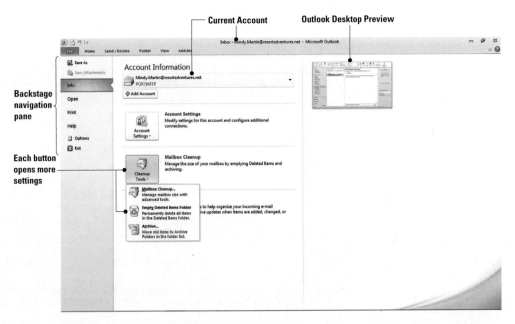

2. The right pane of the Backstage view window is the Preview pane. On the Info page, the preview simply shows you the current state of your main Outlook window. The Preview pane also appears on the Backstage view's Print page. Click the Print in the left navigation pane. The Print page opens and a preview appears in the right Preview pane.
3. Click the Table Style command in the Settings area and then the Memo Style. Notice how the preview changes.

PAUSE. LEAVE Outlook open to use in the next exercise.

Setting General Options

You can use the Microsoft Office Backstage to control many of the settings and options that used to be located on the Tools menu. When you click the Options command in Outlook's Backstage navigation pane, the Outlook Options dialog box opens. This one dialog box contains all of the options that you can use to customize the Outlook environment to suit your personal needs. These options are grouped according to type. The Outlook Options dialog box opens to the General

Options page. You can use the general options to set your user name, the color scheme, and the style of ScreenTip you want. You can also use these options to turn the Live Preview and the Mini Toolbar on or off. In this exercise, you'll set your user name and try modifying some of the options.

STEP BY STEP   **Set General Options**

GET READY. LAUNCH Outlook if it is not already running.

1. In the Outlook window, click the Microsoft Office Test Message and then click the File tab. This opens the Backstage view, with the Info page active (refer to Figure 1-17).
2. Click Options in the Navigation Pane. The Outlook Options dialog box opens to the General Options page.
3. Personalize Outlook by typing your name in the User Name box and your initials in the Initials box, as shown in Figure 1-18. When you personalize Outlook in Backstage view, your name will automatically be added to every Outlook item you create.

Figure 1-18

General Options page of the Outlook Options dialog box

Hover over the information circle for more information

Each item in the Navigation Pane opens an entire page of associated settings you can customize

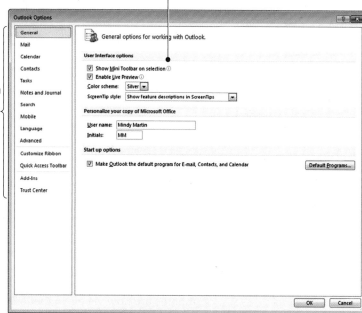

4. In the *User Interface options* area, click the color scheme dropdown box and select Blue. Click OK. Outlook applies the color to the Outlook window.
5. Click the File tab. This opens the Microsoft Office Backstage again.
6. Click Options in the navigation pane. The Outlook Options dialog box opens to the General Options page.
7. In the *User Interface options* area, click the color scheme dropdown box again and select Silver. Click OK. This will restore the default color to the Outlook window.

PAUSE. LEAVE the Outlook Options dialog box open to use in the next exercise.

CERTIFICATION READY   **1.1.1**

How do you set Outlook's General program options?

Setting Advanced Options

Outlook 2010 gives you more control than ever when it comes to personalizing Outlook. You can use the Advanced options page of the Outlook Options dialog box to customize how the various panes of the Outlook window appear. You can also control specific aspects of the program to suit your needs, such as determining which folder appears when Outlook opens, or how Outlook should handle dial-up connections and international e-mails. You can also determine how often Outlook performs tasks like sending and receiving messages, AutoArchiving, and receiving RSS feeds. In this exercise, you'll change some of these settings to familiarize yourself with the process.

STEP BY STEP   Set Advanced Options

GET READY. LAUNCH Outlook if it is not already running.

1. Click the **File** tab again and select **Options** and then **Advanced**. The Advanced options page of the Outlook Options dialog box appears.

2. Click the top of the Outlook Options dialog box and drag it to the middle of your Outlook window. The Navigation Pane and To-Do Bar should be visible on either side of the Outlook Options dialog box, as shown in Figure 1-19.

Figure 1-19

Advanced Options page of the Outlook Options dialog box

Changes to the Outlook pane area change the layout of the main Outlook window

Click to open the Advanced Outlook Options page

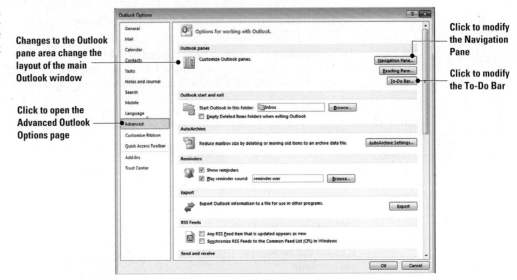

Click to modify the Navigation Pane

Click to modify the To-Do Bar

3. The first section on the Advanced page is the Outlook panes area. In this section, click the **Navigation Pane** button. The Navigation Pane Options dialog box appears.

4. With the Mail option highlighted, click the **Move Down** button two times, then click **OK**. Notice that the Mail button in the bottom of the Navigation Pane is now the third item in the list.

5. In the Outlook panes area of the dialog box, click the **To-Do Bar** button. The To-Do Bar Options dialog box appears.

6. In the *Number of month rows* box, type **3** and click **OK**. Notice that three calendar months are now visible in the To-Do Bar.

7. Scroll down, reading each of the available options. When you get to the *Send and receive* area, deselect the *Send immediately when connected* option. This change means that you need to manually tell Outlook when you're ready to send and receive messages.

8. Click **Cancel**. This will restore the default layout and settings.

PAUSE. LEAVE Outlook open to use in the next exercise.

CERTIFICATION
READY   **1.1.6**

How do you set Outlook's Advanced program options?

Setting Language Options

Outlook 2010 also allows you to select your default language. You can choose to match the rest of Office or choose a different language as your default. If you prefer to use English as your default language but correspond with non-English speaking friends or coworkers on a regular basis, you can add the languages you need to the Editing Languages. When your create e-mails in another language, Outlook will look up your editing languages and offer you all the same spell-check and grammar tools that you're used to in Office. In this exercise, you'll set English as your default language and add Spanish to your Editing Languages.

STEP BY STEP   **Set Language Options**

GET READY. LAUNCH Outlook if it is not already running.

1. Click the File tab again and select Options and then Language. The Language options page of the Outlook Options dialog box appears.

2. Click the [Add additional editing languages] box in the Choose Editing Languages area of the dialog box. A long list of available languages appears.

3. Scroll down the list and select Spanish (United States). Click Add. Outlook adds the language to the Editing Languages list, which turns on all of its proofing tools for that language.

4. You can use the *Choose Display and Help Languages* area to change the language that appears onscreen, in ScreenTips and in the Help window. In the Display Language window, select English, if necessary. Your screen should look like Figure 1-20.

Figure 1-20

Language Options page of the Outlook Options dialog box

Changing the Editing Language changes the proofing tools that Outlook uses to check your writing

Changing the Display Language changes the language of menus and onscreen text

Changes the Screen-Tip Language

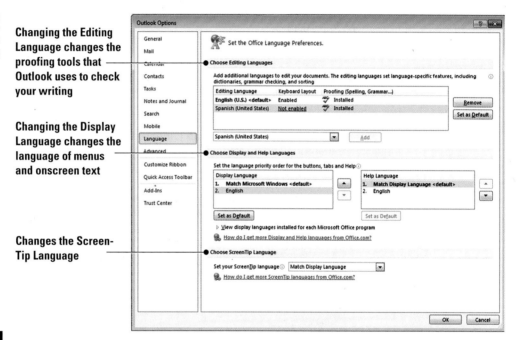

CERTIFICATION READY 1.1.7

How do you set Outlook's Language program options?

5. Click Cancel. Outlook will restore the default language options and return you to the main window.

PAUSE. LEAVE Outlook open to use in the next exercise.

As you've seen, you can use Outlook's Backstage view to access a wide variety of settings to help you customize the way Outlook looks and works to suit your needs (see Table 1-3).

Table 1-3

Options within Outlook's Backstage view

General	Personalize Outlook with your user name, turn on and off Live Preview, and change the color scheme.
Advanced	Customize the Outlook window's Navigation Pane, Reading Pane, and To-Do Bar. You can also AutoArchive your mailbox, set reminders, export Outlook information, synchronize RSS feeds, and set rules for international correspondence.
Language	You can add proofing tools for additional languages and set your own default language.

PERSONALIZING OUTLOOK

You can arrange the elements in the Outlook window to fit your needs. You have a great deal of control over the Outlook environment. In the previous exercise, you learned how to change the views for each Outlook feature, but you can go even further. You can resize, rearrange, hide, or display Outlook features to create an environment that meets your requirements. In this section, you'll learn how to rearrange your Outlook window by moving the Reading Pane and the To-Do Bar; add or delete columns in a List view; and add and remove elements from the To-Do Bar. In addition, you'll learn how to use the new People Pane to better connect to your contacts.

Changing the Reading Pane View

You can show, hide, or move the Reading Pane to fit your needs. Do you get a lot of long e-mail messages? Display the Reading Pane vertically on the right to display as much text as possible. Perhaps the messages you receive contain a lot of information in the item listing area. Display the Reading Pane horizontally. In this exercise, you'll learn to show, hide, and move the Reading Pane.

STEP BY STEP   **Change the Reading Pane View**

GET READY. LAUNCH Outlook if it is not already running.

1. Click Mail in the Navigation Pane to display Outlook's default opening screen. Notice that the Reading Pane is visible on the right of the main content pane.

2. On the View tab, click the Reading Pane button in the Layout group. Select the Bottom option. The Reading Pane is displayed horizontally, across the bottom of the message viewing area. If you have any e-mails in your mailbox, you'll see a preview of the message contents in the Reading Pane, as shown in Figure 1-21.

Figure 1-21

Reading Pane displayed in the bottom position

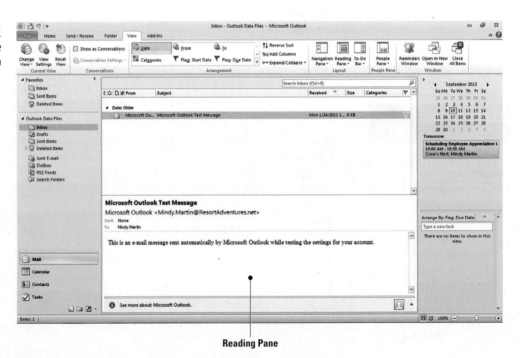

Reading Pane

3. On the View tab, click the Reading Pane button in the Layout group. Select the Off option. The Reading Pane is hidden, as shown in Figure 1-22.

Figure 1-22

The Reading Pane is hidden.

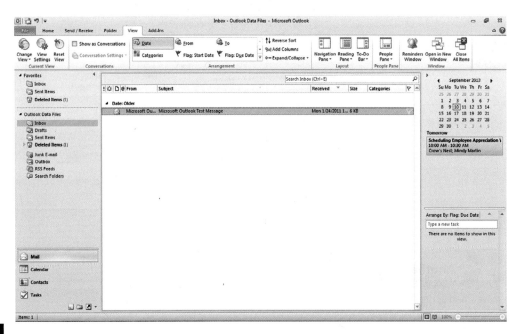

4. On the View tab, click the Reading Pane button again and select Right to restore the default view.

PAUSE. LEAVE Outlook open to use in the next exercise.

Showing or Hiding Fields in a List View

Another way you can personalize your Outlook window is by deciding which fields you want to see in a list view. In Outlook, **fields** are specific bits of information about an item. For example, an incoming e-mail message might contain fields of information, such *From, Subject, To, Received, Flag Status, Attachments*, and so on. You can click the View Settings button on the View tab to access the Advanced View Settings dialog box to add and remove fields that appear as columns in a List view. In this exercise, you'll add and remove a field from a List view.

STEP BY STEP   **Show or Hide Fields in a List View**

GET READY. LAUNCH Outlook if it is not already running and ensure that it shows the mailbox with the Reading Pane hidden.

1. Click the View tab and then click the Change View. Select Preview from the Change Views gallery.

2. Click View Settings to open the Advanced View Settings: Preview dialog box.

3. Click Columns. The Show Columns dialog box opens listing all of the available columns, as shown in Figure 1-23.

Figure 1-23

Figure 1-23

The Show Columns dialog box

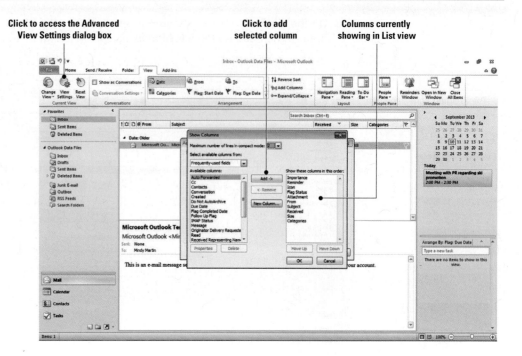

Click to access the Advanced View Settings dialog box

Click to add selected column

Columns currently showing in List view

Another Way
You can also remove a field by right-clicking the field header in the List view and selecting *Remove this column* from the content menu.

4. Select From in the *Show these columns in this order* box, and then click the Remove button. Click OK twice to apply your changes and close the dialog boxes. The column changes have been applied to the mailbox, as shown in Figure 1-24.

Figure 1-24

The mailbox with modified columns

Click to revert back to the defaults for the selected view

Click to access the Advanced View Settings dialog box

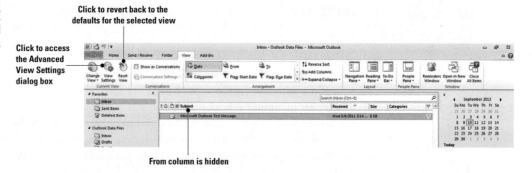

From column is hidden

Another Way
You can also change the column order by selecting the field name in either the Show Columns dialog box or in the List view itself and dragging the field to the desired location.

CERTIFICATION
READY   1.3.1

How do you show or hide fields in a list view?

5. Click the View Settings button, then click Columns in the Advanced View Settings: Preview dialog box.

6. Select From in the Available Columns box on the left of the dialog box and click the Add button. Notice that the From column is at the bottom of the *Show these columns in this order* list, meaning that it will appear at the far right column in Preview view list.

7. Click the Move Up button below the list repeatedly until the From column appears at the top of the list. Click OK twice to apply your changes and close the dialog boxes. The From column is visible again, but is located at the far left of the column headers.

8. Click Reset View in the Current View group on the View tab. Click Yes at the prompt to restore the mailbox to the default view.

PAUSE. LEAVE Outlook open to use in the next exercise.

Viewing, Hiding, and Minimizing the To-Do Bar

You can show, hide, or minimize the To-Do Bar in the same way that you worked with the Reading Pane. The **To-Do Bar** summarizes the current items that need your attention. In this exercise, you'll learn to show, hide, and minimize the To-Do Bar.

STEP BY STEP   **View, Hide, and Minimize the To-Do Bar**

GET READY. LAUNCH Outlook if it is not already running.

1. If necessary, click the Mail button in the Navigation Pane to display the mailbox.

2. Click the View tab and click the To-Do-Bar button in the Layout group. Select the Minimized option. The To-Do Bar is minimized to a slim pane on the right side of the Outlook window, as shown in Figure 1-25.

Figure 1-25

Minimized To-Do Bar

Click to change the To-Do Bar view

Click to expand the To-Do Bar

Another Way
You can also minimize the To-Do Bar simply by clicking the minimize button at the top left of the To-Do Bar.

3. Click the To-Do Bar button and select the Off option. The To-Do Bar is hidden.

4. Click the To-Do Bar button and select the Normal option. The To-Do Bar is restored to its original size and position.

PAUSE. LEAVE Outlook open to use in the next exercise.

Customizing the To-Do Bar

You can select the elements to include on the new To-Do Bar. The To-Do Bar summarizes the current Outlook items that need some follow-up. With a single glance, you can see your appointments, tasks, and e-mail messages that require some action. You can customize the To-Do Bar by changing which elements are visible and by rearranging its elements. In this exercise, you'll work with the To-Do Bar Options and the To-Do Bar button on the View tab to remove and add elements to the To-Do Bar.

STEP BY STEP   **Customize the To-Do Bar**

GET READY. LAUNCH Outlook if it is not already running.

1. If necessary, click the Mail button in the Navigation Pane to display the default mailbox view and verify that the To-Do Bar is displayed.

2. Click the View tab, click the To-Do Bar button, and select Options. The To-Do Bar Options dialog box is displayed, as shown in Figure 1-26.

Figure 1-26

To-Do Bar Options dialog box

Click to open the To-Do Bar Options dialog box

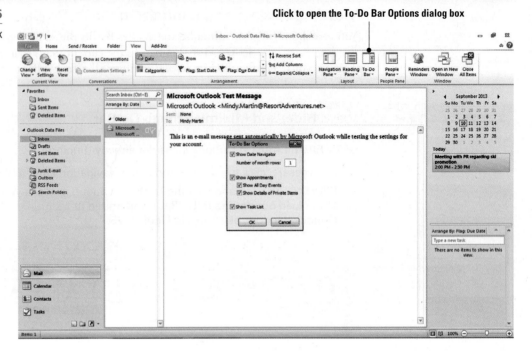

 Ref

This is the same dialog box that you accessed earlier in the lesson using the Advanced page of the Outlook Options dialog box.

3. Examine the options. The checkmark indicates that the element is currently displayed. The numbers indicate the number of months you want to display in the Date Navigator.

 **Another Way**
You can also show or hide each of the other To-Do Bar elements by opening the View tab and selecting the To-Do Bar button.

4. Click the Show Task List checkbox and click the OK button. The dialog box closes and the Task List is removed from the To-Do Bar.

5. Click the View tab, click the To-Do Bar, and select the Task List option. Click OK. The Task List is again displayed on the To-Do Bar.

PAUSE. LEAVE Outlook open to use in the next exercise.

The To-Do Bar contains many different elements that can be added, removed, or modified using either the To-Do Bar Options dialog box or the Advanced page of the Outlook Options dialog box (see Table 1-4).

Table 1-4

To-Do Bar Element Descriptions

To-Do Bar Element	Description
Appointments	The Appointments element displays appointments scheduled in Outlook. You can select the number of appointments to be displayed.
Date Navigator	The Date Navigator displays a small calendar. You can select the number of months to be displayed.
Task Input Panel	Key new tasks into the Task Input Panel.
Task List	The Task List displays the tasks that have been assigned to you.

Using the People Pane

The People Pane is a new feature in Outlook 2010. When you select an e-mail item, the **People Pane** shows you thumbnail images for the sender and all recipients. When you click on a person's thumbnail in the People Pane, the pane expands to show you all the e-mails, meetings, and attachments related to the selected person. This new shortcut lets you see at a glance every contact you've had with that person without having to open different windows. You can also use the People Pane to sync your Contacts list with your friends and contacts on social networking sites like Facebook and LinkedIn. In this exercise, you'll learn to show, hide, and minimize the People Pane and familiarize yourself with some of the People Pane's features.

STEP BY STEP   **Use the People Pane**

WileyPLUS Extra! features an online tutorial of this task.

Another Way
You can also find the People Pane at the bottom of each Contact window. Just double-click on a name in the Contacts list to view all their information and see their People Pane.

GET READY. LAUNCH Outlook if it is not already running and ensure that it is open, in the default Mail view.

1. Click Mail in the Navigation Pane to display your mailbox. Select the Microsoft Outlook Test Message or another e-mail in your Inbox. If you don't have this message, you can click any message in the Inbox for the exercise.

2. On the View tab, click the People Pane button. When Outlook initially opens, the People Pane is turned off.

Take Note   Your screen will look different if default settings have been changed or other content has been added to your PC. Use these figures as a reference.

3. Select the Normal option. The People Pane appears at the bottom of the Reading Pane, as shown in Figure 1-27. The People Pane appears in the bottom third of the Reading Pane. You'll notice a large picture placeholder and beside it is a box with a row of icons. At the top-right corner of the People Pane is a smaller thumbnail image.

Figure 1-27

The People Pane's default view

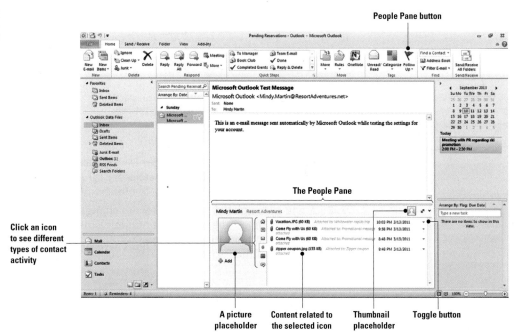

Take Note   Because the Test Message is from Outlook to you using your e-mail address as the sender, you see only one picture placeholder, which represents you. However, in most cases, you'll see multiple picture placeholders in the People Pane because most messages are conversations between two or more people.

4. In the People Pane, point to each of the icons next to the picture placeholder. The ScreenTips tell you what kind of information is available about this person. For example, in Figure 1-27, we've clicked the paperclip icon, which opens a list of every attachment that you've received from this person. In this case, there have been four attachments received. From here you could click the name of the attachment to open it or click the down arrow to the right of the attachment to open the original message.

5. Click the toggle button shown in Figure 1-28 to change People Pane views. The tabs and the content box are hidden so that the People Pane now shows a larger picture placeholder for you.

Take Note   If you click on a message to or from another person, you'll see picture placeholders for the sender and each recipient. This is the default People Pane view for messages with multiple people listed.

Figure 1-28

The People Pane in large thumbnail view

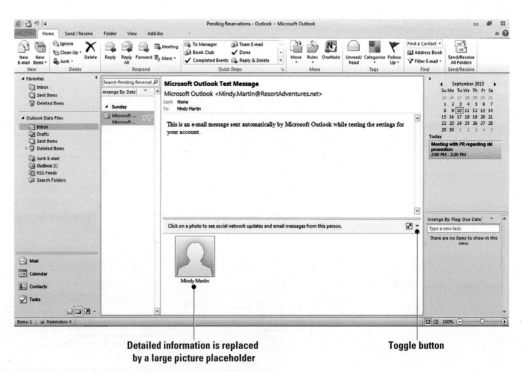

Detailed information is replaced
by a large picture placeholder

Toggle button

6. If you have other messages in your Inbox, click on another message. The People Pane will change to show a picture placeholder for the sender and every recipient. If you don't have another message, use the following figures as a reference.

7. Click one of the picture placeholders to change back to the default view. In the top bar of the People Pane, you'll see multiple small thumbnail placeholders, as shown in Figure 1-29. Outlook highlights the thumbnail for the person currently displayed in the bottom part of the People Pane.

Figure 1-29

The People Pane with multiple contacts

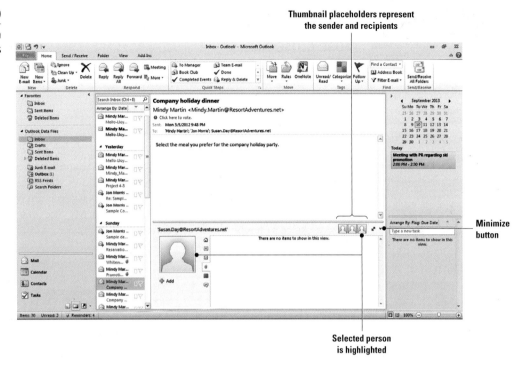

Thumbnail placeholders represent the sender and recipients

Minimize button

Selected person is highlighted

Take Note   As you build your Contacts list, you'll notice that each contact record includes a similar picture placeholder. You can replace the placeholders with actual photos of your contacts. When you click on a message to or from a contact for whom you've added a photo, you'll see their actual photo in the People Pane instead of the silhouette.

8. Click one of the non-highlighted placeholders. The People Pane changes to reflect the items related to the selected person.

9. Click the minimize button in the top-right corner of the People Pane to minimize it. The pane becomes a small bar at the bottom of the Reading Pane that shows only the thumbnail picture placeholder for the sender and each recipient, as shown in Figure 1-30.

Figure 1-30

The minimized People Pane

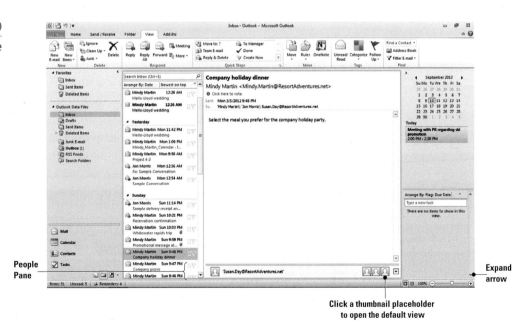

People Pane

Expand arrow

Click a thumbnail placeholder to open the default view

CERTIFICATION READY   **1.3.4**

How can you use the People Pane?

10. Click the People Pane button again on the View tab, and select Off to turn off the People Pane.

PAUSE. CLOSE Outlook.

 Ref

You'll learn more about working with the People Pane in Lessons 3 and 7.

You can also use Outlook to sync contacts with a SharePoint MySite account. SharePoint is a cloud computing system set up by Microsoft. It allows you to store documents, contacts, and links in a convenient Internet server so that you can access it anywhere. If you are using a Share-Point account to store your contacts, syncing your My Site and Outlook together means that you won't have to retype all of your contacts.

SKILL SUMMARY

In This Lesson You Learned How To:	Exam Objective	Objective Number
Start Outlook.		
Work in the Outlook window.		
Use Backstage view to manage Outlook.	Set General options.	1.1.1
	Set Advanced options.	1.1.6
	Set Language options.	1.1.7
Personalize Outlook.	Change the reading view.	1.3.2
	Show or hide fields in a List view.	1.3.1
	Use the People Pane.	1.3.4

Knowledge Assessment

True/False

Circle T if the statement is true or F if the statement is false.

T   F   1. In the To-Do Bar, you can see your appointments, tasks, and e-mail messages that require some action.

T   F   2. The Outlook Contacts list is stored in the People Pane.

T   F   3. Backstage view is a new help feature in Outlook.

T   F   4. The Reading Pane can be hidden.

T   F   5. You can hide columns from a list by selecting the field and pressing the Delete key.

T   F   6. The Status bar identifies the application and the active feature.

T   F   7. In Outlook, messages, appointments, contacts, tasks, and notes are called items.

T   F   8. The Viewing Pane displays the text of a selected e-mail message.

T   F   9. The Calendar feature contains an appointment book.

T   F   10. The Date Navigator in the To-Do Bar can only display one month.

Multiple Choice

Select the letter of the term that best responds to or completes the following statements and questions.

1. A(n) _____ is a record stored in Outlook.
   a. message
   b. item
   c. object
   d. note

2. You can _____ a pane to save room in the Outlook window.
   a. compress
   b. minimize
   c. rotate
   d. shrink

3. You can use the _____ to control almost every aspect of the Outlook environment.
   a. Options menu
   b. Options tab
   c. Backstage view
   d. Preferences tab

4. What new feature groups all of your messages from a person in one place?
   a. Reading Pane
   b. Contact Pane
   c. Filter Pane
   d. People Pane

5. Click the _____ button to access the Show Columns dialog box where you can add and remove fields from a List view.
   a. View Settings
   b. Show Columns
   c. View Options
   d. Custom Views

6. How many views are available for the To-Do List feature?
   a. 3
   b. 11
   c. 6
   d. 7

7. Which pane provides access to the Outlook features, such as the Contacts and Calendar?
   a. Navigation Pane
   b. Navigation menu
   c. Home menu
   d. File tab

8. What pane displays the text of a selected e-mail message?
   a. Preview Pane
   b. Viewing Pane
   c. Message Pane
   d. Reading Pane

9. The _____ contains menus and commands available in Outlook 2010.
   a. Toolbar
   b. Options menu
   c. Ribbon
   d. Banner

10. The _____ button is the first feature listed in the Navigation Pane.
   a. Tasks
   b. Contacts
   c. Calendar
   d. Mail

Project 1-1: View the Outlook Ribbon

Become familiar with the Outlook Ribbon.

GET READY. LAUNCH Outlook if it is not already running.

1. If necessary, click the Mail button in the Navigation Pane to display the mailbox and verify that the To-Do Bar is displayed.
2. Click the Home tab. Click each of the dropdown buttons to see what options are available.
3. Click the Send/Receive tab. Click each of the dropdown buttons to see what options are available.
4. Click the Folder tab. Click each of the dropdown buttons to see what options are available.
5. Click the View tab. Click each of the dropdown buttons to see what options are available.
6. Click the Add-Ins tab, if you have one. Click each of the dropdown buttons to see what options are available.

LEAVE Outlook open for the next project.

Project 1-2: Use the Folder List

Use the Folder List to display the Outlook folders.

GET READY. LAUNCH Outlook if it is not already running.

1. Click the Folder List button in the Navigation Pane. The Folder List is displayed in the upper area of the Navigation Pane.
2. Click the Calendar folder in the Folder List. The Calendar is displayed.
3. Click the Contacts folder in the Folder List. The Contacts folder is displayed.
4. Click the Folder List button again. Click the Deleted Items folder in the Folder List. The Deleted Items folder is displayed. Any deleted Outlook items are stored here until this folder is emptied.
5. Right-click the Deleted Items folder in the Folder List. Note the Empty "Deleted Items" Folder option. Selecting this option permanently deletes these items.
6. Click the Inbox folder in the Folder List. By default, the Inbox folder contains any e-mail messages you have received.
7. Click the Notes folder in the Folder List. The Notes folder is displayed.
8. Click the Tasks folder in the Folder List. The Tasks folder is displayed.
9. Click the Mail button in the Navigation Pane to return to Outlook's default view.

LEAVE Outlook open for the next project.

Project 1-3: Use Keyboard Shortcuts to View Outlook Features

The main Outlook features can be accessed by keyboard shortcuts. Use the shortcuts to display the folders data.

GET READY. LAUNCH Outlook if it is not already running.

1. Identify the keyboard shortcuts used to display the Mail, Calendar, Contacts, Tasks, Notes, and Folder List tools.
2. Use the keyboard shortcuts to display the Outlook features.

LEAVE Outlook open for the next project.

Project 1-4: Customize the To-Do Bar

Change the number of months and appointments displayed in the To-Do Bar.

GET READY. LAUNCH Outlook if it is not already running.

1. If necessary, click the Mail button in the Navigation Pane to display the mailbox and verify that the To-Do Bar is displayed.
2. Display the options for Outlook's To-Do Bar.
3. Change the options to display two months and five appointments.
4. Return to the main Outlook window to see the changes in the To-Do Bar.
5. Display the options for Outlook's To-Do Bar again.
6. Change the options to the default values to display one month and three appointments.
7. Return to the main Outlook window to see the changes in the To-Do Bar.

LEAVE Outlook open for the next project.

Project 1-5: Identify the New Features in Outlook 2010

The People Pane discussed in this lesson is only one of many new features in Outlook 2010. Use Microsoft Office Help to locate information about the various new features in Outlook 2010.

GET READY. LAUNCH Outlook if it is not already running.

1. Use Backstage view to access Microsoft Office Help.
2. Do a help search. Key What's new in Microsoft Outlook 2010.
3. Read through the article to identify the new features that could affect how you use Outlook 2010.

LEAVE Outlook open for the next project.

Project 1-6: Customize a List View

The columns in a list view can be added, deleted, and rearranged.

GET READY. LAUNCH Outlook if it is not already running.

1. Click the Tasks button in the Navigation Pane to display the To-Do List and verify that the To-Do Bar is displayed.
2. Change to the Active view so that the tasks are shown as a list.

3. Remove the Due Date and Folder columns.

4. Using the Show Columns dialog box, add the Sensitivity and Company columns to the far left of the list.

5. Add the Reading Pane in the bottom position.

6. Collapse the Navigation Pane.

7. Remove the To-Do Bar.

8. Close Outlook. Start Outlook and use the Tasks keyboard shortcut to open the Task List. The customized view should be displayed.

9. Reset the Active view to the default columns and restore the Navigation Pane and the To-Do Bar.

CLOSE Outlook.

INTERNET READY

Unfortunately, you might not be the only user on your computer. You might share your computer with a coworker at the office or a family member at home. How can you keep your e-mail private without requiring passwords or a series of arcane gestures and dance steps? Use the Internet or Microsoft Office Outlook Help to investigate the different options you can use to secure your Outlook communications.

LESSON SKILL MATRIX

Skills	Exam Objective	Objective Number
Creating Messages	Specify message content format.	2.1.2
Sending Messages	Show or hide the From and Bcc fields.	2.1.3
Reading and Responding to Messages	Save a message in an external format.	3.1.3
Formatting Messages	Use formatting tools. Apply styles. Create styles. Specify a message theme. Create themes. Use Paste Special.	2.4.1 2.4.2 2.4.3 2.1.1 2.4.4 2.4.5
Personalizing Messages	Manage signatures.	3.4.1
Creating and Formatting Graphic Message Content	Insert graphical elements. Format graphical elements. Insert a hyperlink.	2.3.1 2.4.6 2.3.2
Working with Attachments	Attach external files. Attach an Outlook item. Save message attachments. Print attachments.	2.5.2 2.5.1 3.1.2 1.5.1

KEY TERMS
- attachment
- AutoComplete
- AutoPreview
- character
- clip art
- crop
- font
- Format Painter
- formatting attributes
- hyperlink
- Hypertext Markup Language (HTML)
- plain text
- Quick Access Toolbar
- Quick Styles
- Rich Text Format (RTF)
- signature
- SmartArt graphics
- style
- subject
- theme

Mindy Martin and Jon Morris own and operate Resort Adventures, a luxury resort. They stay busy throughout the day, and frequently work different shifts to stay on top of the activities going on at different times. Sometimes, they rely on e-mail to keep each other informed. Outlook is the perfect tool for this task. Mindy and Jon also use Outlook to contact clients and create press releases. Outlook 2010's new ability to format and enhance messages makes it a great way to send professional and polished messages. In this lesson, you'll learn how to create, save, format, and print messages.

SOFTWARE ORIENTATION

Microsoft Outlook's Message Window

E-mail is the most frequently used Outlook component. The Message window, shown in Figure 2-1, should be familiar to every Outlook user.

Figure 2-1

Outlook Message window

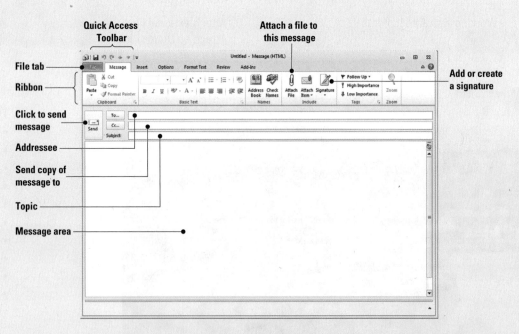

Many of the elements in the Message window are familiar to you if you use Microsoft Word 2010. The editor used to create messages in Outlook is based on Microsoft Word 2010. Your screen may vary if default settings have been changed or if other preferences have been set. Use this figure as a reference throughout this lesson as well as the rest of this book.

CREATING MESSAGES

The Bottom Line

Creating e-mail messages is probably the most common user activity in Outlook. Creating a simple e-mail message is not much harder than jotting a note on a Post-It®. In this section, you'll create a basic e-mail message and specify its format.

Composing a Message

Microsoft Outlook's e-mail component is a full-featured composition tool that provides many of the same functions found in Microsoft Word. Keying, copying, cutting, and deleting text in an Outlook message are identical to the same functions in Microsoft Word 2010. The **AutoComplete** function is another Word feature available in Outlook. It helps you quickly enter the names of the months and days of the week. AutoComplete cannot be turned off in Outlook 2010. In this exercise, you create a new e-mail message.

STEP BY STEP   **Compose a Message**

WileyPLUS Extra! features an online tutorial of this task.

GET READY. LAUNCH Outlook if it is not already running.

1. If necessary, click the Mail button in the Navigation Pane to display the Mail folder, as shown in Figure 2-2.

Figure 2-2

The Inbox—Outlook's opening screen

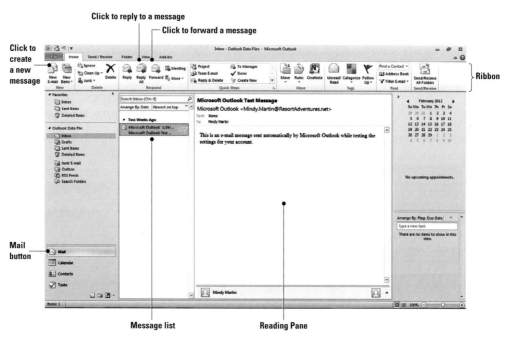

2. Click the New E-mail button on the Home tab. The Message window is displayed, as shown in Figure 2-1.

Take Note

Throughout this chapter you will see information that appears in text within brackets, such as [Press Enter] or [your e-mail address]. The information contained in the brackets is intended to be directions for you rather than something you actually type word for word. It will instruct you to perform an action or substitute text. Do not type the actual text that appears within brackets.

3. Click the message area.
4. Press Enter twice to add a blank line.
5. Key Hi Jon, [press Enter twice].

6. Key **Blue Yonder Airlines is running a contest in January. The winner gets free round-trip airfare to Cincinnati. Terry Crayton, a marketing assistant at Blue Yonder, asked if we would be interested in offering a free weekend at Resort Adventures as part of the prize. What do you think?** [Press **Enter** twice.]

7. Key **Let me know.** [Press **Enter** twice.]

8. Key [your name]. [Press **Enter.**]

PAUSE. LEAVE the Outlook Message window open to use in the next exercise.

Regardless of the tool you use, the task of writing a message is the same. In normal business correspondence, you would be more formal in addressing the correspondence. However, this example is just a quick note between the partners at Resort Adventures.

Specifying Message Content Format

The most attractive e-mail messages contain formatted text. Formatting, including bullets, font sizes, font colors, and bold text, can convey just the right impression. Microsoft Outlook can send messages in Hypertext Markup Language (HTML), Rich Text Format (RTF), and plain text—formats described in Table 2-1. Because of its flexibility and the formatting options it provides, HTML is the default format for the message you compose and send. However, not all e-mail applications can display these effects. In this exercise, you will change the format for a message to plain text.

Table 2-1

Message Formats

Format	Description
HTML	*Hypertext Markup Language (HTML)* is used by web browsers to display information. HTML enables you to format text and insert items such as horizontal lines, pictures, and animated graphics. Older and less robust e-mail programs may not be able to display HTML.
RTF	*Rich Text Format (RTF)* uses tags to format text. It can be read by most word processors and newer e-mail programs, but it can't display animated graphics and some web page formatting.
Plain text	*Plain text* does not use any formatting. It can be read by all e-mail programs. Without formatting, though, the impression you can convey in your message is limited.

STEP BY STEP **Select a Message Format**

USE the message you created in the previous exercise.

1. **OPEN** *Picture Signature* in the data files for this lesson. Select the table containing the picture and Mindy Martin's contact information. Right-click the table and click Copy on the shortcut menu. Close the *Picture Signature* document.

@ The *Picture Signature* file is available on the book companion website or in WileyPLUS.

2. Select the text Mindy Martin in the message window that you opened in the previous exercise and right-click.

3. Click Paste on the shortcut menu. Mindy's signature, including the picture of the stained-glass window, is pasted into the message.

4. In the Subject field, key Plain Text Message.

5. Click the Format Text tab, as shown in Figure 2-3.

6. In the Format group, click Plain Text. The Microsoft Outlook Compatibility Checker dialog box shown in Figure 2-3 is displayed. The items listed in the dialog box identify the changes that will occur in this particular message.

Figure 2-3

Formatted message and
Microsoft Outlook Compatibility
Checker dialog box

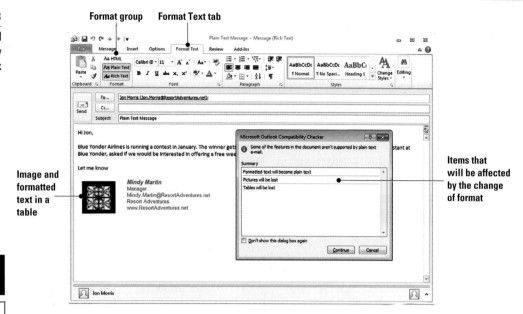

Image and
formatted
text in a
table

Items that
will be affected
by the change
of format

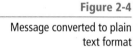

CERTIFICATION
READY   2.1.2

How do you specify the plain
text format for an individual
message?

7. Click the Continue button. The picture and formatting are removed from the message, as shown in Figure 2-4.

Figure 2-4

Message converted to plain
text format

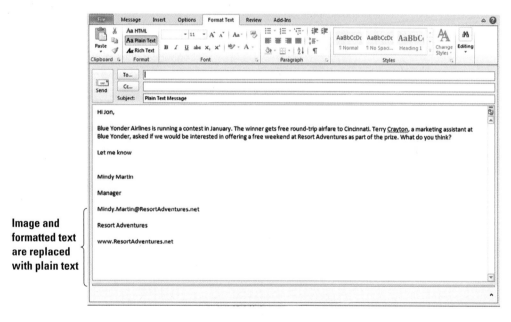

Image and
formatted text
are replaced
with plain text

CERTIFICATION
READY   2.1.2

How do you specify the Rich
Text Format for an individual
message?

PAUSE. LEAVE the Plain Text Message—Message window open to use in the next exercise.

Take Note   When you reply to a message, Outlook automatically uses the format of the received message as the format for your reply. Thus if you receive a message in plain text, your reply will automatically be sent in plain text.

CERTIFICATION READY   2.1.2

How do you specify HTML for an individual message?

In the previous exercise, you saw how you can choose to use RTF or plain text for an individual message. If you find that most of the people you need to send messages to can't read messages in HTML format, you can change the default message format for all your outgoing messages. To change the default format, click the File tab to open Backstage view and select Options from the navigation pane. In the left navigation pane of the Outlook Options dialog box, select Mail. In the Compose messages area, click the *Compose messages in the format* dropdown arrow and select either Plain Text or RTF. Click OK to save your changes.

SENDING A MESSAGE

The Bottom Line

Sending an e-mail message is easier than addressing and mailing a letter. An e-mail message can be sent to one or more recipients, resent if necessary, and saved for future reference. Table 2-2 describes the function of each element in the Message window. In this section, you'll address a message and send it. You'll then reopen the message, change the recipient, and resend it.

Table 2-2

Message Window Elements

NEW
to Office 2010

Element	Description
File tab	Use the File tab to access common Outlook settings and options.
Quick Access Toolbar	Use the **Quick Access Toolbar** to save, print, or undo your recent actions and redo your recent actions. The position and content of the Quick Access Toolbar can be customized.
Ribbon	The Ribbon organizes commands into logical groups. The groups are placed under tabs that focus on a particular activity. In the Message window, the tabs include Message, Insert, Options, and Format Text. The content of the Ribbon varies by the task. The Ribbon in the Message window contains different options from the Ribbon in the Contact window.
To	Key the name or e-mail address of the person or people who will receive the message you are sending. To send the message to several addressees, key a semicolon after a name before adding the next addressee.
Cc	The *Cc* field is optional. You can send a message without entering anything in the *Cc* field. Generally, you would use this to send a copy of the message to individuals who you think should be informed about the message content but from whom you don't expect any action.
Subject	Key a brief description of the information in the message. The **Subject** tells the recipient what the message is about and makes it easier to find the message later.

Showing and Hiding the *From* and *Bcc* Fields

The Outlook message window contains four standard fields that you can use to create and address your messages. However, there are two additional fields that you can use or hide as needed: *From* and *Bcc*. These fields are hidden by default, but you can use the Options tab to display them in the Message window.

Using the From field can be quite convenient when you use more than one e-mail account. For example, you might use one account for work and a different one for personal messages.

The Bcc field enables you to send a blind copy to someone. You would use this to send a copy of the message to an individual who should be informed about the message's content without notifying the recipient(s) listed in the *To* and *Cc* fields. The *Bcc* field is different from the *Cc* field in that no one else who receives the e-mail message knows that someone else received a blind copy. In this exercise, you'll turn on and off the From and Bcc fields.

STEP BY STEP   **Show or Hide the *From* and *Bcc* Fields**

USE the message you created in the previous exercise.

1. Click the Options tab. The Option tab displays the sending and delivery options as well as many options you can use to customize the message.

Ref   You'll learn more about Outlook's advanced messaging options in Lesson 3.

2. In the Show Fields group, click Bcc. The *Bcc* field appears in the Message window, as shown in Figure 2-5.

3. In the Show Fields group, click From. The *From* field appears in the Message window, as shown in Figure 2-5.

Figure 2-5

Displaying the *From* and *Bcc* fields

Click to toggle on and off the From and Bcc fields

Click the From button to select an alternate email address

The Bcc field

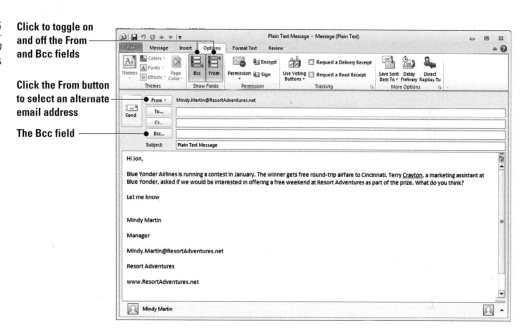

4. In the *Bcc* field, key [your e-mail address].

Take Note   Displaying and hiding the *From* and *Bcc* fields affects only the current Message window.

CERTIFICATION READY   2.1.3

How do you display or hide the *From* and *Bcc* fields?

5. In the Show Fields group, click From. The *From* field is once again hidden from view.
PAUSE. LEAVE Outlook open to use in the next exercise.

Sending a Message

Addressing an e-mail message is similar to addressing a letter. In seconds, you can send an e-mail message to one or more recipients. In this exercise, you'll address an e-mail message and send it to the recipient.

STEP BY STEP   **Send a Message**

USE the message you worked on in the previous exercise.

1. Click the *To* field. Key someone@example.com or key [the e-mail address of a friend or coworker]. To send the message to more than one recipient, key a semicolon (;), and then key another e-mail address.

2. Select the text in the *Subject* field. Key Blue Yonder Airlines contest and press Enter. The message is now ready to send, as shown in Figure 2-6.

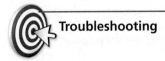 **Troubleshooting** The e-mail addresses used in this book are owned by Microsoft Corporation. Because they are not real e-mail addresses, you will receive either an error message or a message thanking you for using Microsoft products.

Figure 2-6

Message ready to be sent

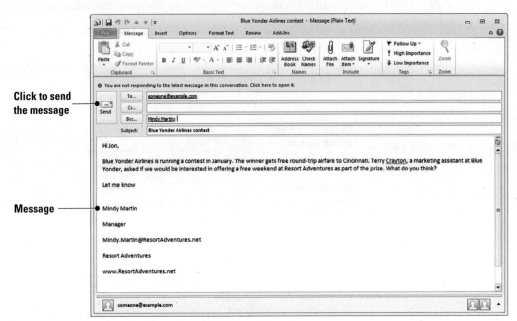

3. Click the Send button. The Message window closes, and the message is moved to the Outbox.

Take Note If your computer is connected to the Internet, the message is sent to the addressee as soon as you click the Send button. If your computer is not connected to the Internet, the message will remain in the Outbox until you connect to the Internet and the message can be sent.

PAUSE. LEAVE Outlook open to use in the next exercise.

In the previous exercises, you used the Message window to compose and send an e-mail message. If your computer has not been connected to the Internet since you started this lesson, the message you sent will still be in the Outbox. Outgoing messages are moved to the Outbox when you click the Send button. They are moved to the Sent Items folder when you connect to the Internet and the messages are sent.

Resending a Message

Occasionally, you may want to resend a message. This commonly occurs when you want to send the same message to additional recipients or the recipient has accidentally deleted the message and needs another copy. In this exercise, you'll resend the message that you just sent.

STEP BY STEP **Resend a Message**

USE the message you created in the previous exercise.

1. In the Navigation Pane, click the Sent Items folder. The e-mail messages you sent will be listed as items in the Sent Items folder, as shown in Figure 2-7.

Figure 2-7

Sent Items folder

Sent message in
the message list

Sent Items
folder selected

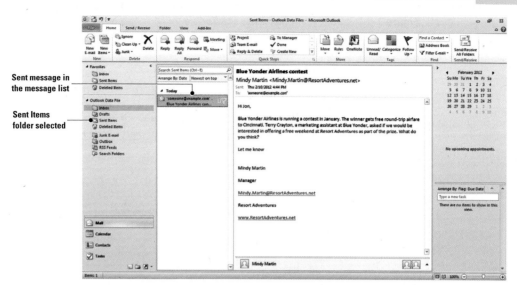
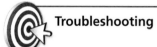

Troubleshooting If you haven't been connected to the Internet and your message is still sitting in the Outbox, click the Outbox folder instead of the Sent Items folder. Then continue with step 2.

---

2. In the list of items that have been sent, double-click the message you sent in the last exercise. The message is displayed in a new window, as shown in Figure 2-8. The title bar of the new window is the subject of the message.

Figure 2-8

Sent message

Title bar matches the subject ———   ——— Actions button

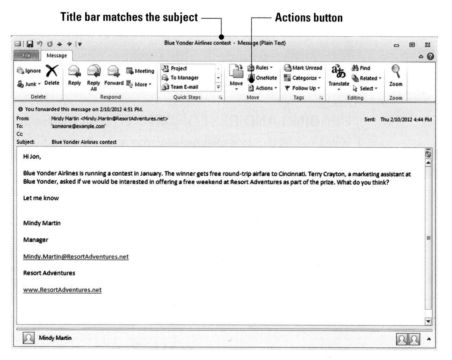

3. Click the Actions button in the Move group on the Home tab. Select the Resend This Message option from the menu that appears. This opens the message in a new window, which enables you to make modifications to the original message.

4. Click after the addressee in the To field. Key a semicolon (;) and an additional e-mail address, as shown in Figure 2-9. For this exercise, use your e-mail address as the addressee. By default in Outlook, someone who is listed as both a recipient in the *To* field and the *Bcc* field will only receive the message once.

Figure 2-9

Message ready to be resent

Addressee added before resending the message   Original message window

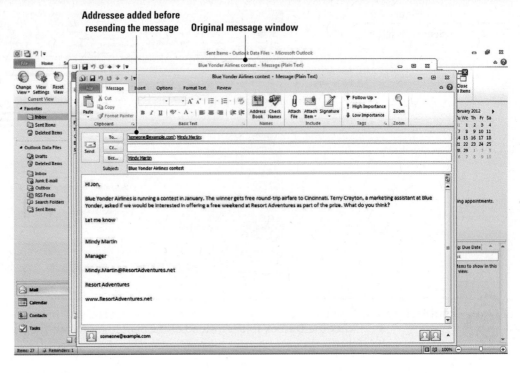

5. Click the Send button. The Message window closes, and the message is moved to the Outbox. The message is sent when your computer is connected to the Internet.

6. Close the original Message window.

PAUSE. LEAVE Outlook open to use in the next exercise.

In the previous exercise, you resent a message. When you resend a message, you can delete the original addressee, add new addressees, and edit the message content.

READING AND RESPONDING TO MESSAGES

The Bottom Line

When you receive an e-mail message, you naturally want to read it and, in many cases, send a reply. Outlook enables you to preview and reply to a message with a few mouse clicks. In this section, you'll preview and read a new e-mail message and flag it as a reminder for yourself. Finally, you'll reply to the message and then forward to a colleague.

Automatically Previewing Messages

If you return to your desk after a meeting to find 20 messages in your Inbox and another meeting to attend in 5 minutes, it might be impossible to read all the messages and still get to the meeting on time. In this exercise, you learn how to use **AutoPreview** to view the first three lines of every message in the message list.

STEP BY STEP   **Automatically Previewing Messages**

USE the message you created in the previous exercise.

1. In the Navigation Pane, click the Inbox folder. The Inbox is displayed.

2. On the View tab, click the Change View button. The available views for this folder appear below the Current View group.

3. Select the Preview option. The Inbox folder's layout changes: The Reading Pane disappears, and the messages appear in a list format. Notice that the first three lines of text in each unread message is displayed, as shown in Figure 2-10.

Figure 2-10

AutoPreview messages

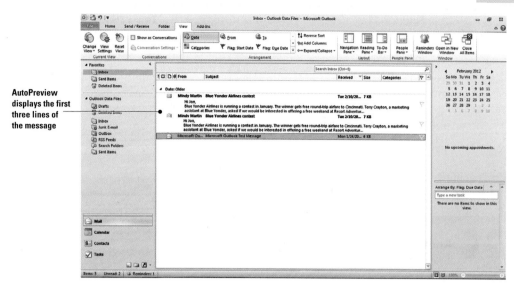

AutoPreview
displays the first
three lines of
the message

Take Note

By default, AutoPreview only displays a preview of the unread messages. If you want to view all messages this way, click the View Settings button and select Other Settings. In the AutoPreview area of the Other Settings dialog box, select the Preview All Items option and then click OK twice to close the dialog boxes.

4. On the View tab, click the Change View button. Select Compact from the available views. This turns off the AutoPreview function and returns to the default view.

PAUSE. LEAVE Outlook open to use in the next exercise.

AutoPreview requires more space in the message list. Therefore, you probably want to turn off the feature most of the time.

Sending a Reply to a Message

Not every message is going to require a reply, but many messages do need a response of some type. When you use the Reply function, your response is automatically addressed to the person who sent the message to you. In this exercise, you'll send a reply to a message.

STEP BY STEP   **Send a Reply to a Message**

USE the message you received when you sent a message to yourself in a previous exercise.

1. In the Inbox, click the message with the subject Blue Yonder Airlines contest. The message is selected and a preview appears in the Reading Pane.

2. Click the Reply button on the Home tab. The message is displayed in a new window, as shown in Figure 2-11. Note that the *To* and *Subject* fields are already filled and the contents of the original message are included at the bottom of the window. They are sent as part of the reply.

Take Note

In the *Subject* field, the text "RE:" was inserted before the original subject line. "RE:", which stands for "regarding," tells the recipient that the message is a reply about the Blue Yonder Airlines contest topic.

Figure 2-11

Replying to a message
you received

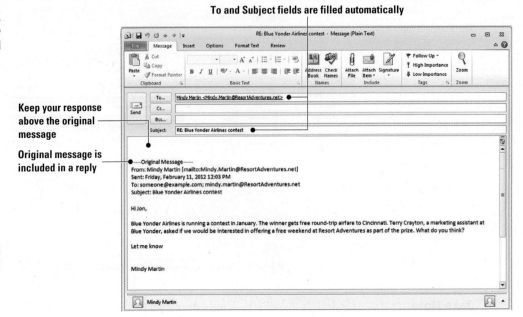

Figure 2-11

Replying to a message
you received

Another Way
If you want to send
a reply to everyone who received
an e-mail message, you can
click the Reply All button on
the Home tab.

Take Note   Before responding to a message, check the *To* line to ensure that you did not reply to all message recipients if you intended to reply to the sender only.

3. Key **The contest could be a good idea. Let's set up a meeting**.

4. Click the **Send** button. The Message window closes, and the reply is moved to the Outbox. The message is sent when your computer is connected to the Internet.

PAUSE. LEAVE Outlook open to use in the next exercise.

When a reply has been sent, the icon next to the original message is changed. An arrow pointing left, as shown in Figure 2-12, indicates that you replied to the message. When you view the main Outlook window, this icon tells you which messages you have answered.

Figure 2-12

Icon indicating that a reply
was sent

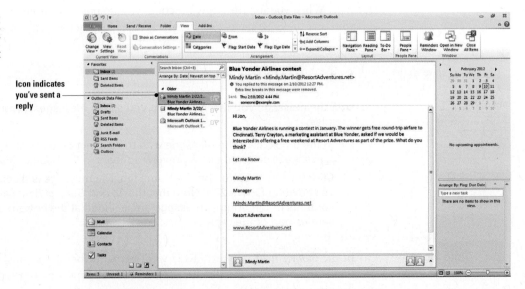

Forwarding a Message

Occasionally, you receive a message that should be sent to additional people. Outlook's Forward function is a quick method of sending the message to additional people without re-creating the original message. In this exercise, you'll forward a message to a colleague.

STEP BY STEP   **Forwarding a Message**

USE the message you received when you sent a message to yourself in a previous exercise.

1. In the Inbox, click the message with the subject Blue Yonder Airlines contest. The message is selected.
2. Click the Forward button on the Home tab. The message is displayed in a new window, as shown in Figure 2-13. The original message is included at the bottom of the window.

Take Note   Note that the *Subject* field is already filled. In the *Subject* field, the text "FW:" has been inserted before the original subject line. "FW:" tells the recipient that the message has been forwarded by the sender.

3. In the *To* field, key someone@example.com.
4. Click the message area above the original message. Key What is the value of the airfare and weekend at Resort Adventures?
5. [Press Enter.] Key [your name].

Figure 2-13

Forwarding a message you received

Subject field filled automatically

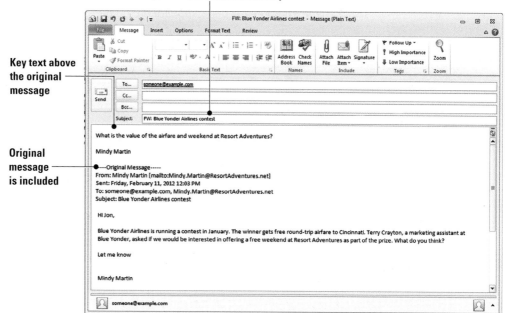

Key text above the original message

Original message is included

6. Click the Send button. The Message window closes, and the message is moved to the Outbox. The message is sent when your computer is connected to the Internet.

PAUSE. LEAVE Outlook open to use in the next exercise.

When a message has been forwarded, the icon next to the original message is changed. An arrow pointing right, as shown in Figure 2-14, indicates that you forwarded the message.

Figure 2-14

Icon indicating the message was forwarded

Forwarded message

Printing an E-mail Message

In Outlook 2010, each message is actually a document. As with any other documents you create or receive, you might want to have a hard copy of the information. You can use the tools on the Print page in Backstage view to preview and print the selected message. The Print page includes a preview pane that shows you how the message will look when printed so that you can make any necessary changes before sending it to the printer. The Print page also contains the various printing options you can select, such as the number of copies and the range of pages to print. You can choose printing options each time or simply print using the default options. In this exercise, you'll print a message.

STEP BY STEP   **Print an E-mail Message**

 Troubleshooting Before printing your document, you will need to make sure you have selected a printer. If your computer is already set up to print, you will not need to complete step 5 of this exercise.

USE the message you created in the previous exercises.

1. In the Inbox, click the message with the subject Blue Yonder Airlines contest. The message is selected.

2. Click the File tab to open the Backstage view and click the Print option in the navigation pane. The preview pane appears on the right of the page, as shown in Figure 2-15.

Figure 2-15

Printing a message

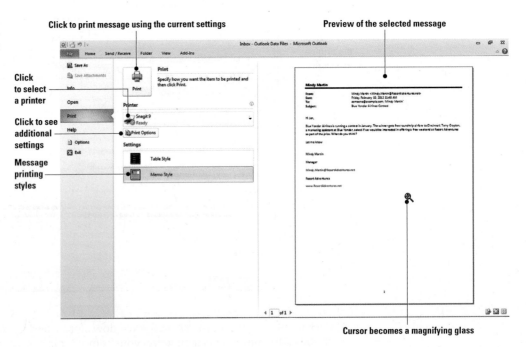

Take Note   Memo Style is the default style for printing messages. If you want to print the message list for the current folder, you can click Table Style.

3. Move the pointer over the document preview and notice that it changes to a magnifying glass, as shown in Figure 2-15.

4. Click the document to zoom in to 100% and again to zoom out to 50%.

5. Click the Printer button to display a list of available printers. Select the printer you want to use from the list.

 Troubleshooting You may need to set up a new printer before you can proceed.

6. Click the Print Options button to display the Print dialog box, as shown in Figure 2-16. Notice the available printing options.

Figure 2-16

Print dialog box

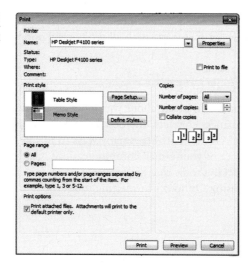

Another Way
If you already have a printer selected, you can simply click the large Print button to print the message using the default settings.

7. In the copies area, click the upward-pointing arrow next to the *Number of copies* box to change it to 2.
8. Click Print to print two copies of the letter.
PAUSE. LEAVE Outlook open to use in the next exercise.

You chose to print two copies of the message in this activity. If the message were longer, you could have chosen other options, such as printing a range of pages, collating the pages, or printing multiple pages per sheet.

 Ref   You will learn more about printing multiple messages in Lesson 3.

Saving a Message in an External Format

Outlook stores a copy of every message you write or receive in one of its folders until you delete it. Saving messages in Outlook's folder structure in Outlook Message Format is often all you need. However, if you need a message available in a different format, you can choose to save it as a .txt file or as a fully formatted .html file. In this exercise, you'll save a copy of a message as a text file.

STEP BY STEP   **Save a Message in an External Format**

USE the message you created in the previous exercises.

1. Click the File tab to open the Backstage view and then click Save As. The Save As dialog box is displayed, showing the Documents folder.
2. Navigate to the Outlook Lesson 2 folder. You can also choose a folder in which to store the file from the folder list.

Take Note   To create a new folder in the folder list to store your message, click the New Folder button in the menu bar.

 **Another Way**
You can also choose any of the other types listed. If the message is in the default HTML format, saving it as an HTML document will also be a choice.

3. In the *Save As type* box, click the downward-pointing arrow and choose Text Only.
4. In the File Name box, key Sample Saved Message.
5. Click Save to close the dialog box and save the document.
6. Close the message window.
PAUSE. LEAVE Outlook open to use in the next exercise.

You can save a message as a file to a folder on your hard drive, a network location, a CD, the desktop, or another storage location. You just saved the message letter you created as a .txt file.

If you had chosen Outlook Message Format in the *Save as type* box, the message would be stored as a functioning Outlook message, which means that when you open the file it opens as a fully functioning message window, complete with all the normal options.

FORMATTING MESSAGES

The Bottom Line

Your e-mail messages convey an image about you and your business. In order to present the best image to clients and business contacts, the best business communications are as eye-catching and polished as possible. Outlook provides many ways to format the text in your message so as to improve the appearance of your e-mail communications. Outlook includes most of the same formatting and spellchecking tools that are available in Microsoft Word 2010. In this section, you'll format messages using Outlook's formatting tools, themes, and styles.

SOFTWARE ORIENTATION

Formatting Outlook Messages

As you learn to format messages, it is important to become familiar with the tools you will use. The Format Text tab displayed in Figure 2-17 contains the formatting commands that you will use to enhance the appearance of the messages you create.

Figure 2-17

Message window's Format Text tab

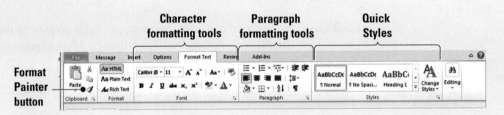

You will use commands from every group on the Format Text tab as you learn to apply formatting to text, copy formatting, and apply styles and themes.

Using Formatting Tools

Microsoft has a variety of fonts and font sizes to help you communicate your intended message, whether it is casual for your personal life or formal for the workplace. In addition to changing the font and font size, you can apply special **formatting attributes**, such as bold or italic, to characters within your text to give them special emphasis. A **character** can be a letter, number, punctuation mark, or symbol. In this exercise, you'll use Outlook's formatting tools to enhance the appearance of a message.

You can use the **Format Painter** to copy formats, including font, font size, font style, font color, alignment, indentation, number formats, borders, and shading. To copy formatting from one location to another, select the text that has the formatting you want to copy. Click Format Painter in the Clipboard group. The mouse pointer turns into a white plus sign with the paintbrush beside it. Drag the mouse pointer across the text you want to format.

To copy formatting to several locations, double-click the Format Painter button, and then drag the mouse pointer across each text item you want to format. When you're done, click the Format Painter again or press Esc to turn off the Format Painter.

E-mail Basics   47

STEP BY STEP   **Use Formatting Tools**

GET READY. LAUNCH Outlook if it is not already running.

1. If necessary, click the Mail button in the Navigation Pane to display the Mail folder.
2. Click the New E-mail button on the Home tab. The Message window is displayed, as shown in Figure 2-1.
3. Open the **Promotional Flyer** document in the data files for this lesson and select the text. Right-click and click Copy on the shortcut menu.
4. Back in Outlook, right-click the message area.
5. Click Paste on the shortcut menu. The text of the Promotional Flyer is pasted into the message.
6. Select all the text in the message area.
7. Click the Format Text tab to display the Font group, as shown in Figure 2-18.

The **Promotional Flyer** file is available on the book companion website or in WileyPLUS.

Figure 2-18

The Font group

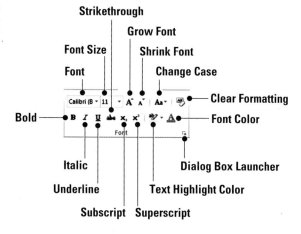

8. In the Font group click the dialog box launcher. The Font dialog box appears.
9. Click ++Body in the selection pane under the Font box. Press the down arrow to scroll through the list to select Verdana, as shown in Figure 2-19. Notice that the Preview area displays how your selected text will look with each font selected.

Another Way
You can also access the Font dialog box from the Basic Text group on the Home tab.

Figure 2-19

The Font dialog box

Another Way
You can also click the Font arrow button on the ribbon to open a menu that you can use to change the font of the selected text.

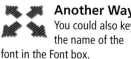

Another Way
You could also key the name of the font in the Font box.

10. Click OK to close the dialog box.

Another Way
You can also use the keyboard to apply bold. Select text and press Ctrl+B.

Another Way
You can also use the keyboard to apply Underline. Select text and press Ctrl+U.

Another Way
You can also use the keyboard to apply italics. Select text and press Ctrl+I.

Another Way
The Format Painter is available on the Mini toolbar as well as in the Clipboard group.

Another Way
You can use the Format Painter to change multiple selections. With the source formatting selected, double-click the Format Painter button. You can click any text to change it. Double-click to turn off the Format Painter.

11. Select the first sentence in the message area (be sure to select both lines). Click the Font Size arrow in the Font group and select 36. The text size changes to 36.

12. With the text still selected, click the Font Size box and key 22 and press Enter. The text size shrinks considerably.

13. With the text still selected, click the Grow Font button three times and then the Shrink Font button one time. The text is now resized to 26.

14. With the text still selected, click the Font Color arrow and select Blue, Accent 1, Darker 25% from the gallery that appears. The text changes to medium blue color.

15. Select the text Resort Adventures near the bottom of the message and click Bold. The text is made bold to draw more attention to it.

16. Select the web address at the bottom of the message and click Underline.

17. Select the text The Zipper and click Italic.

18. Select the text Resort and click the Format Painter button in the Clipboard group. The formatting details are stored in the clipboard.

19. Click one of the zeros in 2,500 in the main paragraph. The text 500 becomes bold, but the rest of the number doesn't. The Format Painter applies the format to the entire word, but because there is a comma in this number, Format Painter interprets it as two different words.

20. Click the Format Painter button again and this time click and drag the cursor across the entire number 2,500. The format is applied to the entire number.

21. In the Subject field, key Come Fly with Us, as shown in Figure 2-20.

Figure 2-20

A formatted message

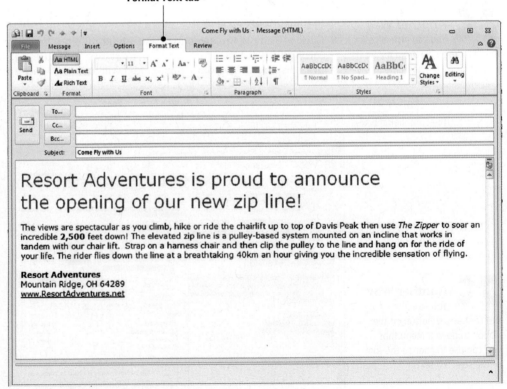

PAUSE. LEAVE the Outlook Message window open to use in the next exercise.

The font group in the Format Text tab contains the Font menu for changing the font, and the Font Size menu for changing its size. You can also access these commands on the Mini toolbar. Table 2-3 provides extra information about each character formatting tool.

Table 2-3

Formatting Tools

Button	Example	Description
Bold	**Sample bold text**	Emphasis formatting attribute that makes the selected text look darker and thicker.
Change Capitalization	Hello world hello world HELLO WORLD Hello World hELLO wORLD	The Change Case menu in the Font group has five options for changing the capitalization of text.
Font	Calibri Times New Roman Comic Sans	A **font** is a set of characters that have the same design. Each font has a unique name.
Font Color	Sample font color	Changes the color of the selected text. Click the down arrow next to the button to select a different font color.
Font Size	Size 8 Size 10 Size 12	Font sizes are measured in points. Point sizes refer to the height of text characters, with one point equaling approx. 1/72 of an inch.
Grow Font	Grow Grow Grow	Click the Grow Font button to increase the size of the selected text by one increment.
Italic	*Sample italic text*	Emphasis formatting attribute the makes the selected text look lighter and tilted to the right.
Shrink Font	Shrink Shrink Shrink	Click the Shrink Font button to decrease the size of the selected text by one increment.
Strikethrough	~~Sample strikethrough text~~	Emphasis formatting attribute that places a line through the center of the selected text.
Subscript	Sample $_{subscript}$	Emphasis formatting attribute that places the selected text just below the line of the surrounding text.
Superscript	Sample$^{2\ superscript}$	Emphasis formatting attribute that places the selected text just above the line of the surrounding text.
Text Highlight	Sample highlight	Use the Text Highlight Color button in the Font group to highlight text, making it look as if it was marked with a highlighting pen. Click the down arrow next to the button to select a different highlight color. To remove highlighting select the highlighted text and choose No Color from the menu.
Underline	Sample underlined text	Emphasis formatting attribute that places an underline beneath the selected text. You can select the style and thickness of the line by click the Underline button arrow.
Clear Formatting	Sample unformatted text	Removes all formatting from the selected text.

Formatting Paragraphs

Depending on the type of information you want to convey in your message, you might want to apply paragraph formatting to make your message more understandable. Outlook contains a number of tools that you can use to change the appearance of paragraphs. You can change alignment and line spacing, create numbered and bulleted lists, sort paragraphs, and use shading and borders. To apply paragraph formatting, place the insertion point anywhere in a paragraph. Outlook will apply the formatting you chose to the entire paragraph. In this exercise, you will try out the different paragraph formatting options.

STEP BY STEP   **Format Paragraphs**

USE the message you created in the previous exercise.

1. If necessary, open the Come Fly with Us message that you worked on in the previous exercise and click the Format Text tab to display the Paragraph group, as shown in Figure 2-21.

Figure 2-21

The Paragraph group

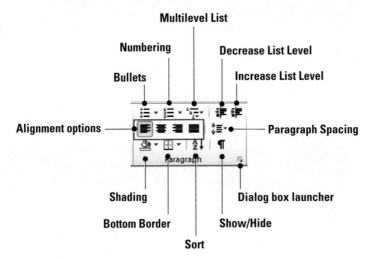

2. Click the Show/Hide button in the Paragraph group of the Format Text tab. The paragraph symbol (¶) appears at the end of each paragraph.
3. Select the paragraph symbol (¶) at the end of the first line and press Delete. Press Spacebar. The first sentence becomes one paragraph.
4. Click anywhere in the first paragraph and click the Paragraph group dialog box launcher. The Paragraph dialog box is displayed, as shown in Figure 2-22.

Figure 2-22

The Paragraph dialog box

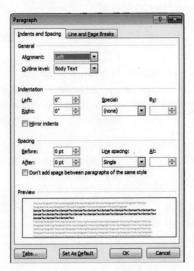

5. In the After box in the Spacing area, key 18. Click OK to close the dialog box. The spacing between the first paragraph and the second paragraph is increased.

6. Click the Align Center button in the Paragraph group of the Format Text tab. The paragraph where the insertion point is located is centered at the top of the message.

7. Click the Shading button arrow and select Dark Blue. Dark blue shading appears behind the main paragraph. Notice that the font color automatically changes to white to make text more readable.

8. Click the Shading button arrow again and select Olive Green, Accent 3, Lighter 40%. Since you've applied a lighter shading option, the font color automatically changes back to black to make text more readable.

9. Select the last three rows of text and click Align Right.

10. Click anywhere in the text Resort Adventures and click the Borders button arrow. A menu of border styles is displayed.

11. Click the Top Border button in the menu. A thin line appears above the text. Your message should look like the one in Figure 2-23.

<table>
<tr><td>Figure 2-23

Shading and aligning paragraphs</td><td>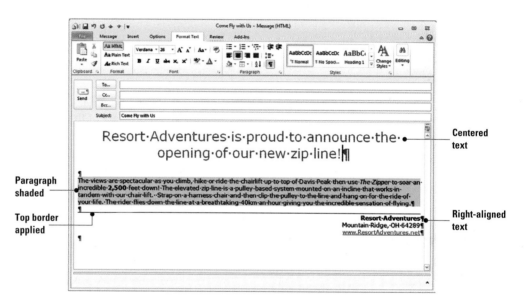</td></tr>
</table>

PAUSE. LEAVE the Outlook Message window open to use in the next exercise.

Applying Styles to a Message

Although formatting your messages makes them more appealing, it can also be time consuming. You can save time by selecting a style from Outlook's Quick Style gallery. A **style** is a set of formatting attributes that you can apply to text more easily than setting each formatting attribute individually. **Quick Styles** are predefined formats that you can apply to your document to instantly change its look and feel. Outlook eliminates the guesswork by allowing you to preview the formatting changes in your message before you commit to a style. In this exercise, you will apply Quick Styles to a message.

STEP BY STEP | **Apply Styles to a Message**

USE the message you created in the previous exercise.

1. If necessary, open the Come Fly with Us message that you worked on in the previous exercise and click the Format Text tab to display the Styles group, as shown in Figure 2-17.

2. Click anywhere in the first sentence and click the More button in the Styles group to display the Quick Styles gallery, as shown in Figure 2-24.

Figure 2-24

Quick Styles gallery

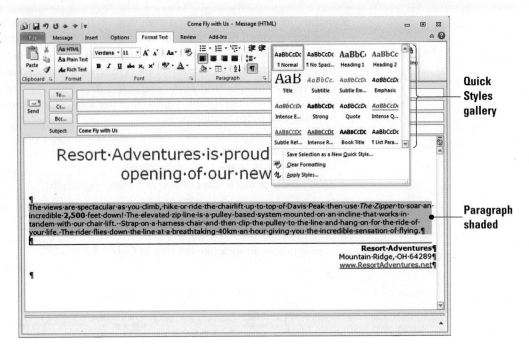

Figure 2-24

Quick Styles gallery

3. Place your pointer over any choice on the Styles Set menu and notice that your document changes to show you a preview of that style.

4. Click **Title**. The text changes font, color, and alignment to reflect the Title style.

5. Select the body paragraph that begins "*The views are spectacular...*" Click the **More** button to open the Quick Styles gallery again.

6. Place your pointer over any thumbnail in the gallery and notice that the paragraph changes to show you a preview of that style.

Take Note   You will notice that some of the thumbnails remove the background formatting and some do not. When you select a paragraph style, all the previous formatting for the paragraph is replaced with the new style.

7. Click the **Quote** thumbnail. Notice that style is applied to the paragraph you selected. Your message should look similar to Figure 2-25.

Figure 2-25

Message formatted with Quick Styles

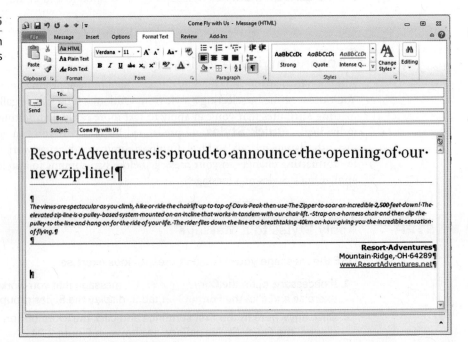

8. Click the Change Styles button in the Styles group. Point to Style Set and point to each of the Style Sets listed. Notice that the formatting of the entire message changes to reflect the style set.

9. Click on Traditional. The message changes to reflect the Traditional styles, as shown in Figure 2-26.

Figure 2-26

Message formatted with a Style Set

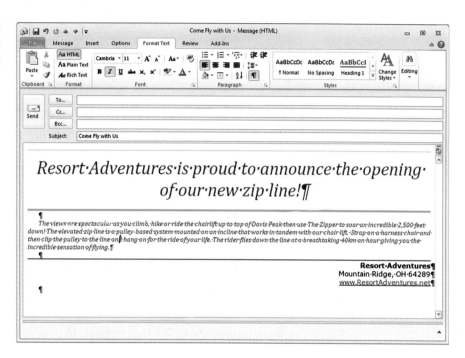

PAUSE. LEAVE the Outlook Message window open to use in the next exercise.

CERTIFICATION READY   **2.4.2**

How do you apply Quick Styles to a message?

There are two kinds of Quick Styles—paragraph styles and character styles. A paragraph mark to the right of the style's name denotes a style created for paragraphs. When you choose paragraph styles, the formats are applied to all the text in the paragraph in which your insertion point is located, whether or not you have it all selected.

Character styles have the lowercase letter a beside them. Character styles are applied to individual characters you have selected within a paragraph rather than affecting the entire paragraph.

Style Sets are collections of Quick Style formats that go well together. When you select a Style Set from the Change Styles button, the entire message is changed to reflect the combination of styles in the set.

Creating Styles

Outlook allows you to create custom styles that you can save to the Styles list. You can then apply the custom style to future messages. You can also modify Quick Styles to suit your needs. In this exercise, you'll create a custom style.

STEP BY STEP   **Create Styles**

USE the message you created in the previous exercise.

1. If necessary, open the Come Fly with Us message that you worked on in the previous exercise and click the Format Text tab to display the Styles group (refer to Figure 2-17).

2. Select the text Mountain Ridge, OH 64289. Click the dialog box launcher for the Styles group. The Styles list is displayed as a floating box in the Message window.

3. Click the top of the Styles list and drag it to the left edge of the message window. The Styles list is docked to the side of the message, as shown in Figure 2-27.

Figure 2-27

Docked Styles list

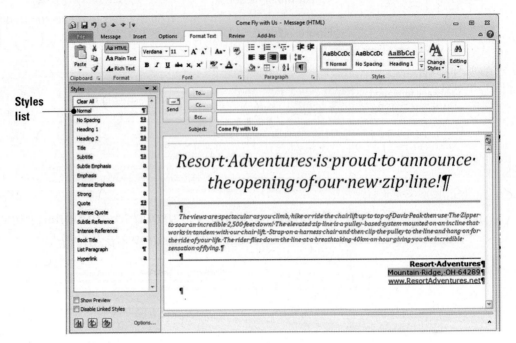

4. Click the Subtle Emphasis style. The style is applied to the selected text.

5. Click the arrow to the right of Subtle Emphasis to display the shortcut menu. Click Modify. The Modify Style dialog box appears, as shown in Figure 2-28.

Figure 2-28

Modify Style dialog box

6. Click the Bold button in the dialog box. Click the Font Color down arrow and click Dark Blue, Text 2, Lighter 60% in the standard colors section. Notice that the preview in the dialog box changes.

7. Click OK to apply your changes and close the dialog box. The appearance of the selected text changes.

8. Select the text Resort Adventures. Click the Italic button in the Font group.

9. Click the Font down arrow and select Cooper Std Black. Click the Font Color down arrow and select Dark Blue.

10. Click the Increase Font button twice to change the font size to 14.

11. Click the More button is the Styles group. Select Save Selection as a new Quick Style. The Create New Style from Formatting dialog box opens, as shown in Figure 2-29.

Figure 2-29

Create New Style from
Formatting dialog box

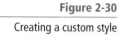

12. Key Resort Adventures in the Name box and click OK. The Resort Adventures style is
displayed in the Styles list, as shown in Figure 2-30.

Figure 2-30

Creating a custom style

13. Close the Come Fly with Us message window. Be sure to allow Outlook to save a copy
of the message.

PAUSE. LEAVE Outlook open to use in the next exercise.

You just learned that the Modify Style dialog box has basic formatting commands like the Font
menu; Font Size menu; Bold, Italic, and Underline buttons; and Font Color menu. When you
modify paragraph fonts you can also change alignment indents and spacing.

Applying a Message Theme

Message themes are another way to quickly change the overall design of your document using
formatting choices that are predefined in Outlook. A **theme** is a predefined set of colors, fonts,
and lines that can be applied to an entire message. Outlook contains the same collection of
themes that are available in the rest of Microsoft Office. You can apply an entire theme to your
message or choose from a variety of theme fonts, colors, and effects. In this exercise, you'll use a
theme to format an e-mail message.

Apply a Message Theme

USE the message you created in the previous exercise.

1. Click **Drafts** in the Navigation Pane. Double-click the **Come Fly with Us** message that you worked on in the previous exercise and click the **Options** tab to display the Themes group, as shown in Figure 2-31.

Figure 2-31

The Themes group

2. In the Themes group, click **Page Color**. The Page Color gallery is displayed.
3. Select the **Tan, Accent 2** color from the Theme colors area.
4. In the Themes group, click **Themes** as shown in Figure 2-32.

Figure 2-32

The Themes gallery

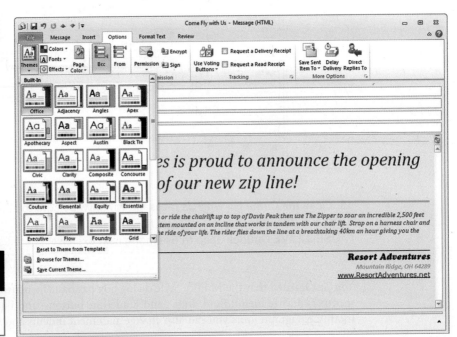

CERTIFICATION READY 2.1.1

How do you apply a theme to a message?

5. Place your pointer over any built-in theme and notice that the document changes to show you a preview of that theme.
6. Click **Executive**. The colors, fonts, and effects for that theme are applied to your message. Notice that the text *Resort Adventures* does not change because it uses a custom style.

PAUSE. LEAVE the Outlook Message window open to use in the next exercise.

Creating a New Theme

Although you used a theme to change the overall design of the entire message, you can also change individual elements by using the Theme Colors, Theme Fonts, and Theme Effects buttons. If you make any changes to the colors, fonts, or effects of the current theme, you can save it as a custom message theme and then apply it to other messages.

STEP BY STEP   **Create a New Theme**

USE the message you created in the previous exercise.

1. If necessary, open the Come Fly with Us message that you worked on in the previous exercise and click the Options tab to display the Themes group.

2. In the Themes group, click Theme Fonts as shown in Figure 2-33.

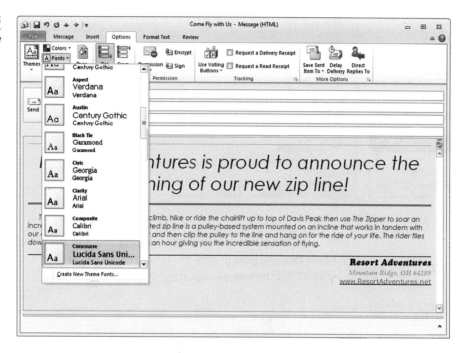

3. Place your pointer over any of the theme fonts and notice that the document changes to show you a preview of that theme.

4. Click the Concourse theme font. The fonts for that theme are applied to your message.

5. In the Themes group, click Theme Colors as shown in Figure 2-34.

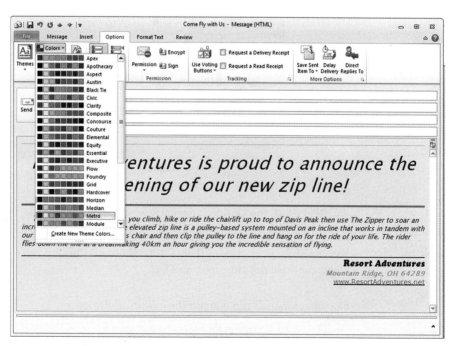

6. Click the Metro theme color. The colors for that theme are applied to your message.

7. In the Themes group, click Themes. Click the Save Current Theme option at the bottom of the Themes gallery. The Save Current Theme window is displayed with the text Theme1 already displayed in the *File name* box, as shown in Figure 2-35.

Figure 2-35

The Save Current
Theme window

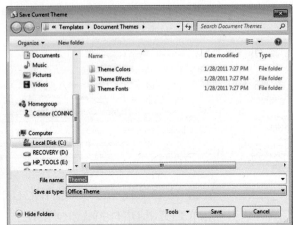

CERTIFICATION
READY   2.4.4

How do you create a
custom theme?

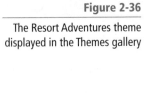

8. In the *File name* box, select the existing text and key Resort Adventures. Click Save.

9. In the Themes group, click Themes. The new custom theme appears in the Custom area of the Themes gallery, as shown in Figure 2-36.

Figure 2-36

The Resort Adventures theme
displayed in the Themes gallery

New theme
added to
the gallery

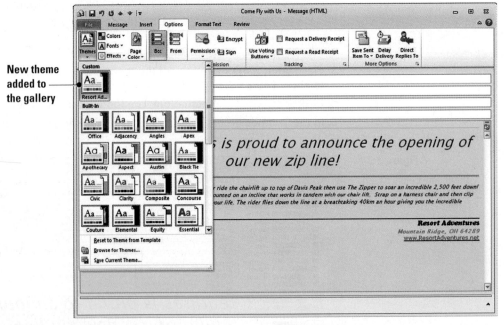

PAUSE. LEAVE the Outlook Message window open to use in the next exercise.

Take Note   You can share your custom theme throughout all Office programs, so all of your Office documents can have the same look and feel.

Document themes can contain the following elements:

• Theme colors contain four text and background colors, six accent colors, and two hyperlink colors. Click the Theme Colors button to change the colors for the current theme (refer to Figure 2-34).

- Theme fonts contain a heading font and a body text font. Click the Theme Fonts button to change the fonts for the current theme (refer to Figure 2-33).
- Theme effects are sets of lines and fill effects. Click the Theme Effects button to change the effects for the current theme (refer to Figure 2-37).

Figure 2-37

The Theme Effects gallery

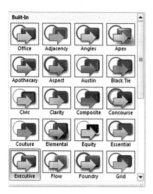

Using Paste Special

When you copy something from one source and paste it into an Outlook message, Outlook assumes you want to keep the source formatting. Sometimes this formatting works with your existing formatting, but often the pasted text clashes with the existing message. You can use the Paste Special feature to have more control over how the text appears. In this exercise, you'll use the Paste Special feature to copy and paste text into your message.

STEP BY STEP   **Use Paste Special**

USE the message you created in the previous exercise.

1. If necessary, open the Come Fly with Us message that you worked on in the previous exercise and click the Home tab to display the Clipboard group.
2. Place the insertion point at the end of the main paragraph in the message. Press Enter twice to add some space between the paragraph and the horizontal line.

@ The *Zipper Rates* file is available on the book companion website or in WileyPLUS.

3. In your Internet browser, open the *Zipper Rates* web page document in the data files for this lesson.
4. Scroll down the web page. Select the text Some Highlights You Could Experience: and the bulleted list that follows. Press Ctrl+C, which is the keyboard shortcut for the Copy command.

Take Note   The Ctrl+C keyboard shortcut is a powerful tool. Using the shortcut allows you to copy text in almost any application and then paste it (by using the Paste button or the keyboard shortcut Ctrl+V) into Outlook.

5. Back in Outlook, click the message area one line below the main paragraph.
6. In the Clipboard group, click the Paste button. The copied text is pasted into the message using the original formatting from the web page and the Paste Options button appears at the end of the text. In this case, the new text does not match the text in the original message, as shown in Figure 2-38.

Figure 2-38

Pasting into a message

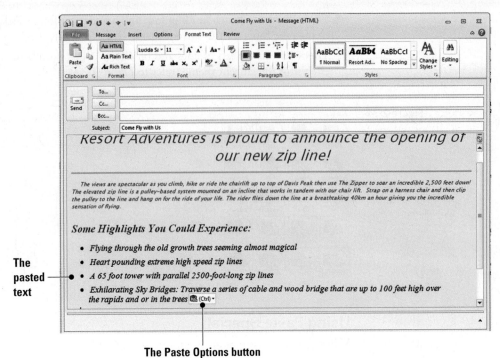

The
pasted —
text

The Paste Options button

7. Click the Undo button. In the Clipboard group, click the Paste down arrow. The Paste Options are listed beneath the Paste button, as shown in Figure 2-39.

Figure 2-39

The Paste Options

Click to keep the text only

**Click to keep the
original formatting**

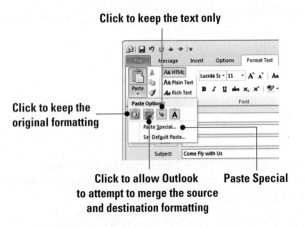

**Click to allow Outlook
to attempt to merge the source
and destination formatting**

Paste Special

8. Select Paste Special. The Paste Special dialog box is displayed, as shown in Figure 2-40.

Figure 2-40

Paste Special dialog box

**Inserts only the
unformatted text**

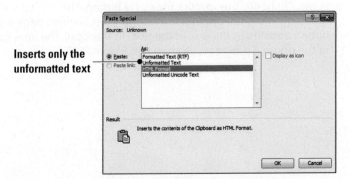

Another Way
You can also paste unformatted text by clicking the Paste Options button and selecting the Keep Text Only option.

CERTIFICATION
R E A D Y   2.4.5

How would you use the Paste Special dialog box to paste unformatted text into a message?

9. Select Unformatted Text and click OK. The dialog box closes and the text is pasted into the message without any formatting. Click the Format Text tab.

10. Select the text Some Highlights You Could Experience: and select Heading 1 from the Style gallery in the Styles group to apply the Heading 1 Quick Style to just this text selection.

11. Select the pasted list under the heading. Click the Bullets button in the Paragraph group. The new text is bulleted as it was in the browser window.

12. Click the More button to open the Style gallery. Select Emphasis from the Style gallery to give the bulleted items a style that blends well with the rest of the message.

13. Click the Bullets down arrow and select the large circle from the Bullet Library to change the bullets in the list, as shown in Figure 2-41.

Figure 2-41

Formatting the pasted text

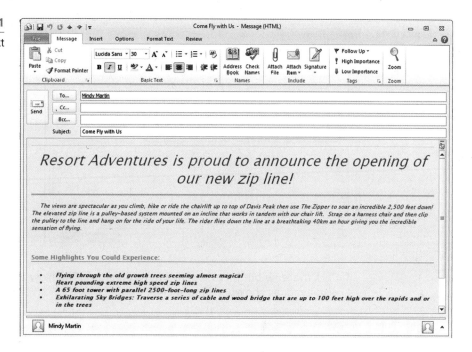

14. In the *To* field, key [your e-mail address].

15. Close the Come Fly with Us – Message window. Be sure to allow Outlook to save a copy of the message.

PAUSE. LEAVE Outlook open to use in the next exercise.

PERSONALIZING MESSAGES

The Bottom Line

You can personalize your messages in many ways. Formatting, colors, and images probably come to mind first. However, the signature is one of the most useful places to personalize your messages. In this section, you'll create a personal signature and attach it to a message. You'll also look into attaching your personal signature to all outgoing messages.

Creating a Personal Signature

A **signature** is text or images that Outlook automatically places at the end of your outgoing messages. A signature can be as fancy or as plain as you like. In this exercise, you'll create a personal signature.

STEP BY STEP   **Create a Personal Signature**

> **GET READY. LAUNCH** Outlook if it is not already running.
>
> 1. If necessary, click the Mail button in the Navigation Pane to display the Mail folder.
> 2. Click the New E-mail button on the Home tab. The Message window is displayed.
> 3. Click the Signature button in the Include group on the Ribbon. In the dropdown list, click Signatures. The Signatures and Stationery dialog box is displayed, as shown in Figure 2-42.

Take Note   If you share your e-mail account with other users or if additional Outlook profiles have been created, signatures created by other users may be listed in the Signatures and Stationery dialog box.

Figure 2-42

Signatures and Stationery dialog box

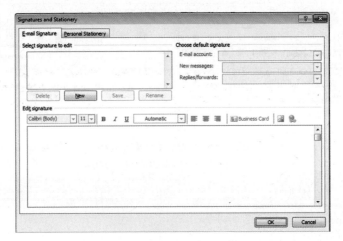

> 4. Click the New button to create a new signature. The New Signature dialog box is displayed, as shown in Figure 2-43.

Figure 2-43

New Signature dialog box

> 5. To name the new signature, key Lesson 2 into the *Type a name for this signature* field. Click OK. The New Signature dialog box is closed, and Lesson 2 is highlighted in the *Select Signature To Edit* list box.
> 6. Click in the empty Edit signature box. Any changes you make here are applied to the selected Lesson 2 signature. If additional signatures were listed, you could select a different signature and make changes to it.
> 7. Key [your name]. [Press Enter.]
>
>   Key [your title]. [Press Enter.]
>
>   Key [your e-mail address]. [Press Enter twice.]
>
>   Key [the name of your company]. [Press Enter.]
>
>   Key [the web address of your company]. [Press Enter.]
>
>   If you do not have a title, company, or company website, key the information that applies to you.
> 8. Select all the text in the signature. In the toolbar above the *Edit Signature* box, click the Font dropdown box arrow and select Arial from the list.
> 9. In the Font Size box on the toolbar, key 10. Click the Font Color dropdown box arrow (the current selection is Automatic) to open a palette of Font colors, as shown in Figure 2-44.

Figure 2-44

Editing a signature

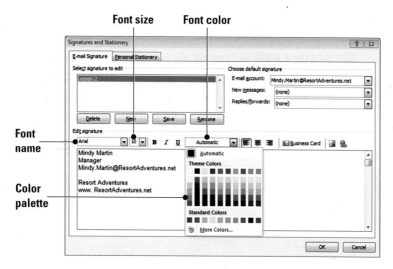

10. Select the color Blue.

11. Click in the *Edit Signature* box to deselect the text. Now select just your name in the Edit Signature box. Click Bold and Italic to apply those formatting attributes to the selected text. Change the font size to 12, as shown in Figure 2-45.

Figure 2-45

New signature

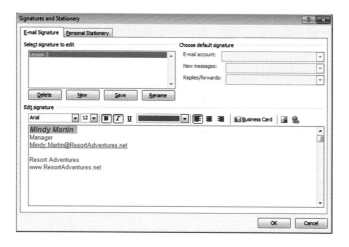

12. Verify that (none) is still selected in the *New Messages* and *Replies/Forwards* fields. Click OK. The dialog box is closed, and the signature is saved. Close the Message window.

PAUSE. LEAVE Outlook open to use in the next exercise.

 Ref   You can find more information on creating signatures in Lesson 7.

Although you can include images and more complicated formatting, the formatting you can do in the Signatures and Stationery dialog box is limited. For example, you can't resize an image in the Signatures and Stationery dialog box. However, you can open a new message, use the formatting tools in the new Message window to create a signature you like, cut the signature, and paste it into the Signatures and Stationery dialog box as a new signature.

Adding a Signature to a Single Message

You can choose to add a signature to an individual message. This enables you to create and use more than one signature.

STEP BY STEP **Add a Signature to a Single Message**

GET READY. LAUNCH Outlook if it is not already running.

1. If necessary, click the Mail button in the Navigation Pane to display the Mail folder.
2. Click the New E-mail button on the Home tab. The Message window is displayed.
3. In the message area, key I'm testing my new signature. Press Enter twice.
4. In the Include group on the Ribbon, click Signature. In the dropdown list, select Lesson 2. The signature is inserted into the message, as shown in Figure 2-46.

Figure 2-46

Message using the new signature

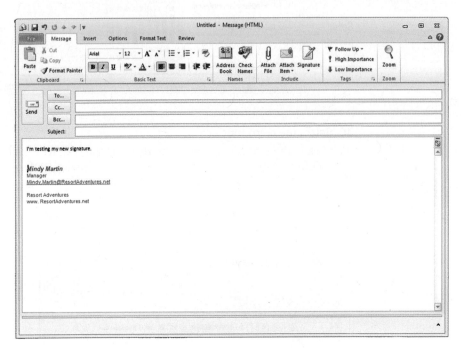

5. Click the To field and key your e-mail address.
6. Click the Subject field and key Testing signature in a single message. Click the Send button.
7. If the message has not been received, click the Send/Receive All Folders button.
8. Click the message in the message list. Click the File tab and select the Save As option. The Save As dialog box is displayed.
9. Navigate to folder where you want to save the file and click the Save button. The message is saved as Testing signature in a single message.htm.

PAUSE. LEAVE Outlook open to use in the next exercise.

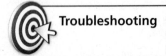
Troubleshooting If formatting has been applied to your e-mail messages or other signatures, the same formatting may be applied to the signature as you key the text. You can change the formatting after you key the signature.

You might want to create several signatures. This enables you to select the signature to match the message. When you send a personal message, use a signature that includes a picture from your favorite sport or a photo of your new puppy. When you send a business message, use a signature that includes your business information.

Adding a Signature to All Outgoing Messages

If you primarily use your e-mail account for the same type of e-mail (business or personal), you can select a signature that is automatically inserted into every outgoing message. This gives you a quick, consistent way to insert your signature.

Add a Signature to All Outgoing Messages

GET READY. LAUNCH Outlook if it is not already running.

1. If necessary, click the Mail button in the Navigation Pane to display the Mail folder.
2. Click the New E-mail button on the Home tab. The Message window is displayed.
3. Click the Signature button in the Include group on the Ribbon. In the dropdown list, click Signatures. The Signatures and Stationery window is displayed.
4. In the *New Messages* field, select Lesson 2, if necessary. Click OK. The Lesson 2 signature will automatically be added to every outgoing message. Close the message window.

PAUSE. LEAVE Outlook open to use in the next exercise.

Even if you use your e-mail account to send business and personal messages, you can save time by automatically adding a signature. When the automatic signature isn't appropriate, delete it from the message and insert the correct signature.

CREATING AND FORMATTING GRAPHIC MESSAGE CONTENT

Adding a chart, picture, or other illustration to a message captures attention and immediately portrays an idea of what the worksheet is all about. In this section, you'll add hyperlinks and graphics to a message.

SOFTWARE ORIENTATION

The Insert Tab

Microsoft Office includes a gallery of media images you can insert into worksheets such as pictures, clip art, shapes, and SmartArt graphics. You can also insert external picture files. The insert tab, shown in Figure 2-47, contains a group of features that you can use to add graphics to your document. The Illustrations group has options for several types of graphics you can use to enhance your messages.

Figure 2-47

The Insert tab

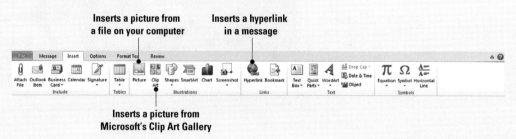

Use this figure as a reference through this section as you become skilled in inserting and formatting illustrations within a worksheet.

Inserting a Graphical Element

While the old adage "A picture is worth a thousand words" is perhaps an exaggeration, a visual element adds interest and calls attention to your messages. Unlike a message background that is displayed but does not print, pictures and other graphic objects are included in message printouts.

Graphics can be an integral part of creating a compelling message. You can insert or copy pictures into a worksheet from image providers, Microsoft's clip art organizer (Microsoft Clip Organizer), or files on your computer. A well-chosen picture can portray a powerful message. In this exercise, you will insert a graphic element into a message.

STEP BY STEP   **Insert a Graphical Element**

USE the Come Fly with Us message you created in a previous exercise.

1. If necessary, click the Drafts button in the Navigation Pane to display the Mail folder. In the last exercise, you saved and closed the message window. Outlook automatically places messages that you've worked on but haven't sent in the Drafts folder.

2. Open the Come Fly with Us message that you worked on in the previous exercise and click the Insert tab to display the Illustrations group, as shown in Figure 2-47.

3. Place the insertion point at the end of the main paragraph in the message. Press Enter twice to add two lines of blank space.

4. In the Illustrations group, click Picture. The Insert Picture dialog box is displayed.

@ The *Vista* file is available on the book companion website or in WileyPLUS.

5. Select the *Vista.jpg* file in the data files for this lesson.

6. Click Insert. A large picture of a landscape near the resort is displayed in the message and the Picture Tools Format tab is displayed in the Ribbon, as shown in Figure 2-48.

7. Maximize the message window to see more of the image.

Figure 2-48

Inserting a graphic in a message window

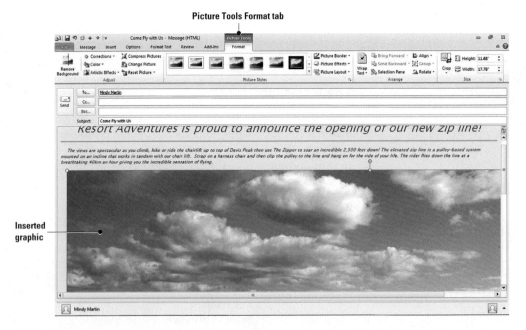

Picture Tools Format tab

Inserted graphic

PAUSE. LEAVE the Outlook Message window open to use in the next exercise.

The Insert Picture technique enables you to customize a message with selected photographs. The pictures you inserted in this exercise are digital photographs.

You can also insert clip art images in your messages. **Clip art** refers to picture files from the Clip Art task pane that can be inserted into a document. In the Clip Art task pane, you can also search for photographs, movies, and sounds. To include any of those media types, select the check box next to each in the *Result Should Be* box in the Clip Art task pane.

You can also insert SmartArt graphics. **SmartArt graphics** are visual representations of information that can help communicate your message or ideas more effectively.

CERTIFICATION READY   **2.3.1**

How do you insert pictures from files and clip art?

Formatting Graphical Elements

Once you've inserted a graphic, you can alter it using the Picture Tools Formatting tab. There are many options for changing the graphic. For example, you can add shapes to the graphic, alter its direction, change the layout, and change the colors. In this exercise you make multiple formatting changes to the picture in an e-mail message. The same formatting options are available when you work with clip art, SmartArt, and shapes. You can quickly make adjustments to a picture or graphic that has been inserted into a message by using the tools in Table 2-4.

Table 2-4

Formatting Tools for Graphics

Tool	Description
Crop	When you crop a picture, you trim the horizontal or vertical edges to get rid of unwanted areas.
Resize	Change the size or scale of a graphic using the Shape Height and Shape Width tools in the Size group.
Picture Style	You can use Picture styles to change the shape of the image or add borders or 3D effects.
Corrections	You can make an image brighter or darker and improve the sharpness and contrast of the image.
Color	You can turn the picture into a grayscale, sepia-toned, washed-out, or black-and-white version.
Wrap Text	You can use text wrapping to change the way text wraps around the picture or drawing object.

STEP BY STEP

Format Graphical Elements

USE the Come Fly with Us message you created in a previous exercise.

1. If you closed the message window, click the Drafts button in the Navigation Pane to display the Mail folder. Double-click on the Come Fly with Us message that you worked on in the previous exercise. Click the image to display the Picture Tools Format tab, as shown in Figure 2-49.

Figure 2-49

The Picture Tools Format tab

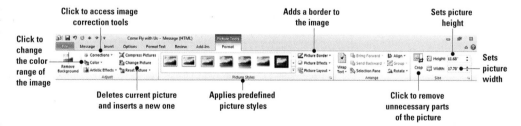

2. Click the Height box in the Size group and key 6.5 and press Enter. The image height changes to 6.5" and the image width changes as needed to avoid warping the image.

3. In the Size group, click Crop. Crop handles appear at each corner and side of the image, as shown in Figure 2-50. Drag each of the crop handles toward the center of the image, as shown in Figure 2-50.

Figure 2-50

Cropping an image

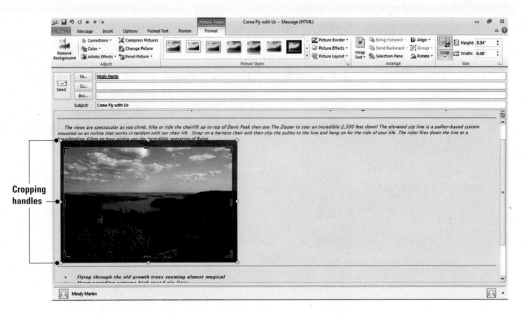

4. Click the Crop button again to save your changes.

5. In the Picture Styles group, select the Drop Shadow Rectangle style. The image changes to match the style.

6. Click the Picture Border button in the Picture Styles group. Select Dark Blue from the color palette that appears. A thin blue-gray border is displayed around the image, as shown in Figure 2-51.

Figure 2-51

Applying Picture Styles to the image

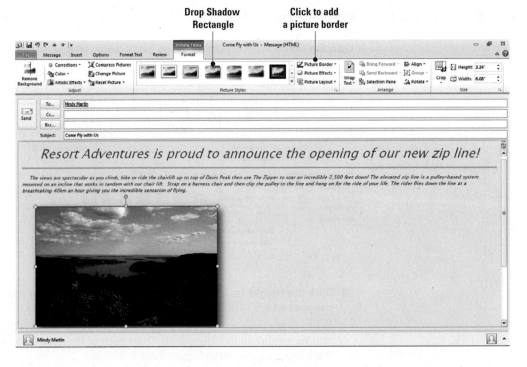

7. In the Adjust group, click Color and select Saturation: 200% in the Color Saturation area. The image is now brighter than the original.

8. Click the Corrections button and select Brightness: 0%, Contrast: +20% in the Brightness and Contrast area. The image is now brighter and warmer than the original.

9. Click Wrap Text in the Arrange group. Select Square from the list. The remaining text for the message moves up next to the image, as shown in Figure 2-52.

Figure 2-52

Adjusting an image

10. Click the Save button on the Quick Access Toolbar.

PAUSE. LEAVE the Outlook message window open to use in the next exercise.

Take Note   If at any time you want to revert back to the original graphic, click the Reset Picture button in the Adjust group to discard the formatting changes you have made.

Inserting a Hyperlink

For quick access to related information in another file or on a web page, you can insert a hyperlink in a message. A **hyperlink** is an image or sequence of characters that opens another file or Web page when you click it. The target file or web page can be on the World Wide Web, on the Internet, or on your personal computer. Hyperlinks enable you to supplement message information with additional materials and resources. It is easy to embed a hyperlink in a message. Just click where you want to create a hyperlink, or select the text or object you want to become a hyperlink, and click the Hyperlink button on the Insert tab. In this exercise, you'll insert a hyperlink into a message.

STEP BY STEP   **Insert a Hyperlink**

USE the Come Fly with Us message you created in a previous exercise.

1. If necessary, click the Drafts button in the Navigation Pane to display the Mail folder. Open the Come Fly with Us message that you worked on in the previous exercise.

2. If necessary, click the image in the message and click the Insert tab.

3. Click Insert Hyperlink in the links group. The Insert Hyperlink dialog box opens, as shown in Figure 2-53.

Figure 2-53

Insert Hyperlinks
dialog box

 The *Zipper Rates*
file is available on the
book companion website
or in WileyPLUS.

4. In the Address box, enter the URL of the *Zipper Rates.htm* file in your data files.

5. Click ScreenTip in the upper-right corner of the Insert Hyperlinks dialog box. The Set Hyperlink ScreenTip dialog box is displayed, as shown in Figure 2-54.

Figure 2-54

Set Hyperlink ScreenTip
dialog box

6. Key For more information click here in the ScreenTip Text textbox. Click OK twice to apply your changes and close the dialog boxes.

CERTIFICATION
READY **2.3.2**

How do you insert a hyperlink
into a message?

7. Click the message window's Send button to send the message to yourself.

8. If the message has not been received, click the Send/Receive All Folders button.

9. Click the message in the message list. Click the File tab and select the Save As option. The Save As dialog box is displayed.

10. In the *File name* box, key Come Fly with Us.

11. Navigate to the folder where you save your solution files and click the Save button. The message is saved as Come Fly with Us.msg.

PAUSE. LEAVE Outlook open to use in the next exercise.

WORKING WITH ATTACHMENTS

The Bottom Line

Attachments are files sent as part of an e-mail message. An attachment is a convenient way to send pictures, spreadsheets, and other types of files to e-mail recipient. In this section, you'll attach files and items to e-mail messages. You'll then preview, save, and print an attachment.

The Attachment Tools Tab

Outlook's new Attachment Tools tab contains all of the tools you need to work with e-mail attachments.

Figure 2-55

The Attachment Tools tab

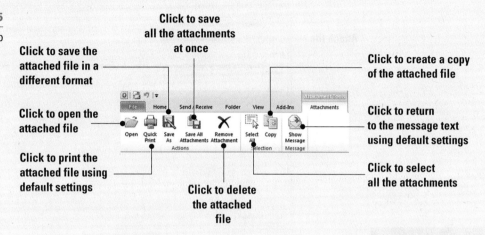

The tools on the Attachment Tools tab are the same tools available when you right-click on an attachment icon.

Attaching an External File to a Message

Do you need to submit a five-page report to your supervisor at the home office? Perhaps you have a new product brochure to distribute to all the sales representatives, or you want to share a picture of your new puppy with a friend. Attach the file to an e-mail message and send it. When you attach a file to a message, the filename, size, and an icon representing the file are displayed in the *Attached* field. If you attach more than one file, the files are listed separately in the *Attached* field. In this exercise, you'll attach a file to a message.

STEP BY STEP   **Attach an External File to a Message**

GET READY. LAUNCH Outlook if it is not already running.

1. If necessary, click the Mail button in the Navigation Pane to display the Mail folder.
2. Click the New E-mail button on the Home tab. The Message window is displayed.
3. In the *To* field, key your e-mail address. You will send this message to yourself so you can use the attachment in the following exercises.
4. In the *Subject* field, key Zipper coupon attached.
5. Click the message area. Key Hi Jon, [Press Enter twice].
6. Key the following note: I attached a copy of the coupon for the new Zipper attraction. I'd like to get your opinion of it before sending it out with the Come Fly with Us promotional message we discussed earlier. [Press Enter twice.]
7. Key Thanks, [press Enter].
8. Key [your name].
9. Click the Attach File button in the Include group on the Ribbon. The Insert File dialog box is displayed.
10. Navigate to the data files for this lesson. Click the *Zipper Coupon* file and click Insert. The Insert File dialog box is closed, and the file is listed in the *Attached* field, as shown in Figure 2-56.

@ The *Zipper Coupon* file is available on the book companion website or in WileyPLUS.

Figure 2-56

Sending an attachment

Attach File button

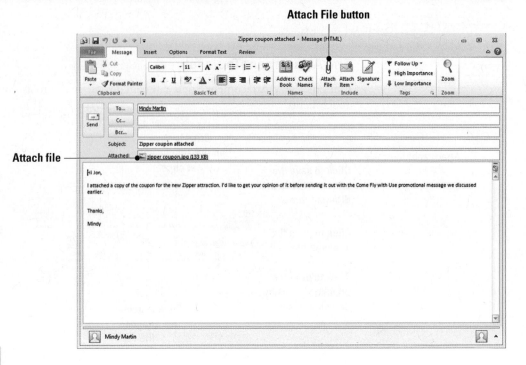

Attach file ──────

CERTIFICATION READY   2.5.2

How do you attach a file to a message?

11. Click the Send button. The Message window closes, and the message is moved to the Outbox. The message is sent when your computer is connected to the Internet.

PAUSE. LEAVE Outlook open to use in the next exercise.

In the previous exercise, you attached an external file to an Outlook message window using the Attach Items button. You can also open a Windows Explorer window containing the file you want to attach and simply click and drag it to the message window. It will attach itself to the message and you're ready to share.

Attaching an Outlook Item to a Message

An attachment can also be an Outlook item, such as a contact, a note, or a task. In this exercise, you'll attach an Outlook message to another message.

STEP BY STEP   **Attach an Outlook item to a Message**

GET READY. LAUNCH Outlook if it is not already running.

1. If necessary, click Mail button in the Navigation Pane to display the Mail folder.
2. Click the New E-mail button on the Home tab. The Message window is displayed.
3. In the *To* field, key [your e-mail address].
4. In the *Subject* field, key Promotional message attached.
5. Click the message area. Key Hi Jon, [Press Enter twice].
6. Key the following note: I attached a copy of the Come Fly with Us promotional message we discussed. [Press Enter twice.]
7. Key Let me know what you think. [Press Enter.]
8. Key [your name].
9. Click the Attach Item button in the Include group on the Ribbon. Select Outlook Item. The Insert Item dialog box is displayed, as shown in Figure 2-57.

Figure 2-57

Attaching an Outlook item
to a message

Attach Item button

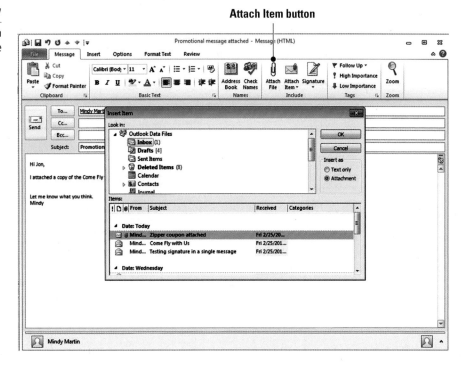

10. If necessary, click Inbox in the *Look in* window. In the Items window, select Come Fly with Us.

11. Make sure that Attachment is selected in the *Insert As* area. Click OK. The Insert Item dialog box is closed, and the file is listed in the *Attached* field.

12. Click the Send button. The Message window closes, and the message is moved to the Outbox. The message is sent when your computer is connected to the Internet.

PAUSE. LEAVE Outlook open to use in the next exercise.

Previewing an Attachment in Outlook

Outlook's Attachment Previewer enables you to view attachments in the Reading Pane. Without needing to save and open an attachment, you can make critical decisions quickly and efficiently. In this exercise, you'll preview an attachment in Outlook.

STEP BY STEP **Preview an Attachment in Outlook**

USE the Zipper coupon attached message with the attachment you sent a message to yourself in an earlier exercise.

1. If the message with the coupon attachment has not arrived yet, click the Send/ Receive All Folders button on the Home tab to check for new messages. The paper clip icon with the message, as shown in Figure 2-58, indicates that the message has an attachment.

Figure 2-58

Message with attachment
received

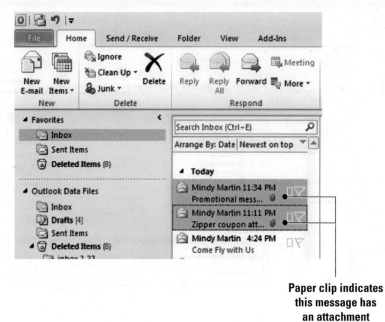

Paper clip indicates
this message has
an attachment

2. Click the Zipper coupon attached message. The message is displayed in the Reading
Pane, as shown in Figure 2-59.

Figure 2-59

Reading Pane containing the
message with attachment

Click to view the attached file

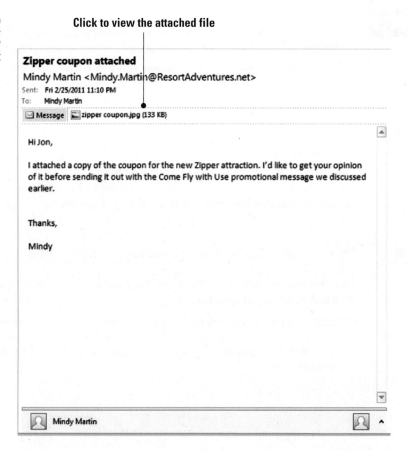

3. In the Reading Pane, click the attachment's filename. The attachment is displayed in the
Reading Pane, as shown in Figure 2-60.

Take Note   For some types of files, you may be asked if you want to preview the file before the attachment
is displayed.

Figure 2-60

Attachment displayed in the
Reading Pane

**Click to view
the attached file**

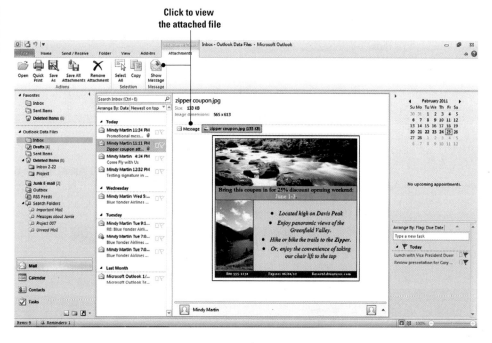

Figure 2-60

Attachment displayed in the
Reading Pane

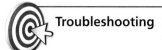**Troubleshooting** For your protection, all scripts, macros, and ActiveX controls are disabled in a previewed
document.

4. In the Reading Pane, click the Show Message icon to close the preview and display the
message.

PAUSE. LEAVE Outlook open to use in the next exercise.

Saving an Attachment from the Message List

Attachments in the message list can be saved without having to preview the attachment. In the
following exercise, you will save an attachment from the message list.

STEP BY STEP   **Save an Attachment from the Message List**

USE the Zipper coupon attached message with the attachment you sent a message to
yourself in an earlier exercise.

1. Click the Zipper coupon attached message in the message list.

2. Click the File tab to open Backstage view.

3. Click Save Attachments in the navigation pane. The Save All Attachments dialog box is
displayed, as shown in Figure 2-61.

Figure 2-61

Save All Attachments dialog box

4. Select Zipper Coupon.jpg. Click OK. The Save Attachment dialog box is displayed. By default, the My Documents folder is displayed. Navigate to the folder where you save your solution files, as shown in Figure 2-62.

Figure 2-62

Save Attachment dialog box

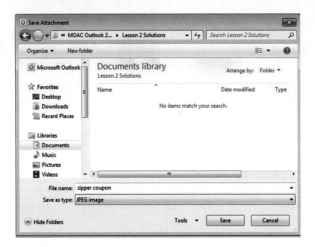

CERTIFICATION READY   3.1.2

How do you save a message attachment?

5. In the *File name* field, key Zipper Coupon from message list.

6. Click the Save button. A copy of the attachment is stored in your solutions folder.

PAUSE. LEAVE Outlook open to use in the next exercise.

Saving an Attachment from the Reading Pane

When you preview an attachment in the Reading Pane, you can use the new Attachment Tools tab to quickly save the attachment. In the following exercise, you will save an attachment from the Reading Pane.

STEP BY STEP   Save an Attachment from the Reading Pane

USE the Zipper coupon attached message with the attachment you sent a message to yourself in an earlier exercise.

1. Click the Zipper coupon attached message in the message list.

2. In the Reading Pane, click the Zipper Coupon.jpg attachment. The Attachment Tools tab is displayed, as shown in Figure 2-63.

Figure 2-63

Saving an attachment using the
Attachment Tools tab

Click to save the attached file

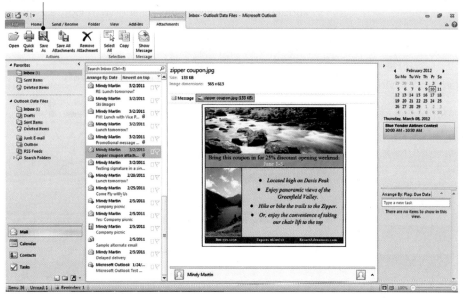

3. Click the Save As button on the Attachment Tools tab. The Save Attachment dialog box is displayed, as shown in Figure 2-62.

4. If necessary, navigate to the folder where you save your solution files. In the *File name* field, change the name of the file to Zipper Coupon from Reading Pane. Click the Save button.

PAUSE. LEAVE Outlook open to use in the next exercise.

Another Way
If the message contains multiple attachments, click Save All Attachments to save them all in one step.

Saving an Attachment from an Open Message

It is easy to save an attachment from an open message window. You can use the Save Attachments option on the File tab, but you can also save the attachment from the attachment's shortcut menu. In the following exercise, you will save an attachment from an open message window.

STEP BY STEP   **Save an Attachment from an Open Message**

USE the Zipper coupon attached message with the attachment you sent a message to yourself in an earlier exercise.

1. Double-click the Zipper coupon attached message in the message list. The message is opened in a new window.

2. In the new window, right-click the Zipper Coupon.jpg attachment. The attachment's shortcut menu is displayed, as shown in Figure 2-64.

Figure 2-64

Attachment's shortcut menu

3. Select Save As on the shortcut menu. The Save Attachment dialog box is displayed.
4. If necessary, navigate to the folder where you save your solution files. In the *File name* field, change the name of the file to Zipper Coupon from message window. Click the Save button.

PAUSE. LEAVE Outlook open to use in the next exercise.

Opening an E-mail Attachment

You can open an attachment from the Reading Pane or from an open message. In the following exercise, you will open an attachment from each location.

STEP BY STEP **Open an E-mail Attachment**

USE the Promotional Message message with the attachment that you sent to yourself in an earlier exercise.

1. Click the Promotional Message message in the message list.
2. In the Reading Pane, double-click the attachment icon. The Come Fly with Us message window is displayed. Close the message window.

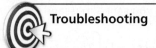 **Troubleshooting** It is safer to save an attachment and scan the file with an antivirus software program before opening an attachment. Do not open attachments from unknown sources.

3. Back in the Reading Pane, click the attachment icon once and click Open on the Attachments tab. The zipper coupon.jpg file opens in the default image viewing program, as shown in Figure 2-65.

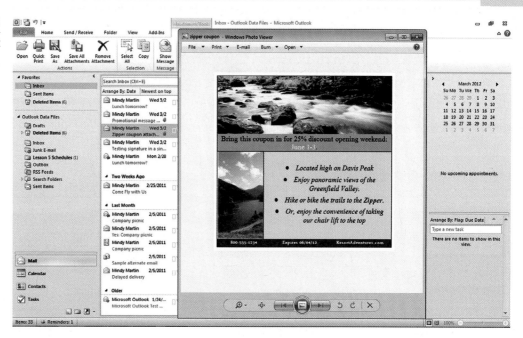

Figure 2-65

Opening an attachment

4. Close the message window. In the message list, double-click the Promotional Message message in the message list. The Promotional Message message window is displayed.

5. Double-click the Come Fly with Us attachment. The Come Fly with Us - Message window is displayed.

6. **CLOSE** both message windows.

PAUSE. LEAVE Outlook open to use in the next exercise.

Printing an Attachment

Printing an attachment is simple once you've set up your default printer in Outlook. Just use the Quick Print tool on the Attachments tab. In this exercise, you'll print an attachment from a message you received.

STEP BY STEP   **Printing an Attachment**

USE the Zipper coupon attached message with the attachment you sent a message to yourself in an earlier exercise. You need to have set up the printer in a previous exercise to complete this exercise.

1. Click the Zipper coupon attached message in the message list.

2. In the Reading Pane, click the zipper coupon.jpg attachment to display it in the Reading Pane.

3. Click the Quick Print button on the Attachments tab.

PAUSE. LEAVE Outlook open to use in the next exercise.

CERTIFICATION READY   **1.5.1**

How would you print an attachment?

If you have not set up a printer previously, you can still print an attachment. Just click the attachment icon in the Reading Pane and click the Open button on the Attachments tab to open the attachment in a new window. From there, click the File tab and click the Print button in the Navigation Pane. In the Printer area, click the Printer dropdown arrow and select the printer you would like to use.

SKILL SUMMARY

In This Lesson You Learned How To:	Exam Objective	Objective Number
Create messages	Specify message content format.	2.1.2
Send messages	Show or hide the From and Bcc fields.	2.1.3
Read and respond to messages	Save a message in an external format.	3.1.3
Format messages	Use formatting tools.	2.4.1
	Apply styles.	2.4.2
	Create styles.	2.4.3
	Specify a message theme.	2.1.1
	Create themes.	2.4.4
	Use Paste Special.	2.4.5
Personalize messages	Manage signatures.	3.4.1
Create and format graphic message content	Insert graphical elements.	2.3.1
	Format graphical elements.	2.4.6
	Insert a hyperlink.	2.3.2
Work with attachments	Attach external files to an e-mail message.	2.5.2
	Attach an Outlook item to an e-mail message.	2.5.1
	Save message attachments.	3.1.2
	Print attachments.	1.5.1

Knowledge Assessment

Multiple Choice

Select the letter of the text that best completes the following statements.

1. The _____ feature automatically completes the names of the months and days of the week.

   a. Live Preview

   b. AutoComplete

   c. AutoDate

   d. AutoPreview

2. Text or images that are automatically placed at the end of your outgoing messages are called _____.

   a. stationery

   b. templates

   c. closing

   d. signatures

3. A file sent as part of an e-mail message is called a(n) _____.

   a. enclosure

   b. add on

   c. attachment

   d. supplement

4. To preview a style or theme _____.
   a. place your pointer over the choice
   b. print the document
   c. use Print Preview
   d. It is not possible to preview a style or theme.

5. Choosing the number of copies or range of pages are options that are available when performing what process on a message?
   a. Previewing
   b. Assigning properties
   c. Printing
   d. Saving in a different format

6. The _____ indicates the topic of a message.
   a. Reference
   b. Topic
   c. RE:
   d. Subject

7. Use the _____ tab to alter the look of a graphic.
   a. Format
   b. Format Graphics tab
   c. Graphic Tools Format tab
   d. Picture Tools Format tab

8. The _____ command can be used to save a copy of a message with a new filename in a new location.
   a. Save
   b. Save as
   c. Print preview
   d. Save new

9. A document theme includes sets of _____.
   a. Colors
   b. Effects
   c. Fonts
   d. All of the above

10. Before a message can be sent, the _____ field(s) must be filled in.
    a. From
    b. Bcc
    c. To
    d. A and B

True/False

Circle T if the statement is true or F if the statement is false.

T F   1. Use the Message window to compose and send an e-mail message.

T F   2. To send a message to several recipients, key a colon (:) after a name before adding the next addressee.

T F   3. The Drawing Tools Format tab only appears when a picture is selected.

T F   4. A message is moved to the Sent Items folder when you click the Send button.

T F   5. When you send a reply, the text "RE:" is inserted before the original subject line.

T F   6. When you make changes to the colors, fonts, or effects of the current theme, you permanently change the original theme.

T F   7. Use the AutoComplete function to insert your signature before you send a message.

T   F   8. You can restore a picture to its original formatting without reverting to a saved file.

T   F   9. Use the Default Print button to print an attachment with the default settings.

T   F   10. If you have a personal signature, it can be used as the default address to save time.

Competency Assessment

Project 2-1: Create an E-mail Message

Send an e-mail message to a friend inviting him to lunch tomorrow.

GET READY. LAUNCH Outlook if it is not already running.

1. On the Standard toolbar, click the New E-mail button to open a new Message window.
2. Key [a friend's e-mail address] in the *To* field. If you are not completing these exercises with a friend or coworker, key [your e-mail address] in the *To* field. This will give you a message to reply to in the next exercise.
3. In the Subject field, key Lunch tomorrow?
4. Click in the message area. Key Hi, [press Enter twice].
5. Key How about lunch tomorrow? [press Enter twice]. Key [your name].
6. Click the Send button.

LEAVE Outlook open for the next project.

Project 2-2: Reply to a Friend's E-mail Message

Reply to a friend's lunch request.

USE the e-mail you received at the end of Project 2-1 before starting this project.

1. If the message sent in Project 2-1 has not arrived, click the Send/Receive All Folders button on the Home tab.
2. In the message list, click the message sent in Project 2-1.
3. Click the Reply button on the Home tab.
4. Key I'll pick you up at 1:00 PM. Don't be late! [press Enter twice]. Key [your name].
5. Click the Send button.
6. Click the Send/Receive All Folders button on the Home tab.
7. In the message list, click the reply message.
8. Click the File tab and select the Save As option. The Save As dialog box is displayed.
9. Navigate to your solutions folder for Lesson 02. Save the message as RE Lunch tomorrow.htm.

LEAVE Outlook open for the next project.

Proficiency Assessment

Project 2-3: Send an Attachment

The last guest in the best suite at Resort Adventures accidentally broke the stained-glass window in the suite. You must replace the window before you can accept any reservations for the suite.

GET READY. LAUNCH Outlook if it is not already running.

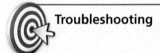 **Troubleshooting** The e-mail addresses provided in these projects belong to unused domains owned by Microsoft. When you send a message to these addresses, you will receive an error message stating that the message could not be delivered. Delete the error messages when they arrive.

1. Create a new e-mail message to Nancy Anderson at the Graphic Design Institute. Nancy's e-mail address is Nancy@graphicdesigninstitute.com. Ask Nancy if she can design a window similar to the stained-glass window that was broken. Ask Nancy how long the project will take and how much it will cost.

@ The *Window.jpg* file is available on the book companion website or in WileyPLUS.

2. Attach the *Window.jpg* file located in the data files for this lesson.

3. Be sure to include the signature you created in this lesson.

4. Send the message.

LEAVE Outlook open for the next project.

Project 2-4: Insert Pictures and Clip Art

Resort Adventures is in the progress of putting together a new brochure to publicize the resort's ski facilities. Put together a new e-mail message to a colleague containing two pictures and two clip art images.

GET READY. LAUNCH Outlook if it is not already running.

1. Create a new e-mail message and address it to yourself.

2. In the Subject field, key Ski Images.

3. In the Insert tab, click Pictures.

@ The *Ski 1.jpg* file is available on the book companion website or in WileyPLUS.

4. Navigate to the Data Files for Lesson 2 and insert *Ski 1.jpg*. Press Enter twice.

5. Repeat the process to insert the file *Ski 2.jpg* from your data files. [Press Enter twice.]

6. On the Insert tab, click Clip Art. The Clip Art task pane opens.

@ The *Ski 2.jpg* file is available on the book companion website or in WileyPLUS.

7. In the *Results should be* field, select Illustrations. All other media types should be deselected.

8. Key ski in the *Search for* field and click Go.

9. Scroll through the search results and double-click an image you like that represents skiing.

10. Close the Clip Art task pane.

11. Save the message to your Drafts folder in Outlook.

LEAVE Outlook open for the next project.

Mastery Assessment

Project 2-5: Format and Reset a Picture to Its Original State

Apply formatting to the images in your Ski Images message. You'll then reset one of the images back to its original state.

USE the e-mail you created at the end of Project 2-4 in this lesson.

1. Open Ski Images message in the Drafts folder.

2. Click the first picture. Increase the width to 6".

3. Click Corrections and select Sharpen: +50% and Brightness: +20% Contrast: +20%.

4. In the Picture Styles group, click Soft Edge Oval.

5. Click Color and click Grayscale.

6. Click the second picture. In the Picture Styles group, click Simple Frame, Black.

7. Click Picture Border and select Red in the Standard Colors.

8. In the Picture Border menu, select Weight and click 2 1/4 pt.

9. In the Picture Effects menu, select Perspective Diagonal Upper Right.

10. Select the second picture. Click Crop and crop excess from each side of the image. Change the height to 4". Place the crop tool at the lower-right corner and drag up to the desktop in the picture. Click Crop to complete the crop.

11. Select the third picture. In the Picture Styles group, select Drop Shadow Rectangle.

12. Click **Corrections** and select **Brightness: 0% (Normal)**, **Contrast: -40%**.

13. Click **Color** and select **Aqua, Accent color 5, Light**.

14. Save the message as **Ski Images.htm**.

15. Select the first picture and click **Reset Picture**.

16. Send the message.

LEAVE Outlook open for the next project.

Project 2-6: Create a Custom Theme

Blue Yonder Airlines has decided to give all their documents a branded look by creating a new custom theme to be used for all client-facing business documents.

GET READY. LAUNCH Outlook if it is not already running.

1. Open a new e-mail message and address it to **someone@example.com**.

2. In the *Subject* field, key **Custom Theme for Blue Yonder Airlines**.

3. Use the Outlook Help button to get more information about creating a custom theme.

4. Choose a custom set of colors, fonts, and/or effects that you feel would be a good choice for Blue Yonder Airlines.

5. Save the theme as **Custom_xxx** (where xxx are your initials).

6. Key a short paragraph explaining that you are creating a custom theme. Include a bulleted list outlining which colors, fonts, or effects you used. Format the paragraph with your custom theme.

7. SAVE the message in Outlook Message Format as **Custom Theme** and save the message then click **Send**.

CLOSE Outlook.

INTERNET READY

When creating a message, you are not limited to inserting only the clip art and other media that come installed with Outlook. A single click can open up a whole new world of options. At the bottom of the Clip Art task pane, notice the More at Office.com link. Click the link to connect to the clip art and media home page, as shown in Figure 2-66. You can browse dozens of categories, download the clip of the day, view featured collections, and more. Next time you need to enhance your messages with clip art or other media, expand your options by going online.

Figure 2-66

Office.com's Images and More page

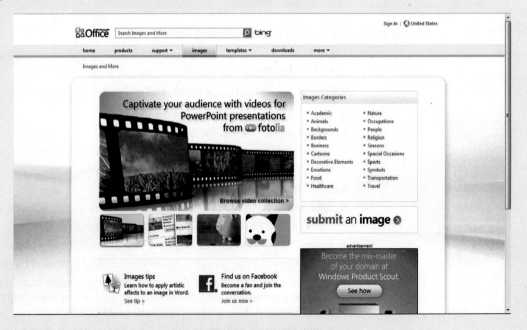

Workplace *Ready*

SENDING A WEEKLY CUSTOMER NEWSLETTER

Although sending unsolicited e-mail ads to people is frowned upon, sending newsletters and promotions to your customers is more popular than ever. The more professional these materials look, the more likely customers are to respond and to share them with others.

Steven Jacobs is the owner of a growing business that delivers locally grown fruits and vegetables. He has worked hard to develop a co-op of local farmers who supply him with produce for his expanding client list. Each week he sends his clients an e-mail newsletter containing information about the types of produce that are going to be included in their weekly deliveries, as well as information about how to prepare and cook the different food items.

Recently he has started including articles that spotlight the different farms and orchards in his co-op group. He has found that the customers have really responded to this information and feel a stronger connection to the farmer as well as the community. In fact, since he expanded the newsletter, he has been getting more and more calls from people who found out about his service because a friend or family worker had forwarded the newsletter to them.

Steven can't wait to introduce the next expansion to his newsletter. He is going to start offering boutique gourmet food products. He is putting together profiles of a wide variety of interesting food producers. He knows this type of content will appeal to the foodies in the community.

3 Advanced E-mail Tools

LESSON SKILL MATRIX

Skill	Exam Objective	Objective Number
Managing Automatic Message Content	Set Mail options.	1.1.2
	Specify options for replies.	3.4.3
	Specify options for forwards.	3.4.4
	Specify the font.	3.4.2
	Set a default theme for all HTML.	3.4.5
Using Advanced Message Options	Set the Sensitivity Level.	1.2.3
	Set a reminder for message recipients.	2.1.4
	Configure tracking options.	2.1.9
	Configure message delivery options.	2.1.7
	Specify the sent item folder.	2.1.6
	Specify the sending account.	2.1.5
Working with Voting Options	Configure voting options.	2.1.8
Working with Security	Manage signatures.	3.4.1
Locating Messages	Use the People Pane.	1.3.4
	Use built-in Search folders.	1.4.1
Printing Multiple Messages	Print multiple messages.	1.5.3

KEY TERMS

- attribute
- delivery receipt
- digital ID
- encryption
- InfoBar
- Information Rights Management (IRM)
- Instant Search
- read receipt
- sensitivity
- theme

Business is booming. Mindy and Jon have accepted reservations for several major events to be held at the Resort Adventures resort. Two weddings, a company retreat, and a confidential marketing meeting for a major toy company have been scheduled for next month. As the dates for the events get closer, e-mail messages have been flying. The toy company insists on using security features, such as a digital ID, for all e-mail communications. One of the ways that Outlook 2010 helps you save time is by allowing you to automate how Outlook creates and processes messages. In this lesson, you'll use some of Microsoft Outlook's advanced e-mail tools to take advantage of this capability as you finalize the arrangements for the new clients.

SOFTWARE ORIENTATION

Microsoft Outlook's Message Options

The mail component in Microsoft Outlook 2010 can do more than just send basic e-mail messages. Many of the advanced e-mail options in Microsoft Outlook are set through the New Message window's Options tab, as shown in Figure 3-1.

Figure 3-1

The New Message window's Options tab

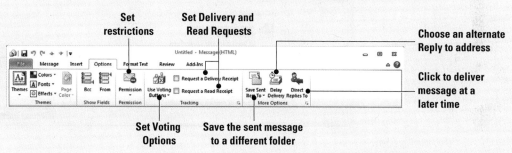

The advanced options in Microsoft Outlook enable you to change the message settings, address security issues, vote for selected items, set tracking options, and determine delivery options.

MANAGING AUTOMATIC MESSAGE CONTENT

The Bottom Line

You can use the Microsoft Office Backstage to control many of the settings and options that Outlook uses to determine how to handle e-mails messages you create and receive. You can also use Outlook's Mail options to create a format for all new messages, complete with background, colors, and fonts. Creating a default format for all messages provides continuity and a professional finish to your messages without requiring you to spend time formatting each message.

Setting Mail Options

When you open the Outlook Options dialog box and click Mail in the navigation pane, the Mail Options page is displayed. You can use the Mail Options to control how messages are sent and received, as well as how they are tracked and saved. You can adjust these settings to have Outlook automatically save your messages, notify you when new mail arrives, check spelling in messages, and more. In this exercise, you'll learn how to set Outlook Mail options.

STEP BY STEP   **Set Mail Options**

GET READY. LAUNCH Outlook if it is not already running.

1. Click the File tab to open Backstage view, then select Options on its navigation page to display the Outlook Options dialog box.
2. Click Mail on the left navigation pane. The Mail Options page of the Outlook Options dialog box is displayed, as shown in Figure 3-2.

Figure 3-2

Setting Mail Options

3. In the Message Arrival area, click the Desktop Alert Settings button. The Desktop Alert Settings dialog box is displayed.
4. Click the Preview button to see an example of the default message alert, as shown in Figure 3-3. Change the alert duration to 10 seconds and click OK to apply your changes and close the Desktop Alert Settings dialog box.

Figure 3-3

Desktop Alert Settings dialog box and Message preview

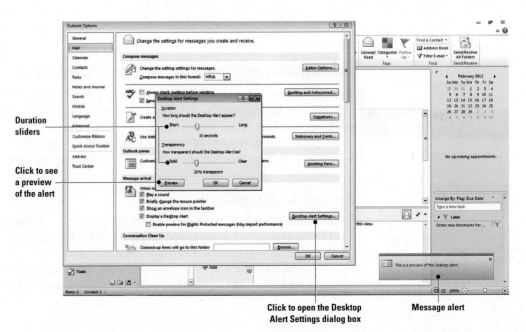

Duration sliders

Click to see a preview of the alert

Click to open the Desktop Alert Settings dialog box

Message alert

5. Scroll down to the Save Messages area of the Mail Options page and change the *Automatically save items that have not been sent after this many minutes* option to reflect 1 minute.

6. Click OK to save your changes, close the Outlook Options dialog box, and return to the main Mail window.

7. Click New E-mail button on the Home tab. The Untitled—Message (HTML) window is displayed.

8. In the *To* field, key someone@example.com. In the *Subject* field, key This is a timed test and press Tab. Minimize the This is a timed test—Message window.

9. Click Drafts in the Navigation Pane to open the Drafts folder. After a minute the *This is a timed test* message will appear in the Drafts folder.

10. Close the *This is a timed test* message window. Click No when prompted whether to save changes.

11. Click the File tab to open the Backstage view. Open the Outlook Options dialog box.

12. In the Save Message area of the Mail page, change the *Automatically save items that have not been sent after this many minutes* option back to 3 minutes.

13. Click OK to save your changes.

PAUSE. LEAVE Outlook open to use in the next exercise.

CERTIFICATION READY 1.1.2

How do you set up message alerts?

In the previous exercise, you keyed the basic information for a contact. Once a contact has been created, his or her information is stored in the Outlook Address Book.

Specifying Options for Replies and Forwards

You can also use the Mail Options to control how Outlook handles messages when you send replies or when you forward a message to someone. These options include things like determining whether you want Outlook to include the text of an original message when you send a reply and where you want Outlook to store your reply messages. In this exercise, explore Outlook's default way of handling replies and forwards.

STEP BY STEP | **Specify Options for Replies and Forwards**

GET READY. LAUNCH Outlook if it is not already running.

1. Click Inbox in the Navigation Pane to open the default Mail folder.

2. Double-click on your Microsoft Test Message. The Microsoft Outlook Test Message window is displayed.

 Troubleshooting If you don't have a Microsoft Outlook Test Message in your inbox, you can open any received message for this exercise.

3. Click Reply on the Home tab. A new RE: Microsoft Outlook Test Message window is displayed on top of the original message, as shown in Figure 3-4.

Figure 3-4

Outlook's default reply handling

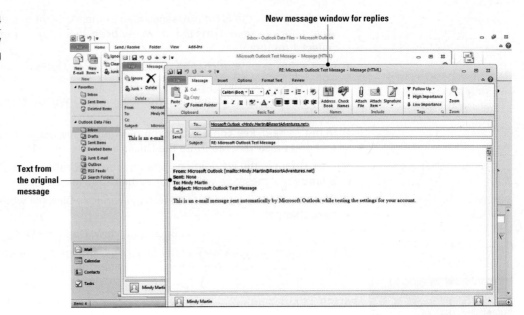

4. By default, when you reply to a message or forward it to someone else, Outlook keeps the original message open and includes the text of the original message at the bottom of the new message window. Close the RE: Microsoft Outlook Test Message window.

5. Click the File tab to open Backstage view, and select Options on its navigation page to display the Outlook Options dialog box.

6. Click Mail on the left navigation pane. The Mail options page of the Outlook Options dialog box is displayed. Scroll down to see the options for Replies and Forwards.

7. In the Replies and Forwards area, click the Close original message window when replying and forwarding check box to activate this option.

8. Click the When forwarding a message dropdown arrow. A list of options is displayed, as shown in Figure 3-5.

Figure 3-5

Setting options for replies and forwards

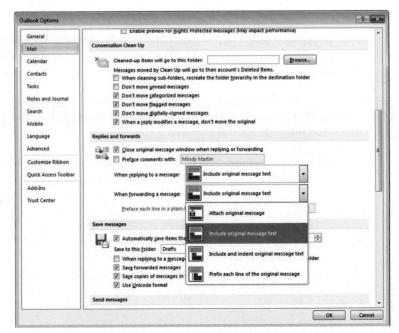

9. Select Attach original message and click OK to apply your changes and close the Outlook Options dialog box.

10. Click the Microsoft Outlook Test Message window to display it again.

11. Click the Forward button on the Home tab. The original message window closes and the FW: Microsoft Outlook Test Message—Message window is displayed. Notice that the original message now appears as an attachment. Close the window without saving changes.

12. Click the File tab to open the Backstage view. Open the Outlook Options dialog box, and click Mail in the navigation pane.

13. In the Replies and Forwards area of the Mail page, deselect the *Close original message window when replying and forwarding* option.

14. Click the When forwarding a message dropdown arrow. Select Include original message text.

15. Click OK to restore the default settings.

PAUSE. LEAVE Outlook open to use in the next exercise.

Specifying the Default Font for New Messages

In the previous lesson, you learned how to format your message content to make it more appealing and professional looking. You may want to streamline that process by choosing a default font for all new messages. You can also set options to change the color of text for replies and forwards. In this exercise, you'll specify the font to use for new messages.

STEP BY STEP   **Specify the Default Font for New Messages**

GET READY. LAUNCH Outlook if it is not already running.

1. Click the File tab and select Options in the Backstage view navigation pane to display the Outlook Options dialog box.

2. Click Mail on the left navigation pane. The Mail options page of the Outlook Options dialog box is displayed.

3. In the Compose Message area, click the Stationery and Fonts button. The Signatures and Stationery dialog box is displayed, as shown in Figure 3-6.

Figure 3-6

The Signatures and Stationery dialog box

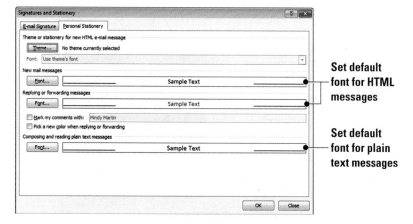

4. In the New Mail Messages area, click the Font button. The Font dialog box is displayed.

5. In the Font box, select Century Schoolbook.

6. Click the Font Color dropdown arrow and select Olive Green, Accent 3, Darker 50%. Click OK to apply your changes and close the Font dialog box.

7. In the Replying or Forwarding Messages area of the Signatures and Stationery dialog box, click the Font button. The Font dialog box is displayed.

8. Click the Font Color dropdown arrow and select Red. Click OK.

CERTIFICATION
READY   3.4.2

How would you change the
default font of a new plain
text message?

9. In the *Composing and reading plain text messages* area, click the Font button and select Arial. Click OK.

10. Notice the change in the *Sample Text* boxes.

11. Click Close and then Cancel to close both dialog boxes without saving the changes.

PAUSE. LEAVE Outlook open to use in the next exercise.

Setting a Default Theme for All New HTML Messages

In Outlook 2010, you can specify a default theme for all the new HTML messages you create. In Outlook, **themes** are a set of formatting choices that include colors, fonts (including heading and body text fonts), and theme effects (including lines and fill effects). In this exercise, you'll specify a new default theme to use for future messages and create a test message to see how your new theme looks.

STEP BY STEP   **Set a Default Theme for All New HTML Messages**

GET READY. LAUNCH Outlook if it is not already running.

1. Select Options on the Backstage view navigation bar to display the Outlook Options dialog box.

2. Click Mail on the left navigation pane to display the Mail options page of the Outlook Options dialog box.

3. In the Compose Message area, click the Stationery and Fonts button. The Signatures and Stationery dialog box is displayed (refer to Figure 3-6).

CERTIFICATION
READY   3.4.5

How would you specify the
default stationery to be used
for all HTML messages?

4. In the *Theme Or Stationery for New Html E-Mail Message* area, click the Theme button. The Theme or Stationery dialog box is displayed.

5. Click Bears (Stationery) in the *Choose a Theme* box. Notice the change in the Sample of Theme window. Selecting one of the options marked by *(Stationery)* will set the default stationery for all of your future HTML messages.

6. Press the down arrow repeatedly to scroll downward in the *Choose a Theme* box until you come to the Evergreen theme, as shown in Figure 3-7. Selecting one of the options without *(Stationery)* will set the default theme for all of your future HTML messages.

Figure 3-7

The Theme or Stationery dialog box

Specifies the default stationery

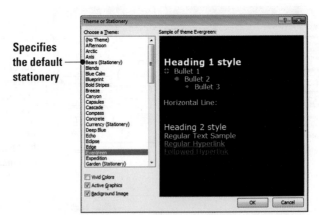

7. Click OK to apply the new theme and close the Theme or Stationery dialog box. Click OK to close the Signatures and Stationery dialog box, then click OK again to close the Outlook Options dialog box.

Take Note

Each theme has an associated font. If you want to override the theme's font, you can select *Use my font* when replying and forwarding messages or *Always use my fonts* from the Font dropdown under the selected Theme.

**CERTIFICATION
READY   3.4.5**

How would you specify
a font for all HTML
messages?

8. In the main Mail window, click the New E-Mail button on the Home tab. The Untitled—Message window is displayed.

Take Note

Throughout this chapter you will see information that appears in black text within brackets, such as [Press Enter], or [your e-mail address]. The information contained in the brackets is intended to be directions for you rather than something you actually type word for word. It will instruct you to perform an action or substitute text. Do **not** type the actual text that appears within brackets.

9. In the To field, key [your e-mail address or the address of someone you know]. In the Subject field, key Sample Theme.

10. In the Message area, key This is a sample of the Evergreen theme. Click Send.

11. Click the File tab and select Options, then Mail. The Mail options page is displayed.

**CERTIFICATION
READY   3.4.5**

How would you specify the
default theme for all HTML
messages?

12. Click the Stationery and Fonts button, then select (No Theme) in the Signatures and Stationery dialog box.

13. Click OK three times to close all the open dialog boxes and restore the default settings.

PAUSE. LEAVE Outlook open to use in the next exercise.

Outlook offers two ways to specify the default formatting for every message you send.

- You can specify the font style and color to be used for new mail messages, replies and forwards, and plain text messages.

- Or, you can make it even easier by formatting all the colors, fonts, and graphics at once using themes.

USING ADVANCED MESSAGE OPTIONS

The Bottom Line

Advanced message options enable you to specify settings that attract attention to the messages you send. You can use these advanced options to alert message recipients to the sensitive nature or importance of a message's contents, to remind the recipient that a reply is expected, and to trigger notification when a message you've sent has been delivered and/or read. You also can use these settings to direct message replies to a specific e-mail address, to configure message delivery options, to specify where Outlook will save sent items, or to send messages from multiple e-mail accounts. Many of these options are set in the Properties dialog box shown in Figure 3-1 or on the Options tab of the message window.

SOFTWARE ORIENTATION

Microsoft Outlook's Message Options

Some Microsoft Outlook 2010 options require more detail than is available on the Options tab. You can access the Properties window, shown in Figure 3-8, by clicking on the More Options dialog box launcher.

Figure 3-8

The Properties dialog box

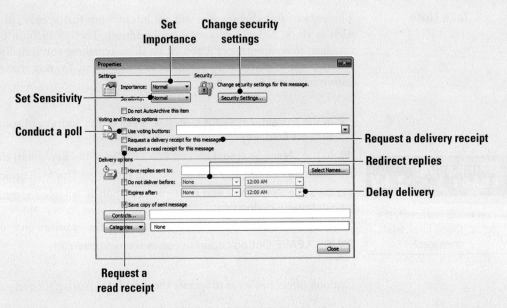

In the Message Properties dialog box, you can make decisions about these options for the message you are creating. These changes affect only the current message; they do not affect all messages you send.

Setting the Sensitivity Level

The **sensitivity** level of a message is an indicator of how secret the message's contents are. Although sensitivity does not affect how the message is sent or received, it does suggest how the recipient should treat the message and the type of information in the message. You set Outlook's Sensitivity settings—Normal, Personal, Private, and Confidential—in the Properties dialog box. In this exercise, you'll create a message and set the sensitivity level.

Set the Sensitivity Level

GET READY. LAUNCH Outlook if it is not already running.

1. If necessary, click the Mail button in the Navigation Pane to display the Mail folder.
2. Click the New E-mail button on the Home tab. The Untitled—Message window is displayed. By default, the Message tab is selected.

3. Click the More Options dialog box launcher on the Options tab. The message Properties dialog box is displayed, as shown in Figure 3-9.

Figure 3-9

Setting the Sensitivity level of a message

Set Sensitivity

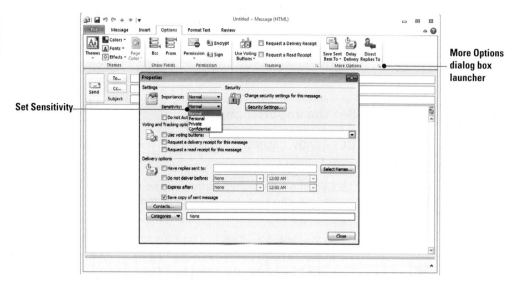

More Options dialog box launcher

4. In the Settings area, click the Sensitivity setting dropdown arrow, as shown in Figure 3-9. Then select Confidential from the dropdown list.

5. Click the Close button to accept the Confidential setting and return to the message window.

6. In the message area, key Sample confidential message.

7. In the *To* field, key [your e-mail address]. In the *Subject* field, key Sample confidential message.

8. Click the Send button. The message is moved to the Outbox and it is sent when your computer is connected to the Internet.

9. When your computer is connected to the Internet, click the Send/Receive All Folders button on the Home tab if the message has not arrived yet.

10. When the new message appears in your Inbox, click the received message to select it. The message has the text *Please treat this as Confidential* in the InfoBar at the top of the message, as shown in Figure 3-10.

Figure 3-10

Confidential message received

Message flagged as confidential

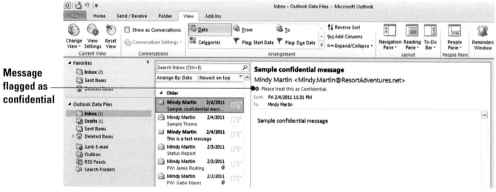

PAUSE. LEAVE Outlook open to use in the next exercise.

In this exercise, you saw that an InfoBar was added to the recipient's confidential message. An **InfoBar** is a banner containing information added automatically at the top of a message. An InfoBar is added for personal, private, and confidential messages. The messages are handled the same as any other message you send—the text in the InfoBar is the only difference.

The default sensitivity is normal. The InfoBar is not added to messages with a normal sensitivity.

Setting the Importance Level

Some e-mail messages are more important than others. Use the Importance setting to draw attention to a message. The importance level of a message can be set to High, Low, or Normal. High-importance messages are identified for the recipient by a red exclamation point in the message list and noted in the message InfoBar. Low-importance messages are marked with a blue down arrow in the message list and noted in the InfoBar. Normal-importance messages are not marked. In this exercise, you'll create a sample message with a high importance level.

STEP BY STEP   **Set the Importance Level**

GET READY. LAUNCH Outlook if it is not already running.

1. If necessary, click the Mail button in the Navigation Pane to display the Mail folder.
2. Click the New E-mail button on the Home tab. The Message window is displayed. By default, the Message tab is selected.

Another Way
Select the importance in the message Properties dialog box.

3. Click the High Importance button in the Tags group.
4. In the message area, key Sample important message.
5. In the *To* field, key [your e-mail address]. In the *Subject* field, key Sample important message, as shown in Figure 3-11.

Figure 3-11

Creating an important message

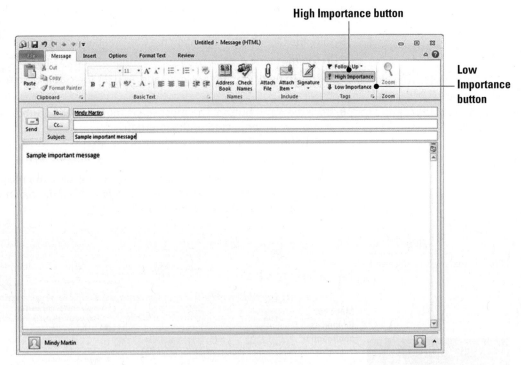

6. Click the Send button. The message is moved to the Outbox and it is sent when your computer is connected to the Internet.
7. Return to your Inbox, and click the Send/Receive All Folders button if the message has not arrived yet.

8. Select the new message, which is flagged with a red exclamation mark in your Inbox list. The text *This message was sent with High importance* appears in the InfoBar at the top of the message, as shown in Figure 3-12.

Figure 3-12

Important message received

High Importance message in the message lists

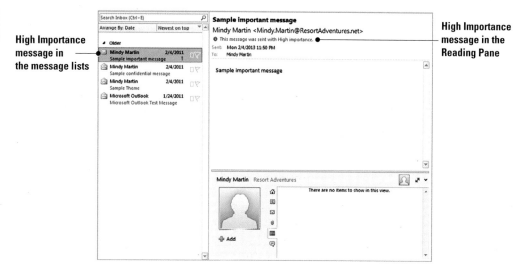

High Importance message in the Reading Pane

PAUSE. LEAVE Outlook open to use in the next exercise.

If you set the importance level of a message too high or low, you can reset the importance level to normal before you send it. Simply click the High Importance button or the Low Importance button that is currently selected.

Setting a Reminder for Recipients

When you send a message, you can mark it with a follow-up flag that will be seen by the recipient and act as a reminder that he or she is expected to take some action based on the information in the message you sent. In this exercise, you'll create a sample message with a reminder.

STEP BY STEP   **Set a Reminder for Recipients**

GET READY. LAUNCH Outlook if it is not already running.

1. If necessary, click the Mail button in the Navigation Pane to display the Mail folder.

2. Click the New E-mail button on the Home tab. The Untitled—Message window is displayed. By default, the Message tab is selected.

3. In the *To* field, key [your e-mail address]. In the *Subject* field, key Lunch tomorrow with Alan Brewer.

4. In the message area, key the following message: Don't forget lunch tomorrow with Alan Brewer from Fabrikam, Inc. He wants to discuss arrangements for the conference scheduled for our Blue Conference Room at the end of next month. Come prepared!

5. In the Tags group on the Message tab, click the Follow-Up dropdown button and select Custom from the dropdown menu to select additional options. The Custom dialog box shown in Figure 3-13 is displayed.

Figure 3-13

Custom dialog box

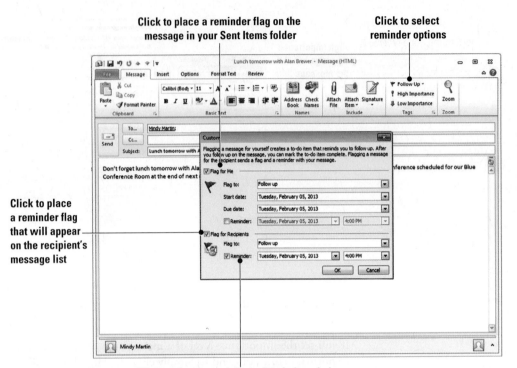

Figure 3-13

Custom dialog box

Click to place a reminder flag on the message in your Sent Items folder

Click to select reminder options

Click to place a reminder flag that will appear on the recipient's message list

Click to give the recipient a Reminder window

6. Click the Flag For Recipients option and select the Reminder check box to activate that option.

7. Click OK to save the settings. The dialog box is closed. As shown in Figure 3-14, the InfoBar in the message you're creating indicates that the recipient will receive the Follow-Up flag.

Figure 3-14

Creating a message with a reminder for a recipient

InfoBar indicates that this message will be flagged for follow-up for the recipient

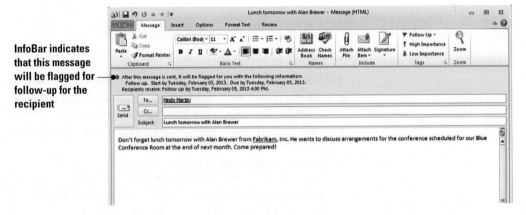

Troubleshooting The text *After this message is sent, it will be flagged for with you the following information* in the InfoBar appears while the message is being composed. This text is not displayed to the recipient.

8. Click the Send button. The message is moved to the Outbox and it is sent when your computer is connected to the Internet.

PAUSE. LEAVE Outlook open to use in the next exercise.

How do you set a follow-up
flag for the recipient?

When the computer is connected to the Internet and a message is sent, the message in
the Sent Items folder will have a flag. When the message is received it will have a flag
and the recipient will receive a reminder window at the appointed time, as shown in
Figure 3-15.

Figure 3-15

Sent message with follow-up
flag for the recipient

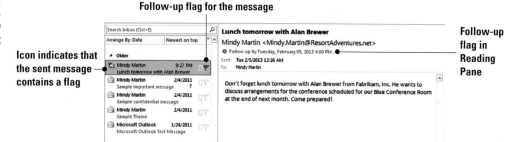

When the message arrives in the recipient's Inbox, the message is marked by a flag, as shown
in Figure 3-16. This draws attention to the message and indicates that some action might be
required. A flag set by a sender contains a small silhouette, making it look different from a
flag you set for yourself. If the recipient clicks the flag in the message list, it is added to the recipient's task list.

Figure 3-16

Received message with
follow-up flag set by
the sender

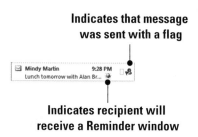

 Ref   You can find more information about tasks in Lesson 11.

Requesting Delivery and Read Receipts

Did she get the message? Requesting delivery and read receipts takes the mystery out of sending
a message because you will know that the message was delivered to the recipient and opened for
reading. A **delivery receipt** tells you that the message has arrived in the recipient's mailbox; the
message has been delivered. A delivery receipt does not guarantee that the recipient has opened or
read the message. A **read receipt** tells you that the message has been opened in the recipient's
mailbox. In this exercise, you'll send a sample message with a delivery and read receipt request.

STEP BY STEP   **Request Delivery and Read Receipts**

GET READY. LAUNCH Outlook if it is not already running.

1. If necessary, click the Mail button in the Navigation Pane to display the Mail folder.

2. Click the New E-mail button on the Home tab. The Message window is displayed. By
   default, the Message tab is selected.

Another Way
Click the Request a delivery receipt for this message check box and click the Request a read receipt for this message check box in the Message Options dialog box.

3. In the *To* field, key [your e-mail address]. In the *Subject* field, key Sample delivery receipt and read receipt.

4. In the message area, key Sample delivery receipt and read receipt.

5. Click the Options tab on the Ribbon.

6. In the Tracking group, click the Request a Delivery Receipt and the Request a Read Receipt check boxes, as shown in Figure 3-17.

Figure 3-17
Creating a message requesting a delivery receipt and a read receipt

Tracking options

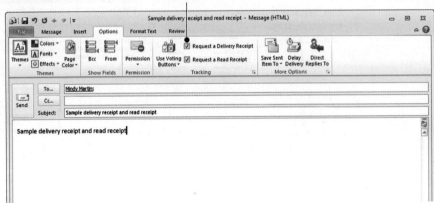

CERTIFICATION READY   2.1.9

How do you request a read receipt and a delivery receipt?

7. Click the Send button. The message is moved to the Outbox and it is sent when your computer is connected to the Internet.

PAUSE. LEAVE Outlook open to use in the next exercise.

A read receipt tells you that the message has been opened in the recipient's mailbox, but the recipient can choose to send or not send a read receipt, as shown in Figure 3-18. This means that you might not receive a read receipt, even when the recipient has read the message.

Figure 3-18
Recipient can choose to send a read receipt

If the recipient chooses to send the read receipt, it is sent to your mailbox by default, as shown in Figure 3-19.

Figure 3-19
Read receipt received in mailbox

Read receipt in the message list   Read receipt in the Reading Pane

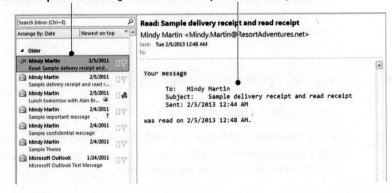

Directing Replies to a Specific Address

Directing replies to an e-mail address other than the one from which you sent the message can be a surprisingly useful tool. By sending a message with the replies directed elsewhere you prevent your inbox from being flooded with messages that you'll need to forward to someone else. For example, the president of a company could send out a message about an upcoming event, but direct any replies to the message to the event coordinator. Or, a human resources manager might want to send out an announcement of a job opening and direct the replies to her assistant for processing. In this exercise, you'll create a sample message and direct replies to it to go to HR@ResortAdventures.net.

STEP BY STEP   **Direct Replies to a Specific Address**

GET READY. LAUNCH Outlook if it is not already running.

1. In the Mail folder, click the New E-mail button on the Home tab. The Message window is displayed, with the Message tab selected.

2. Click the Options tab in the Ribbon and click the Direct Replies To button in the More Options group. The Properties dialog box is displayed.

3. In the Delivery Options area, the *Have replies sent to check box* is selected, and your e-mail address is displayed.

4. Select your e-mail address and key HR@ResortAdventures.net, as shown in Figure 3-20.

Figure 3-20

Directing message replies to an alternate address

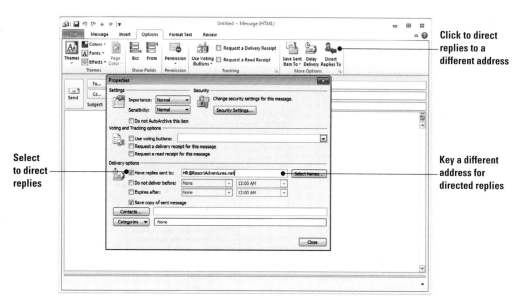

Click to direct replies to a different address

Select to direct replies

Key a different address for directed replies

5. Click Close. Close the message window without saving or sending a message.

PAUSE. LEAVE Outlook open to use in the next exercise.

Take Note   Some spam filters interpret messages with a different sender and reply to address as spam. If you are going to use this technique, you should also add a delivery receipt to ensure that your recipients receive your message.

When you send an e-mail message, the message header includes information about where to send replies. This information tells the recipient's e-mail application what e-mail address to use in the *To* field of a reply message. (When you request replies to be directed to a different address, Outlook replaces your Reply To information in the message coding with the alternate address you requested.)

If you have contacts entered in Outlook, you can choose a contact for the Have Replies Sent To field rather than keying an address. Using contact information in Outlook simplifies the process of directing replies to a different address.

 Ref | You can find more information about contacts in Lesson 6.

Configuring Message Delivery Options

Occasionally, you might want to delay the delivery of a message. For example, a Human Resources specialist can write a message explaining a change in benefits, but delay sending the message until the announcement is made later in the day. Delayed messages are held in the Outbox until the specified time, regardless of how often you click the Send/Receive button during the day. In this exercise, you learn how to specify specific details about a delivery delay using the message Properties dialog box.

STEP BY STEP | **Configure Message Delivery Options**

GET READY. LAUNCH Outlook if it is not already running.

> **Another Way**
> Click the More Options dialog box launcher to open the message Properties dialog box.

1. Click the New E-mail button on the Home tab. The Message window is displayed. By default, the Message tab is selected.

2. Click the Options tab in the Ribbon and click the Delay Delivery button. The message Properties dialog box is displayed and the *Do not deliver before* check box is selected. The current date and 5:00 PM are selected.

3. Click the Time dropdown arrow. Select the next available time from the dropdown list, as shown in Figure 3-21.

Figure 3-21

Message Properties dialog box with delayed delivery selected

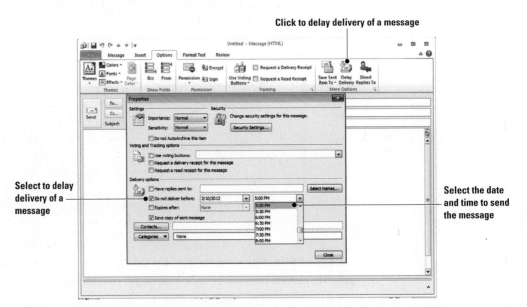

Click to delay delivery of a message

Select to delay delivery of a message

Select the date and time to send the message

4. Do not change the date. Click the Close button at the bottom of the dialog box. Note that the Delay Delivery button is highlighted.

5. In the *To* field, key [the e-mail address of a coworker or friend]. In the *Subject* field, key Delayed delivery.

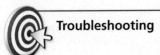 **Troubleshooting** | If you are using a POP3 e-mail account rather than an internal company network, you must keep Outlook open until the message is sent. Your computer must be connected to the Internet at the time specified for delivery.

6. In the message area, key Sample delayed delivery.

7. Click the Send button. The message is moved to the Outbox. The message is sent at the specified time if your computer is connected to the Internet.

PAUSE. LEAVE Outlook open to use in the next exercise.

Be sure that Outlook is running and your computer is connected to the Internet at the specified delivery time, in order to receive a delayed message at the scheduled time.

Saving a Sent Item to a Specific Folder

By default, sent messages are saved in the Sent Items folder. You might want to save a copy of a message in a different location. For example, you can keep messages about a specific project in a different folder. Or, you can keep correspondence with a specific individual in a separate folder. Organizing your messages can help you stay on top of a hectic day. In this exercise, you'll create a sample message and change the options to have the sent message saved in a specific folder.

STEP BY STEP   **Save a Sent Item to a Specific Folder**

GET READY. LAUNCH Outlook if it is not already running.

1. Click the New E-mail button on the Home tab. The Untitled—Message window is displayed.

2. Click the *To* field. Key [the e-mail address of a friend or coworker].

3. Click the *Subject* field. Key Different Save Location. In the message area, key Different Save Location.

4. Click the Options tab on the Ribbon.

5. Click the Save Sent Item To button and select the Other Folder option. The Select Folder dialog box is displayed, as shown in Figure 3-20.

Figure 3-22

Select Folder dialog box

Click to specify an alternate folder to store the sent message

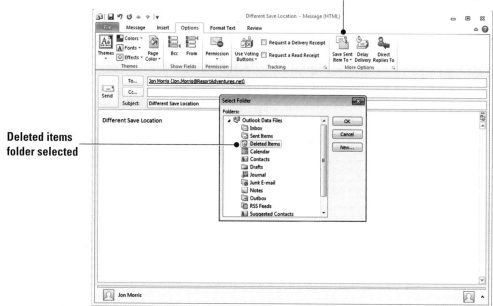

Deleted items folder selected

6. Select the Deleted Items folder, and click OK to close the dialog box.

Troubleshooting Normally, you will create a new folder or save the message to a folder you created earlier. That isn't necessary for this exercise.

7. Click the Send button. The Message window closes, and the message is moved to the Outbox. The message is sent when your computer is connected to the Internet.

8. In the main Outlook window, click the Deleted Items folder in the Navigation Pane. The message will be displayed in the Deleted Items folder when it has been sent.

 Ref   You will learn more about creating and using folders in Lesson 4.

9. Click the Inbox in the Navigation Pane.

PAUSE. LEAVE Outlook open to use in the next exercise.

CERTIFICATION READY   2.1.6

How do you change the location for saving a sent message?

Saving sent messages in different folders determined by the message content or addressee is a great way to keep your mailbox organized. Later, you will learn to create rules that automatically move messages to different folders.

Specifying the Sending Account

Many people have more than one e-mail account, such as a business account and a personal account. You can add all of your e-mail accounts to Outlook so that you can keep up with all of them at once. If you have more than one account, it is important that you specify the appropriate e-mail account as the sending account for your outgoing messages. If you have multiple e-mail accounts set up, you'll have an extra From button in your message window. Click this button to choose the e-mail account from which you want to send the message. In this exercise, you'll create a sample message and send it from an alternate e-mail address.

STEP BY STEP   Specify the Sending Account

 Troubleshooting In order to complete this exercise, you'll need to have at least two e-mail accounts set up in Outlook.

GET READY. LAUNCH Outlook if it is not already running and be sure that you have more than one e-mail account set up.

1. Click the New E-mail button on the Home tab. The Message window is displayed. By default, the Message tab is selected.

2. Click the From button in the Ribbon. A dropdown list is displayed showing each of your e-mail accounts, as shown in Figure 3-23.

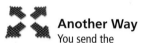

Figure 3-23

Selecting a sending account

The sending email address

Click to select an
alternate sending
account

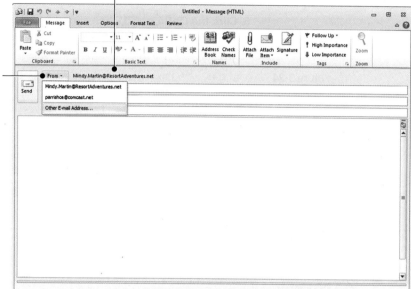

Another Way
You send the
message from another e-mail
address by selecting the Other
E-mail Address option and
keying a different address
into the From field.

3. Select your alternate e-mail account from the dropdown list.

4. In the *To* field, key your main e-mail address. In the *Subject* field, key Sample alternate e-mail.

5. In the message area, key Sample alternate e-mail.

6. Click the Send button. The Message window closes, and the message is moved to the Outbox. The message is sent when your computer is connected to the Internet and the message will be displayed in the Inbox when it has been sent.

PAUSE. LEAVE Outlook open to use in the next exercise.

CERTIFICATION READY   2.1.5

How do you send a message
from a specific e-mail address?

WORKING WITH VOTING OPTIONS

The Bottom Line

Often the most time-consuming part of planning a project or event is getting everyone's consensus on specific aspects of the activity at hand. You can use Outlook's voting options to poll messages recipients. If the standard voting buttons do not meet your need, you can create customized voting buttons.

Troubleshooting Microsoft Exchange Server is required to use voting buttons.

Using Standard Voting Buttons

Outlook's standard sets of voting buttons include Approve and Reject; Yes and No; and Yes, No, and Maybe. These three standard voting options can handle most of your voting needs. In this exercise, you'll create a sample message containing a standard set of voting buttons.

STEP BY STEP   **Use Standard Voting Buttons**

GET READY. LAUNCH Outlook if it is not already running.

1. Open a new message window.

2. In the *To* field, key [your e-mail address and the addresses of two friends or coworkers.]

3. In the *Subject* field, key Company picnic.

4. In the message area, key Do you plan to attend the company picnic next month? [Press Enter.]

5. Click the Options tab, then click the Use Voting Buttons button on the Ribbon. The three sets of standard voting buttons are listed, as shown in Figure 3-24.

Figure 3-24

Recipient's voting options

Click to select a voting option

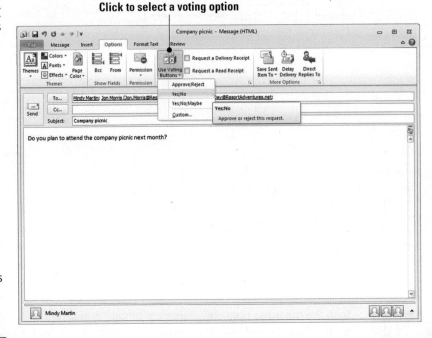

Another Way
Click the Use voting buttons check box in the message Properties dialog box. To display the Message Options dialog box, click the dialog box launcher in the Tracking group on the Options tab.

CERTIFICATION READY   2.1.8

How do you create a poll using standard voting buttons?

6. Click the Yes;No option.

7. Click the Send button. The message is moved to the Outbox, and it is sent when your computer is connected to the Internet.

PAUSE. LEAVE Outlook open to use in the next exercise.

When the message arrives in a recipient's mailbox, the InfoBar displays the text "Vote by clicking Vote in the Respond group above." When the recipient clicks the Vote button in the Respond group, the voting options are displayed. The recipient simply clicks the choice she wants. A dialog box asks the recipient to confirm her choice, as shown in Figure 3-25. When the recipient confirms her choice, a message is automatically sent to the source of the poll. In this case, you are the source of the poll.

Figure 3-25

Responding to a message with voting options

Click to vote

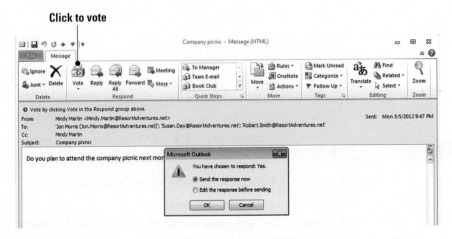

As replies arrive, the votes are tracked in the original sent message containing the poll question. The message used to send the poll is saved in the Sent Items folder like other sent messages. However, it is identified in the message list by the Tracking icon (see Figure 3-26), which resembles the Tracking button.

Figure 3-26

Sent message with voting options

Tracking icon ——

To view the results of the voting, double-click the message to open it. Click the Tracking button in the Ribbon, as shown in Figure 3-27.

Figure 3-27

Viewing poll results

Results tallied on the InfoBar

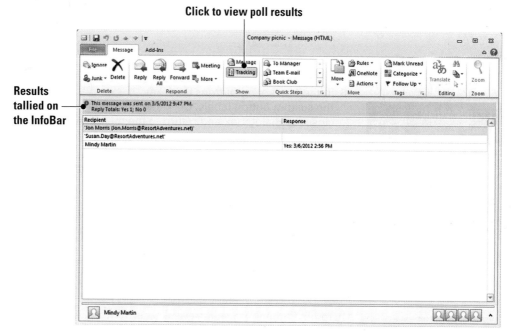

Configuring Custom Voting Buttons

Sometimes a simple Yes/No answer is not enough. When the standard voting buttons don't provide the options you need, you can create custom voting buttons. For example, if your company's holiday party is catered, you can ask employees who plan to attend if they want chicken or steak. In this exercise, you'll create a sample message with custom voting buttons.

STEP BY STEP   **Configure Custom Voting Buttons**

GET READY. LAUNCH Outlook if it is not already running.

1. Open a new message window.

2. In the *To* field, key [your e-mail address and the addresses of two friends or coworkers].

3. In the *Subject* field, key Company holiday dinner.

4. In the message area, key Select the meal you prefer for the company holiday party. [Press Enter.]

5. Click the Options tab, then click the Use Voting Buttons button on the Ribbon. Click the Custom option. The Properties dialog box is displayed. The *Use voting buttons* option is selected and *Approve; Reject* is displayed in the field, as shown in Figure 3-28.

Figure 3-28

Message Properties dialog box with *Use voting buttons* selected

Click to choose voting buttons

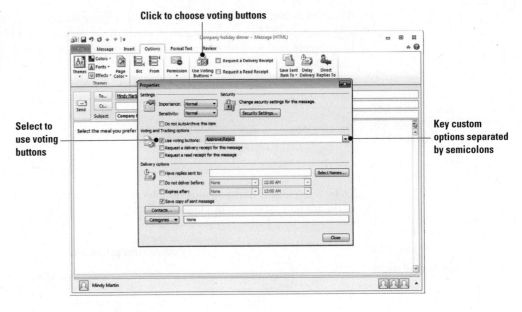

Select to use voting buttons

Key custom options separated by semicolons

6. In the *Use voting buttons* field, key Chicken;Steak. Always insert a semicolon between the custom button labels. Click the Close button at the bottom of the dialog box to close the dialog box and return to the message.

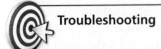

CERTIFICATION READY   2.1.8

How do you create a poll using custom voting buttons?

7. Click the Send button. The message is moved to the Outbox and it is sent when your computer is connected to the Internet.

PAUSE. LEAVE Outlook open to use in the next exercise.

Customized buttons provide flexibility when conducting polls. Choosing dinner is only one of the many types of polls you can create. Any time you need to gather opinions from several people, consider using a poll.

WORKING WITH SECURITY

The Bottom Line

Microsoft Outlook provides several security features to protect your e-mail correspondence. These features include encryption, a digital signature, and restricting permissions to a message. In this section, you'll create sample messages using each of these security features.

Troubleshooting   To use a digital signature or encrypt a message, you must have a digital ID. If you do not have a digital ID, consult your system administrator or purchase a digital ID from a certificate authority.

Using a Digital Signature

A **digital ID** is a way to authenticate that a message is coming from you and to add a level of encryption to the message. Digital IDs enable a recipient to verify that a message is really from you and decrypt any encrypted messages received from you. A digital ID contains a private key that remains on your computer and a public key you give to your correspondents to verify that you are the message sender. The keys unlock the encryption. When you give a recipient a digital ID, you are giving their computer the codes to unlock your encrypted messages. In this exercise, you'll create a sample message and add a digital signature.

STEP BY STEP   Use a Digital Signature

GET READY. LAUNCH Outlook if it is not already running.

1. Open a new message window.
2. In the *To* field, key [the address of a friend or coworker].
3. In the *Subject* field, key Digitally signed message.
4. On the Options tab, click More Options dialog box launcher. The message Properties dialog box opens.
5. Click the Security Settings button. The Security Properties dialog box is displayed, as shown in Figure 3-29.

Figure 3-29

Security Properties dialog box

Click to digitally sign messages once the initial security settings have been set up

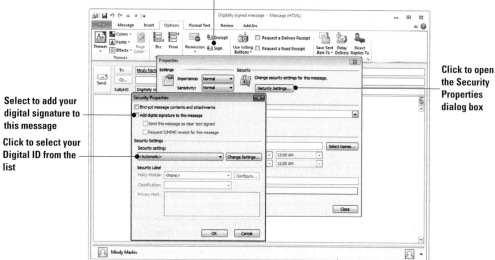

Select to add your digital signature to this message

Click to select your Digital ID from the list

Click to open the Security Properties dialog box

Another Way
Once you've set up your Security Settings with your Digital ID, you can simply click the Digitally Sign Message button on the Options tab to sign future messages.

CERTIFICATION READY   3.4.1

How do you use a digital signature?

6. Click the Add digital signature to this message check box.
7. Click the Security setting dropdown box and select your Digital ID from the list. Click OK to close the dialog box. Click the Close button to close the message Properties dialog box.
8. In the message area, key Sample digitally signed message. Click the Send button. The message is moved to the Outbox and it is sent when your computer is connected to the Internet.

PAUSE. LEAVE Outlook open to use in the next exercise.

When a digitally signed message arrives in the Inbox, an icon in the message list indicates that the message is digitally signed, as shown in Figure 3-30. Remember that messages with a digital ID contain the codes you will need to unlock encrypted messages from that person. So the first time you receive a digitally signed message for any sender, you should use the digital ID to add the person to your contact list or to update existing contact information so that their private key information is added to their contact record.

Figure 3-30

Digitally signed message

Icon indicates a digitally signed message

Ref   You can find more information about contacts in Lesson 6.

Using Encryption

Encryption is a great way to protect the privacy of important messages. When you use **encryption**, your message contents are scrambled so that only a recipient with the encryption key can decipher the message. To send an encrypted message and decrypt an encrypted message, you must have exchanged digital ID certificates with the recipient. In other words, both you and the recipient need to send each other a digitally signed message and add each other's digital ID to the Contacts list. In this exercise, you'll create a sample encrypted message.

STEP BY STEP   **Use Encryption**

GET READY. LAUNCH Outlook if it is not already running.

Take Note   Before you exchange encrypted messages, both you and the recipient need to send each other a digitally signed message and add each other's digital ID to the Contacts list.

1. Open a new message window.
2. In the *To* field, key [the address of the friend or coworker who has exchanged digital ID certificates with you].
3. In the *Subject* field, key Sample encrypted message.

@ The *Content* file is available on the book companion website or in WileyPLUS.

4. Open the *Content* file in the data files for this lesson. Select and copy all the text. Paste it in the message area.
5. On the Options tab, click the Encrypt button, as shown in Figure 3-31.

Figure 3-31

Encrypting a message

Click to encrypt a message

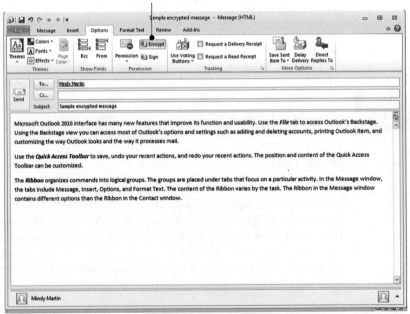

6. Click the Send button. The message is moved to the Outbox, and it is sent when your computer is connected to the Internet.

LEAVE Outlook open to use in the next exercise.

When an encrypted message arrives in the Inbox, an icon in the message list indicates that the message is encrypted, as shown in Figure 3-32. An encrypted message cannot be viewed in the Reading Pane. It must be opened to be read.

Figure 3-32

Encrypted a message

Icon indicates encrypted message

Encrypted messages cannot be viewed in the Reading Pane

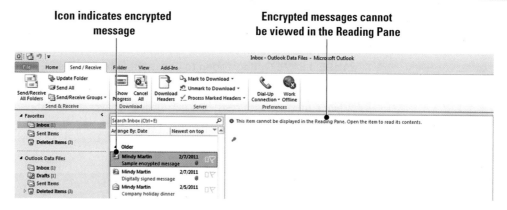

Restricting Permissions to a Message

Information Rights Management (IRM) is an Outlook feature that allows you to control how the recipient can use a message. When you restrict a message using IRM, Outlook encodes the message with instructions that prevent the recipient from printing, forwarding, or copying sensitive messages. In this exercise, you will create a sample message with restricted permissions.

STEP BY STEP   **Restrict Permissions to a Message**

WILEY PLUS EXTRA

WileyPLUS Extra! features an online tutorial of this task.

Take Note

GET READY. LAUNCH Outlook if it is not already running.

You must have Microsoft Windows Rights Management Services (RMS) installed to perform this activity.

IRM for the 2010 Microsoft Office system requires Microsoft Windows Rights Management Services (RMS).

Another Way
To restrict permissions to a message, click the Permissions button in the Options group of the Message tab on the Ribbon.

1. Open a new message window.
2. In the *To* field, key [the address of a friend or coworker with whom you've exchanged digital ID certificates].
3. In the *Subject* field, key Sample message with restricted permissions.
4. On the Options tab, click the Permission dropdown arrow. Select the Do Not Forward option. An InfoBar is displayed in the message window as shown in Figure 3-33.

Figure 3-33

Creating a message with restricted permissions

Click to add a restriction to the message

InfoBar indicates the nature of the restriction on the message

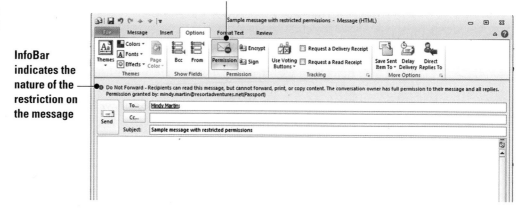

5. In the message area, key Sample message with restricted permissions.

6. Click the Send button. The message is moved to the Outbox, and it is sent when your computer is connected to the Internet.

PAUSE. LEAVE Outlook open to use in the next exercise.

When a message with restricted permissions arrives in the Inbox, an icon in the message list indicates that the message has restricted permissions, as shown in Figure 3-34. The same InfoBar that was displayed in the message window as you created the message is displayed in the window pane when the message is received.

Figure 3-34

Message with restricted permissions in the message list

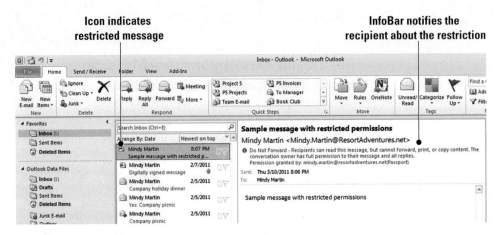

Icon indicates restricted message

InfoBar notifies the recipient about the restriction

Troubleshooting   Remember that IRM is not failsafe. IRM cannot protect your messages from being corrupted, erased, or duplicated by hand.

LOCATING MESSAGES

The Bottom Line

What was the cost of that item? When is the project deadline? Important information is often exchanged through e-mail messages and finding that information can be critical. Outlook 2010 has several powerful tools that make it easy to locate the right message when you need it.

You can easily locate all messages and attachments from a specific contact using the People Pane. You can sort any Mail folder by any attribute. You can filter search results using Instant Search with its companion Search Contextual tab and Search Suggestions list. If you find that you need to perform the same search on a regular basis, you can create a custom search folder that will always contain your filtered items.

Sorting Messages by Attributes

In the message list, e-mail messages are usually listed by date. The newest messages are displayed at the top of the message list. One of the easiest ways to locate messages is by sorting the message list by another **attribute** such as size, subject, or sender. In this exercise, you'll sort the message list by different file attributes.

STEP BY STEP   **Sort Messages by Attributes**

GET READY. LAUNCH Outlook if it is not already running.

1. If necessary, click the Mail button in the Navigation Pane of the main Outlook window.

2. Click Arranged By above the message list. Select the Attachment option. Messages are grouped by whether they include an attachment or not.

Another Way
To sort messages, click the View menu, click the Arrange By, and select an attribute.

3. Click Arranged By above the message list. Select the Subject option. Messages are grouped by sender. Groups are listed in alphabetic order.

4. Click Arranged By above the message list. Select the Date option. Messages are grouped by date. Groups are listed in chronological order.

PAUSE. Leave Outlook open to use in the next exercise.

By default, messages are sorted by the date they are received. Sometimes, you can get a better picture of a situation by viewing all the messages from a particular sender or subject. Another way to see all the messages from a particular sender is by using the People Pane.

Using the People Pane to Find a Message

NEW to Office 2010

Outlook 2010's People Pane is a convenient way to locate messages and attachments based on the sender information. The Show e-mail messages page and Show attachments page in the People Pane (visible in both the Mail folder and individual contact records) collect everything from each contact in one convenient place. In this exercise, you'll locate an attachment using the People Pane.

STEP BY STEP | **Use the People Pane to Find an Attachment**

GET READY. LAUNCH Outlook if it is not already running.

Instant Search must be enabled.

1. If necessary, click the Mail button in the Navigation Pane of the main Outlook window.

2. In the Inbox, select a message you sent to yourself.

3. If the People Pane is not visible, click the People Pane button on the View tab and select Normal. The home page of the People Pane displays a list of messages that you've sent to yourself.

4. Click the attachment icon to open the *Show Attachments That You Have Received From This Person* list. A list of only those messages that included an attachment is displayed. The list is sorted by message date, as shown in Figure 3-35.

Figure 3-35

Locating an attachment in the People Pane

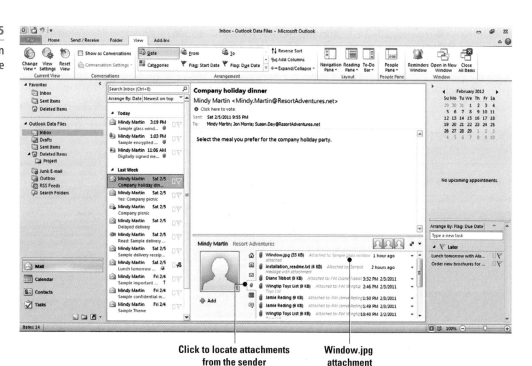

Click to locate attachments from the sender

Window.jpg attachment

CERTIFICATION
READY   1.3.4

How do you search for
messages from a specific
contact?

5. Click on the message you sent to yourself that had an attachment called Window.jpg. The message window opens, showing the message that contained the Window.jpg attachment.

6. Close the message window.

PAUSE. Leave Outlook open to use in the next exercise.

You can use the People Pane to show all the messages from a particular sender stored anywhere within your mailbox. This can be the simplest way to find more messages from a contact. However, if you've received several messages from the same person, you might find that the list is too long to be convenient. As an alternative, you can use Instant Search to search for a specific message that contains specific attributes.

Using Instant Search

One of the biggest problems with searching through e-mail messages over time is that the searches usually produce far too many results. **Instant Search** now includes two features that you can use to filter through the results: Search Suggestions List and the Search Contextual tab. As you begin typing a keyword in the Instant Search box, results are immediately displayed in the mail list rather than waiting to complete the search to display the results. In this exercise, you'll locate an Outlook item using Instant Search to filter your results.

STEP BY STEP   **Use Instant Search**

GET READY. LAUNCH Outlook if it is not already running.

1. Click the **Mail** button in the Navigation Pane of the main Outlook window.

2. If necessary, click the **Inbox** folder in the Navigation Pane. The Instant Search box is displayed at the top of the Inbox, as shown in Figure 3-36.

Take Note   The Instant Search feature works in every Outlook folder.

3. In the Instant Search box, key **Sample**. As you key the search text; three things happen. Outlook displays the messages that match the text; the Search Suggestions list appears, allowing you to choose which part of the message includes the keyword; and the Search Tools tab appears, as shown in Figure 3-36.

Figure 3-36

Instant Search features

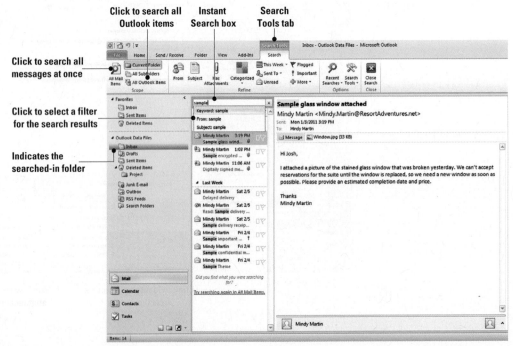

Take Note

CERTIFICATION
READY 1.4

How do you use Instant
Search to locate a message?

Instant Search searches only the specific Outlook folder you're currently viewing—in this case, the Inbox. You can search any mail folder or search everywhere in Outlook at the same time by clicking the All Outlook Items link in the Search Tools tab.

4. Click the Subject: Sample from the Search Suggestions list. Only messages that include the word Sample in the subject line are displayed.

5. Click the Attachments button in the Search Tools tab. Only messages that include the word *Sample* in the subject line and have attachments are displayed, as shown in Figure 3-37.

Figure 3-37

Filtered search list

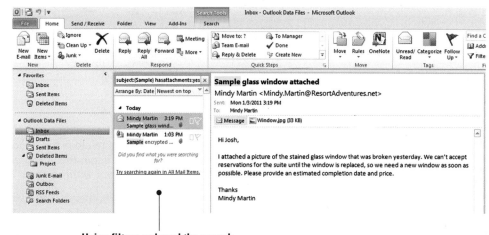

Using filters reduced the search
results to a more manageable list

6. Click Inbox in the Navigation Pane to clear the search.

PAUSE. LEAVE Outlook open to use in the next exercise.

CERTIFICATION
READY 1.4

How do you use search
filters to locate a message?

As you begin typing a search parameter in the Instant Search box, Outlook begins populating the mail list with items that contain your keyword, and the Search Suggestions list appears below the Instant Search box. By selecting one of the options in this list, you can filter the results based on where the keyword appears in the message.

Using Built-in Search Folders

If you find that you need to perform the same kind of search on a regular basis, you can save time by creating a custom search folder. Search folders are virtual folders stored in the Folder List in the Navigation Pane. A virtual folder looks and acts like a normal folder, but a virtual folder is really just a collection of links to messages that are stored in other folders. This allows you to maintain your folder organization while still offering you easy access to messages that fit your search needs. For example, you can access every unread e-mail message from every folder using the Unread Mail search folder.

STEP BY STEP **Use Built-in Search Folders**

GET READY. LAUNCH Outlook if it is not already running.

1. If necessary, click the Mail button in the Navigation Pane.

2. On the Folder tab, click New Search Folder in the New group. The New Search Folder dialog box is displayed, as shown in Figure 3-38.

Figure 3-38

New Search Folder dialog box

Click to create a new search folder —

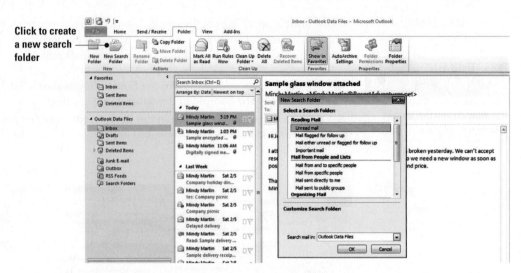

Figure 3-38

New Search Folder dialog box

3. In the *Select a Search Folder* section of the dialog box, select **Important Mail** in the *Reading mail* portion of the list. Click **OK** to close the dialog box. Outlook displays a new folder at the bottom of the folder list in the Navigation Pane called Search Folders. The Important Mail folder appears within Search Folders, as shown in Figure 3-39.

Figure 3-39

Important Mail search folder

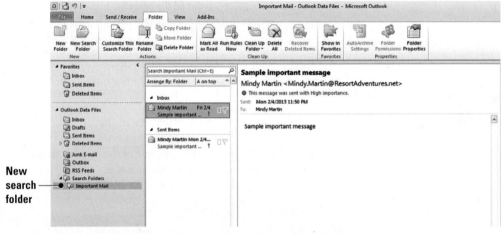

New search folder —

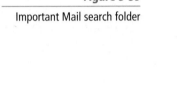

CERTIFICATION READY   **1.4.1**

How would you create an Unread Mail search folder?

PAUSE. LEAVE Outlook open to use in the next exercise.

Outlook provides a number of built-in search folders (see Table 3-1) for everything from unread mail to mail flagged for follow-up to mail containing specific keywords. You can also create a custom search folder containing any criteria you want.

Search Folder	What Items Will Appear in the Search Folder
Unread mail	Holds any message from any folder that is marked as unread.
Mail flagged for follow up	Holds any message from any folder that has been flagged.
Mail either unread or flagged for follow-up	Holds any message from any folder that is marked as unread or flagged.
Important mail	Holds any message from any folder that is marked as important.
Mail from and to specific people	Holds any message from any folder that is either from or to contact(s) you choose. When selected, a new box is displayed in the lower portion of the New Search Folder dialog box. Click Choose to open your address book and select the names of people you want included in the search.
Mail from specific people	Holds any message from any folder that is from contact(s) you choose. When selected, a new box is displayed in the lower portion of the New Search Folder dialog box. Click Choose to open your address book and select the names of people you want included in the search.
Mail sent directly to me	Holds any message from any folder that specifically lists you in the *To* field.
Mail sent to public groups	Holds any message from any folder that is addressed to a contact group or distribution list chosen by you. When selected, a new box is displayed in the lower portion of the New Search Folder dialog box. Click Choose to open your address book and select the contact group(s) you want included in the search.
Categorized mail	Holds any message from any folder that you've organized using categories. When selected, a new box is displayed in the lower portion of the New Search Folder dialog box. By default, any category is included, but you can click Choose to open a new window in which you can specify the words you want included in your search.
Large mail	Holds any message from any folder that is at least a specified size. When selected, a new box is displayed in the lower portion of the New Search Folder dialog box. By default, the size limit is 100 KB, but you can click Choose to open a new window in which you can specify the size limit you want.
Old mail	Holds any message from any folder that is older than a specific date. When selected, a new box is displayed in the lower portion of the New Search Folder dialog box. By default, anything older than 1 week is included, but you can click Choose to open a new window in which you can specify the number of days, weeks, or months you want included.
Mail with attachments	Holds any message from any folder that has an attachment.
Mail with specific words	Holds any message from any folder that contains words that you specify. When selected, a new box is displayed in the lower portion of the New Search Folder dialog box. Click Choose to open a new window in which you can specify the words you want included in your search.
Create a custom Search Folder	Holds any message from any folder that meets the specified criteria. When selected, a new box is displayed in the lower portion of the New Search Folder dialog box. Click Choose to open a new window in which you can specify the name for the folder and the specific criterion you want to use.

PRINTING MULTIPLE MESSAGES

The Bottom Line

With Outlook 2010, printing multiple messages is just as easy as printing one. Printed messages include the header and the body of the message. You can control all the printing settings in Backstage view.

Printing Multiple Messages

In this exercise, you learn how to print multiple messages in Outlook 2010.

STEP BY STEP   **Print Multiple Messages**

GET READY. LAUNCH Outlook if it is not already running.

1. If necessary, click the Mail button in the Navigation Pane of the main Outlook window. The Inbox is displayed.

2. Select the most recent e-mail messages. Press Ctrl and then click the next message in the list to select. Click the File tab to open Backstage view.

3. Click Print in the navigation pane to open the print settings page. The preview pane on the right displays a message saying that it might take a few minutes to display the preview of multiple messages, as shown in Figure 3-40.

Figure 3-40

Printing multiple messages

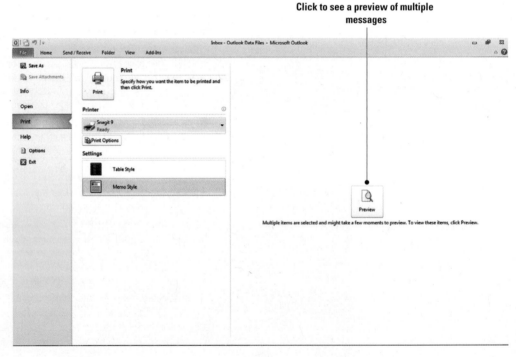

Click to see a preview of multiple messages

4. Click the Preview button. A preview of the first of the selected messages is displayed, as shown in Figure 3-41. Click the Next Page button to see the next selected message, as shown in Figure 3-41.

Figure 3-41

Print Settings in
Backstage view

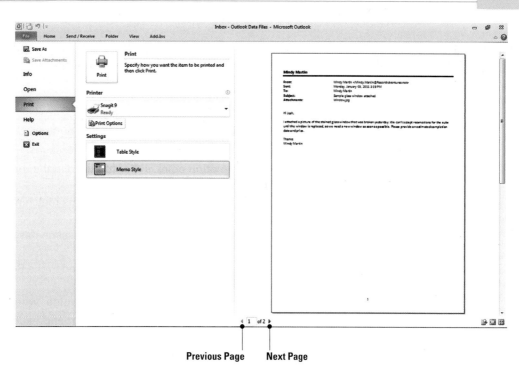

Previous Page   Next Page

CERTIFICATION
READY   1.5.3

How would you print
multiple messages?

5. Click the Printer dropdown arrow and select your printer from the list.

6. Click Print to print the selected messages.

CLOSE Outlook.

SKILL SUMMARY

In This Lesson You Learned How To:	Exam Objective	Objective Number
Manage automatic message content	Set Mail options.	1.1.2
	Specify options for replies.	3.4.3
	Specify options for forwards.	3.4.4
	Specify the font.	3.4.2
	Set a default theme for all HTML.	3.4.5
Use advanced message options	Set the Sensitivity Level.	1.2.3
	Set a reminder for message recipients.	2.1.4
	Configure tracking options.	2.1.9
	Configure message delivery options.	2.1.7
	Specify the sent item folder.	2.1.6
	Specify the sending account.	2.1.5
Work with voting options	Configure voting options.	2.1.8
Work with security	Manage signatures.	3.4.1
Locate messages	Use the People Pane.	1.3.4
	Use built-in Search folders.	1.4.1
Print multiple messages	Print multiple messages.	1.5.3

True/False

Circle T if the statement is true or F if the statement is false.

T   F   1. "Maybe" is one of the standard voting buttons.

T   F   2. Plain text is the default format for all messages.

T   F   3. A red exclamation point is the icon used in the message list to indicate that a message is confidential.

T   F   4. The Instant Search feature displays items matching the search criterion before the search is complete.

T   F   5. A delivery receipt indicates that the message has been opened by the recipient.

T   F   6. An encrypted message can be previewed in the Reading Pane when the message arrives.

T   F   7. A message is moved to the Sent Items folder when you click the Send button.

T   F   8. An InfoBar is a banner containing information added automatically at the top of a message.

T   F   9. When you create custom voting buttons, insert a colon between the options.

T   F   10. When you delay the delivery of a message, it is held in the Outbox until it is time to be sent.

Multiple Choice

Select the letter of the text that best completes the following statements.

1. A _____ assures the recipient the identity of the sender of a message.
   a. message header
   b. digital ID
   c. secure ID
   d. all of the above

2. Which of the following tells you that the message has been opened in the recipient's mailbox?
   a. Read receipt
   b. Delivered flag
   c. Delivery receipt
   d. Read flag

3. Which of the following suggests how the recipient should treat the message and the type of information in the message?
   a. permission restriction
   b. tags
   c. flags
   d. categories

4. The _____ contains all the messages for a given contact.
   a. message header
   b. contact record
   c. People Pane
   d. Received folder

5. What is the name of the banner containing information added automatically at the top of a message?
   a. Context bar
   b. InfoBar
   c. ScreenTip
   d. Trust Center

6. Which of the following allows you to filter search results?
   a. Arrange by field
   b. Search Context
   c. Search Suggestions List
   d. All of the above

7. What formatting language enables you to format text and insert into messages items such as horizontal lines, pictures, and animated graphics?
   a. Theme
   b. Format
   c. Template
   d. HTML

8. Which of the following contains a private key that remains on your computer and a public key you give to your correspondents to verify that you are the message sender?
   a. digital ID
   b. same server transfer
   c. encryption
   d. confidential e-mail

9. Which of the following tells you that the message has arrived in the recipient's mailbox?
   a. Read receipt
   b. Delivered flag
   c. Delivery receipt
   d. Read flag

10. What scrambles the text so that only the recipient with a key can decipher the message?
    a. encryption
    b. blending
    c. digital remixing
    d. encoding

Competency Assessment

Project 3-1: Create a Message with a Read Request

Mindy Martin, a co-owner of Resort Adventures, is supervising the arrangements for a wedding scheduled for next month at the resort. She needs to send them a message confirming the date and notifying them of the cancellation policy. Because she doesn't want any question as to whether the message was received, she is going to send the message with a Read Request.

GET READY. LAUNCH Outlook if it is not already running.

1. On the Home tab, click the New E-mail button to create a new message.

2. In the *Subject* field, key Keyser wedding confirmation.

3. In the message area, key the following message.

   Today's date. [Press Enter twice.]

   Mrs. Keyser, [Press Enter twice.]

As per our conversation of today, I am pleased to confirm the date of June 26 for the Keyser wedding. [Press Enter twice.]

Please be advised that our policy requires a four-week notice for wedding cancellations. Any cancellations after that date will result in forfeiture of your down payment. [Press Enter twice.]

Please let me know if you have any additional questions, [Press Enter twice.]

Mindy Martin [Press Enter.]

Resort Adventures [Press Enter.]

4. On the Home tab, click the High Importance option.

5. Click the Options tab. Select the Request a read receipt.

6. Click the File tab and select the Save As option. Save the message in Outlook Message Format as *Keyser wedding confirmation*.

7. Close the message without resaving, addressing, or sending it.

LEAVE Outlook open for the next project.

Project 3-2: Create a Confidential Message

Doug Hite is the personal assistant for a well-known actor. The actor has reservations for next week-end. To avoid publicity, the actor will use the alias "Jeff Hay" when he registers. Create a confidential message confirming the reservation.

GET READY. LAUNCH Outlook if it is not already running.

1. Click the New E-mail button to create a new message.

2. In the *To* field, key your e-mail address.

3. In the *Subject* field, key Reservation confirmation.

4. In the message area, key the following message.

Today's date [Press Enter twice.]

Mr. Hite, [Press Enter twice.]

This message confirms the reservation for Jeff Hay, arriving after 5 PM on Friday and leaving Sunday afternoon. As you requested, five pounds of dark chocolate nonpareils have been placed in the suite's refrigerator. [Press Enter twice.]

Please contact me if you need any further assistance. [Press Enter twice.]

Mindy Martin [Press Enter.]

Resort Adventures [Press Enter.]

5. Click the Tags dialog box launcher. Change the Sensitivity option to Confidential. Close the message Properties dialog box.

6. Click the File tab and select the Save As option. Save the message in Outlook Message Format as *Confidential confirmation* in the location specified by your instructor.

7. Close the message without addressing or sending it. Let Outlook save a copy

LEAVE Outlook open for the next project.

Proficiency Assessment

Project 3-3: Specify a Default Theme and Create a Message with Voting Options

You work for the Resort Adventures resort. Mindy Martin, one of the owners, asked you to select a default theme to be used for the resort. You need to select a theme and send a message to Mindy for her review.

GET READY. LAUNCH Outlook if it is not already running.

1. Open the Signatures and Stationery dialog box from the Mail Options page in Backstage view.

2. Open the Theme or Stationery dialog box, and select the Water theme.

3. Close the open dialog boxes, saving your changes, and open a new message. The new theme will be applied.

4. In the *Subject* field, key Proposed theme.

5. In the message area, key the following message using the same line spacing between paragraphs and signature lines that you've used in the previous projects.

Today's date

Mindy,

I think Water might be a good theme for our stationery as it meets the requirements we discussed.

It is brighter than the previous theme proposed.

It is colorful without being too intense.

Please let me know what you think.

Your Name

Resort Adventures

6. Select the two sentences that begin with It is and make them bullet points.

7. Add the Accept;Reject voting option to the message.

8. Save the message in HTML format as ***Proposed theme*** in the location specified by your instructor.

9. Close the message and save it in drafts. Do not address or send it.

10. Go back to the Mail options dialog box and restore the original theme.

PAUSE. LEAVE Outlook open to use in the next exercise.

Project 3-4: Locate and Print Messages

Mindy Martin, co-owner of Resort Adventure, received your message containing the latest sample theme; however, before she votes on it, she would like to sit down with you and Jon to discuss the pros and cons of each. You need to locate each of the theme styles that have been proposed (be sure to include the themed message that you created in Lesson 2). Print a copy of all three messages and bring them to the meeting.

GET READY. LAUNCH Outlook if it is not already running.

1. Click the Sent Items folder.

2. In the *Instant Search* field, key theme.

3. From the Search Suggestions list, select subject: theme.

4. On the Search Tools tab, click All Mail Items in the Scope group.

5. Select the three messages that remain in the search results list.

6. Click the File tab to open Backstage view and select Print on the navigation pane.

7. Click the Preview button.

Mastery Assessment

Project 3-5: Press Announcement

Its natural surroundings, luxurious facilities, and exceptional reputation have made Resort Adventures a hometown favorite location for weddings. Later today, another well-known local couple will send wedding invitations to a few close friends and the press. Mindy wants to provide her contact informa-tion for the press, but it will be a busy afternoon. She decides to write the message, but delay the delivery of the message until the couple announces the wedding date and location an hour from now.

GET READY. LAUNCH Outlook if it is not already running.

1. Open a new message window.

2. In the *To* field, key your e-mail address.

3. In the *Subject* field, key Mello-Lloyd wedding.

4. In the message area, write a brief message stating that you are confirming that the Mello-Lloyd wedding will be held at Resort Adventures. Provide a link to your website at www.resortadventures.net and your contact information at 800-555-1234. Don't forget to include your name at the end of the message.

5. Set the delivery delay for 90 minutes from now. (You must be able to leave the computer running and connected to the Internet until the specified time.)

6. Send the message without saving it.

PAUSE. LEAVE Outlook open to use in the next exercise.

Project 3-6: Send Your Digital Signature

A large corporation in a nearby city has decided to hold its spring sales convention at Resort Adventures. However, the Marketing Department in charge of the convention requires digital signatures on every message. You must exchange your digital signature with the marketing team member in charge of the convention.

GET READY. LAUNCH Outlook if it is not already running.

1. Open a new message window.

2. In the *To* field, key the address for a friend or coworker.

3. In the *Subject* field, key Spring Conference.

4. In the message area, write a brief message stating that your digital signature has been added to the message.

5. Add your digital ID to the message.

6. Send the message without saving it.

CLOSE Outlook.

INTERNET READY

A certificate authority sells digital IDs. Make a list of three to five certificate authorities. Compare the prices and functionality of the products they provide. (Hint: Select Options on the File tab. Click Trust Center. Click the Trust Center Settings button. In the Trust Center dialog box, click E-mail Security and click the Get a Digital ID button.)

Workplace *Ready*

SENDING A MESSAGE

E-mail is a common form of business correspondence. In many situations, it has replaced "snail mail," written correspondence delivered by the U.S. Postal Service. E-mail software has made electronic messages a timely, creative, efficient method of communication.

Suppose you are the owner of a small candy company. You have a bricks-and-mortar store in a small town in New Hampshire. It's a great place to raise a family, but your store does not get as much foot traffic in a month as a prime location in a big-city mall sees in a single day. To reach additional customers, you have created an electronic storefront on the Internet.

As your business grows, the sales from your electronic storefront increase at a phenomenal rate. You communicate with customers daily as they place orders or request information.

To your surprise, though, e-mail messages are useful in running your bricks-and-mortar store as well. You communicate with vendors, equipment providers, and other small business owners through e-mail. In a single day, you might send dozens of messages to

- Respond to customer inquiries.
- Confirm orders from customers.
- Send invoices to customers.
- Send shipping notifications to customers.
- Send a list of monthly specials to customers subscribed to your mailing list.
- Set up a meeting with a vendor.
- Place orders for ingredients.
- Request information about new equipment.
- Place an ad for more employees in the local newspaper.

Yes, business is booming. Your small-town store has sold candy to customers in Los Angeles, Cincinnati, Phoenix, and Montreal.

Fabrikam, Inc. is an older company. This family business was established by Rob Caron in 1973 to sell, install, and maintain swimming pools. As the second generation has taken over management of the company, Fabrikam has expanded by increasing the Fabrikam line of products. Fabrikam now sells patio furniture, house awnings, and hot tubs. Over time, they plan to add almost every product that makes your back yard more fun or more comfortable.

Project 1: Signature

Nicole Caron, the Marketing Manager, asked you to create a signature for e-mail messages. She asked you to use a graphic she likes.

GET READY: Outlook should not be running.

1. Launch Outlook from a desktop shortcut.
2. Click the New E-mail button. A new message window is opened.
3. In the *To* field, key Nicole@fabrikam.com. In the Subject field, key New Signature.

Take Note   Throughout this Circling Back you will see information that appears in black text within brackets, such as [Press Enter] or [your e-mail address]. The information contained in the brackets is intended to be directions for you rather than something you actually type word for word. It will instruct you to perform an action or substitute text. Do not type the actual text that appears within brackets.

4. Click the Options tab and click Bcc to display the Bcc field. In the Bcc field, key [your e-mail address].
5. Click in the message area. Key Hi Nicole, do you like this signature? [Press Enter three times.]
6. On the Insert tab on the Ribbon, click the Table button in the Tables group. Click the second square in the fifth row of boxes in the dropdown list. An empty table with two columns and five rows is inserted in the message area.
7. Select all the cells in the first column of the table and click the Layout tab in the Ribbon. Because table cells are selected, the displayed layout options on the Ribbon apply to tables.
8. Click the Merge Cells button in the Merge group on the Ribbon. The cells in the first column are merged.
9. Click in the merged cell. Click the Insert tab on the Ribbon.

@ The *Sun.gif* file is available on the book companion website or in *WileyPLUS*.

10. Click the Picture button in the Illustrations group. Select the *Sun.gif* file in the Data files. Click the Insert button on the dialog box. The image is inserted, but it is much too large to use in a signature. The image is automatically selected in the table.
11. With the picture still selected, click the Dialog Box Launcher in the Size group on the Picture Tools Format tab. The Size dialog box is displayed.

Take Note   Hint: The dialog box is the small arrow on the bottom-right corner of a group.

12. In the Scale area, click the Lock aspect ratio check box to select the option if necessary. This option will keep the image in proportion as you resize it.
13. Click in the Height box. Key 5%, and press Tab. Click the OK button to return to the message window. The sun image has been resized.
14. Drag the vertical center border of the table to the left so the first column is barely wider than the sun image.

15. Click in the first row of the second column and enter the following information in that column:

First row   Nicole Caron
Second row   Marketing Manager
Third row   Fabrikam, Inc.
Fourth row   www.fabrikam.com
Fifth row   800-555-8734 or Nicole@fabrikam.com

[Press Enter.]

16. Select all the text in the table. Click the Message tab if necessary. In the Basic Text group, change the font to Verdana. (Use *Arial* font if you don't have Verdana.).

17. Select Nicole Caron in the first row of the second column. Change the font to Freestyle Script. (If you don't have Freestyle Script font, use any font that looks like handwriting or leave the font unchanged.).

18. Increase the font size of Nicole's name to 24 and click the Bold button.

19. Select all the text in the table. Click the Font Color arrow. Click More Colors. In the displayed colors, click a dark orange shade that coordinates with the color of the sun image. Click OK to close the dialog box.

20. Drag the right border of the table to the left so that the second column is barely wider than the widest text in the column.

21. Click the sun image. Click the Table Tools Layout tab. Click the Align Center button in the Alignment group.

22. Select the table. Click the Design tab. In the Table Styles group, click the Borders arrow. Click the No Border option.

23. Click the File tab and select Save As. The Save as dialog box is displayed.

24. In the *File name* field, key CB Project 1. In the *Save as type* field, select HTML. Click Save.

25. Click Send.

LEAVE Outlook and the message window open for the next project.

Project 2:   Send a Digital ID with a Default Theme

Nicole likes the new signature and has asked you to create a default theme to go with the "look" you are designing. Create and send a message using the new signature and theme. Mark the message as High Importance and flag the message for the recipient to follow up. If you have a digital ID, include your digital ID in the message.

GET READY. Outlook must be running for this project.

1. Click the File tab and select Options. The Outlook Options dialog box is displayed.

2. Click Mail in the navigation pane. In the *Compose messages* area, click the Stationery and Fonts button. The Signatures and Stationery dialog box opens.

3. Click the Personal Stationery tab. Click the Theme button to display the Theme or Stationery dialog box.

4. In the list of themes and stationery, scroll down and click Network. Click OK to close the Theme or Stationery dialog box.

5. Click the Font dropdown arrow, select font. Use my fonts.

6. Click OK to close the Signatures and Stationery dialog box. Note that changes to the theme or stationery are not displayed until you open a new message window. Click OK again to close the Outlook Options dialog box.

7. On the Home tab, click the New E-mail button. A new message window is opened and the Message tab is selected.

8. Click in the message area. Key Hi Jon, and press Enter twice. Notice that the theme you selected changed the fonts used in the message area.

9. Key I'm looking forward to our lunch appointment tomorrow. [Press Enter twice.]

10. In the *To* field, key [the e-mail address of a friend or coworker].

11. In the *Subject* field, key CB Project 2.

12. In the Tags group, click the Follow Up button. Click the Custom option. The Custom dialog box is displayed.

13. Click the Flag for Recipients check box so the option is selected. Click OK to close the dialog box.

14. In the Tags group, click the High Importance button.

15. In the Show Fields group, click Bcc to deselect it.

16. Click the Send button. The message is moved to the Outbox and sent when the computer is connected to the Internet.

17. Click Send/Receive All Folders on the Home tab. Click the Sent Items folder and locate the CB Project 2 message.

Take Note   If you have already set up a digital ID account, proceed with the steps below. If you do not have digital ID, proceed to Project 3.

18. If you have already set up a digital ID account, double-click the CB Project 2 message. In the Move group, click the Actions button and select Resend this message in the dropdown list.

19. In the new message area, click at the end of the message and key I'm sending my digital ID.

20. In the Permission group, click the Digitally Sign Message button.

21. In the Permission group, click Permission and select Do Not Forward.

22. Click Send to send the message a second time.

LEAVE Outlook open for the next project.

Project 3: Send Voting Message with Attachments

When the New signature message arrives, Nicole previews it and saves the signature table as a personal signature. Afterwards, she needs to create and send a message with two attachments asking the recipient to vote on which of the two images should be included in the upcoming brochure.

USE the New Signature message you created in the previous projects.

1. Click the Folder List button in the Navigation Pane.

Take Note   Hint: The Folder List button is at the bottom of the Navigation Pane. If needed, use ScreenTips to identify the correct button.

2. Click the Minimize the Navigation Pane button at the top right of the Navigation Pane. The Navigation Pane collapses to a bar along the left side of the screen.

3. On the View tab, click the To-Do Bar button in the Layout group. Select Off in the dropdown list.

4. Click in the Instant Search box, and key Caron. Messages to Nicole Caron appear in the message list.

5. Click once on the New Signature message to select it. The Reading Pane displays a preview of the message.

6. From the Reading Pane, select the table containing the signature for Nicole Caron and press Ctrl+C to copy the table.

7. Click the New E-mail button. A new message window is opened.

8. In the *To* field, key [the e-mail address of a friend or coworker]. In the *Cc* field, key [your e-mail address]. In the *Subject* field, key New brochure photo.

9. Click in the message area. Key Please view the two attached images and vote on whether they will be okay to use in the new brochure. [Press Enter three times.]

10. On the Message tab in the Include group, click the Signature button. Click the Signatures option to display the Signatures and Stationery dialog box.

11. Click the New button. The New Signature dialog box is displayed.

12. Key CB Project 3 and click OK to return to the Signatures and Stationery dialog box.

13. Click in the *Edit signature* area. Press Ctrl+V to paste the new signature into the box. Click the OK button to return to the message window.

14. In the Include group, click the Signature button. Click the CB Project 3 option to insert the signature.

15. In the Include group, click the Attach File button. The Insert File dialog box is displayed.

@ The *Patio.jpg* and *Porch.jpg* files are available on the book companion website or in *WileyPLUS*.

16. Select the *Porch.jpg* file in the Data files for this activity. Press Ctrl and click the *Patio. jpg* file that is also in the data files. Click Insert.

17. Click the Options tab. Click the Use Voting Buttons and select Yes; No; Maybe. An InfoBar appears at the top of the message to notify you that voting buttons have been added to the message.

18. Click the Send button. The message is moved to the Outbox and sent when the computer is connected to the Internet. Click Send/Receive All Folders on the Home tab.

19. If necessary, click the Mail button on the Navigation Pane to return to the Inbox. In the *Instant Search* box, key Nicole. Click the All Mail Items button in the Scope group of the Search Tools tab. All the messages to or from Nicole are displayed in the message list.

20. Select both the New Signature and New brochure photo messages.

21. Click the File tab and select Print in the Navigation Pane. Double-click the Preview button to view the messages in the preview pane.

22. If you have a printer connect to your PC, click Print to print the messages using your default settings.

CLOSE Outlook.

4 Managing E-mail Messages

LESSON SKILL MATRIX

Skills	Exam Objective	Objective Number
Working with Folders		
Working with Conversations	Ignore a Conversation.	3.1.4
Managing the Mailbox	Mark items as read or unread.	1.2.4
	Set flags.	1.2.2
	Use the Reminder window.	1.3.3
Using Outlook's Cleanup Tools	View mailbox size.	3.1.1
	Use cleanup tools.	3.1.5
Managing Junk Mail	View message properties.	1.2.5
	Filter junk mail.	3.3.2
	Allow a specific message (Not Junk).	3.3.1

KEY TERMS

- archive
- AutoArchive
- Conversation
- Deleted Items folder
- Drafts folder
- Inbox folder
- Junk E-mail folder
- MailTips
- Outbox
- restore
- retention rules
- Really Simple
  Syndication (RSS)
- Sent Items folder
- spam
- split

Mindy Martin, Adventure Works' co-owner, started using Outlook a couple of months ago. She was amazed to see that her Inbox currently contains 180 messages. Clearly, she needs some way to organize them. After a bit of thought, she decides to mimic the organization she uses with her paper documents. She begins creating folders for the main categories of vendors, events, and guests. If you don't take the time to organize and maintain your mailbox, things can quickly get out of hand. In this lesson, you'll learn how to manage your mailbox to organize and maintain your information.

SOFTWARE ORIENTATION

Microsoft Outlook's Folder List

The Folder List, shown in Figure 4-1, provides a complete list of Outlook's initial folders. It includes a folder for each Outlook component, such as the Calendar and Notes.

Figure 4-1

Outlook's Folder List

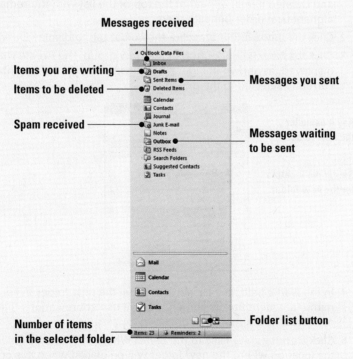

Although the Folder List includes every component, you will normally work only with the mail folders identified in Figure 4-1. The status bar at the bottom of the Outlook window displays the number of items in the selected folder. Create new folders to organize Outlook items by projects or individuals.

WORKING WITH FOLDERS

The Bottom Line

How often do you wander around your house looking for your car keys? If your answer is "rarely," you are already in the habit of putting things away so you know where to find them later. Organize your Outlook items in folders for the same reason. Items are easier to find when you put them away. In this section, you'll work with Outlook folders by creating, moving, deleting, and restoring them. You'll also move mail items from folder to folder.

Creating and Moving a Mail Folder

In your office, new documents arrive in your Inbox regularly. You look at the document, perform the associated tasks, and file the paper in a folder you labeled for that type of item. You don't place it back in your Inbox. If you piled up all your documents in your Inbox, in a few weeks or months you would have a stack of paper that was several inches tall. In the same way, you don't want to keep all your messages in your Inbox in Microsoft Outlook. In this exercise, you'll create and move Outlook folders.

STEP BY STEP   **Create and Move a Mail Folder**

GET READY. LAUNCH Outlook if it is not already running.

1. Click the Folder List button in the bottom of the Navigation Pane to display the Folder List shown in Figure 4-1. The four main Outlook folders (Inbox, Drafts, Sent Items, and Deleted Items) appear at the top of the list with the remaining Outlook folders in alphabetical order beneath them.

2. Click the Inbox folder and click the Folder tab to display Outlook's folder tools.

3. Click the New Folder button in the New group. The Create New Folder dialog box is displayed, as shown in Figure 4-2. Since you selected the Inbox in step 2, the Inbox is currently selected in the dialog box

Figure 4-2

Create New Folder dialog box

Key a name for the new folder

Select the location for the new folder

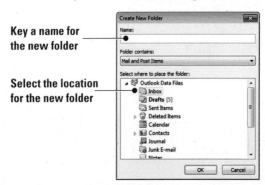

Another Way
To create a new folder, right-click any folder in the folder list and select New Folder.

4. In the *Name* field, key Lesson 4 to label the new folder. When creating a folder, use a name that identifies its contents. Don't use abbreviations that you won't remember next week or six months from now.

5. Click Outlook Data Files in the Select Where to Place the Folder list. This determines the location where the new folder will be placed when it is created. If you do not have the correct location selected, you can move the new folder later.

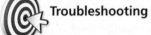
Troubleshooting For this exercise, you want to select the top-level folder. It's the folder that holds your Inbox, Sent Items folder, and so on. Depending on the settings on your computer and the type of e-mail account you have, this might be called Outlook Data Files, Personal Folders, or simply your e-mail address.

6. Click the OK button to close the dialog box and create the folder. The new folder is added to the Folder List.

7. In the Folder List, click the Lesson 4 folder to select it and then drag the folder down to the Notes folder. When the Notes folder is highlighted, drop the folder. An expand arrow is displayed next to the Notes folder, indicating that it contains a folder, as shown in Figure 4-3.

**Outlook Data
Files folder**

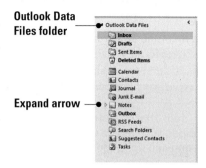

Expand arrow

8. Click the expand arrow next to the Notes folder. The Folder List expands to display the Lesson 4 folder, as shown in Figure 4-4.

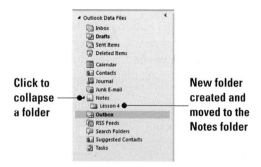

**Click to
collapse
a folder**

**New folder
created and
moved to the
Notes folder**

9. Drag the Lesson 4 folder and drop it on the Outlook Data Files icon in the Folder List. The Lesson 4 folder is placed alphabetically in the Folders List, and the expand arrow is removed from the Notes folder.

PAUSE. LEAVE Outlook open to use in the next exercise.

Outlook provides several default mail folders that meet your most basic organizational needs. Table 4-1 identifies the default mail folders and describes their content.

Folder	Description
Deleted Items	The **Deleted Items folder** holds your deleted messages. Items in the Deleted Items folder can be restored to full use. However, if the item is deleted while in the Deleted Items folder, it will be permanently deleted from your computer. Emptying the Deleted Items folder permanently removes every item in the folder.
Drafts	The **Drafts folder** holds Outlook messages you write but haven't sent. You can return to a draft later to complete and send the message. If you close a message without sending it, a dialog box will ask if you want to save the draft. Click Yes to save the draft. Click No to discard the draft.
Inbox	By default, new messages to you are placed in this **Inbox folder** when they arrive.
Junk E-mail	The **Junk E-mail folder** contains messages identified as spam when they arrive.
Outbox	The **Outbox** holds outgoing messages in this folder until you are connected to the Internet. When an Internet connection is detected, the message is sent.
RSS Feeds	**Really Simple Syndication (RSS)** allows you to subscribe to content from a variety of websites offering the service. RSS is not covered in this book. Use Outlook's Help feature to find more information on RSS.
Sent Items	Items are automatically moved to the **Sent Items folder** after they have been sent.

Deleting and Restoring a Folder

You can delete an Outlook folder you no longer need. When you delete a folder, it is moved to Outlook's Deleted Items folder. Items in the Deleted Items folder are still on your computer. You can **restore** these items, that is, make them available for use again, by moving them out of the Deleted Items folder. In this exercise, you'll delete the Lesson 4 folder and restore it.

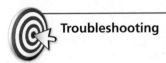 **Troubleshooting** Use caution. If you *delete* an item that is stored in the Deleted Items folder instead of moving the item to another folder, such as the Outlook Data File, the item is permanently removed from your computer and can no longer be restored.

STEP BY STEP   **Delete and Restore a Folder**

GET READY. USE the folder you created in the previous exercises.

1. If necessary, click the Folder List button in the Navigation Pane to display the complete list of Outlook folders.

2. Right-click the Lesson 4 folder created in the previous exercise. Click Delete Folder from the shortcut menu. A warning dialog box is displayed, as shown in Figure 4-5.

Figure 4-5

Deleting a folder

Expand arrow

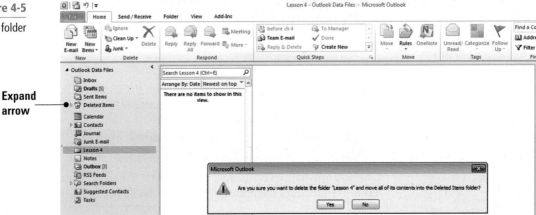

3. Click Yes to close the warning dialog box. The Lesson 4 folder is moved to the Deleted Items folder. It will not be removed from your computer until you empty the Deleted Items folder.

4. In the Folder List, click the expand arrow next to the Deleted Items folder. The Lesson 4 folder is displayed in the Deleted Items folder.

5. Drag the Lesson 4 folder and drop it on the Outlook Data Files icon in the Folder List. The Lesson 4 folder is placed in the Outlook Data Files, and the expand arrow is removed from the Deleted Items folder. The Lesson 4 folder has been restored, and it is now available for use.

PAUSE. LEAVE Outlook open to use in the next exercise.

Moving Messages to a Different Folder

Outlook uses folders to organize Outlook items. Messages arrive in the Inbox. Messages you send are stored in the Sent Items folder. To effectively organize your messages, create new folders for projects or individuals, and move the related messages into the new folders. In this exercise, you'll start organizing your mailbox by moving messages to different folders.

STEP BY STEP   **Move Messages to a Different Folder**

GET READY. LAUNCH Outlook if it is not already running, and complete the previous exercises.

1. If necessary, click the Mail button in the Navigation Pane to display the Inbox.

Ref

In Lesson 5, you will create and use rules to automatically move messages.

2. Click the New E-mail button on the Home tab. The Message window is displayed. By default, the Message tab is selected.

3. In the *To* field, key [your e-mail address]. In the *Subject* field, key Sample Message for Lesson 4.

4. In the message area, key Sample Message for Lesson 4.

5. Click the Send button. The message is moved to the Outbox, and it is sent when your computer is connected to the Internet.

6. Return to your Inbox. Click the Send/Receive All Folders button if the message has not arrived yet. Because the message was sent to your e-mail address, the message is moved to the Sent Items folder and it arrives in your Inbox. You will move both copies of the message into the Lesson 4 folder.

7. Right-click the Sample Message for Lesson 4 message that just arrived in your Inbox. Click Move on the shortcut menu. A list of potential folders is displayed.

8. Click Other Folder at the bottom of the list. The Move Items dialog box is displayed, as shown in Figure 4-6.

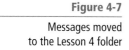 **Another Way**
You can also open the Move Items dialog box by selecting the message and pressing Ctrl+Shift+V.

Figure 4-6

Move Items dialog box

9. Click the Lesson 4 folder in the dialog box, if necessary. Click the OK button to close the dialog box and move the received message from the Inbox to the Lesson 4 folder.

10. Click the Sent Items folder in the Folder List. A list of the messages you have sent is displayed in the message list.

11. Click the Sample Message for Lesson 4 message and drag it to the Lesson 4 folder. The message is moved from the Sent Items folder to the Lesson 4 folder.

12. Click the Lesson 4 folder in the Folder List. The two messages you moved are displayed in the message list, as shown in Figure 4-7.

Figure 4-7

Messages moved to the Lesson 4 folder

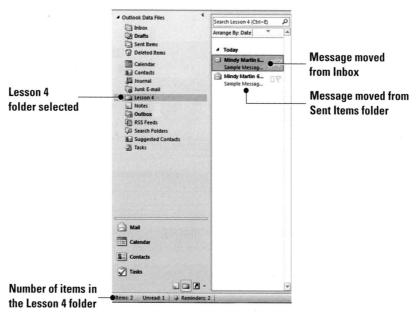

PAUSE. LEAVE Outlook open to use in the next exercise.

USING CONVERSATION VIEW

The Bottom Line

NEW
to Office 2010

In previous versions of Outlook, the only way to group all of the messages related to a single stream of correspondence together was to move them into a separate folder. In Outlook 2010, Microsoft has introduced a new function called **Conversation view**, which enables you to organize every e-mail message you send or receive about the same subject together into one **Conversation** group right there in your Inbox. In this section, you'll turn on Conversation view and learn how to work with it. You'll also learn how to ignore a Conversation that you no longer want to follow.

SOFTWARE ORIENTATION

Microsoft Outlook's Conversation View

Outlook's newest way to streamline your Inbox is Conversation view, shown in Figure 4-8. Conversation view groups all the messages related to a single subject (based on the Subject line) in one convenient location.

Figure 4-8

Message list in
Conversation view

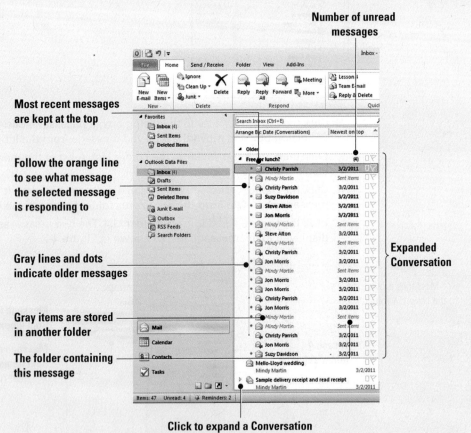

Number of unread messages

Most recent messages are kept at the top

Follow the orange line to see what message the selected message is responding to

Gray lines and dots indicate older messages

Gray items are stored in another folder

The folder containing this message

Expanded Conversation

Click to expand a Conversation

Conversation view uses colors and symbols to let you know the status of each message in the Conversation. Every related message is included in the Conversation group, even if it has been stored in a different folder. Use this figure as a reference throughout this lesson as well as the rest of this book.

Turning on Conversation View

Conversations are a great new way to organize your messages. Conversations can greatly reduce the clutter in your Inbox by grouping like information together. For example, say you send an e-mail called *Lunch Tomorrow* to four friends asking what restaurant they want to go to for lunch. All replies are grouped into a Conversation along with the original message you sent, as well as any other messages that the five of you send back and forth as replies or forwards to the original e-mail message. In this lesson, you'll turn on Conversation view.

NEW to Office 2010

Another of Outlook's new tools to help you work more efficiently is MailTips. **MailTips** are messages that can appear in a message's InfoBar alerting you to potential dangers. For example, in a Conversation a common mistake that people make is replying to the wrong message. In most cases, you'll want to reply to the most recent message in the Conversation thread. When you have a list of messages with the same name it can be easy to click Reply while selecting an older message. When this happens, Outlook will give you a MailTip letting you know that you are not replying to the most recent message. If you still want to the reply to the open message, just ignore the MailTip. To follow the MailTip's advice, click the InfoBar to see your options.

STEP BY STEP   **Turn on Conversation View**

USE the *Sample message for Lesson 4* message you created in the previous exercise.

1. If necessary, click the Mail button in the Navigation Pane to display the mailbox. Click the Lesson 4 folder and select the bottom message.

2. Click the View tab and select Show as Conversations in the Conversations command group. A message box is displayed, as shown in Figure 4-9.

Figure 4-9

Turning on Conversation view

---

3. Click This Folder. The message list changes into a Conversation, as shown in Figure 4-10.

Figure 4-10

Message list in Conversation view

Select to view Conversations

Conversation

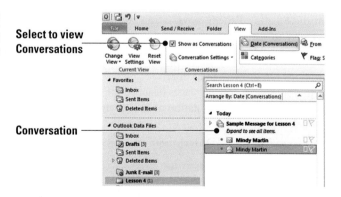

---

4. Right-click the bottom message and select Reply from the shortcut menu. The *Re: Sample message for Lesson 4* window is displayed. The message window contains an InfoBar warning you that you are not responding to the latest message, as shown in Figure 4-11. This is one of Outlook's new MailTips designed to help you work smarter.

Figure 4-11

A Conversation message displaying a MailTip

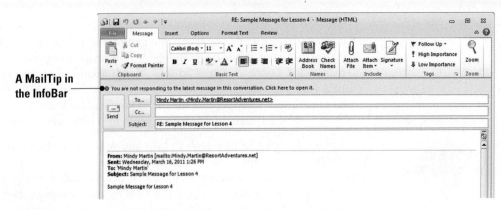

A MailTip in the InfoBar

Take Note Microsoft spent a lot of time analyzing the kinds of mistakes people make when they send messages. If Outlook thinks you might be about to make a mistake, it will display a MailTip warning you of possible dangers.

5. Click the MailTip in the InfoBar. Select the Open the Latest Message in a Conversation option. The latest Sample Message for Lesson 4 window is displayed.

Take Note The MailTip options will vary depending on the kind of issue you are being warned about.

6. Click Reply on the Message tab. A *RE: Sample Message for Lesson 4—message* window is displayed.

7. Close both message windows without saving or sending the messages.

8. Click the View tab. Click Conversation Settings in the Conversation group on the View tab, and verify that the Show Messages from Other Folders option in selected in the menu that appears. This ensures that Outlook will show you entire Conversations regardless of the folder the messages are stored in.

PAUSE. LEAVE Outlook open to use in the next exercise.

Working with Conversations

In Conversation view, your Inbox will only show the latest message in the Conversation. To let you know that more information is available, Outlook displays an expansion arrow beside the message. When you click the header of the Conversation message, the most recent message appears in the Reading Pane. Conversation view uses a series of symbols and connecting lines to makes it easy to see who replied to whom. Click any message in the Conversation and follow the orange line back to its source. In this exercise, you'll practice working with Conversations.

Conversations can grow to hold dozens of messages. When working with Conversations, it is important to understand how messages relate to the Conversation and to each other. To help you in this task, Outlook uses a combination of notes, symbols, and lines, which are described in Table 4.2.

Table 4-2

Conversation View Symbols

Conversation Cues	Description
Split	A **split** occurs when more than one person responds to a message; Outlook indicates this has happened by adding a Split note to the Conversation group listing. Future messages related to the split will be tracked as mini Conversation groups within the split.
Large orange dot	This symbol marks the latest message in the Conversation, (or within each split).
Small orange dot	When you click on a message within a Conversation, an orange line will drop down the list. The small orange dot at the end of the orange line indicates what message triggered the selected message.
Gray lines and dots	Older messages in the Conversation are marked with a gray line and dot. These markers indicate that the messages are still related but are not the most recent in the Conversation.

WileyPLUS Extra! features an online tutorial of this task.

STEP BY STEP   **Work with Conversations**

GET READY. LAUNCH Outlook if it is not already running.

1. If necessary, click the Mail button in the Navigation Pane to display the Inbox. On the View tab, ensure that Show as Conversation is selected.
2. Click the New E-mail button on the Home tab to open a new message window.
3. In the *To* field, key [the e-mail address of a friend]. In the *Subject* field, key Sample Conversation. In the message area, key Initial message. Click Send. Click the Send/ Receive All Folders button on the Home tab.
4. When the Sample Conversation message with the text *Initial message* arrives from your friend, select it and click Reply in the Respond group to open a RE: Sample Conversation message window.

Take Note   Because Conversations are typically with two or more people, you should try to complete this exercise with a friend or coworker. If none is available, you can complete the exercise by sending and receiving messages to yourself.

5. In the message area, key First response. Click Send. Click the Send/Receive All Folders button on the Home tab. Notice that an expansion arrow appears next to the Sample Conversation message to let you know that it is now a Conversation, as shown in Figure 4-12.

Figure 4-12

Beginning a Conversation

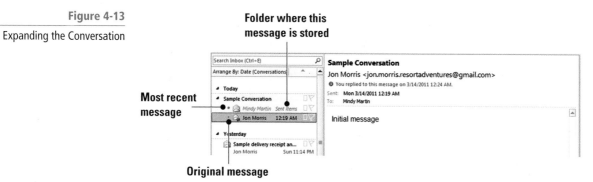

6. Click the expansion arrow to expand the Conversation, as shown in Figure 4-13. Two messages appear in the Conversation. The Sample Conversation message from your Inbox is highlighted. Notice that there is an orange dot next to each of the messages. The smaller dot indicates that it is the original message. A larger dot indicates that it is the most recent message.

Figure 4-13

Expanding the Conversation

7. Click the gray and italicized message in the Conversation. Its text appears at the top of the Reading Pane. This is the "first response" message from you. Notice that there is now an orange line that shows the connection between the two messages, as in Figure 4-14.

Take Note   Below this message there is a thin line that divides it from the previous message in the Conversation.

Figure 4-14

Viewing messages from other folders in the Conversation

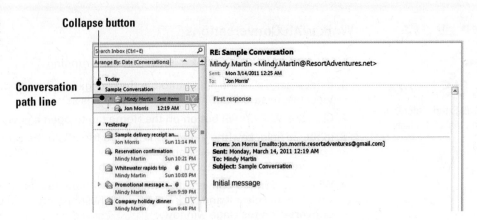

Collapse button

Conversation path line

8. When the *RE: Sample Conversation* message arrives from your friend with the text *First response*, select it and click Reply in the Respond group to open a RE: Sample Conversation message window.

9. In the message area, key Reply to the "first response" message. Click Send. Click the Send/Receive All Folders button on the Home tab. The RE: Sample Conversation message arrives from your friend and is added to the Conversation, as shown in Figure 4-15.

Take Note   You can read and respond to any of the messages in a Conversation just as you would any other message.

Figure 4-15

Continuing the Conversation

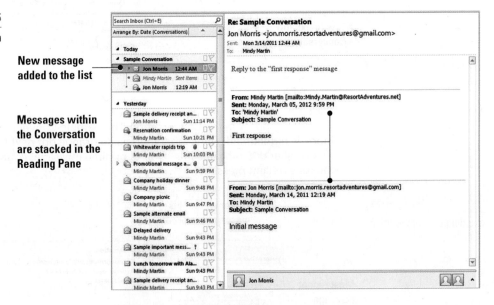

New message added to the list

Messages within the Conversation are stacked in the Reading Pane

10. When the RE: Sample Conversation message arrives from your friend with the text *Reply to first response*, select it and click Forward in the Respond group to open a FW: Sample Conversation message window.

11. In the message area, key Forward final message to a friend. Click Send. Click the Send/Receive All Folders button on the Home tab. The message that you sent appears at the top of the expanded Conversation.

12. In the Reading Pane, scroll down through the previous messages in the Conversation. Point to the right end of the line that appears above the *"First response"* message. Two navigation buttons appear just below the line, as shown in Figure 4-16.

Figure 4-16

Completing the Conversation

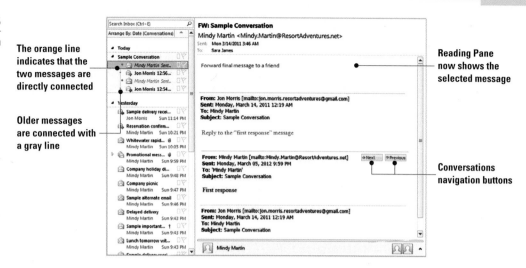

The orange line indicates that the two messages are directly connected

Older messages are connected with a gray line

Reading Pane now shows the selected message

Conversations navigation buttons

13. Click the Next button. As you can see by the arrow on the button, clicking the Next button jumps you up to the beginning of the next Conversation.

Take Note

Remember that because Conversations flow from newest to oldest, the next button takes you to the next highest message.

14. Click the black collapse arrow next to the Conversation heading. The Conversation compresses down to one item with an expansion arrow.

PAUSE. LEAVE Outlook open to use in the next exercise.

One of the convenient things about working with Conversations is that Outlook is able to group messages from any folder into the Conversation. So no matter how you organize your messages, you can still see them in one convenient place. When Outlook displays a message from another folder, the message information appears gray and italicized in the message list.

Ignoring a Conversation

Although Conversations are a great organizing tool, you might find that you no longer want to be included in a particular Conversation. You can stop following a Conversation by selecting the Conversation header and clicking Ignore in the Delete group. All future messages related to this Conversation (as indicated by the Subject line) will automatically move to your Deleted Items folder. In this exercise, you'll ignore a Conversation.

STEP BY STEP **Ignore a Conversation**

USE the Sample delivery receipt and read receipt messages you sent to yourself in Lessons 3 and 4.

1. If necessary, click the Mail button in the Navigation Pane to display the mailbox and click the Sample delivery receipt and read receipt message in the message list.

2. Click the Home tab to display the Delete group.

3. Click Ignore in the Delete group. Outlook asks you to confirm that you want to ignore the Conversation, as shown in Figure 4-17.

Figure 4-17

Ignoring a Conversation

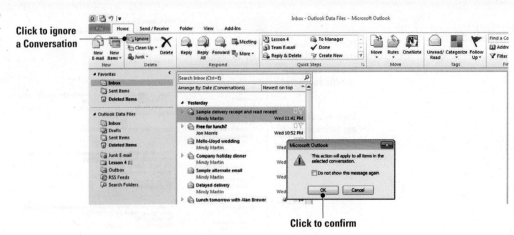

4. Click **OK.** The Ignore Conversation message box is displayed, as shown in Figure 4-18.

Figure 4-18

Ignore Conversations
message box

5. Click **Ignore Conversation.** The Conversation moves out of the Inbox and into the Deleted Items box. Outlook will move all future messages related to this Conversation to your Deleted Items folder, as soon as they are received by your e-mail account.

6. Click the **View** tab and deselect **Show as Conversations** in the Conversations command group. A message box is displayed asking whether you want to stop using Conversations view. Click **All Folders** to turn off Conversation view.

PAUSE. LEAVE Outlook open to use in the next exercise.

CERTIFICATION READY   3.1.4

How do you ignore a Conversation?

Take Note

When you receive replies or forwards, the text from the previous e-mail appears at the end. This is the same text that is in some of the messages in the Conversation. To get rid of even more clutter, you can click Clean Up in the Delete group and select Clean Up Conversations. The extra messages will be deleted.

MANAGING THE MAILBOX

The Bottom Line

Although organizing your messages into folders and Conversations is a good way to cut down the clutter in your mailbox, you still need to manage the items that remain. Managing your messages means keeping track of what you've read or haven't read, and following up on messages that require a response or action from you in a timely fashion. In this section, you'll learn to manually mark items as read or unread, add follow-up reminders for yourself, and work with the Reminder windows that Outlook uses to keep you on your toes.

Marking a Message as Read or Unread

Have you ever been called away in the middle of reading an e-mail message? Once you've opened a message or even paused on it for a few seconds, Outlook considers it read (whether or not you actually finished reading it) and displays it as such in the Inbox listing. When your Inbox shows no unread messages, it can be easy to forget which messages you need to return to. To help you avoid this confusion, you can manually mark a message as read or unread. In this exercise you'll mark messages as read and unread.

Mark a Message as Read or Unread

USE the *Blue Yonder Airlines contest* messages you sent to yourself in Lesson 2.

1. If necessary, click the Mail button in the Navigation Pane to display the mailbox and click the Blue Yonder Airlines contest message in the message list. Because you sent a reply to this message, Outlook shows the message as read.

2. On the Home tab, click Unread/Read in the Tags group. The message status changes to Unread and its header appears as bold in the message list.

3. With the message still selected in the message list, on the Home tab, click Unread/Read in the Tags group. The message status changes to Read and its header is no longer bolded in the message list.

PAUSE. LEAVE Outlook open to use in the next exercise.

CERTIFICATION READY   1.2.4

How do you mark a message as unread?

Setting a Flag as a Reminder for a Message

The easiest way to keep track of messages that you need to follow up on is to mark them with a flag. When you see a flag you know that there is still something that you need to do in regard to that message. You can choose whether or not you want Outlook to give you a Reminder window at a specified time to remind you of your deadline. Once you've completed the required task or response, you can clear the flag to remove the reminder. In this exercise, you'll add a reminder flag to a message.

Set a Flag as a Reminder for a Message

GET READY. USE the Sample Important Message messages you sent to yourself in Lesson 3.

1. If necessary, click the Mail button in the Navigation Pane to display the mailbox and double-click the Sample Important Message item in the message list. Because this is an important message, you want to be sure to follow up.

2. In the Tags group, click Follow Up. A list of options is displayed beneath the button, as shown in Figure 4-19.

Figure 4-19

Follow Up options

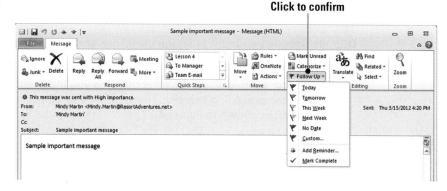

Another Way
The Follow Up button is also available on the Home tab in the Tags group.

Take Note   The color of the flag becomes darker the closer you get to the deadline.

3. Click Custom in the dropdown menu to open the Custom dialog box, as shown in Figure 4-20.

Figure 4-20

The Custom dialog box

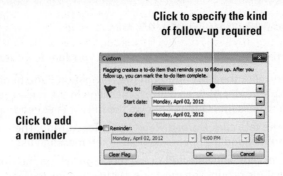

Click to specify the kind of follow-up required

Click to add a reminder

4. Click the Flag To down arrow and select Review from the list.

5. Click the Reminder check box near the bottom of the dialog box.

6. Set a reminder for five minutes from now. Click OK and close the message window. The message list now shows the message with a reminder flag in the far-right column, as shown in Figure 4-21.

Figure 4-21

A reminder flag in the message list

Dark reminder flag indicating that the action is due today

PAUSE. LEAVE Outlook open to use in the next exercise.

Working with Reminder Windows

Once you've set a reminder flag for a message, Outlook uses the Reminder window as a way to prompt you that a due date is approaching. Outlook uses the same Reminder window to remind about tasks and calendar appointments. In this exercise, you'll open an Outlook item from the Reminder window, dismiss the reminder, and clear the flag on a message.

 Ref

You can read more about setting reminders for tasks in Lesson 11 and for Calendar appointments in Lesson 8.

STEP BY STEP   **Work with Reminder Windows**

USE the Sample Important Message messages and complete the preceding exercise.

1. If necessary, click the Mail button in the Navigation Pane to display the mailbox.

2. A Reminder window is displayed at the time you indicated in the Custom dialog box in step 5 of the preceding exercise. The window lists all reminders that have not yet been completed, as shown in Figure 4-22.

Figure 4-22

Reminder window

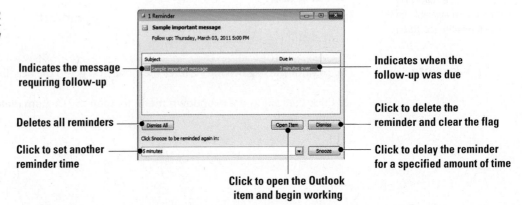

Indicates the message requiring follow-up

Deletes all reminders

Click to set another reminder time

Indicates when the follow-up was due

Click to delete the reminder and clear the flag

Click to delay the reminder for a specified amount of time

Click to open the Outlook item and begin working

3. When your Reminder Window appears, the highlighted entry within the Subject area of the window indicates the Outlook item to which the reminder is attached and how much time has passed since the Reminder time. With the entry still highlighted, click Open Item. The original message window is displayed for your review.

4. Click the Close button in the top-right corner of the message window to close the message and return to the Reminder window. Click Dismiss. The reminder item is deleted from the Subject area. If that was the only item in the Reminder window, the window closes as well.

5. Click the flag in the message list. The flag disappears and a check mark takes its place, indicating that you've already followed up, as shown in Figure 4-23.

Figure 4-23

A completed reminder in the message list

Indicates that you've already followed up on the message

PAUSE. LEAVE Outlook open to use in the next exercise.

The Reminder window is a great way to stay on top of all your obligations. When the Reminder window appears, it might not be a convenient time to complete the follow-up. If this occurs, click the *Click Snooze to be reminded again in:* down arrow and select the amount of time you want before the next reminder. Then click Snooze. You'll get another Reminder window at the appointed time.

USING OUTLOOK'S CLEANUP TOOLS

The Bottom Line

To maintain your folders, you should also delete or archive old items. This prevents you from keeping old items past the date when they are useful. In this section, you'll delete and archive older messages. Outlook 2010 makes it easier than ever to maintain a neat and organized mailbox by consolidating its Cleanup tools in one convenient location in Backstage view. In this section, you'll work with Outlook's Cleanup tools to reduce the size of your mailbox.

Viewing Mailbox Size and Cleanup Tools

Outlook stores all of your items in one large .pst file on your computer. Over time, this file can become huge. Rather than saving every single item, it makes more sense to remove any item that you no longer need. You can use the Mailbox Cleanup option within the Cleanup Tools in Backstage view. In the Mailbox Cleanup window, you can view the mailbox size and choose options to delete items, archive items, and find large e-mails with attachments. In this exercise, you'll view the mailbox size and explore the Mailbox Cleanup tools.

STEP BY STEP   **View Mailbox Size and Cleanup Tools**

GET READY. LAUNCH Outlook if it is not already running.

1. Click the File tab to open the Backstage view.

2. Click Cleanup Tools in the Mailbox Cleanup section. A list of available cleanup tools is displayed, as shown in Figure 4-24.

Figure 4-24

Outlook's Mailbox
Cleanup tools

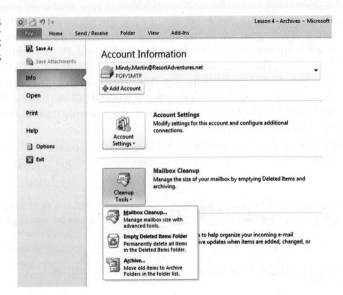

Figure 4-24

Outlook's Mailbox
Cleanup tools

3. Click **Mailbox Cleanup**. The Mailbox Cleanup dialog box is displayed, as shown in Figure 4-25.

Figure 4-25

Mailbox Cleanup dialog box

Click to view the size of each folder in your mailbox

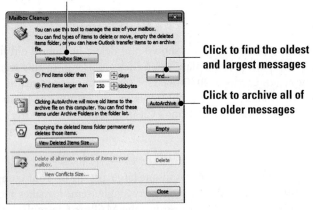

Click to find the oldest and largest messages

Click to archive all of the older messages

4. Click **View Mailbox Size** in the top section of the dialog box. The Folder Size dialog box is displayed, as shown in Figure 4-26.

Figure 4-26

Folder Size dialog box

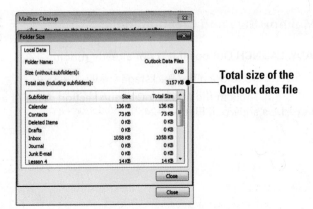

Total size of the Outlook data file

5. Locate the **Total Size** item to see the total size of your mailbox file.

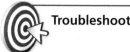

Troubleshooting Remember that your mailbox size might differ substantially from this one depending on the mailbox items that you've created or received.

6. Scroll through the list of folders in the dialog box to see which are the largest. Click Close twice to close the Folder Size dialog box and the Mailbox Cleanup dialog box and return to Backstage view.

PAUSE. LEAVE Outlook open to use in the next exercise.

CERTIFICATION
READY   3.1.1

How do you view the size of your mailbox?

The Mailbox Cleanup tools dialog box contains several useful tools to help you keep a handle on your mailbox size.

• View Mailbox Size—Enables you to see which folders are using up the most space.
• Find—Helps you to locate either the largest or oldest messages in the mailbox. These are the messages that can make the biggest difference when cleaning up your mailbox.
• Archive—Uses Outlook's default AutoArchive settings to take the oldest items out of your mailbox and store them in a separate archive file.
• Empty—Empties the items in the Deleted Items folder.

Emptying the Deleted Items Folder

When you delete an Outlook item, it is moved to the Deleted Items folder. It is held in the Deleted Items folder indefinitely. Items in the Deleted Items folder can be moved to another folder or permanently deleted from the computer. Rather than deleting each item manually, you can use the Empty Folder tool to permanently delete every item from the Deleted Items folder at the same time. When you use the Empty Folder tool, the contents of the folder are removed from your computer and can no longer be restored. The same procedure can be used to empty the Junk E-mail folder. In this exercise, you'll empty the Deleted Items folder.

STEP BY STEP   **Empty the Deleted Items Folder**

GET READY. LAUNCH Outlook if it is not already running.

1. If necessary, click the File tab to open the Backstage view.
2. Click Cleanup Tools in the Mailbox Cleanup section. A list of available cleanup tools is displayed (refer to Figure 4-24).
3. Click Empty Deleted Items Folder. A warning dialog box is displayed, as shown in Figure 4-27.

Figure 4-27

Emptying the Deleted Items folder

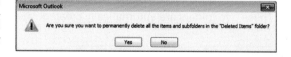

4. Click the Yes button to remove the items from your computer; those items are now permanently deleted, and you can no longer restore them.

PAUSE. LEAVE Outlook open to use in the next exercise.

CERTIFICATION
READY   3.1.5

How do you use Outlook's Cleanup tools to manage the size of your mailbox?

Archiving Outlook Items

It is easy to accumulate messages. Some messages are no longer related to your current projects, but you don't want to delete them. Also, some companies or departments have to follow **retention rules** that specify the length of time correspondence must be kept. When you **archive** a message, you store it in a separate folder, reducing the number of messages in the folders you use most often. You can still access archived messages in Outlook. By default, items are archived automatically using the **AutoArchive** function, but you can change the AutoArchive settings and archive items manually. In this exercise, you'll manually archive Outlook items.

STEP BY STEP   **Archive Outlook Items**

GET READY. LAUNCH Outlook if it is not already running.

1. If necessary, click the File tab to open the Backstage view.
2. Click Cleanup Tools in the Mailbox Cleanup section. A list of available cleanup tools is displayed (refer to Figure 4-24).
3. Click Archive. The Archive dialog box is displayed, as shown in Figure 4-28. This dialog box displays the AutoArchive options that are currently active.

Figure 4-28

Archive dialog box

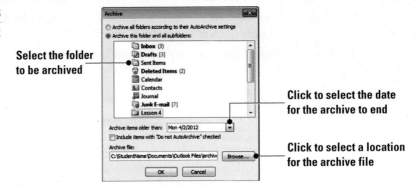

Select the folder to be archived

Click to select the date for the archive to end

Click to select a location for the archive file

4. Ensure that *Archive this folder and all subfolders* option is selected and click the Lesson 4 folder in the dialog box.

 Troubleshooting   Be careful! If you select the wrong folder, whatever folder you click will be emptied of items.

5. Click the Archive Items older than down arrow, and select [tomorrow's date].
6. Click Browse and select the Solutions folder for this lesson. In the File name box, key Archive_xxx (where *xxx* is your initials). Click OK. The items are automatically moved to the Archives file you created and the dialog box closes.
7. Click the Home tab. If necessary, click the Folder List button in the Navigation Pane and click the Lesson 4 folder you created earlier in this lesson. Notice that it is now empty and that a new Archives folder appears at the bottom of the Folder List.
8. Click the Archives folder expansion arrow to open the archive. The Archives folder includes a Search folder and a Deleted Items folder, in addition to the Lesson 4 folder, as shown in Figure 4-29. These two folders are automatically created whenever you archive folders.

Figure 4-29

The new Archives folder

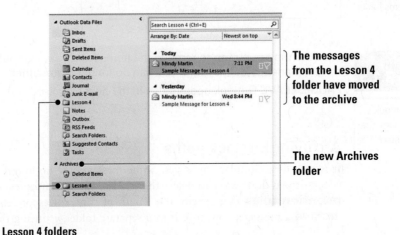

The messages from the Lesson 4 folder have moved to the archive

The new Archives folder

Lesson 4 folders

9. Click the empty Lesson 4 folder in the Outlook Data Files list and then click the Folder tab on the Ribbon. Click Delete Folder to delete the empty Lesson 4 folder. When prompted, click Yes to move the folder to the Deleted Items folder.

10. Right-click the Archives folder and select Close folder from the shortcut menu to close the Archives folder.

PAUSE. LEAVE Outlook open to use in the next exercise.

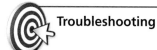

Troubleshooting   Check your state and company retention policies before deleting any business-related messages.

MANAGING JUNK MAIL

The Bottom Line

Nearly every day, the average inbox receives *spam*—unwanted junk mail messages from advertisers and con artists. Aside from the nuisance factor, many junk mail messages are designed to plant viruses on your computer or lure you into divulging your identity information. In this section, you'll learn to spot and manage junk mail messages.

CERTIFICATION READY   3.1.5

How do you use Outlook's Cleanup tools to manage the size of your mailbox?

Viewing Message Properties

Having your mailbox flooded with ads is annoying, but falling prey to someone who is misrepresenting himself in a spam message is downright dangerous. Some spammers format and design their messages to look as though they are coming from someone else. You can spot most of these "spoofing" messages by examining the message header to ensure that its properties are in keeping with the content of the message. The message header is text that is encoded into every e-mail message. Though not visible when reading the actual message, it contains detailed information about the sender, the sender's domain, and the sender's e-mail service. In this exercise, you'll examine a message header's properties.

STEP BY STEP   **View Message Properties**

GET READY. LAUNCH Outlook if it is not already running.

1. If necessary, click the Mail button in the Navigation Pane to display the Inbox.

2. Double-click a message that you sent to yourself. The message window opens, displaying the selected message.

3. Click the File tab and click Properties in Backstage view. The Properties dialog box is displayed, as shown in Figure 4-30.

Figure 4-30

Properties dialog box

The Internet headers contain information about the person who sent the message

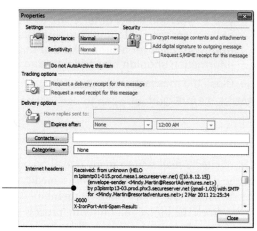

4. Click anywhere in the Internet Headers area at the bottom of the dialog box. The Internet Headers area can contain a lot of information that can be hard to read. To make it easier to locate the information you're looking for, it helps to copy the header information and paste it into a blank document or message window.

5. Press Ctrl+A to select all the information listed there. Press Ctrl+C to copy it. Click Close to close the Properties dialog box.

6. On the Message tab, click Reply. In the message area, press Ctrl+V to paste the information about the message header into your Reply message, as shown in Figure 4-31.

Figure 4-31

Reading a message header

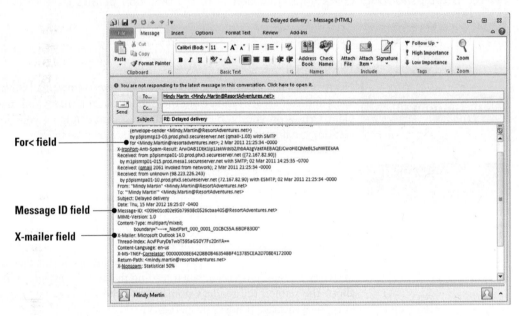

For< field

Message ID field

X-mailer field

7. Scroll through the information you've pasted in the Reply message area. Locate the *Message ID* field. This should end in the domain name of the sender. For example, if you received a message from PayPal asking to confirm your account settings, the domain name listed should match the paypal.com that the official PayPal site uses. If you see any other error in spelling, capitalization, or suffix, you know the message is a fake.

8. Locate the *X-mailer* field. This lists the e-mail software used by the sender. In most cases, a major corporation won't be sending messages from a webmail system, such as Hotmail or Yahoo Mail. They are more likely to use a business e-mail program like Outlook 2010.

9. Scroll through the message header again and locate the *for<* field. This field lists all the people to whom the message was sent. Now obviously you'll receive messages to you, to you and a few others, and to a group to which you belong. The key is to look at the message content in combination with the for< field. For example, messages from your bank (or a similar kind of business) containing supposedly confidential information shouldn't be addressed to a bulk mailing list.

10. Close the message without sending or saving.

PAUSE. LEAVE Outlook open to use in the next exercise.

CERTIFICATION READY   1.2.5

How do you view a message's properties?

Filtering Junk Mail

NEW to Office 2010

Unsolicited e-mail sent to many e-mail accounts is **spam** or junk e-mail. It arrives at all times of the day containing offers of cheap medication, knock-off jewelry, and bad stock tips. If you don't manage the junk e-mail, your Inbox could easily be buried in spam. Outlook 2010 has streamlined the junk e-mail filtering process to make it easier than ever to keep your Inbox free from spam. In this exercise, you'll explore Outlook's options for filtering junk e-mail and learn how to add someone to your Blocked Senders list.

STEP BY STEP   **Filter Junk Mail**

GET READY. LAUNCH Outlook if it is not already running.

1. If necessary, click the Mail button in the Navigation Pane to display the Inbox.
2. On the Home tab, click Junk in the Delete group. A list of options for handling junk mail is displayed.
3. Select Junk E-mail Options. The Junk E-mail Options dialog box is displayed, as shown in Figure 4-32.

Figure 4-32

Junk E-mail Options dialog box

Current
security
level

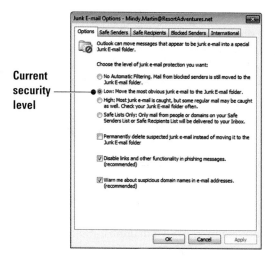

4. The default protection level is Low. If you click the High option, less junk e-mail will be delivered to your Inbox, but some messages that you want to see might be sent to the Junk E-mail folder as well. A higher setting will filter out more messages, but you'll find that more of the messages you want keep will get sent to the Junk E-mail folder. The question is whether the extra level of security is worth the hassle of hunting for messages in the Junk E-mail folder. There is no one right answer. If you are receiving a lot of junk messages, you'll want to use the High setting.
5. For now, you will leave the setting at Low so you don't miss any important messages. Click the Cancel button to close the dialog box and return to the main Outlook window.
6. If a message from a friend or coworker is in your Inbox, right-click the message in the message list. Point to Junk on the shortcut menu. A list of Junk E-mail options is displayed, as shown in Figure 4-33.

Figure 4-33

Selecting a Junk E-mail option

7. Click the Block Sender option. A message is displayed notifying you that the sender has been added to your Block Senders List, as shown in Figure 4-34.

Figure 4-34

Blocking a specific message

8. Click **OK**. The message moves from the Inbox to the Junk E-mail folder.

PAUSE. LEAVE Outlook open to use in the next exercise.

Increasing the level of protection decreases the amount of spam that will be directed to your Inbox. However, it increases the chance that a non-spam message will also be delivered to the Junk E-mail folder. If you choose to increase your protection level, check your Junk E-mail folder frequently.

Using Not Junk to Return a Specific Message to the Inbox

Outlook uses your filter settings to make a guess as to what is spam and what isn't. Sometimes a good message will slip into the Junk E-mail list. If this happens, you can easily move the message back to your Inbox and add the sender to your Safe Senders list, which will ensure that future messages don't get caught in the spam filter. In this exercise, you'll find a message in the Junk E-mail folder and mark it as Not Junk to return it to the Inbox.

STEP BY STEP   **Use Not Junk to Return a Specific Message to the Inbox**

GET READY. LAUNCH Outlook if it is not already running and complete the previous exercise.

1. If necessary, click the Folder List button in the Navigation Pane to display the mailbox.

2. Click the Junk E-mail folder in the Folder List and right-click on the message. Point to Junk in the shortcut menu. A list of Junk E-mail options is displayed as a fly-out menu.

3. In the Junk E-mail options list, select Never Block Sender. Outlook notifies you that it will move the selected message's Sender e-mail address to the Safe Senders List, as shown in Figure 4-35. Click **OK** to complete the process.

Figure 4-35

Using Never Block Sender
to add a person to your Safe
Senders List

4. Your friend's e-mail address is now considered safe, but the message remains in the Junk E-mail folder.

5. Right-click the message again and click Junk in the shortcut menu to open the list of options.

6. Click Not Junk. The Mark as Not Junk dialog box is displayed, as shown in Figure 4-36.

Figure 4-36

Mark as Not Junk dialog box

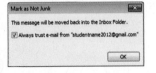

7. Click **OK**. The message moves back to the Inbox.

CLOSE Outlook.

Outlook's Junk E-mail options are outlined in Table 4-3 below.

Table 4-3

Junk E-mail Filtering Options

Option	Description
Block Sender	Add the sender to the Blocked Senders List. All future messages from this sender's e-mail address will go straight to the Junk E-mail folder.
Never Block Sender	Add the sender to the Safe Senders List. Future messages from this sender will be regarded as safe.
Never Block Sender's Domain	Add the sender's domain to the Safe Senders List. Future messages from anyone at the same domain will be considered safe.
Never Block this Group or Distribution List	Add the distribution list or contact group to the Safe Senders List. Future messages from the group will be considered safe.
Not Junk	Regardless of other settings, Not Junk marks the message as safe and returns it to the inbox.

CERTIFICATION READY   3.3.2

How do you add a person to your Safe Senders List?

CERTIFICATION READY   3.3.2

How do you add a domain name to your Safe Senders List?

CERTIFICATION READY   3.3.2

How do you add a contact group or distribution list to your Safe Senders List?

As you receive messages from people you want to correspond with, add their e-mail addresses to the Safe Senders List. Messages from senders on the Safe Senders List are never directed to the Junk E-mail folder.

SKILL SUMMARY

In This Lesson You Learned How To:	Exam Objective	Objective Number
Work with folders		
Work with conversations	Ignore a Conversation.	3.1.4
Manage the mailbox	Mark items as read or unread.	1.2.4
	Set flags.	1.2.2
	Use the Reminder window.	1.3.3
Use Outlook's Cleanup tools	View mailbox size.	3.1.1
	Use cleanup tools.	3.1.5
	View message properties.	1.2.5
	Filter junk mail.	3.3.2
	Allow a specific message (Not Junk).	3.3.1

Knowledge Assessment

Fill in the Blank

Complete the following sentences by writing the correct word or words in the blanks provided.

1. _____ determine the length of time correspondence should be kept.
2. Spam is stored in the _____ folder.
3. Messages are automatically moved to the _____ after they are sent.
4. To permanently remove deleted items from your Outlook data file, use the _____ tool.

5. Messages you send are stored in the _____ until your computer is connected to the Internet.

6. Messages from senders on the _____ are never delivered to the Junk E-mail folder.

7. The _____ contains messages you have written but not sent yet.

8. To eliminate clutter in your mailbox, _____ your older and no longer relevant messages to a separate folder.

9. In _____ view, Outlook groups all the messages in an e-mail thread.

10. Set a _____ so that Outlook will prompt you when a deadline approaches.

Multiple Choice

Select the best response for the following statements.

1. If you want to stop following a Conversation, you can select it and click _____.

   a. Delete
   b. Ignore
   c. Stop
   d. Block

2. In a message header, the _____ field contains the sender's domain name.

   a. Message ID
   b. X-mailer
   c. Domain ID
   d. Sender ID

3. In Conversation view, the Conversation _____ when more than one person responds to an e-mail.

   a. grows
   b. expands
   c. breaks
   d. splits

4. If you want to remember to go back to reading a message again later, you can _____.

   a. flag it
   b. mark it as read
   c. mark it as unread
   d. Both a and c

5. How do you remove an Outlook item from your computer?

   a. Delete the item and then delete again from within the Deleted Items folder
   b. Move the item to the Deleted Items folder
   c. Select the item and press the Delete key
   d. Delete the item and close Outlook

6. By default, where does e-mail arrive?

   a. Inbox
   b. Outbox
   c. Junk E-Mail
   d. Sent Items

7. By default, what attribute does AutoArchive use to determine which messages should be archived?

   a. Attachments
   b. Sender
   c. Size
   d. Date

8. How do you restore a folder?

   a. Delete the folder

   b. Archive the folder

   c. Move the folder from the Deleted Items folder to the Outlook Data Files in the Folder List

   d. Delete items from the folder

9. Outlook's Mailbox Cleanup tools are accessed _____.

   a. on the Tools menu

   b. in the Options dialog box

   c. in Backstage view

   d. in the Outlook data file

10. When you receive a junk e-mail message, select the message and click the _____ button in the Delete group.

    a. Spam

    b. Delete

    c. Block Sender

    d. Junk

Competency Assessment

Project 4-1: Create a Mail Folder

The Alpine Ski House is just a brisk walk away from Resort Adventures. Joe Worden, Mindy Martin's cousin, is the owner of the Alpine Ski House, which sells ski equipment. To attract and hold local customers when it isn't ski season, Joe started a ski club for local residents. During the off season, club members meet to hike, bike, and exercise together to stay in shape for skiing. As the ski club becomes more active and gains more members, Joe decides he needs to organize his ski club messages.

Create a folder to store ski club messages and send a message to the club about an upcoming hike

GET READY. LAUNCH Outlook if it is not already running.

1. Click the Folder List button in the Navigation Pane to display the Folder List.
2. On the Folder tab, click the New Folder button. The Create New Folder dialog box is displayed.
3. In the *Name* field, key Ski Club to identify the new folder.
4. Click Outlook Data Files folder at the top of the Navigation Pane to place the folder in the main level of folders.
5. Click the OK button to close the dialog box and create the folder.
6. Click the New E-mail button on the Home tab. The Message window is displayed.
7. In the *To* field, key your e-mail address. In the *Subject* field, key Ski Club Hike Saturday!
8. In the message area, key the following message:

   Hi Ski Club members! [Press Enter twice.]

   This is just a reminder. We'll be hiking the Mountain Dancer trail this Saturday. Meet in the Mountain Dancer camp site. Bring sandwiches for lunch and plenty of water for the hike. The weather forecast says it will be hot, hot, hot! Be sure you stay hydrated! [Press Enter twice.]

   I'll see you Saturday at 9 AM! Call by Friday afternoon if you can't make it for the hike! [Press Enter twice.]

   Joe Worden [Press Enter.]

   Alpine Ski House [Press Enter.]

9. Click the Send button. The message is moved to the Outbox, and it is sent when your computer is connected to the Internet.

LEAVE Outlook open for the next project.

Project 4-2: Use Junk Mail Options

Add your own name to the Safe Senders List using the Never Block Sender option.

GET READY. LAUNCH Outlook if it is not already running.

1. Return to your Inbox if necessary. Click the Send/Receive All Folders button if the message you sent during Project 4-1 has not arrived yet. Select the message you just sent to yourself.

2. Click the Junk E-mail button on the Home tab and select Block Sender. Click OK. The message moves the selected message to the Junk E-mail folder and future messages sent to you from your own e-mail account will be blocked.

3. Open the Junk E-mail folder and right-click the message to yourself to open the shortcut menu.

4. Point to Junk E-mail on the shortcut menu and select Never Block Sender from the menu that appears. Click OK.

5. Right-click the message to yourself again and point to Junk E-mail on the shortcut menu. Select Not Junk from the shortcut menu to send the message back to the Inbox.

LEAVE Outlook open for the next project.

Proficiency Assessment

Project 4-3: Ski Club Conversation

Joe Worden of the Alpine Ski House is planning a hike for the ski club members this weekend. He sent a message about the hike and wants to use Conversation view to view the responses more efficiently.

GET READY. LAUNCH Outlook if it is not already running.

1. If necessary, click the Mail button in the Navigation Pane to display the mailbox.
2. Select the Ski Club Hike Saturday! message and click Reply.
3. In the message area, key Great! and click Send.
4. Select the Ski Club Hike Saturday! message and click Reply.
5. In the message area, key Sorry, I can't make it. Click Send.
6. On the View tab, select Show as Conversations. When prompted, select All Folders to apply the Conversation view everywhere.
7. If the new messages haven't arrived, click Send/Receive All Folders on the Home tab.
8. Click the expansion arrow beside the Conversation to see all the messages.

LEAVE Outlook open for the next project.

Project 4-4: Organize Ski Club E-mails

Now that more e-mails have arrived it's time to organize them. Move the messages to the Ski Club folder. And set up a reminder so that you don't forget about Saturday's hike.

GET READY. LAUNCH Outlook if it is not already running.

1. If necessary, click the Mail button in the Navigation Pane to display the mailbox.
2. Right-click the Ski Club Hike Saturday! Conversation header and select Move on the shortcut menu.
3. Select Ski Club from the list of folders. Click OK.

4. Click the Ski Club folder and expand the Conversation.

5. Select all three messages and click Unread/Read in the Tags group.

6. Select the original message and click Follow Up in the Tags group. Select Custom from the list.

7. In the *Start Date* box, key [Saturday's date].

8. Select the *Reminder* box, and change the time to 6:00 am. Click OK.

LEAVE Outlook open for the next project.

Mastery Assessment

Project 4-5: Manually Archive the Ski Club Folder

GET READY. LAUNCH Outlook if it is not already running.

1. If necessary, click the Mail button in the Navigation Pane to display the mailbox.

2. On the View tab, deselect Show as Conversation. Click All Folders.

3. Click the Ski Club folder in the list of mail folders and click the File tab.

4. Click Cleanup Tools and select Archive from the list. The Archive dialog box is displayed.

5. Click the Archive this folder using these settings option.

6. Select the Ski Club folder. If necessary, change the Archive Items Older Than date to [tomorrow's date].

7. Click Browse. Select the solution folder for this lesson and key Project 4-5.

8. Click OK. Click Yes to initiate the Archive process.

LEAVE Outlook open for the next project.

Project 4-6: Permanently Delete the Ski Club Folder

Joe Worden thought about the ski club while he sipped his coffee. With only one event per month, perhaps it wasn't necessary to create a folder just for the ski club. Delete the Ski Club folder and empty the Deleted Items folder.

GET READY. LAUNCH Outlook if it is not already running.

1. If necessary, click the Folder List button in the Navigation Pane to display the complete list of Outlook folders.

2. Right-click the Ski Club folder created in a previous project. Click Delete folder from the shortcut menu. A warning dialog box is displayed.

3. Click Yes to close the warning dialog box.

4. Right-click the Deleted Items folder. Select Empty Folder from the list. Click Yes to confirm.

CLOSE Outlook.

INTERNET READY

Data management is essential for growing businesses. Hunting for messages is not only a nuisance, it costs money. In most businesses, efficiency is directly tied to profitability. Make a list of 10 file management tips that you can use to keep your mailbox organized.

Workplace *Ready*

ORGANIZING OUTLOOK ITEMS

Nicole Richards is an instructor at Forsyth College. Every session, a batch of new students registers for Nicole's classes. Nicole teaches several courses and many of her assignments require students to submit electronic files. The student messages from all the courses come directly to Nicole's e-mail account, so she uses Outlook to help her stay organized.

Every session, Nicole sets up a new e-mail folder for her classes. She sets up a mail folder for each student and places the student folders in the main course folder. Throughout the semester, she places the messages from each student in the folder she created for them. A few weeks after classes end, Nicole archives the class folders that are no longer needed.

Because she takes a bit of extra time at the beginning of each semester to get organized, she is able to keep up with her busy schedule and still have time for her students.

LESSON SKILL MATRIX

Skills	Exam Objective	Objective Number
Creating and Running Rules	Create rules.	3.2.1
	Modify rules.	3.2.2
Managing Rules	Delete rules.	3.2.3
Working with Automated Replies	Specify options for replies.	3.4.3
Using Quick Steps	Perform Quick Steps.	2.2.1
	Edit Quick Steps.	2.2.3
	Duplicate Quick Steps.	2.2.5
	Create Quick Steps.	2.2.2
	Delete Quick Steps.	2.2.4
	Reset Quick Steps to default settings.	2.2.6

KEY TERMS

- action
- condition
- exception
- Quick Steps
- rule
- template
- wizard

Mindy Martin is a co-owner of Resort Adventures, a luxury resort. As in any business, a steady stream of information goes in and out of her office. Reservations, schedules, vendor orders, maintenance requests, and menus for the resort's restaurant are only a small sample of the information flying in and out of Mindy's e-mail folders. To keep things straight, Mindy uses message rules to organize her messages as they arrive.

SOFTWARE ORIENTATION

Microsoft Outlook's Rules and Alerts Window

Message rules are displayed in the Rules and Alerts dialog box, as shown in Figure 5-1. You can refer to this figure as you work through this lesson and throughout the book.

Figure 5-1

Outlook's Rules and Alerts window

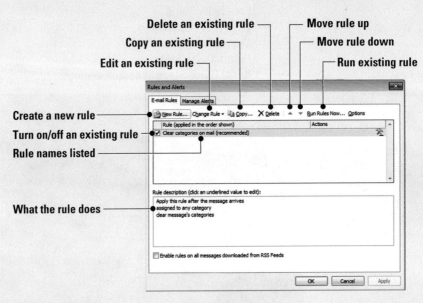

The rules that help you organize your messages are displayed in the Rules and Alerts window. In this window, you can edit existing rules, create new rules, enable rules, and disable rules.

CREATING AND RUNNING RULES

A **rule** defines an action that happens automatically when messages are received or sent. Rules can be created in a number of different ways. Using a template is the easiest method for creating a new rule. A **template** is an existing rule provided by Outlook that contains specific pieces of information that can be customized to create new rules. You also can create a rule from an existing message or copy an existing rule and edit one or more of the rule's components. If a rule is simple, you can create it quickly from scratch. In this section, you'll use a variety of methods to create rules.

Creating a Rule from a Template

One of the best ways to organize your mailbox is to move messages out of the Inbox and into folders that group related messages together. For example, you can place messages about your active projects in project folders and messages from vendors in separate vendor folders. Create and use as many folders as you need to keep yourself organized. Manually locating and moving a lot of messages can be time consuming and prone to errors. Instead, automate the process by creating a rule to move the messages for you. The simplest method of creating rules is to let the Rules Wizard helps you create a template from a template. A **wizard** consists of steps that walk you through completing a process in Microsoft Office applications. In this exercise, you'll use a template to create a rule for moving messages.

A rule consists of three parts: a condition, an action, and an exception. In simple terms, a rule says if A happens (the condition), then B (the action) occurs unless C (the exception). Table 5-1 describes these parts of a rule.

Table 5-1

Default Mail Folders

Part	Description
Condition	The **condition** identifies the characteristics used to determine the messages affected by the rule. Use caution when you define the conditions. If your conditions are too broad, the rule will affect more messages than intended. If your conditions are too narrow, the rule will not identify some of the messages that should be affected.
Action	The **action** determines what happens when a message meets the conditions defined in the rule. For example, the message can be moved, forwarded, or deleted.
Exception	The **exception** identifies the characteristics used to exclude messages from being affected by the rule.

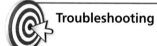

STEP BY STEP   **Create a Rule from a Template**

GET READY. LAUNCH Outlook if it is not already running.

1. If necessary, click the Mail button in the Navigation Pane to display the mailbox. Right-click Outlook Data Files in the Folders List, and click New Folder in the shortcut menu. The Create New Folder dialog box is displayed.

Troubleshooting For this exercise, you want to select the top-level folder. It's the folder that holds your Inbox, Sent Items folder, and so on. Depending on the settings on your computer and the type of e-mail account you have, this might be called Outlook Data Files, Personal Folders, or simply your e-mail address.

2. In the *Name* field, key Lesson 5 Schedules. If necessary, click Outlook Data Files in the *Select Where to Place the Folder* section. Click OK to create the folder and close the dialog box. You will create a rule to move messages into this folder.

3. Click the File tab. In Backstage view, click the Manage Rules and Alerts option. The Rules and Alerts window shown in Figure 5-1 is displayed. Click the New Rule button. The Rules Wizard window is displayed, as shown in Figure 5-2. Step 1 of this wizard involves choosing a template or blank rule.

Figure 5-2

Rules Wizard window with default selections

Wizard step 1

Rule names listed

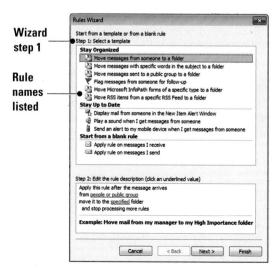

Another Way
You can also open the Rules and Alerts window by clicking Rules on the Home tab and selecting Manage Rules and Alerts.

4. In the Stay Organized category of the Step 1 templates and rules list, click Move messages with specific words in the subject to a folder. This rule will move messages about the selected topic. The rule description in the lower area of the window changes, as shown in Figure 5-3.

Figure 5-3

Rules Wizard window with template to move messages selected

Template selected

Customized underlined text

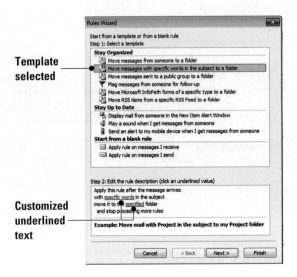

Troubleshooting To ensure that a rule looking for a specific subject moves the messages, the subject line must contain the exact words shown in the editing area of the Rules Wizard window.

5. In the Step 2 area, click specific words. The Search Text window is displayed, as shown in Figure 5-4.

Figure 5-4

Search Text window

Key specific words that must appear in the subject

List of words that must be in the subject to move the message

Click to add keyed text to the search list

Take Note In this exercise, you will use a single phrase as the search text. To add more words or phrases to the search list, key the text into the Search Text window and click the Add button.

6. In the *Specify words or phrases to search for in the subject* field, key Lesson 5 Schedule. Click the Add button. The Lesson 5 Schedule phrase is enclosed by quotation marks and added to the search list for this rule. Click OK to close the Search Text window. The Rules Wizard window is displayed. The Lesson 5 Schedule search phrase is identified, as shown in Figure 5-5.

Figure 5-5

Rules Wizard window with the search phrase identified

Template selected

Search text specified as "Lesson 5 Schedule"

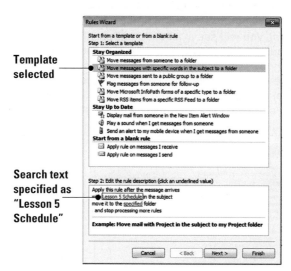

7. In the Step 2 area of the Rules Wizard window, click specified to identify the destination folder. The Folder List is displayed in the Rules and Alerts window, as shown in Figure 5-6.

Figure 5-6

Select the destination folder.

Outlook folders

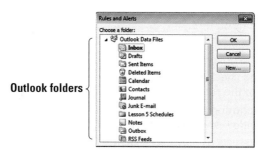

8. Click the Lesson 5 Schedules folder in the Choose a Folder list, and click OK. The specified destination folder is identified in the Rules Wizard window, as shown in Figure 5-7.

Figure 5-7

Rules Wizard window with the destination folder identified

Outlook folders

Template customized

Click the Next button to continue the Wizard

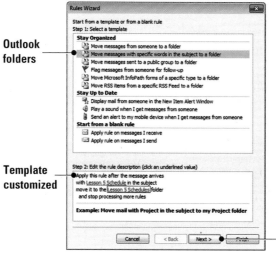

9. Click the Next button to continue to the next Wizard window. Under *Step 1: Select condition(s)*, you will see a list of conditions that can be added to the rule. You don't want to add conditions to this rule, so click the Next button to continue to the third Wizard window. Under *Step 1: Select action(s)*, you will see a list of actions that can be taken if the conditions are met. Without any conditions, you don't want to add actions to this rule, so click the Next button to continue to the next window of the Wizard. A list of exceptions to the rule is displayed, as shown in Figure 5-8.

Figure 5-8

Rules Wizard window with exceptions that can be added to the rule

Exceptions that can be added to the rules

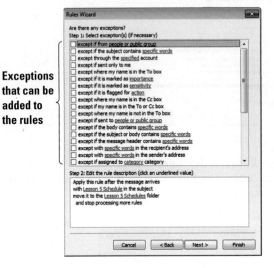

10. Click the second check box on the list: except if the subject contains specific words. Text is added to the rule description at the bottom of the Rules Wizard window.

11. In the rule description area at the bottom of the window, click specific words. The Search text window shown in Figure 5-4 is displayed.

12. In the *Specify words or phrases to search for in the subject* field, key RE:. Making RE: an exception prevents replies to the Lesson 5 Schedule messages from being moved to the destination folder. Click the Add button. The RE: text is enclosed by quotation marks and added to the search list for this rule. Click OK to close the Search Text window. The Rules Wizard window is displayed. The exception is added to the rule, as shown in Figure 5-9.

Figure 5-9

Rules Wizard window with exception added to the rule

Exception that is part of the rule

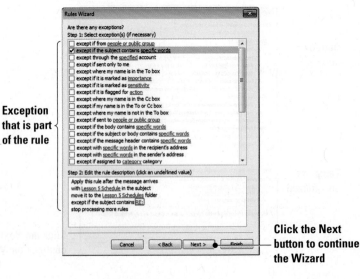

Click the Next button to continue the Wizard

13. Click the Next button to continue the Wizard. The rule is displayed for your approval, as shown in Figure 5-10.

Figure 5-10

Rules Wizard window with rule displayed for approval

Name the rule ———

Enable the rule ———

Review the rule ———

Click to complete the rule

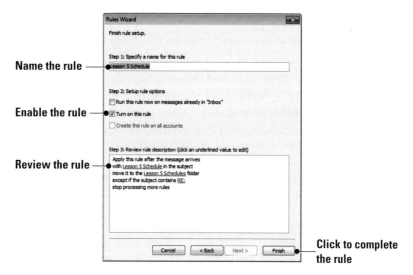

14. Examine the rule carefully to verify that it is correct. Click the Finish button. The new rule is displayed in the Rules and Alerts window, as shown in Figure 5-11.

Figure 5-11

Rules and Alerts window with the new rule displayed

New rule created

Description of the new rule

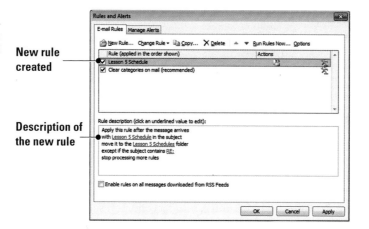

CERTIFICATION READY 3.2.1

How do you create a rule to move messages?

15. Click the OK button to close the Rules and Alerts window.

PAUSE. LEAVE Outlook open to use in the next exercise.

Using the wizard to create a new rule simplifies the process. If you try to advance to the next step without completing the current step, an error message is displayed. It instructs you to finish the current step.

Testing a Rule

Whenever you create a rule, it is a good idea to test it to ensure that it works the way you expect. The easiest way to test a rule is to create a message that will meet the conditions of your rule to see if it handles the message properly. In this exercise, you'll send yourself a message that meets the rule's conditions to verify that the action is carried out as intended.

STEP BY STEP   **Test a Rule**

GET READY. Before you begin these steps, be sure to complete the previous exercise creating a rule.

1. Click the New E-mail button on the Home tab. The Message window is displayed.
2. In the *To* field, key [your e-mail address].
3. In the *Subject* field, key Lesson 5 Schedule. When this message arrives, it will meet the condition defined in the Lesson 5 Schedule rule.
4. In the message area, key Lesson 5 Schedule rule test.
5. Click the Send button. The message is moved to the Outbox and sent when the computer is connected to the Internet.
6. Click the Lesson 5 Schedule folder. If necessary, click the Send/Receive All Folders button to receive the message. When the message arrives, the rule runs automatically and places the message in the Lesson 5 Schedules folder, as shown in Figure 5-12.

Figure 5-12

Rule moved the received message

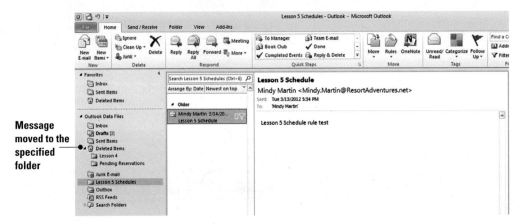

Message moved to the specified folder

PAUSE. LEAVE Outlook open to use in the next exercise.

After creating a rule, test the rule to verify that it works. For example, to test the rule created in the previous exercise, you sent a message with *Lesson 5 Schedule* as the subject to yourself. Over time, you might need to add conditions to the rule because not everyone who sends schedules to you uses the correct subject. You can add a condition such as the *Lesson 5 Schedule* phrase in the body of the message or add a condition identifying any message with the word *schedule* in the subject.

Creating a Rule from a Selected Message

Repeating the same action over and over is one of the most common reasons for creating a rule. For example, another common organization tool that requires repetitive tasks is categorizing messages. When you categorize messages, you assign messages about related topics a specific color code so that they are easy to locate. Automatically categorizing messages is a common organizational task that you can automate by creating a rule. The next time you select a message on which you plan to perform an often-repeated action, use the message to create a rule. In this exercise, you'll create a rule from an existing message. The rule will categorize messages by color.

STEP BY STEP   **Create a Rule from a Selected Message**

USE the message you sent in the previous exercise.

1. If necessary, click the Mail button in the Navigation Pane to display the mailbox.
2. In the Navigation Pane, click the Lesson 5 Schedules folder. One message is in the folder. It is highlighted in the Message List.

3. Right-click the message. Point to Rules and select Create Rule on the shortcut menu. The Create Rule dialog box is displayed, as shown in Figure 5-13. The conditions of the selected message are displayed in the dialog box.

Figure 5-13

Create Rule dialog box

Conditions of the selected message

Click to specify rule components

4. Click the Subject contains check box. The field contains *Lesson 5 Schedule*, the subject of the selected message.

5. Click the Advanced Options button to specify additional rule components. The Rules Wizard window is displayed. The condition about the message's subject is already selected in the first Rules Wizard window.

6. Click the Next button. The Rules Wizard window lists the available actions for the rule. Actions based on the selected message are displayed at the top of the list.

7. Click the assign it to the category category check box. The selected action is moved to the lower area of the window, as shown in Figure 5-14.

Figure 5-14

Rules Wizard window with available actions based on the selected message

Characteristics of the selected message

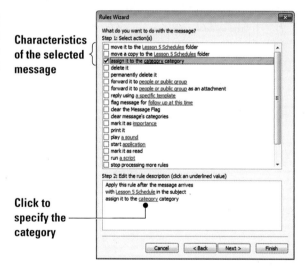

Click to specify the category

8. In the *Step 2: Edit the rule description* area, click the underlined category. The Color Categories dialog box is displayed, as shown in Figure 5-15.

Figure 5-15

Color Categories dialog box

Select the category

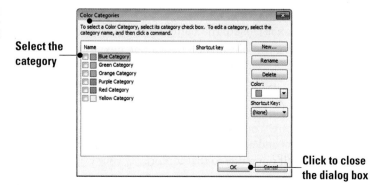

Click to close the dialog box

9. Click the Green Category check box. Click OK. When you complete the exercise and run the rule, messages that match the conditions you've outlined will be highlighted with green, making them easier to spot in a message list.

 Ref

You can find more information on Color Categories in Lesson 12.

10. If a Rename Category window is displayed, click the No button. The Color Categories dialog box is closed, and you are returned to the Rules Wizard window.

Take Note You can rename categories, but it isn't necessary in this lesson.

11. The condition and action for the rule are complete. You don't want to identify any exceptions. Click the Finish button. The rule is saved. The Rules Wizard window is closed, and you are returned to the main Outlook window. In the following steps, you will rename and test the new rule.

Another Way
You can also access the Rules and Alerts window by right-clicking a message, pointing to Rules, and selecting Manage Rules and Alerts.

12. On the Home tab, click Rules in the Move group and select Manage Rules and Alerts option. The Rules and Alerts window is displayed, as shown in Figure 5-16. The new rule you just created is identified as Lesson 5 Schedule (1). The name was inherited from the rule already applied to the message when you selected the message.

Figure 5-16

Rule created from a selected message

Click to change the rule's name

New rule created from a selected message

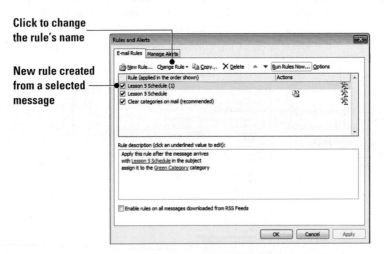

13. If necessary, select the Lesson 5 Schedule (1) rule. Click the Change Rule button, and click the Rename Rule option. The Rename dialog box is displayed, as shown in Figure 5-17.

Figure 5-17

Rename a Rule

14. In the New name of rule field, key Green Lesson 5 Schedule. Click OK. The Rename dialog box is closed. The name of the rule has been changed.
PAUSE. LEAVE Outlook open to use in the next exercise.

Running a Rule

Rules run automatically when new messages arrive. So, what happens to the mail that is already in your mailbox? You can run a rule manually. When you run a rule, it scans the mailbox as if it were new mail and applies the rule's actions on any messages that meet your conditions. In this exercise, you'll run a rule so that it processes your existing messages.

STEP BY STEP   **Test a Rule**

GET READY. LAUNCH Outlook if it is not already running.

1. If necessary, click the File tab to return to Backstage view. Click Manage Rules and Alerts. The Rules and Alerts window shown in Figure 5-1 is displayed.

2. Click the Run Rules Now button. The Run Rules Now dialog box is displayed.

3. In the *Select rules to run* section, click the Green Lesson 5 Schedule check box, as shown in Figure 5-18.

Figure 5-18

Run Rules Now dialog box

Click the Run Now button. The rule runs quietly in the background. In fact, there is no immediately noticeable effect.

4. Click the Close button, and click the OK button to return to the main Outlook window.

5. Click the Lesson 5 Schedule folder. Because you have a message in the Lesson 5 Schedule folder that matches the conditions of this rule, the Green Category has been assigned to the message in the message list, as shown in Figure 5-19.

Figure 5-19

Green Category assigned to a message

Green Category assigned

PAUSE. LEAVE Outlook open to use in the next exercise.

Creating a rule from a selected message has advantages. As you create the rule, the characteristics of the selected message are offered as rule components. This saves time and increases the rule's accuracy.

Creating a Rule by Copying an Existing Rule

Forwarding messages is another common task that can be performed by a rule. When many of the rule components are similar to an existing rule, you can copy the existing rule to create the new rule. In this exercise, you'll create a rule for forwarding messages by copying and modifying an existing rule.

STEP BY STEP   **Create a Rule by Copying an Existing Rule**

USE the message and the rule created in a previous exercise.

1. If necessary, click the Mail button in the Navigation Pane to display the mailbox.

2. On the Home tab, click the Rules command in the Move group. Select the Manage Rules and Alerts option from the menu that appears. The Rules and Alerts window shown in Figure 5-1 is displayed.

3. Click the Green Lesson 5 Schedule rule. Click the Copy button in the Manage Rules and Alerts window. The Copy Rule To dialog box is displayed, as shown in Figure 5-20. The Folder listing in this dialog box identifies the Inbox as being affected by the rule.

Figure 5-20

Copying a rule

Take Note   If your Outlook profile accesses more than one e-mail account, you can choose the Inbox to be affected by the rule. Refer to Outlook's Help for more information about Outlook profiles.

4. Click OK to accept the Folder listing and close the dialog box. A copy of the selected rule is created and added to the list of rules, as shown in Figure 5-21.

Figure 5-21

Copied rule created

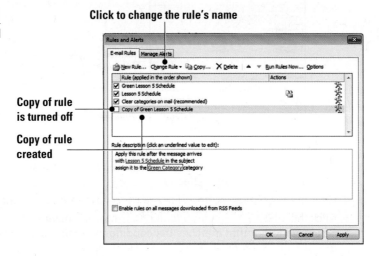

Click to change the rule's name

Copy of rule is turned off

Copy of rule created

5. Select the Copy of Green Lesson 5 Schedule rule, if necessary. Click the Change Rule button, and click Rename Rule. The Rename dialog box is displayed.

6. In the *New name of rule* field, key Forward Lesson 5 Schedule. Click OK. The dialog box is closed, and the rule's name is changed.

7. With the Forward Lesson 5 Schedule rule selected, click the Change Rule button, and click the Edit Rule Settings option. The Rules Wizard window is displayed.

8. The condition about the message's subject is already selected. Click the Next button. The Rules Wizard window lists the available actions for the rule.

9. Click the assign it to the category category check box to deselect the action. Click the forward it to people or people group check box. The action is moved to the rule description in the lower area of the Rules Wizard window.

10. In the *Step 2: Edit the rule description* area, click the underlined people or people group text. The Rule Address dialog box is displayed.

 Ref   Rather than keying an e-mail address into the *To* field, you can select a person from your Outlook Contacts. You will learn more about contacts in Lesson 6.

Take Note   Throughout this chapter you will see information that appears in black text within brackets, such as [Press Enter] or [your e-mail address]. The information contained in the brackets is intended to be directions for you rather than something you actually type word for word. It will instruct you to perform an action or substitute text. Do **not** type the actual text that appears within brackets.

11. In the *To* field, key [the e-mail address of a friend or coworker]. Click the OK button to close the dialog box. The Rules Wizard window is updated, as shown in Figure 5-22.

Figure 5-22

Rule to forward messages

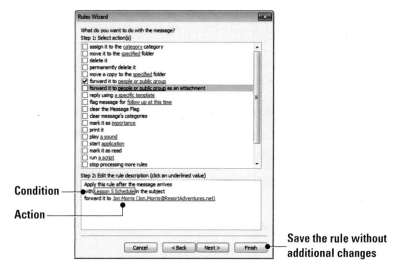

Condition

Action

Save the rule without additional changes

12. This rule does not have exceptions. Click the Finish button to save the rule and return to the Rules and Alerts window.
13. Click the Forward Lesson 5 Schedule check box to turn on the rule.
14. Click the Run Rules Now button. The Run Rules Now dialog box is displayed.
15. Click the Forward Lesson 5 Schedule check box. Click the Run Now button. Outlook looks through your mailbox for messages that meet the conditions you set and forwards them on to the e-mail address you specified in the Rule Address dialog box.
16. Click the Close button. Click OK to return to the main Outlook window. The forwarded message is listed in the Sent Items folder.

PAUSE. LEAVE Outlook open to use in the next exercise.

So far, you have created a rule to move a message, a rule to assign a category, and a rule to forward messages. Rather than creating three separate rules, you could create a single rule that performs all three actions.

When you combine actions into a single rule, keep in mind that you can't simply turn off individual actions. If you turn off a rule with several actions, none of the actions are performed. If one part of the rule or conditions is likely to change periodically, consider keeping that part as a unique rule.

Alternatively, if you do combine it into a single rule and conditions change, you can go in and manually alter the actions within a rule, but you'll have to remember to go back in and alter the actions again when conditions change. Although this is certainly doable, it is time consuming and could easily be forgotten. If an action is likely to change, it is better practice to leave it as a separate rule that you can simply turn on and off.

Let's put that in terms of a real-life situation. Suppose that Jon, the addressee of the forwarded messages you just created, goes on a two-week business trip followed by a two-week vacation in Hawaii. He asked you to stop forwarding schedules to him for four weeks. If the three actions were combined into one rule, you would need to create new rules or edit the combined rule so that the messages are still moved and categorized, but not forwarded to Jon. Then when Jon returns, you'll need to go back in and edit the rule again to add back the third step. If you keep the forwarded action in a separate rule, you just need to deselect the rule in the Rules & Alerts window to turn off the forwarding rule until Jon returns with a tan and too many vacation photos. When he gets back, just select the action again.

Creating a Rule from Scratch

Some rules are simple to write. You want to find messages that meet one condition and perform one action without exceptions. For example, a simple rule might be "Delete all the messages in the Green Category." As you learn in this exercise, you can quickly create simple rules like this from scratch. This is the best method to create simple rules with one condition, one action, and no exceptions.

STEP BY STEP   **Create a Rule from Scratch**

USE the message you sent in the previous exercise.

1. If necessary, click the **Mail** button in the Navigation Pane to display the mailbox.
2. Click the **Rules** on the Home tab and click the **Manage Rules and Alerts** option. The Rules and Alerts window shown in Figure 5-1 is displayed.
3. Click the **New Rule** button. The Rules Wizard window is displayed, as shown in Figure 5-23.

Figure 5-23

Creating a rule from scratch

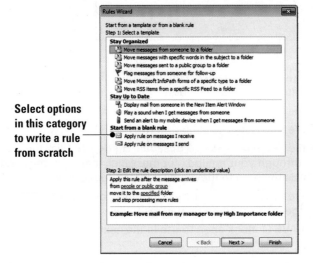

Select options
in this category
to write a rule
from scratch

4. In the *Start from a blank rule* section, click **Apply rule on messages I received**. This identifies when the rule will run automatically. Click the **Next** button to continue creating the rule.
5. In this Rules Wizard window, you identify the conditions of the rule. Click **with specific words** in the subject. This rule will identify messages about the selected topic.
6. In the *Step 2* area, click **specific words**. The Search Text window is displayed.
7. In the *Specify words or phrases to search for in the subject* field, key **Lesson 5 Schedule**. Click the **Add** button. The *Lesson 5 Schedule* phrase is enclosed by quotation marks and added to the search list for this rule.
8. Click **OK** to close the Search Text window. The Rules Wizard window is displayed. The *Lesson 5 Schedule* search phrase is identified. Click the **Next** button to continue creating the rule.
9. Available actions are listed in the Rules Wizard window. Click the **delete it** check box. You don't want to add any additional conditions, actions, or exceptions. Click the **Finish** button. The rule is complete: When a message arrives with Lesson 5 Schedule in the subject, delete it.
10. Select the **Lesson 5 Schedule (1)** rule, if necessary. Click the **Change Rule** button, and click **Rename Rule**. The Rename dialog box is displayed.
11. In the *New name of rule* field, key **Delete Lesson 5 Schedule**. Click **OK**. The dialog box is closed, and the rule's name is changed.
12. Click the **Delete Lesson 5 Schedule** check box to clear it. Click the **OK** button to close the Rules and Alerts window.

PAUSE. LEAVE Outlook open to use in the next exercise.

Another Way
If you wanted to delete all messages from a specific sender instead, select the *from people or distribution list* condition in the *Step 1* area of this first Rules Wizard window. In the *Step 2* area, click *people or distribution list*. At the Rules Address page, you can key or click the sender's e-mail address into the *From* field and click OK to continue creating the rule.

MANAGING RULES

Rules manage your messages. To manage your rules, change their sequence or turn them on or off. In this section, you'll change the order in which rules run, turn rules on and off, and delete rules.

Sequencing Rules

The sequence in which rules are processed can be important. For example, you can change the importance of a message before forwarding it to a coworker. Also, you want to forward a message before you delete it. In this exercise, you'll change the sequence of rules in the Rules and Alerts window.

STEP BY STEP   **Sequence Rules**

USE the rules you created in the previous exercises.

1. If necessary, click the Mail button in the Navigation Pane to display the mailbox.
2. Click the Rules on the Home tab and click the Manage Rules and Alerts option. The Rules and Alerts window shown in Figure 5-1 is displayed.
3. Click the Delete Lesson 5 rule. Click the Move Down button four times. The Delete Lesson 5 Schedule rule becomes last on the list of rules.
4. Click the Clear categories on mail (recommended) rule. Click the Move Up button two times. The sequence of your rules should match the rule sequence in Figure 5-24.

Figure 5-24

Sequenced rules

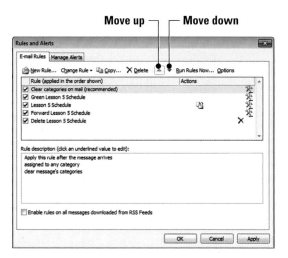

5. Click OK to save the changes and close the Rules and Alerts window.
PAUSE. LEAVE Outlook open to use in the next exercise.

The *Clear categories on mail (recommended)* rule is first on the list of rules. This clears the categories of the arriving message so you can apply your own category in the *Green Lesson 5 Schedule* rule.

Turning Off a Rule

In the Rules and Alerts window, the check box in front of the rule's name controls its status. A rule is either off or on. If a rule is on, the check box in front of the rule is checked. If a rule is off, the check box is empty. Turning off a rule rather than deleting it enables you to turn on the rule if you need it later. It also enables you to keep a rule turned off and run it at a time of your choice In this exercise, you'll turn off a rule.

STEP BY STEP **Turn Off a Rule**

USE the rules you created in the previous exercises.

1. If necessary, click the Mail button in the Navigation Pane to display the Mailbox.
2. Click the Rules on the Home tab and click the Manage Rules and Alerts option. The Rules and Alerts window shown in Figure 5-1 is displayed.
3. Click the Delete Lesson 5 Schedule check box so the check box is empty.
4. Click OK to save the changes and close the Rules and Alerts window.

PAUSE. LEAVE Outlook open to use in the next exercise.

Deleting Rules

If you created a rule that you will not use again, delete it. This keeps your list of rules organized and reduces confusion caused by a long list of old rules that are not used. In this exercise, you'll delete a rule.

STEP BY STEP **Delete Rules**

USE the rules you created in the previous exercises.

1. If necessary, click the Mail button in the Navigation Pane to display the mailbox.
2. Click the Rules on the Home tab and click the Manage Rules and Alerts option. The Rules and Alerts window shown in Figure 5-1 is displayed.
3. Click the Delete Lesson 5 Schedule rule. Click the Delete button. Click Yes in the dialog box to confirm the deletion.
4. Click OK to save the changes and close the Rules and Alerts window.

PAUSE. LEAVE Outlook open to use in the next exercise.

CERTIFICATION READY **3.2.3**

How do you delete a rule?

Use caution when deleting a rule rather than disabling it. You don't want to have to spend time re-creating a rule that you carelessly deleted.

WORKING WITH AUTOMATED REPLIES

The Bottom Line

When you're out of the office, you will still receive e-mail messages. You can set the Automatic Replies function to automatically reply to any e-mail you receive informing the sender that you are out of the office. In this section, you'll create an internal and external Out of Office message.

Creating an Internal Out of Office Message

If you use a Microsoft Exchange Server e-mail account, you can use the improved Out of Office Assistant to send an Internal Out of Office message informing coworkers that you are out of the office. Internal messages are ones that are sent to and from other individuals in the same Exchange Server. In this section, you'll create an internal Out of Office message.

STEP BY STEP **Create an Internal Out of Office Message**

GET READY. You must use a Microsoft Exchange Server account to complete this exercise. If you do not have a Microsoft Exchange Server account, read through the exercise and use it as a reference when preparing for your certification exam.

1. If necessary, click the Mail button in the Navigation Pane to display the mailbox.
2. Click the File tab and click the Automatic Replies option. The Out of Office Assistant dialog box is displayed.

Troubleshooting If you don't have an Exchange Server account, this option won't be visible.

3. Click the Send automatic replies option.

4. Select the Only send during this time range option. Select 12:00 AM [tomorrow] as the Start time. Select 12:00 AM [the following day] as the End time.

5. Click the Inside My Organization tab, if necessary. Key I am out of the office today. I'll respond to your message tomorrow.

Take Note For the Automatic Replies function, Microsoft defines *organization* as people who share an Exchange Server account on your e-mail system.

6. Click OK. The dialog box is closed. The Out of Office message will be sent when you receive messages from other e-mail accounts in your organization.

PAUSE. LEAVE Outlook open to use in the next exercise.

 NEW to Office 2010 Improvements to the Automatic Replies function include additional formatting options, the ability to set the dates that you will be out of the office, and the ability to send an Out of Office message to correspondents outside your organization.

CERTIFICATION READY 3.2.3

How do you create an internal Out of Office message?

Creating an External Out of Office Message

If you use a Microsoft Exchange Server e-mail account, you can use the improved Out of Office Assistant to send an external message informing people outside your organization that you are out of the office. External messages are ones that are sent to and from other individuals who are not in the same Exchange Server. In this section, you'll create an external Out of Office message.

STEP BY STEP **Create an External Out of Office Message**

GET READY. You must use a Microsoft Exchange Server account to complete this exercise. If you do not have a Microsoft Exchange Server account, read through the exercise and use it as a reference when preparing for your certification exam.

1. If necessary, click the Mail button in the Navigation Pane to display the mailbox.

2. Click the File tab and click the Automatic Replies option. The Automatic Replies dialog box is displayed.

 Troubleshooting If you don't have an Exchange Server account, this option won't be visible.

3. Click the Send automatic replies option.

4. Select the Only send during this time range option. In the Start time box, select 12:00 AM [tomorrow]. In the End time box, select 12:00 AM [the following day] as the End time.

5. Click the Outside My Organization (On) tab, and select the Auto-reply to people outside my organization check box. Select My Contacts only.

Take Note For the Automatic Replies function, Microsoft defines My Contacts only as the people listed in your Exchange Server contact list.

6. In the text entry area, key I am out of the office today. I'll respond to your message tomorrow.

7. Click OK. The dialog box is closed. The Out of Office message will be sent when you receive messages from e-mail accounts outside your organization.

PAUSE. LEAVE Outlook open to use in the next exercise.

CERTIFICATION
READY   3.4.3

How do you set up an
internal and external
out of office reply?

The Bottom Line

NEW
to Office 2010

In step 7 of the previous exercise, you set up automatic replies for the people in your contact list. If you want the reply sent to everyone who e-mails you, select *Anyone outside my organization* instead of *My contacts only*.

USING QUICK STEPS

Outlook's new Quick Steps bring the computer power of macros to Outlook for the first time. They enable you to perform a series of tasks with the click of a button. Unlike Rules, you choose when and where to apply the Quick Steps. **Quick Steps** are a type of customizable shortcut that you can use to perform several functions at the same time.

Outlook comes with a set of seven default Quick Steps that you can program with your personal information. For example, you can program the Team E-mail Quick Step with the contact information for the people on your team. When you click the Quick Step, a new message window opens already addressed to your team. In this section, you'll get to know the new Quick Step feature by creating, editing, deleting, performing, duplicating, and resetting Quick Steps.

SOFTWARE ORIENTATION

Microsoft Outlook's Quick Step Group

Outlook's new Quick Step feature (see Figure 5-25) allows you to set up a group of custom shortcuts to perform your common message management. The Quick Step group contains six default Quick Steps for the most commonly performed tasks in Outlook. You can also click the Create New button in the Quick Step group to create your own custom Quick Step shortcuts.

Figure 5-25

Microsoft Outlook's Quick
Step Group

Use this figure as a reference throughout this lesson as well as the rest of this book.

Performing Quick Steps

Quick Steps are easier to run than traditional rules, because they are right there at your fingertips on the Home tab. To perform a Quick Step, you simply select a message and then click the Quick Step icon for the action you want. The first time you perform most Quick Steps, you are asked to add information to personalize the action. For example, if you click the Move to Quick Step, you are asked to specify which folder you want the message moved to. Once you set up the Quick Step, it will always move mail items to the folder you designated during setup unless you go back in and edit the settings. In this exercise, you'll perform a couple of Quick Steps.

STEP BY STEP   **Perform Quick Steps**

GET READY. LAUNCH Outlook if it is not already running.

1. If necessary, click the Mail button in the Navigation Pane to display the mailbox.
2. Select the Sample confidential message in the message list. If you don't have this message, choose any message with the word *Sample* in the subject.

3. On the Home tab, click the Reply & Delete button in the Quick Step group shown in Figure 5-25. A *RE: Sample confidential message* window is displayed and the original is moved to the Deleted Items folder.

4. In the *To* field, key [your e-mail address] and click Send.

5. Click Send/Receive All Folders on the Home tab.

6. Select the newly arrived message and click Done in the Quick Steps group. The First Time Setup dialog box for the Done Quick Step is displayed, as shown in Figure 5-26. The Done Quick Step can perform three actions: mark the message as read, mark it as complete, and move it to a folder you choose.

Figure 5-26

First Time Setup dialog box for Done Quick Step

Another Way
You can also perform a Quick Step by right-clicking on a message, pointing to Quick Steps in the shortcut menu, and selecting the desired Quick Step from the fly-out list.

7. In the Name field, key Completed Events. After the setup process, the Quick Step button will be called Completed Events.

8. Click the Choose Folder down arrow and select the Lesson 5 Schedules folder.

9. Click Save. The First Time Setup dialog box closes and the Completed Events button appears in the Quick Steps group, as shown in Figure 5-27.

Figure 5-27

Newly formatted Quick Step

10. With the message still selected, click the new Completed Events button in the Quick Steps group. The message is moved to the Lesson 5 Schedules folder and is marked as read and completed.

Figure 5-28

The completed message in its new location

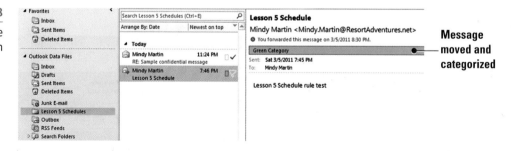

PAUSE. LEAVE Outlook open to use in the next exercise.

**CERTIFICATION
READY   2.2.1**

How do you perform a Quick Step?

The new Outlook Quick Steps (see Table 5-2) are a combination of rules and customized Ribbon buttons. By using Quick Steps, you can perform multiple different actions with a single click.

Quick Steps	Description
Move to	The Move to Quick Step marks the select message as read and moves it to the assigned folder.
To Manager	The To Manager Quick Step forwards the selected message to your manager. If you use Microsoft Exchange Server, Outlook reads your list to determine your manager's name. If you don't use the Exchange Server, you can key the correct e-mail address in the *To* field.
Team E-mail	The Team E-mail Quick Step creates a new message to the members of your team. If you use Microsoft Exchange Server, Outlook reads your list to determine the names of your team members. If not, you can key the correct e-mail addresses in the *To* field.
Done	The Done Quick Step marks the selected message as read and complete and moves it to the selected folder.
Reply & Delete	The Reply & Delete Quick Step deletes the selected message and opens a reply message.
Create New	The Create New Quick Step allows you to create an entirely custom Quick Step.

Editing Quick Steps

Although the default Quick Steps cover many of the most common tasks, you can easily modify them to suit your needs. Using the Manage Quick Steps dialog box, you can rename a Quick Step, change or eliminate actions, or add additional steps to the process. In this exercise, you'll edit a Quick Step.

STEP BY STEP   **Edit Quick Steps**

GET READY. LAUNCH Outlook if it is not already running and be sure to complete the previous exercise.

1. If necessary, click the Mail button in the Navigation Pane to display the mailbox.
2. Click the dialog box launcher in the Quick Steps group to open the Manage Quick Steps dialog box, as shown in Figure 5-29.

Figure 5-29

Manage Quick Steps dialog box

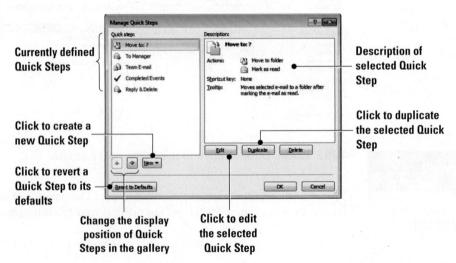

Currently defined Quick Steps

Description of selected Quick Step

Click to create a new Quick Step

Click to duplicate the selected Quick Step

Click to revert a Quick Step to its defaults

Change the display position of Quick Steps in the gallery

Click to edit the selected Quick Step

3. In the *Quick step:* area, select Completed Events. The Description area changes to define the actions performed by this Quick Step, as shown in Figure 5-30.

Figure 5-30

Manage Quick Steps dialog box with Completed Events selected

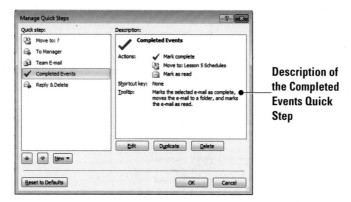

Description of the Completed Events Quick Step

4. Click the Edit button. The Edit Quick Step dialog box is displayed, as shown in Figure 5-31.

Figure 5-31

Edit Quick Steps dialog box

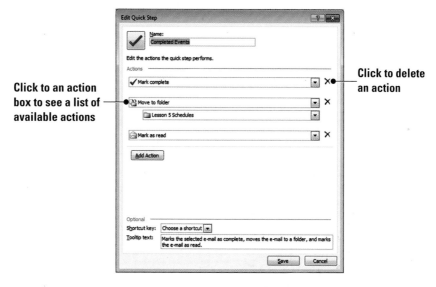

Click to an action box to see a list of available actions

Click to delete an action

Another Way
You can also open the Edit Quick Step dialog box by right-clicking the desired Quick Step in the Quick Step gallery and selecting Edit Quick Step from the shortcut menu.

5. In the *Name* field, select the existing text and key Active Events.

6. Click the Delete button next to the Mark Complete action.

7. Click the Mark as Read action. A drop-down list of options is displayed, as shown in Figure 5-32.

Figure 5-32

Editing a Quick Step

Figure 5-32

Editing a Quick Step

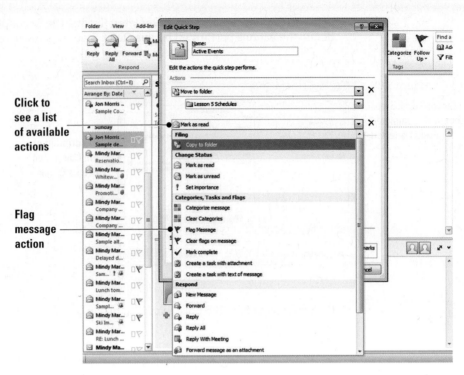

Click to
see a list
of available
actions

Flag
message
action

8. Select the Flag Message option. A new Choose flag action box is displayed.

9. Click the Choose Flag action and select the Today option.

10. Because the actions have changed, the Tooltip information is no longer correct. Select the Tooltip text at the bottom of the Edit Quick Step dialog box and key Moves the selected e-mail to a folder and flags the e-mail for today.

11. Click Save and OK to close the Edit Quick Steps dialog box, then click OK to close the Manage Quick Steps dialog box. The Completed Events Quick Step has been replaced with the new Active Events Quick Step in the Quick Step gallery.

12. Point the cursor at the Active Events icon in the Quick Steps gallery to see the new tip, as shown in Figure 5-33.

Figure 5-33

Edited Quick Step

CERTIFICATION
READY   2.2.3

How do you edit an
existing Quick Step?

13. Click Save and OK to close the Edit Quick Steps dialog box, then click OK to close the Manage Quick Steps dialog box.

PAUSE. LEAVE Outlook open to use in the next exercise.

Duplicating Quick Steps

In many cases, you'll find yourself needing multiple Quick Steps that perform similar functions. For example, you might want to use one Team E-mail Quick Step to send an e-mail to members of your marketing project, another to send e-mails to the members of the Employee Softball team, and another to send e-mails to members of your book club. The easiest way to create new Quick Steps that perform similar actions is by duplication. In this exercise, you'll duplicate a Quick Step.

STEP BY STEP   **Duplicate Quick Steps**

GET READY. LAUNCH Outlook if it is not already running.

1. If necessary, click the Mail button in the Navigation Pane to display the mailbox. Right-click Outlook Data Files in the Folders List, and click New Folder in the shortcut menu. The Create New Folder dialog box is displayed.

2. In the *Name* field, key Pending Reservations. If necessary, click Outlook Data Files in the *Select Where to Place the Folder* section. Click OK to create the folder and close the dialog box. The new folder is displayed in the Folder list in the Navigation Pane.

3. On the Home tab, in the Quick Step group, click the More button to open the Quick Step gallery.

4. Select Manage Quick Steps. The Manage Quick Steps dialog box is displayed (refer to Figure 5-29).

5. Click Active Events in the Quick Step list in the Manage Quick Steps dialog box. Click Duplicate. The Edit Quick Step dialog box is displayed. The text *Copy of Active Events* is automatically entered into the *Name* field, as shown in Figure 5-34.

Figure 5-34

Duplicating a Quick Step

Another Way
You can also duplicate a Quick Step by right-clicking the desired Quick Step in the Quick Step gallery and selecting Duplicate Quick Step from the shortcut menu.

6. Click the Lesson 5 Schedules dropdown box. A dropdown list of available folders appears. Select the Pending Projects folder. The list collapses.

Troubleshooting If necessary, click Other Folders to open the Select Folder dialog box. Select Pending Projects and click OK.

7. In the Name field, key Pending Projects.

8. Click Finish. Click OK. The new Quickstep appears in the Quick Step gallery, as shown in Figure 5-35.

Figure 5-35

New duplicated Quick Step

Figure 5-35

New duplicated Quick Step

Duplicated Quick Step

Original Quick Step

PAUSE. LEAVE Outlook open to use in the next exercise.

Creating Quick Steps

Although the default Quick Steps handle many of the most common tasks in Outlook, you may want to create a unique Quick Step that performs different tasks or a combination of actions. When you click the New button in the Manage Quick Steps dialog box, a blank Edit Quick Steps dialog box opens, allowing you to choose any actions you wish. In this exercise, you'll create a new Quick Step.

STEP BY STEP   **Create Quick Steps**

GET READY. LAUNCH Outlook if it is not already running.

1. If necessary, click the Mail button in the Navigation Pane to display the mailbox.
2. On the Home tab, in the Quick Step group, click Create New. The Edit Quick Step dialog box opens with no actions selected, as shown in Figure 5-36.

Figure 5-36

Creating a custom Quick Step

Click to choose your first action

Click to add another action.

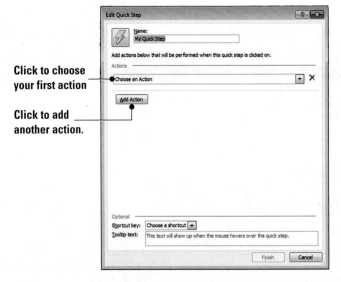

Another Way
You can also create a new Quick Step by clicking the New button in the Manage Quick Step.

3. In the Name box, key Lesson 5.
4. Click the Choose an Action dropdown box, and select Mark as Unread.
5. Click the Add Action button. Click the new action box, and select Categorize message. Select the Yellow category.
6. Click the Add Action button. In the new Choose an Action dropdown box, select Create a task with text of message.
7. In the Optional area, click the Shortcut key down arrow and select Ctrl+Shift+1.
8. In the Tooltip text box, key Sample Lesson 5 Quick Step.
9. Click Finish. The new Quick Step appears in the Quick Step gallery.
10. Open the Lesson 5 Schedule folder. Select the completed message and click the new Lesson 5 Quick Step in the Quick Step gallery. A Sample confidential message Task window is displayed showing the contents of the e-mail message in the body of the task, as shown in Figure 5-37.

Figure 5-37

Lesson 5 Quick Step
created task

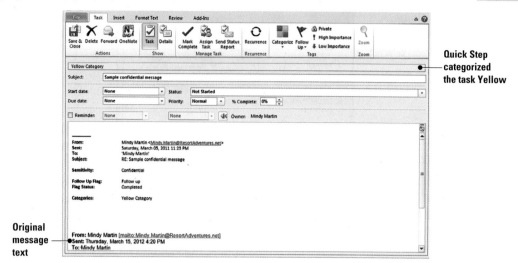

Figure 5-37

Lesson 5 Quick Step
created task

**Quick Step
categorized
the task Yellow**

**Original
message
text**

11. Click the Save and Close button in the Actions group on the Task tab. The message is
now marked as unread and categorized yellow, and the new task appears in the To-Do
bar, as shown in Figure 5-38.

Figure 5-38

Performing the
Lesson 5 Quick Step

New Quick Step

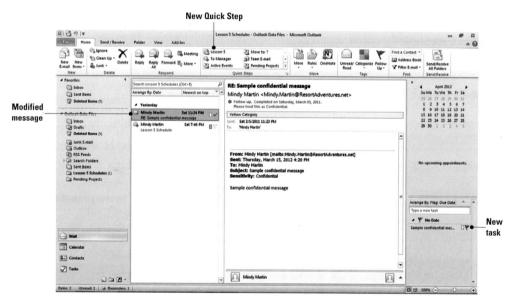

**Modified
message**

**New
task**

PAUSE. LEAVE Outlook open to use in the next exercise.

**CERTIFICATION
READY** **2.2.2**

How do you create
a new Quick Step?

Deleting Quick Steps

Once you embrace the value of Quick Steps, you'll soon find your Quick Step gallery getting
crowded. To keep your Quick Steps easy to find and use, be sure to delete Quick Steps that you
no longer need. In this exercise, you'll delete one of your Quick Steps.

STEP BY STEP   **Delete Quick Steps**

USE the Pending Projects Quick Step that you created in a previous exercise.

1. If necessary, click the Mail button in the Navigation Pane to display the mailbox.
2. Click the dialog box launcher for the Quick Steps group. The Manage Quick Steps
dialog box is displayed, as shown in Figure 5-39.

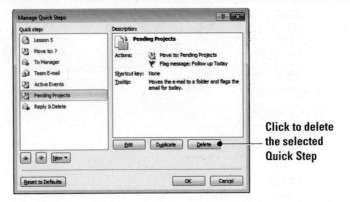

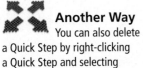**Another Way**
You can also delete
a Quick Step by right-clicking
a Quick Step and selecting
Delete.

**Click to delete
the selected
Quick Step**

3. In the Quick Step list, select Pending Projects.

4. Click the Delete button. The Pending Projects Quick Step is immediately removed from the Quick Step list. Click OK to close the dialog box.

PAUSE. LEAVE Outlook open to use in the next exercise.

**CERTIFICATION
READY 2.2.4**

How do you delete
a Quick Step?

Resetting Quick Steps to Default

If your Quick Steps gallery gets overfilled with items that you no longer need, you might find it easier to simply reset your Quick Step gallery and start over. In this exercise, you'll reset your Quick Steps.

STEP BY STEP | **Resetting Quick Steps to Default**

GET READY. LAUNCH Outlook if it is not already running.

1. If necessary, click the Mail button in the Navigation Pane to display the mailbox.

2. Click the dialog box launcher in the Quick Step dialog box to open the Manage Quick Steps dialog box.

3. Click the Reset to Defaults button. A message is displayed warning you that any changes will be lost, as shown in Figure 5-40.

Figure 5-40

Resetting Quick Steps

4. Click Yes. The Quick Steps in the Manage Quick Steps dialog box revert back to the original list.

CLOSE Outlook.

**CERTIFICATION
READY 2.2.6**

How do you reset
your Quick Steps?

Many people complain that the reason they don't organize their mailboxes and manage their messages is because it is time-consuming. Quick Steps have the power to change all that.

SKILL SUMMARY

In This Lesson You Learned How To:	Exam Objective	Objective Number
Create and run rules.	Create rules.	3.2.1
	Modify rules.	3.2.2
Manage rules.	Delete rules.	3.2.3
Work with automated replies.	Specify options for replies.	3.4.3
Use Quick Steps.	Perform Quick Steps.	2.2.1
	Edit Quick Steps.	2.2.3
	Duplicate Quick Steps.	2.2.5
	Create Quick Steps.	2.2.2
	Delete Quick Steps.	2.2.4
	Reset Quick Steps to default settings.	2.2.6

Knowledge Assessment

Multiple Choice

Select the best response for the following statements.

1. Why would you change the sequence of your rules?
   a. Rules should be in alphabetic order.
   b. Short rules should be processed first.
   c. Some actions should be performed before others.
   d. Rules should be processed in the order they were created.

2. Which Quick Step moves a message to specific folder and marks it as read?
   a. Move to
   b. To folder
   c. Done
   d. Both a and c

3. Why would you turn off a rule?
   a. The rule is no longer needed.
   b. The rule should only be run periodically.
   c. You don't want the rule to run automatically.
   d. All of the above

4. What happens if a rule's conditions are too broad?
   a. The rule will affect more messages than intended.
   b. The rule will affect fewer messages than intended.
   c. The rule will not run.
   d. The affected messages are deleted.

5. What window enables you to add steps in a rule?
   a. Rules and Alerts
   b. Rules Wizard
   c. Steps
   d. New Rule

6. Why would you duplicate an existing Quick Step to create a new rule?

   a. Many of the new Quick Step's characteristics are similar to the existing rule.

   b. The new Quick Step replaces the existing Quick Step.

   c. The existing Quick Step does not work correctly.

   d. This process tests the existing Quick Step.

7. How does a rule identify the messages it affects?

   a. Actions

   b. Cues

   c Conditions

   d. Phrases

8. What window allows you to modify Quick Steps?

   a. Define Quick Steps

   b. Edit Quick Steps

   c. Modify Quick Steps

   d. Manage Quick Steps

9. If you have Exchange Server, you can use the _____ function to create Out of Office messages.

   a. Out of Office Agent

   b. Automatic Replies

   c. Vacation Manager

   d. Calendar

10. How do you decide which actions can be combined in a single rule?

   a. The conditions are the same for all of the actions.

   b. The exceptions are the same for all the actions.

   c. A rule with combined actions is easier to write.

   d. The actions won't need to be turned off separately.

Fill in the Blank

Complete the following sentences by writing the correct word or words in the blanks provided.

1. You should only _____ a rule if you are sure you won't need it again.

2. A(n) _____ is taken only if the conditions are met.

3. When you perform a Quick Step for the first time, you must complete the _____.

4. A(n) _____ provides structure for a rule.

5. A Quick Step can be _____ to create a new one.

6. You must have _____ in order to set up an automatic Out of Office reply.

7. The _____ Quick Step creates a new message with the addressees automatically entered.

8. A(n) _____ walks you through a process.

9. You can use _____ to help you manage your messages automatically.

10. The _____ of the rules changes when you move a rule up or down.

Competency Assessment

Project 5-1: Create Folders and Messages to Test Rules and Quick Steps

Jack Creasey owns a small Internet-based gift shop with a big name. World-Wide Importers sells a variety of crafted objects created by small crafters across the country and by one vendor in Canada, justifying the "World-Wide" portion of his company's name. Jack regularly receives pictures of crafted items from his suppliers and sends invoices to customers who buy his products. Jack decided to create rules to manage his messages automatically. First, he needs to create two folders and a message.

GET READY. LAUNCH Outlook if it is not already running.

1. If necessary, click the Mail button in the Navigation Pane to display the mailbox.
2. Right-click Outlook Data Files in the Folders List. Click New Folder in the shortcut menu. The Create New Folder dialog box is displayed.
3. In the *Name* field, key P5 Products. If necessary, click Outlook Data Files in the *Select where to place the folder* section. Click OK to create the folder and close the dialog box.
4. Right-click Outlook Data Files in the Folders List. Click New Folder in the shortcut menu. The Create New Folder dialog box is displayed.
5. In the *Name* field, key P5 Invoices. If necessary, click Outlook Data Files in the *Select where to place the folder* section. Click OK to create the folder and close the dialog box.
6. Click the New E-mail button on the Home tab. The Message window is displayed.
7. Click the *To* field. Key [your e-mail address].
8. Click the *Subject* field. Key New birdfeeder!
9. In the message area, key Take a look at this new birdfeeder! It's sure to be a big hit!
10. Click the Attach File button on the Ribbon. Navigate to the data folders for this lesson. Click the *Birdfeeder* file, and click the Insert button.
11. Click the Send button. The message is moved to the Outbox and sent when the computer is connected to the Internet.
12. Click the Send/Receive All Folders button on the Home tab.

LEAVE Outlook open for the next project.

The Birdfeeder file is available on the book companion website or in WileyPLUS.

Project 5-2: Perform Quick Step

Suppliers frequently send pictures of new products to Jack. He wants to move these messages to one of the P5 folders.

USE the message and folders you created in Project 5-1 for this project.

1. If necessary, click the Mail button in the Navigation Pane to display the mailbox.
2. Locate the New birdfeeder! message in the message list. If the message has not arrived, you can click Send/Receive All Folders button on the Home tab.
3. Click the Move to Quick Step. The First Time Setup dialog box is displayed.
4. In the *Name* field, key P5 Invoices.
5. Click the Choose Folder box, and select P5 Invoices. Click Finish.

LEAVE Outlook open for the next project.

Project 5-3: Duplicate a Quick Step

Jack wants to move messages about invoices into the P5 Invoices folder. Complete Projects 5-1 and 5-2 before starting this project.

USE the message and folders you created in Project 5-1 for this project.

1. If necessary, click the Mail button in the Navigation Pane to display the mailbox.
2. Click the Quick Steps group's dialog box launcher to open the Manage Quick Steps dialog box.
3. Select the P5 Invoices and click Duplicate to open the Edit Quick Steps dialog box.
4. Click the P5 Invoices box and select P5 Projects.
5. Click Finish and OK to close the boxes.
6. Click the P5 Invoices folder to display the message you moved in the previous project.
7. If necessary, select the message and click the P5 Projects Quick Step to move the message.

LEAVE Outlook open for the next project.

Project 5-4: Create and Run a Rule that Moves Messages

Jack wants to create a rule that will automatically move messages about invoices into the P5 Invoices folder. To test the Invoice rule, Jack will send a message to himself with the word "Invoice" in the Subject field. Complete Project 5-1 before starting this project.

GET READY. LAUNCH Outlook if it is not already running.

1. Click the File tab. In Backstage view, click the Manage Rules and Alerts option to display the Rules and Alerts window.
2. Click the New Rule button. The Rules Wizard window is displayed.
3. In the Stay Organized category, click Move messages with specific words in the subject to a folder.
4. In the Step 2 area, click specific words. The Search Text window is displayed.
5. In the Specify words or phrases to search for in the subject field, key Invoice. Click the Add button. Click OK to close the Search Text window.
6. In the Step 2 area of the Rules Wizard window, click specified to identify the destination folder.
7. Click the P5 Invoices folder, and click OK.
8. Click the Finish button.
9. In the Rules and Alerts window, click Change Rule, and click the Rename Rule option. Key Move Invoices in the New name of rule field. Click OK.
10. Close the dialog boxes and return to the main Outlook window.
11. Create a message addressed to yourself. Use Invoice for the Subject field and Testing for the message body.
12. If necessary, click the Send/Receive All Folders button on the Home tab. The rule is run automatically when messages are received.
13. Click the P5 Invoices folder to verify that the received Invoice message was moved to the P5 Invoices folder.

LEAVE Outlook open for the next project.

Project 5-5: Manage Rules

Jack has made several rules lately. Because he knows that it is important to keep his rules organized, he needs to go back and manage the rules in his Rules and Alerts dialog box. Complete Projects 5-1 and 5-3 before starting this project.

GET READY. LAUNCH Outlook if it is not already running.

1. Click the File tab. In Backstage view, click the Manage Rules and Alerts option to display the Rules and Alerts window.
2. Select the Green Lesson 5 Schedule rule and use the Move Up arrow to move this rule to the top.
3. Click the Lesson 5 Schedule rule and use the Move Down arrow to move it to the bottom of the list.
4. Select the rules you created in this Lesson. Select the Move Invoices rule to deselect it and click the Delete button. Click Yes to confirm.
5. Close the dialog box and return to the mailbox.

LEAVE Outlook open for the next project.

Project 5-6: Create a Quick Step from Scratch to Assign a Category

Jack wants to create a rule that categorizes the messages he sends with "Invoice" in the *Subject* field to assign the messages to the Yellow category. Complete Project 5-1 before starting this project.

GET READY. LAUNCH Outlook if it is not already running.

1. If necessary, click the Mail button in the Navigation Pane to display the mailbox.
2. In the Quick Steps gallery, click Create New to open the Edit Quick Steps dialog box.
3. In the *Name* field, key Project 5.
4. Add the following actions:

Move to folder	select	P5 Invoices
Categorize message	select	Yellow Category

5. Change the Tooltip text to read:

   Categorizes selected message Yellow and moves it to the P5 Invoices folder.

6. To test the Quick Step, select the message in the P5 Invoices folder and click Reply & Delete in the Quick Steps gallery. Click Send in the message window.
7. Click Send/Receive All Folders on the Home tab.
8. Select the new message and click the Project 5 Quick Step. Confirm that the message has moved to the P5 Invoices folder and is categorized as Yellow.

CLOSE Outlook.

INTERNET READY

Another common way to organize messages is based on the sender. Create an e-mail account with a free website such as Yahoo.com. Create a rule to manage messages from the web-based account. Test the rule by sending a message from the web-based account to your Outlook account.

6 Working with Contacts

LESSON SKILL MATRIX

Skills	Exam Objective	Objective Number
Creating and Modifying Contacts	Update a contact in the address book.	4.1.3
Sending and Receiving Contacts	Forward a contact.	4.1.2
Viewing and Deleting Contacts		
Creating and Manipulating Contact Groups	Create a Contact Group.	4.2.1
	Manage Contact Group membership.	4.2.2
	Show notes about a Contact Group.	4.2.3
	Forward a Contact Group.	4.2.4
	Delete a Contact Group.	4.2.5
Sending a Message to a Contact Group	Send a message to a Contact Group.	2.1.10

KEY TERMS

- **contact**
- **Contacts folder**
- **Contact Group**
- **duplicate contact**
- **message header**
- **spoofing**

190

Like many business executives, Mindy Martin will tell you that *who* you know is just as important as *what* you know. Mindy refers to Outlook's contact information dozens of times every day. She calls, writes, and sends messages to suppliers, guests, and other business organizations. Direct contact with the right people can avoid problems or solve small problems before they become catastrophes. Mindy and John have decided to create an outdoor adventure video game based on some of their more popular programs. Mindy needs to set up contact information for her contacts in the software industry so that their information will be readily available. In this lesson, you will learn how to create contacts and Contact Groups, edit and modify contact information, and send a message to a Contact Group.

SOFTWARE ORIENTATION

Microsoft Outlook's Contacts Window

The main Contacts window displays basic information about the contacts in your Contacts folder, as shown in Figure 6-1.

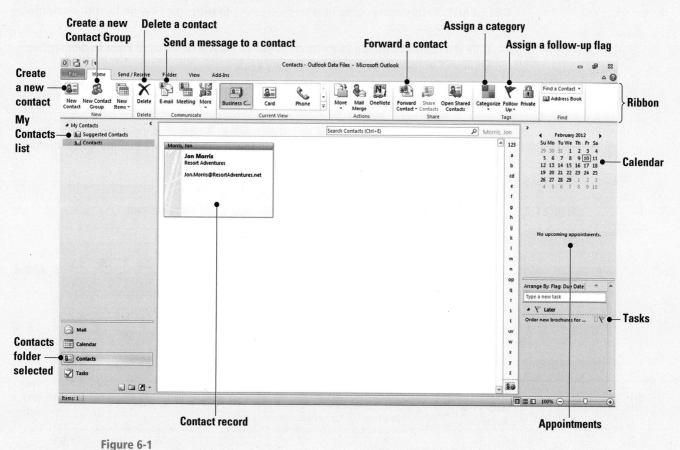

Figure 6-1

Outlook Contacts window

The *Contacts folder* enables you to organize and maintain information about the individuals and businesses you communicate with regularly. In this window, you can select a contact record, create a new contact record, view appointments, view tasks, send a message to a contact, call a contact, assign a contact to a category, and assign a follow-up flag to a contact.

CREATING AND MODIFYING CONTACTS

The Bottom Line

A **contact** is a collection of information about a person or company. Outlook's Contacts feature is an electronic organizer that you can use to create, view, and edit contact information. In this section, you'll learn a number of ways to create a contact and then modify contact information.

(X) Ref

Contacts can be added in many different ways, for example, by exchanging digital signatures. If you exchanged digital signatures with a coworker or friend in Lesson 3, your Contacts list contains a contact for that individual.

Creating a Contact from Scratch

You can use a variety of methods to create contacts. The most basic method of creating a contact is opening a new contact window and keying the necessary information. The blank Contact window has its own Ribbon and command groups. Once a contact has been created, their information is stored in the Outlook Address Book. In this exercise, you'll create a contact using the New Contact button on the Home tab.

STEP BY STEP   **Create a Contact from Scratch**

GET READY. Before you begin these steps, be sure to turn on or log on to your computer, and start Outlook 2010.

1. Click the Contacts button in the bottom section of the Navigation Pane to display the Outlook Contacts window shown in Figure 6-1.

Take Note   The Ribbon options look different in each of Outlook's tools. The Ribbon options now reflect the most commonly used commands for working with contacts.

2. Click New Contact on the Home tab. The Untitled—Contact window is displayed, as shown in Figure 6-2. The blank Contact window is ready to store data for a new contact.

Figure 6-2

Untitled—Contact window

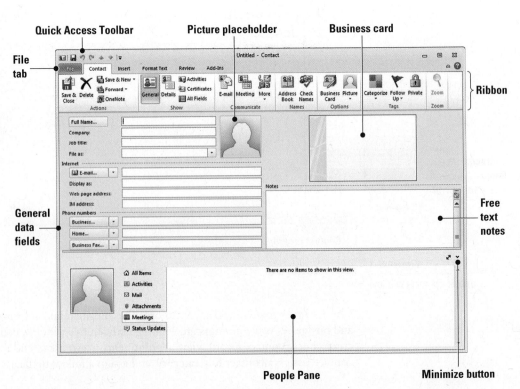

3. Click the *Full Name* field, if your cursor isn't already positioned there. Key Gabe Mares and press Tab. The insertion point moves to the *Company* field. The *File as* field is automatically filled with *Mares, Gabe*, and *Gabe Mares* is displayed in the business card. The name of the window is changed to Gabe Mares—Contact.

4. In the *Company* field, key Wingtip Toys and press Tab. The insertion point moves to the *Job title* field. The company's name is added to the business card.

5. In the *Job title* field, key Sales Support Manager and press Tab. Gabe's job title is added to the business card. The insertion point moves to the *File as* field, highlighting the current value.

6. Click the dropdown arrow in the *File as* field. A short list of alternative ways of filing the contact is displayed. Some methods use the company name to file the contact. Other alternatives file the contact by the contact's first name. Release the mouse button to maintain the default selection, which files contacts by last name.

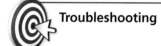

Troubleshooting The e-mail addresses provided in these exercises belong to unused domains owned by Microsoft. When you send a message to these addresses, you will receive an error message stating that the message could not be delivered. Delete the error messages when they arrive.

7. Click the *E-mail* field. Key Gabe@wingtiptoys.com and press Tab. The *Display as* field is automatically filled, and Gabe's e-mail address is added to the business card.

8. You don't want to change the way Gabe's e-mail address is displayed, so press Tab. The insertion point moves to the *Web page address* field.

9. In the *Web page address* field, key www.wingtiptoys.com.

10. Below the *Phone numbers* heading, click the *Business* field. When you move the insertion point out of the *Web page address* field, the Web page address is automatically added to the business card. Key 6155551205 in the *Phone Numbers* field.

Take Note   It isn't necessary to key spaces or parentheses in phone numbers. Outlook automatically formats phone numbers when the insertion point leaves the field.

11. Click the minimize button in the top-right corner of the People Pane at the bottom of the Contact window. The People Pane collapses to a bar at the bottom of the Contact window and additional fields are displayed in the *Address* area of the Contact window.

12. Below the Addresses heading, click the *Business* field. Key 7895 First Street. Press Enter. Key Nashville, TN 76534. Press Tab. The business card is automatically updated and the Map It button is undimmed, as shown in Figure 6-3.

Figure 6-3

Gabe Mares—Contact window

Business card

Outlook automatically formats phone numbers, e-mails, and web addresses

Free text notes

People Pane   Click to open a web page containing a map to the address shown   Expand the People Pane arrow

Take Note   In a contact record, using the postal abbreviation for a state makes it easier to use the information in a mailing list or other data exports.

Troubleshooting   If you press Tab in the *Address* field before keying at least two lines of text, the Check Address dialog box is displayed. Because Outlook expects at least two lines of text in an address, the text you have already keyed might be displayed in the wrong fields in the Check Address dialog box. Click the Cancel button to close the dialog box and continue keying the address.

13. In the Actions group on the Ribbon, click the **Save & Close** button. Gabe Mares' contact information is saved and stored in the Outlook Address Book, and you are returned to the main Contacts window.

PAUSE. LEAVE Outlook open to use in the next exercise.

Take Note   You do not have to key information into every field. To save contact information, you should have a value in the *File As* field. If the *File As* field is empty when you try to save the contact, Outlook displays a warning message asking if you want to save the contact with an empty *File As* field. If you save the contact, it will be placed before any other contacts saved with a value in the *File As* field, because a blank is sorted as a value that occurs before any other value.

In the previous exercise, you keyed the basic information for a contact.

Creating a Contact from an Existing Contact

Often, you will have several contacts who work for the same company. Rather than keying the same data for a new contact, you can create the new contact from the existing contact. When you create a new contact for a person from the same company, the company name, File As, website, phone number, and address are carried over to the new contact. The name, job title, and e-mail address are not carried over to the new contact, because these fields will usually differ between contacts, even if they work for the same company. In this exercise, you'll learn how to create a new contact from an existing contact's record.

STEP BY STEP   **Create a Contact from an Existing Contact**

GET READY. Before you begin these steps, be sure to complete the previous exercise.

1. Click the **Contacts** button in the Navigation Pane to open the Contacts window that now displays the Gabe Mares contact record.

2. Double-click the **Gabe Mares** contact record. The Gabe Mares Contact window is displayed.

3. In the Actions group on the Ribbon, click the **Save & New arrow**. In the dropdown list of options, click **New Contact from Same Company**. A new window titled Wingtip Toys—Contact is displayed.

4. Click the *Full Name* field if necessary. Key **Diane Tibbott** and press **Tab**. The insertion point moves to the *Company* field. The *File As* field is automatically filled with *Tibbott, Diane*, and *Diane Tibbott* is displayed in the business card. The name of the window is changed to Diane Tibbott—Contact.

5. Click the *Job title* field. Key **Marketing Representative** and press **Tab**. Diane's job title is added to the business card. The insertion point moves to the *File As* field, highlighting the current value.

6. Click the *E-mail* field. Key **Diane@wingtiptoys.com** and press **Tab**. The *Display As* field is automatically filled, and Diane's e-mail address is added to the business card.

7. In the Actions group on the Ribbon, click the **Save & Close** button. Diane Tibbott's contact information is saved and her Contact window closes. Close Gabe's contact record window to return to the main Contacts window.

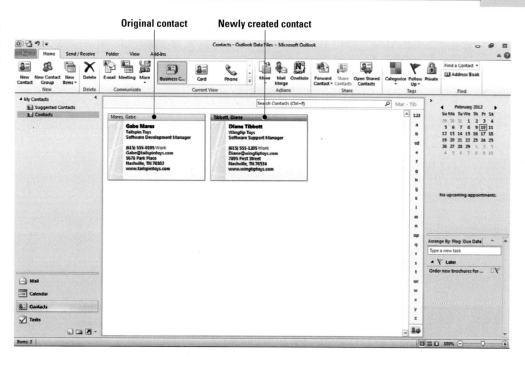

Figure 6-4

Creating a contact from an existing contact

Original contact   Newly created contact

PAUSE. LEAVE Outlook open to use in the next exercise.

Creating a Contact from a Suggested Contact

NEW to Office 2010

One of the ways that Outlook 2010 helps you stay more organized is by recognizing when you send a message to someone who is not listed in your Address Book. Whenever you send a message to a new person, Outlook captures as much contact information as it can and saves it in the Suggested Contacts folder. You can easily save a suggested contact to your Address Book by just dragging it to the Contacts folder. In Lesson 2, you sent a message to someone@example.com. In this exercise, you'll create a contact using the suggested contact that Outlook created from that message.

STEP BY STEP   **Create a Contact from a Suggested Contact**

WILEY PLUS EXTRA

WileyPLUS Extra! features an online tutorial of this task.

GET READY. Before you begin these steps, be sure to have completed the Send a Message exercise in Lesson 2.

1. Click the Contacts button in the Navigation Pane to display the main Contacts window.

2. Click the Suggested Contacts folder in the My Contacts section of the Navigation Pane. The Suggested Contacts window opens and displays a business card for each person you've sent a message to who is not already listed in your Address Book, as shown in Figure 6-5.

Take Note   Depending on which exercises you've completed, you might see additional business cards.

Figure 6-5

Suggested Contacts folder

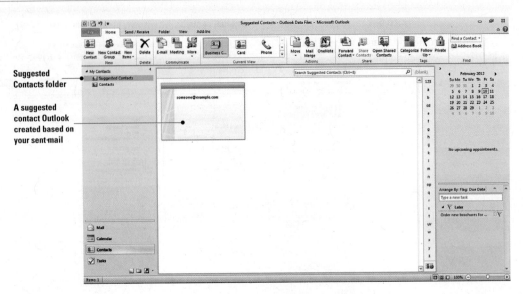

3. Click the someone@example.com business card and drag it to the Contacts folder in the My Contacts section of the Navigation Pane.

4. Click the Contacts folder in the Navigation Pane. The someone@example.com business card appears at the beginning of available contacts because there is no name supplied yet.

PAUSE. LEAVE Outlook open to use in the next exercise.

Updating Contact Information

To keep the information in your Contacts list current, you often need to modify the information for existing contacts. After a contact has been created, you can modify the contact's information using either the main Contact window or the Outlook Address Book. You can modify an existing contact and save it as a new contact rather than overwriting the existing contact. In this exercise, you'll update the contact information in your Address Book and add contact information for a suggested contact.

STEP BY STEP   **Update Contact Information**

GET READY. Before you begin these steps, be sure to complete the preceding exercises and have Outlook open and running on your computer.

1. Click the Contacts button in the Navigation Pane to display the main Contacts window.

2. Double-click the Diane Tibbott contact record. The Diane Tibbott—Contact window is displayed.

3. Click the *Job title* field. Select the existing value, key Software Support Manager, and press Tab. Diane's job title is modified on the business card.

4. In the Actions group on the Ribbon, click the Save & Close button. The modified contact information is saved, and you are returned to the main Contacts window.

5. In the Find group on the Home tab, click Address Book. The Outlook Address Book window is displayed, as shown in Figure 6-6.

Figure 6-6

Outlook Address Book window

Outlook contacts sorted alphabetically

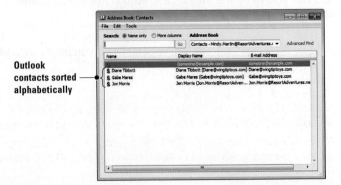

Another Way
To open a contact, select Properties on the File menu.

6. In the list of contacts, double-click the Gabe Mares contact. The Gabe Mares—Contact window opens.

7. Click the following fields and replace the existing values with the new values.

Company	Tailspin Toys
Job title	Software Development Manager
E-mail	Gabe@tailspintoys.com
Web page address	www.tailspintoys.com
Business phone number	6155550195
Business address	5678 Park Place
	Nashville, TN 76502

8. In the Actions group on the Ribbon, click the Save & Close button. The modified contact information is saved and the Gabe Mares—Contact window closes.

9. Right-click the someone@example.com contact record in the Address Book and select Properties from the shortcut menu that appears. The Untitled—Contact window is displayed.

10. Click the following fields and replace the existing values with the new values.

Name	Susan Davis
Company Name	Example Company

The name of the contact record window changes to Susan Davis—Contact.

11. Double-click the picture placeholder in the center of the window. The Add Contact picture dialog box is displayed. Navigate to the data files for this lesson and select the **Susan.jpg** file and click OK. The Add Contact picture dialog box closes and you return to the Susan Davis—Contact window.

12. Click the Expand People Pane arrow if necessary to see how the picture looks in all its locations, as shown in Figure 6-7.

@ The *Susan.jpg* file for this lesson is available on the book companion website or in WileyPLUS.

Figure 6-7

Susan Davis—Contact window

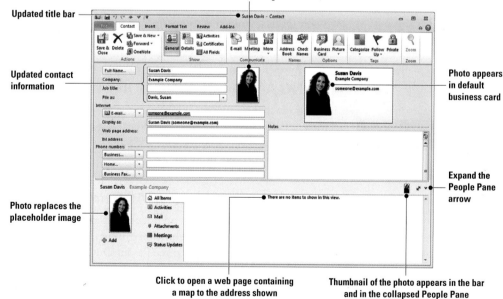

13. In the Actions group on the Ribbon, click the Save & Close button. The modified contact information is saved and the Susan Davis—Contact window closes. Close the Outlook Address Book to return to the main Contacts window.

14. Compare your Contacts folder to Figure 6-8. In your Contacts folder, Jon Morris's contact record is replaced by the individual with whom you exchanged digital signatures in Lesson 3.

Figure 6-8

Modified contacts

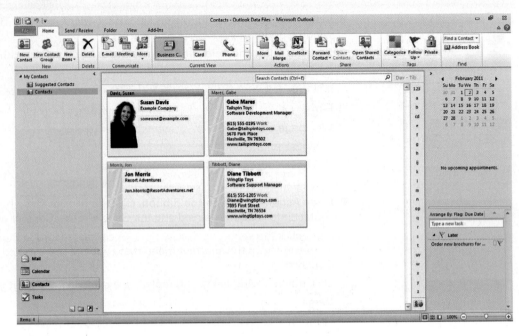

PAUSE. LEAVE Outlook open to use in the next exercise.

In the previous exercise, you updated the information for three contacts. The following changes occurred.

- Gabe Mares left Wingtip Toys. He was hired by Tailspin Toys as the Software Development Manager. Most of his contact information has changed.
- Diane Tibbott was promoted to Gabe's previous position as Software Support Manager. Her e-mail address and phone number remain the same. Only her title has changed. The corner office with a view that came with the promotion is not part of her contact information.
- Susan Davis's name and company name were added to the contact that Outlook suggested for you.

SENDING AND RECEIVING CONTACTS

The Bottom Line

It is easy to exchange contact information via e-mail. You can send and receive contacts as attachments. Every time you send a message, you are also sending your contact information. In Outlook, you can create a contact for the sender of any message you receive, and you can create a contact from a message header.

Forwarding a Contact as an Attachment

You already know that you can send documents and files as attachments. You can also send contacts as attachments. These attachments can be formatted as Outlook contacts, business cards, or plain text. When you send a contact as an Outlook contact, recipients who use Outlook will be easily able to see all the information they need to add the contact to their records. However, if you are unsure what e-mail program the recipient uses, it is safest to send the contact as a business card. Recipients who have Outlook will see it as a contact record and everyone else will see it as an image of the business card. In this exercise, you learn how to send a contact as an attachment in Outlook 2010.

STEP BY STEP   **Forward a Contact as an Attachment**

GET READY. Before you begin these steps, be sure to complete the preceding exercises and have Outlook 2010 open and running on your computer.

1. Click the Contacts button in the Navigation Pane to display the main Contacts window.
2. Double-click the Gabe Mares contact record. The Gabe Mares—Contact window is displayed.
3. In the Actions group on the Ribbon, click the Forward button. In the dropdown menu that appears, click the As an Outlook Contact option. A new message window is displayed. In the *Subject* field, the topic is automatically identified as *FW: Gabe Mares*, and Gabe's contact record is attached to the message, as shown in Figure 6-9.

Figure 6-9

Sending a contact as an attachment

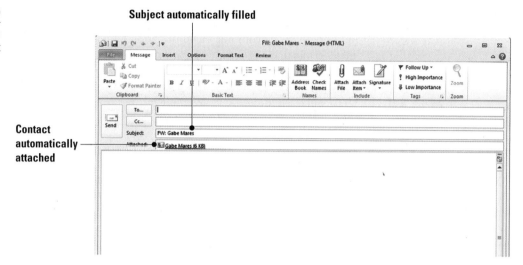

Subject automatically filled

Contact automatically attached

 Troubleshooting If a message is displayed stating that you must save the original item, click OK to continue.

4. In the message area, key Gabe Mares' contact information is attached.

Take Note Throughout this chapter you will see information that appears in black text within brackets, such as [Press Enter] or [next Friday's date]. The information contained in the brackets is intended to be directions for you rather than something you actually type word for word. It will instruct you to perform an action or substitute text. Do **not** type the actual text that appears within brackets.

5. In the *To* field, key [your e-mail address].

Take Note When you send contact information, any text in the *Notes* area of the contact record and items attached to the contact record are also sent. Before you send the contact record, delete any information in the *Notes* area and attachments that you don't want the recipient to see.

6. Click the Send button. The message is moved to the Outbox, and it is sent when your computer is connected to the Internet.
7. **CLOSE** the Gabe Mares—Contact window.

PAUSE. LEAVE Outlook open to use in the next exercise.

CERTIFICATION READY 4.1.2

How would you send a contact as a business card?

In the previous exercise, you sent contact information directly from the Contacts folder as an attachment to a message. This enables you to send contact information without keying it as text in a message.

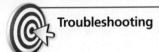

Troubleshooting If the recipient does not use Outlook 2007 or newer, the contact information might not be displayed correctly and the recipient might not be able to create a contact from the attachment.

Saving a Contact Received as a Contact Record

When you request contact information from a coworker's Contacts list, the coworker can send the information as a business card or a contact record in Outlook format. If the contact record is sent in Outlook format, you can open the attachment, view the information, and save it as a contact record. When you try to save a contact with an address that's already in your Address Book, Outlook automatically detects it as a **duplicate contact** and gives you an opportunity to add the new contact or to update the existing contact. However, once a duplicate is detected, you should always combine the information onto one record and delete the duplicate. This eliminates errors that can occur when one record is updated and the other is not. In this exercise, you learn how to save a received contact as a contact record and how to deal with duplicate contacts.

 Ref

You will learn more about electronic business cards in Lesson 7.

STEP BY STEP | **Save a Contact Received as a Contact Record**

GET READY. Before you begin these steps, be sure that Microsoft Outlook is running and that you have completed the preceding exercises in this lesson.

1. Click the Mail button in the bottom section of the Navigation Pane to display the Inbox. If the *FW: Gabe Mares* message has not arrived yet, click the Send/Receive All Folders button on the Home tab.

2. Click the FW: Gabe Mares message. The message is displayed in the Reading Pane.

Troubleshooting If the Reading Pane is not visible, click Reset View on the View tab.

3. In the Reading Pane, double-click the Gabe Mares attachment. The attachment opens in the Gabe Mares—Contact window.

4. In the Actions group on the Ribbon, click the Save & Close button. Because you received this contact information at the same e-mail address used to send the contact information, the contact record is already in your Contacts list, and Outlook detects that this is a duplicate contact. The Duplicate Contact Detected window shown in Figure 6-10 is displayed. If the contact record was not a duplicate, the contact would be saved without any further action needed.

Figure 6-10

Duplicate Contact Detected window

Duplicate Contact Detected window

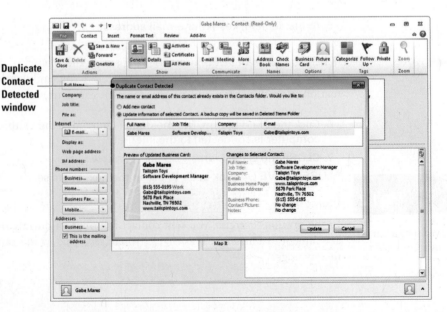

Take Note   As mentioned at the beginning of this exercise, creating duplicate contact records frequently leads to inaccurate information and is not a good practice. You are creating a duplicate record here only so that you can learn additional techniques for eliminating duplicate records in a later exercise.

5. You want to create a new contact, so select the Add new contact option at the top of the window and click the Add button at the bottom of the window. The Duplicate Contact Detected window is closed, the contact record is created, and you are returned to the Mail folder.

6. Click the Contacts button in the Navigation Pane to display the main Contacts window. Now, you have the original Gabe Mares contact record you created by keying the data and the Gabe Mares contact record you created from the attachment. Your Contacts folder should be similar to Figure 6-11. In your Contacts folder, Jon Morris's contact record is replaced by the individual with whom you exchanged digital signatures in Lesson 3.

Figure 6-11

Duplicate Contact record created

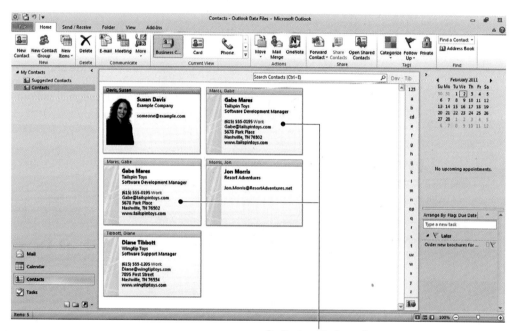

Duplicate contact records

PAUSE. LEAVE Outlook open to use in the next exercise.

Creating a Contact from a Message Header

Every message you send automatically contains your contact information in the message header. The **message header** is the text automatically added at the top of a message. The message header contains the sender's e-mail address, the names of the servers used to send and transfer the message, the subject, the date, and other basic information about the message. In this exercise, you'll learn how to use a message header to create a contact record in your Contacts list for the message's sender.

STEP BY STEP   **Create a Contact from a Message Header**

GET READY. Before you begin these steps, be sure that Microsoft Outlook is running and that you have completed the preceding exercises in this lesson.

1. Click the Mail button in the Navigation Pane to display the Mail folder.

2. Click the FW: Gabe Mares message. The message is displayed in the Reading Pane.

3. In the Reading Pane, point to the sender's name or e-mail address. An information pane appears above the e-mail address and a shortcut menu appears below, as shown in Figure 6-12.

Figure 6-12

Outlook's sender information

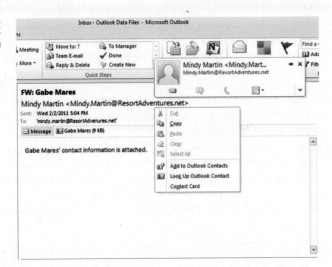

4. Click the Add to Outlook Contacts option on the shortcut menu. A Contact window containing the sender's name and e-mail address is displayed, as shown in Figure 6-13. Because you sent the *FW: Gabe Mares* message, it is your contact information in the Contact window.

Figure 6-13

Creating a contact from a message header

Data automatically entered from a message header

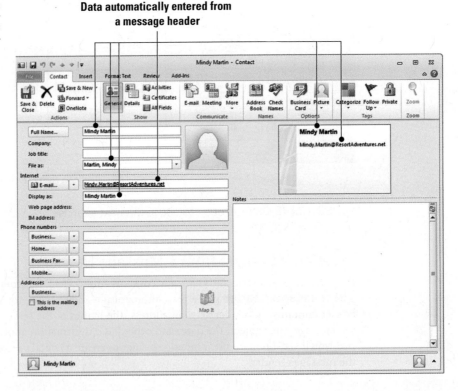

5. In the Actions group on the Ribbon, click the Save & Close button. The contact record is created, and you are returned to the Inbox.

6. Click the Contacts button in the Navigation Pane to display the Contacts window. Now, you have the original Gabe Mares contact record, the Gabe Mares contact record you created from the attachment, the contact record created when you received a digital signature in Lesson 3, Diane Tibbott's contact record created from Gabe's record, the Susan Davis contact created from Outlook's Suggested Contact folder, and your contact record created from a message header.

PAUSE. LEAVE Outlook open to use in the next exercise.

In the previous exercise, you created a contact from a message header. Although a message header contains important information, it is important to note that false information can be provided in the message header. This is known as **spoofing**. Many junk messages contain false information in the message header.

VIEWING AND DELETING CONTACTS

By default, contacts are displayed as business cards. However, other views are available. Selecting a different view lets you focus on specific information. Prevent clutter in your Contacts folder. When a contact is no longer useful or you found a duplicate contact, delete the contact record.

Viewing and Deleting Contacts

In this exercise, you'll explore some Contact window views and delete the duplicate contact record.

STEP BY STEP   **Viewing and Deleting Contacts**

GET READY. Before you begin these steps, be sure that Microsoft Outlook is running and that you have completed the preceding exercises in this lesson.

1. Click the Contacts button in the Navigation Pane to open the Contacts window, displaying the default Business Cards view of the Contacts records, as shown in Figure 6-9. This is the only view that displays any graphics on the business card, such as the contacts photo.

2. Click the Cards button in the Current View group of the Home tab. The view is modified as shown in Figure 6-14. The cards are lined up in narrow columns and any graphics are hidden.

Figure 6-14

The Contact List in Card view

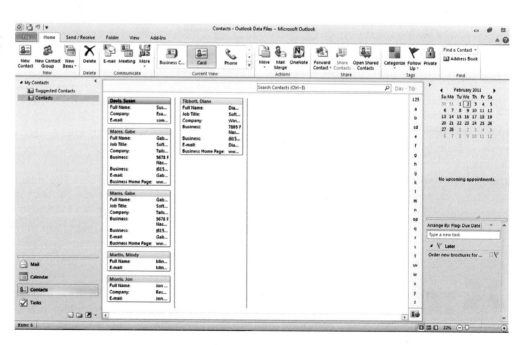

3. Click the Phone button in the Current View group of the Home tab. The view is modified as shown in Figure 6-15. Use this view if you need to call several contacts in your Contacts folder.

Figure 6-15

Contacts in Phone List view

Current View group

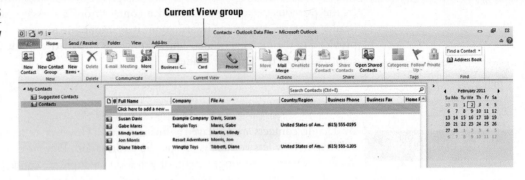

4. Click the View tab to see additional viewing options. In the Arrangement group, you can select to organize the list by category, company name, or location.

5. Click the Categories button. The view is modified to group the contacts by category. Use this view if you need to see all the contacts assigned to a specific color category.

 Ref   You will learn more about organizing your Outlook items using categories in Lesson 12.

6. Click the Company button in the Arrangement group in the View tab. The view is modified to group the contacts by company name, as shown in Figure 6-16. Use this view to see all the contacts working for a specific company.

Arrangement group

Resets view to its default settings

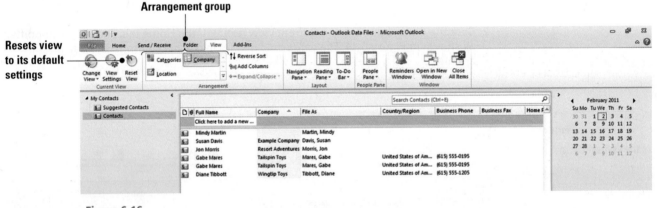

Figure 6-16

Contacts grouped by company name

7. Click the Location button in the Navigation Pane. The view is modified to group the contacts by country/region. Use this view to see contacts with an address in a particular area. This is more useful if your contacts are not located in the same geographic area.

8. Click the Reset View button in the Current View group to return the phone list to its default view.

9. Click Change View button in the Current Views group and select Business Card to return to the default view of the contacts.

10. Click the first Gabe Mares contact record. On the Home tab, click the Delete button. The contact record is moved to the Deleted Items folder. It will not be removed from your computer until the Deleted Items folder is emptied.

PAUSE. LEAVE Outlook open to use in the next exercise.

Another Way
To delete a contact record, right-click the contact and click Delete on the shortcut menu.

Because several views are available, select the view that targets the information you need to see. When you are viewing contact records, you can minimize clutter by deleting contacts that are no longer useful or duplicates that have been accidentally created.

CREATING AND MANIPULATING CONTACT GROUPS

A **Contact Group** is a group of individual contacts saved together as a single contact. A Contact Group simplifies the task of regularly sending the same message to a group of people. If you create a Contact Group, you can make one selection in the *To* field to send the message to all members of the Contact Group. In this section, you'll create a Contact Group, create notes to be stored with it, and make changes to who is in the group. Then you'll forward the Contact Group as an attachment and send a message to the members of the Contact Group.

Creating a Contact Group

To create a Contact Group, you create a contact record that is identified as a Contact Group. Then you select the members of the Contact Group and save the Contact Group. In this exercise, you'll create a Contact Group and add members to it.

STEP BY STEP | **Create a Contact Group**

GET READY. Before you begin these steps, be sure that Microsoft Outlook is running and that you have completed the preceding exercises in this lesson.

1. Click the Contacts button in the Navigation Pane to display the Contacts window.

2. In the New group on the Home tab, click the New Contact Group button. The Untitled—Contact Group window is displayed, as shown in Figure 6-17. The Members button in the Show group on the Ribbon is selected.

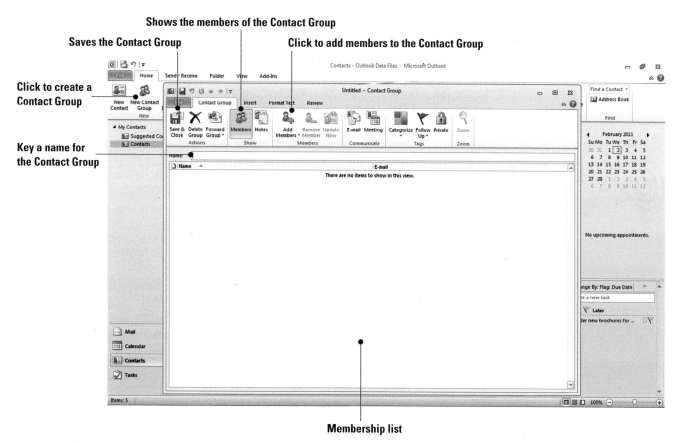

Figure 6-17

Untitled—Contact Group window

3. In the Members group on the Ribbon, click the Add Members button and select the From Outlook Contacts option. The Select Members: Contacts dialog box is displayed, as shown in Figure 6-18. The contacts in your Address Book are listed. The first contact is already selected.

Figure 6-18

Select Members: Contacts window

Select a contact ————————

Click to add selected contact to the Members field ————————

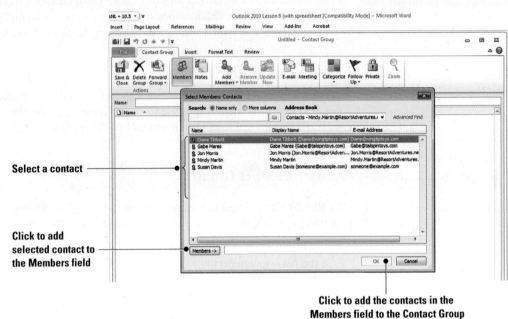

Click to add the contacts in the Members field to the Contact Group

4. Because the first contact you want to include in the Contact Group is already selected, click the Members button at the bottom of the dialog box. The contact's name is added to the *Members* field.

5. Click the second contact in the list, then click the Members button. The second contact is added to the *Members* field.

6. Repeat the actions in Step 5, to select and add the third, fourth, and fifth contacts from the list to the *Members* field.

Troubleshooting If you did not exchange digital signatures in Lesson 3, skip step 8 below and continue.

---

7. Click OK. The Select Members: Contacts dialog box closes, and you return to the Untitled—Contact Group window, which now contains listings for the five contacts you added to this group.

8. Click the *Name* field. Key General Announcements List. This name is used to identify the Contact Group in the Contacts folder.

9. Click the Save & Close button. The General Announcement List Contact Group is saved. The window closes, and you return to the Contacts folder. The General Announcements List contact is displayed, as shown in Figure 6-19.

Figure 6-19

Contact Group created

Contact Group added to Contacts folder

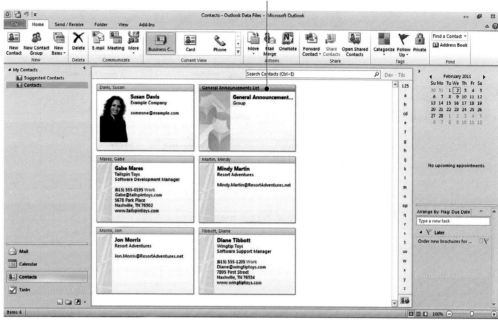

Take Note   When you view the Contact Group in the Contacts folder, the list of members is not visible. To see the list of members, open the contact record.

PAUSE. LEAVE Outlook open to use in the next exercise.

CERTIFICATION READY   4.2.1

How do you create a Contact Group?

In the previous exercise, you created a Contact Group that contains all of your contacts. However, Contact Groups don't usually contain all of your contacts. Instead, they are typically limited to just the contacts working on a specific project.

Creating a Contact Group from an Existing Contact Group

You already know how to create a Contact Group from scratch, but you can also create a Contact Group by duplicating another group and then modifying it. In this exercise, you'll create a new Contact Group by duplicating an existing group.

STEP BY STEP   **Create a Contact Group from an Existing Contact Group**

GET READY. Before you begin these steps, be sure that Microsoft Outlook is running and that you have completed the preceding exercises in this lesson.

1. Click the Contacts button in the Navigation Pane to display the Contacts window.
2. Right-click the General Announcements List contact record and select Copy from the shortcut menu that appears.
3. Press Ctrl+V. A duplicate Contact Group record is displayed in the Contacts window, as shown in Figure 6-20.

Figure 6-20

Creating a duplicate
Contact Group

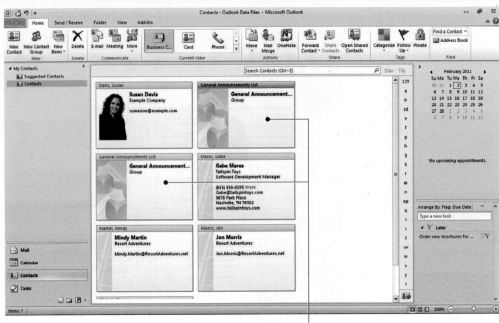

Duplicate Contact Groups

4. Double-click one of the General Announcements List contact records. The General Announcements list—Contact Group window is displayed.

5. Select the text in the *Name* field. Key Wingtip Toys List. This name is used to identify the name of the project this group is working on.

6. Click the Save & Close button. The Wingtip Toys List Contact Group is saved. The window is closed, and you are returned to the Contacts folder, with the Wingtip Toys List contact displayed, as shown in Figure 6-21.

Figure 6-21

Creating a Contact Group from
an existing Contact Group

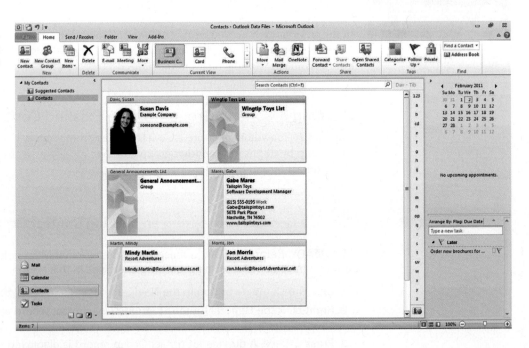

PAUSE. LEAVE Outlook open to use in the next exercise.

In the previous exercise, you created a Contact Group for the Wingtip Toys project you are working on. However, because the Contact Group was created from a Contact Group that contained all of your contacts, you'll need to modify the Contact Group's membership to reflect the members of the project team.

Managing Contact Group Membership

Any Contact Group used over time will eventually require changes. In this exercise, you'll learn how to remove a member from a Contact Group list and edit the contact information.

STEP BY STEP | **Manage Contact Group Membership**

GET READY. Before you begin these steps, be sure that Microsoft Outlook is running and that you have completed the preceding exercises in this lesson.

1. Click the Contacts button in the Navigation Pane to display the default Contacts window.
2. Double-click the Wingtip Toys List contact. The Wingtip Toys List—Contact Group window is displayed.
3. Click Gabe's name in the lower area of the window. In the Members group on the Ribbon, click the Remove Member button. Gabe is removed from the Contact Group.
4. In the list of members, double-click your name. Your contact record is displayed.
5. Click the *Company* field. Key [the name of your company].
6. Click the Save & Close button in your Contact window. Your modified contact record is saved and closed.
7. Click the Save & Close button in the Contact Group window. The Contact Group is saved. The window is closed, and you are returned to the Contacts folder.

PAUSE. LEAVE Outlook open to use in the next exercise.

Another Way
To delete a contact from the group, click the contact and press Delete.

CERTIFICATION READY 4.2.2

How do you modify a Contact Group?

In the previous exercises, you created a Contact Group containing everyone who is working on the Outdoor Adventure software development project. During the weekly management meeting, Mindy and Jon decided to assign Katie Mathews, the resort's PR specialist, the role of lead liaison for the project.

In order for her to take the lead, she will need a copy of the Wingtip Toys Contact Group. Whenever you share Contact Groups with others, it is important to attach notes to the Contact Group so that there is no confusion about who is included and what has changed.

Using Contact Group Notes

You can use the Notes page to keep background information with a Contact Group. As Contact Groups change over time, it can be easy to forget what changes have been made. This is particularly important when the Contact Group list and information is forwarded to someone else. In this exercise, you'll use the Notes page to provide information about a Contact Group before sending it as an attachment to an e-mail message.

STEP BY STEP | **Use Contact Group Notes**

GET READY. Before you begin these steps, be sure that Microsoft Outlook is running and that you have completed the preceding exercises in this lesson.

1. Click the Contacts button in the Navigation Pane to display the default Contacts window.
2. Double-click the Wingtip Toys List contact. The Wingtip Toys List—Contact Group window is displayed with the Contact Group tab opened on the Ribbon.
3. Click the Notes button in the Contact Group tab to show the notes about a Contact Group. The Notes page for this Contact Group is displayed.
4. In the empty text area, key The group includes everyone working on the Outdoor Adventure game project, including Susan Davis, an independent storyboard consultant. Your screen should look similar to the one shown in Figure 6-22.

Figure 6-22

Adding notes to a Contact Group

Click to add or view notes

Include information about the members of the list

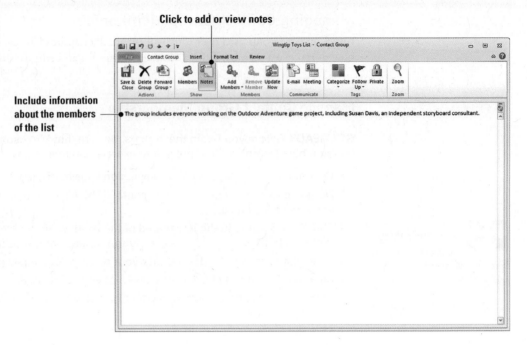

5. Click the **Save & Close** button in the Contact Group window. The Contact Group is saved. The window is closed, and you are returned to the Contacts folder.

6. Double-click the **Wingtip Toys List** contact record to open the Wingtip Toys List—Contact Group window again. **Click the Notes** button in the Contact Group tab to show the notes for this group.

7. Click the **Save & Close** button in the Contact Group window. The Contact Group is saved. The window is closed, and you are returned to the Contacts folder.

8. Double-click the **Wingtip Toys List** contact record to open the Wingtip Toys List—Contact Group window again. **Click the Notes** button in the Contact Group tab to show the notes for this group.

9. Click the **Save & Close** button in the Contact Group window. The Contact Group is saved. The window is closed, and you are returned to the Contacts folder.

PAUSE. LEAVE Outlook open to use in the next exercise.

CERTIFICATION READY   **4.2.3**

How do you look at the notes for a Contact Group?

In the previous exercise, you added an informative note about the Wingtip Toys List Contact Group. You are now ready to send the Contact Group to Katie.

Forwarding a Contact Group

Sending a Contact Group to someone as an e-mail attachment is just as easy as sending a contact. You can forward a Contact Group just by selecting the group's contact record and clicking Forward Contact in the Share group of the Contacts window's Home tab. In this exercise, you'll forward a Contact Group to an e-mail recipient.

STEP BY STEP   **Forward a Contact Group**

GET READY. Before you begin these steps, be sure that Microsoft Outlook is running and that you have completed the preceding exercises in this lesson.

1. Click the **Contacts** button in the Navigation Pane to display the default Contacts window.

2. Click the **Wingtip Toys List** contact record and then click **Forward Contact** in the Share group of the Home tab. In the dropdown menu that appears, select the **As An Outlook Contact** option. A new FW: Wingtip Toys List—Message window is displayed.

3. In the *To* field, key **Katie.Mathews@ResortAdventures.net**.

4. In the message area, key Hi Katie, here is the Contact Group for the game project. as shown in Figure 6-23.

Figure 6-23

Sending a Contact Group as an attachment

Contact Group attachment

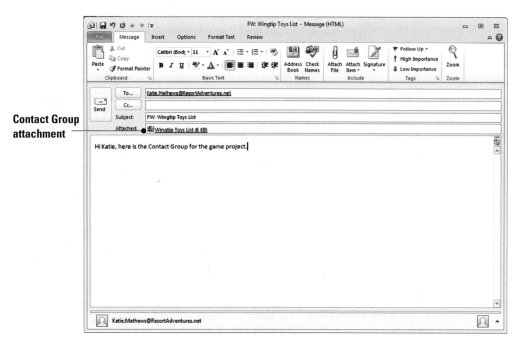

5. Click the Send button. The message is moved to the Outbox, and it is sent when your computer is connected to the Internet.

6. CLOSE the FW: Wingtip Toys List—Message window.

PAUSE. LEAVE Outlook open to use in the next exercise.

<table>
<tr><td>

CERTIFICATION READY   4.2.4

How would you send a Contact Group as an e-mail attachment?

</td></tr>
</table>

Deleting a Contact Group

Contact Groups are a great way to help you keep your contacts organized, but when you no longer need a Contact Group, you should delete it so you don't accidentally send messages to the group. Fortunately, deleting a Contact Group is just as easy as deleting a contact. In this exercise, you'll delete the General Announcements List Contact Group.

STEP BY STEP   **Delete a Contact Group**

GET READY. Before you begin these steps, be sure that Microsoft Outlook is running and that you completed the preceding exercises in this lesson.

1. Click the Contacts button in the Navigation Pane to display the main Contacts window.

2. Click the General Announcements List contact record. On the Home tab, click the Delete button. The Contact Group record is moved to the Deleted Items folder. It will not be removed from your computer until the Deleted Items folder is emptied.

PAUSE. LEAVE Outlook open to use in the next exercise.

<table>
<tr><td>

CERTIFICATION READY   4.2.5

How would you delete a Contact Group?

</td></tr>
</table>

Now that you've sent the Wingtip Toys List to Katie, you want to send a message to the members of the team to introduce Katie.

SENDING A MESSAGE TO A CONTACT GROUP

The Bottom Line

Sending an e-mail message to Contact Group is a simple process. By adding the Contact Group's name in the *To* field, any e-mail message will go to each member of the group. All you need to do to create a group e-mail is select the Contact Group in the Contacts window and click the E-mail button in the Communicate group. In this exercise, you'll create an e-mail message to be sent to a Contact Group.

STEP BY STEP **Send a Message to a Contact Group**

GET READY. Before you begin these steps, be sure that Microsoft Outlook is running and that you completed the preceding exercises in this lesson.

1. Click the Contacts button in the Navigation Pane to display the main Contacts window.
2. Click the Wingtip Toys List contact record.
3. In the Communicate group on the Home tab, click the E-mail button. A blank Message window is displayed. In the *To* field, the Wingtip Toys List contact is automatically entered, as shown in Figure 6-24. The rest of the fields are empty.

Figure 6-24

Message addressed to the Contact Group created

Click to close the message without sending it

Click to expand the Contact Group

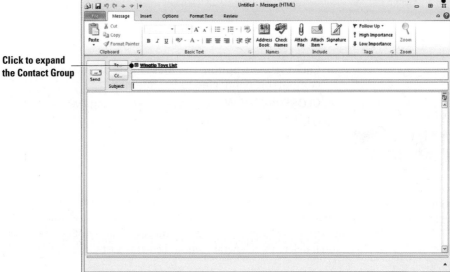

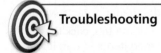 **Another Way**
You can also send a message to a Contact Group by typing the name of the group in the *To* field.

4. Click the plus sign (+) in the *To* field. A warning box is displayed stating that the group name will be replaced with the names of the group's members. Click OK. The individual addressees are displayed in the *To* field.

Troubleshooting It is not necessary to expand the Contact Group in a message. You expanded the Contact Group in this exercise merely for demonstration purposes.

5. Click the Close button to close the message without sending it. Do not save changes to the message.

PAUSE. LEAVE Outlook open to use in the next exercise.

CERTIFICATION READY 2.1.10

How would you address a message to a Contact Group?

When you created the Wingtip Toys Contact Group, you included Gabe Mares. However, he works for Tailspin Toys now. In the previous exercise, you removed Gabe from the Contact Group. You also accessed and modified your contact record through the Contact Group. Finally, you created a message that could be sent to the members of the Contact Group.

SKILL SUMMARY

In This Lesson You Learned How To:	Exam Objective	Objective Number
Create and modify contacts	Update a contact in the address book.	4.1.3
Send and receive contacts	Forward a contact.	4.1.2
View and delete contacts		
Create and manipulate contact groups	Create a Contact Group.	4.2.1
	Manage Contact Group membership.	4.2.2
	Show notes about a Contact Group.	4.2.3
	Forward a Contact Group.	4.2.4
	Delete a Contact Group.	4.2.5
Send a message to a Contact Group	Send a message to a Contact Group.	2.1.10

Knowledge Assessment

Multiple Choice

Select the best response for the following statements.

1. Which field should contain a value when you save a contact?
   a. Display as
   b. Full Name
   c. File As
   d. E-mail

2. How can you simplify the task of regularly sending messages to the same group of contacts?
   a. Resend the message to each contact.
   b. Use the bulk messaging feature.
   c. Set a predetermined time for sending the messages.
   d. Create a Contact Group.

3. _____ should be added to a Contact Group when it is modified or shared.
   a. the contact's name
   b. Notes
   c. protection
   d. track changes

4. A duplicate contact should be
   a. created for every contact.
   b. displayed before the original contact.
   c. deleted.
   d. modified.

5. When you key a phone number in a contact record,
   a. key the parentheses around the area code.
   b. don't key the area code.
   c. key a hyphen between each group of numbers.
   d. don't key spaces or hyphens in the number.

6. Which of the following is a way to send an e-mail message to a Contact Group?
   a. Key the group's name in the *To* field of an e-mail message window.
   b. Select a Contact Group from the Contacts window and click the E-mail button.
   c. Open the group's contact record and click the E-mail button.
   d. All of the above.

7. What value is not carried over to the new contact when you create a new contact record from the same company?
   a. Address
   b. E-mail address
   c. Website
   d. Phone number

8. What provides the information to create a contact from any message you receive?
   a. The attachment
   b. The subject
   c. The message header
   d. The *Subject* field

9. How many views are available in the Contacts feature?
   a. Four
   b. Three
   c. It depends on the number of contact records you have saved
   d. Five

10. What does a recipient need to save a contact received in Outlook format?
   a. Outlook 2007 or 2010
   b. Existing contact records
   c. Any e-mail program
   d. All of the above

Fill in the Blank

Complete the following sentences by writing the correct word or words in the blanks provided.

1. You can _____ a Contact Group to share it with someone else.
2. You can add explanatory information about a Contact Group on the _____ page of the contact record.
3. The default view in the Contacts folder is the _____ view.
4. When sending a message to a Contact Group, you can see which individuals will receive the message by clicking the _____ in the *To* field.
5. If you try to add a contact that already exists in your Contacts folder, Outlook detects a(n) _____.
6. Providing false information in a message header is called _____.
7. A(n) _____ is a group of individual contacts saved together as a single contact record.
8. You can add or delete individuals in a Contact Group using the _____ page.
9. Like documents and files, contact information can be sent as a(n) _____.
10. A(n) _____ is a collection of information about a person or company.

Project 6-1: Create Contacts from Scratch

Gabe Mares recently started a new job at Tailspin Toys. As part of the training program, he will be traveling to different divisions to examine their procedures. At his first stop in Pittsburgh, PA, Gabe collected contact information for the team leader.

GET READY. LAUNCH Outlook if it is not already running.

1. Click the Contacts button in the Navigation Pane to display the Contacts window.
2. Click New on the Standard toolbar. The Untitled—Contact window is displayed.
3. In the *Full Name* field, key Mandar Samant and press Tab.
4. In the *Company* field, key Tailspin Toys and press Tab.
5. In the *Job Title* field, key Software Development Team Lead and press Tab.
6. Click the *E-mail* field. Key Mandar@tailspintoys.com and press Tab.
7. In the *Web Page Address* field, key www.tailspintoys.com.
8. Below the Phone Numbers heading, click the *Business* field. Key 4125551117. Press Tab.
9. Below the Addresses heading, click the *Business* field. Key 4567 Broadway. Press Enter. Key Pittsburgh, PA 14202. Press Tab.
10. In the Actions group on the Ribbon, click the Save & Close button.

LEAVE Outlook open for the next project.

Project 6-2: Create a Contact from a Contact at the Same Company

While Gabe was in Pittsburgh, he interviewed a software developer in Mandar Samant's team. Although Gabe doesn't usually contact developers directly, he wants to save her contact information in case an opening occurs as a team leader.

GET READY. LAUNCH Outlook if it is not already running.

1. If necessary, click the Contacts button in the Navigation Pane to display the Contacts window.
2. Double-click the Mandar Samant contact. The Contact window is displayed.
3. In the Actions group on the Ribbon, click the Save & New arrow. In the dropdown list of options, click New Contact from Same Company.
4. Click in the *Full Name* field if necessary. Key Jamie Reding and press Tab.
5. In the *Job title* field, key Software Developer and press Tab.
6. In the *E-mail* field, key Jamie@tailspintoys.com and press Tab.
7. In the *Notes* field, key Potential team lead.
8. In the Actions group on the Ribbon, click the Save & Close button.
9. **CLOSE** the Mandar Samant contact record without saving changes.

LEAVE Outlook open for the next project.

Project 6-3: Modify Contact Information

Two months later, Jamie Reding was promoted to a team leader in the Pittsburgh office. Gabe modified her contact information.

GET READY. LAUNCH Outlook if it is not already running.

1. If necessary, click the Contacts button in the Navigation Pane to display the Contacts window.

2. Double-click the Jamie Reding contact. The Contact window is displayed.

3. Click the *Job title* field. Change her title to Software Development Team Lead and press Tab.

4. Click the *Notes* field. Change the text to Monitor her progress.

5. In the Actions group on the Ribbon, click the Save & Close button.

LEAVE Outlook open for the next project.

Project 6-4: Send a Contact as an Attachment

Gabe's manager asked for information about the team leader for a new project. Gabe sends Jamie's contact record.

GET READY. LAUNCH Outlook if it is not already running.

1. If necessary, click the Contacts button in the Navigation Pane to display the Contacts window.

2. Double-click the Jamie Reding contact. The Contact window is displayed.

3. In Actions group on the Ribbon, click the Forward button. Select the As an Outlook Contact option. If a message is displayed stating that you must save the original item, click OK to continue.

4. Click the To button. In the *Select Names: Contacts* window, click your contact record. Click the To button. Click OK.

5. Click in the message area. Key The contact information you requested is attached.

6. Click the Send button.

7. **CLOSE** Jamie Reding's contact record without saving changes.

LEAVE Outlook open for the next project.

Mastery Assessment

Project 6-5: Create a Contact Group

Gabe sends several messages to the team leaders each day. To simplify the task, Gabe creates a Contact Group.

GET READY. LAUNCH Outlook if it is not already running.

1. If necessary, click the Contacts button in the Navigation Pane to display the Contacts window.

2. On the Home tab, click the New Contact Group button.

3. In the Members group on the Ribbon, click the Add Members button and select From Outlook Contacts.

4. Add all the Tailspin Toys employees to the *Members* field, including Gabe, and click OK.

5. Name the Contact Group Tailspin Team Leaders.

6. Click the Save & Close button.

LEAVE Outlook open for the next project.

Project 6-6: Modify a Contact Group

Gabe was not surprised to realize that the Tailspin Team Leaders Contact Group needs to be changed. Gabe needs to remove himself from the Contact Group and add Diane Tibbott. Diane just accepted the position of Software Development Team Lead for Tailspin Toys. She will work in the Nashville office with Gabe.

GET READY. LAUNCH Outlook if it is not already running.

1. If necessary, click the Contacts button in the Navigation Pane to display the Contacts window.

2. Use Gabe's contact record to create a new contact record from the same company for Diane Tibbott. Use the following information.

   Full Name   Diane Tibbott

   Job title   Software Development Team Lead

   E-mail   Diane

3. Delete Diane Tibbott's outdated contact record from Wingtip Toys.

4. Open the Tailspin Team Leaders contact record.

5. Click Gabe Mares in the list of members and click the Remove Member button.

6. Click the Add Members button. In the Select Members: Contacts window, add Diane Tibbott to the *Members* field and click OK.

7. SAVE the changes to the Contact Group.

CLOSE Outlook.

INTERNET READY

Looking for a new job with better pay, the right amount of travel, better hours, and a larger office? Use the Internet. Research some companies that interest you. Create contact records for the Human Resources offices in those companies.

LESSON SKILL MATRIX

Skills	Exam Objective	Objective Number
Using Electronic Business Cards	Modify a default business card. Forward a contact. Manage signatures.	4.1.1 4.1.2 3.4.1
Finding Contact Information	Use the People Pane.	1.3.4
Creating a Secondary Address Book		
Printing Contacts and Multiple Contacts	Print multiple contact records.	1.5.4

KEY TERMS

- **address book**
- **custom Search Folder**
- **electronic business cards**
- **import**
- **secondary address book**
- **virtual folder**

The marketing department at Tailspin Toys is holding a contest that is open to all employees. To compete, employees must design an electronic business card. Gabe Mares, the Software Development Manager, wasn't planning to enter the contest. Nevertheless, he had an idea for an electronic business card that he couldn't resist. He thumbed through the Tailspin Toys catalog until he found the perfect picture for his design. After all, who can resist a teddy bear? Outlook is an ideal tool for customizing a business card. Outlook's Edit Business Card window is specifically designed to help you design a custom business card. All you need to do is determine what information you want to include and Outlook's built-in business card template makes it fit. In this lesson, you'll customize a business card and use it as a digital signature. You'll also practice searching for contacts and create a second address book.

SOFTWARE ORIENTATION

Microsoft Outlook's Edit Business Card Window

The default view in the Contacts window is the Business Card view, in which Outlook displays each of your contacts as a business card. By default, the text appears to the right of a wide, gray bar that borders the left side of the card, as shown in Figure 7-1.

Figure 7-1

Outlook's Edit Business Card window

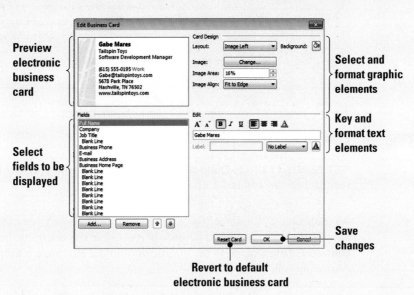

Use the Edit Business Card window to create an electronic business card that fits your company image. Refer to Figure 7-1 as you complete the following exercises.

USING ELECTRONIC BUSINESS CARDS

Electronic business cards are the digital version of paper business cards. They can be sent as attachments, used as signatures, and used to create a contact record. Because the default view in the Contacts window displays the electronic business cards, it is important to design an electronic business card that is memorable and easy to find when several electronic business cards are displayed on the screen. In this section, you'll edit a default business card by adding an image to it, send it to a coworker, and use it as a digital signature.

Editing an Electronic Business Card

The Edit Business Card window has four separate areas, as identified in Table 7-1. The four areas work together to provide a flexible tool that can create an amazing variety of customized business cards.

In this exercise, you'll customize the default Outlook contact record to create a unique electronic business card that is just as eye-catching as a paper business card.

Table 7-1

Edit Business Card window

Area	Description
Preview	View the effects of the changes you make.
Fields	Identify the fields you want to display on the electronic business card. Use the Add button to insert a new field. Select a field in the list and click the Remove button to delete a field. To move a field up or down on the card, select the field and click the Move Field Up (Up arrow) button or the Move Field Down (Down arrow) button.
Card Design	Insert and position a graphic or select a background color for the card. Position the image and define the amount of the card that can be used for the graphic. Although you can edit graphics in Outlook 2010, you cannot edit graphics in the Edit Business Card window.
Edit	Key the value to be displayed in the field. Limited text formatting options are available.

STEP BY STEP   **Edit an Electronic Business Card**

GET READY. LAUNCH Outlook if it is not already running. Use the Gabe Mares contact record that you created in Lesson 6.

Take Note   An electronic business card is created automatically when you create a contact. It is basically another view of the contact record. If you delete the electronic business card, you delete the contact. Changes made to the information on the electronic business card are changed for the contact as well.

1. If necessary, click the Contacts button in the Navigation Pane to display the Contacts window. Minimize the To-Do Bar to provide additional room to display your contact records.
2. Double-click the Gabe Mares contact. The Gabe Mares—Contact window is displayed.

Troubleshooting   The e-mail addresses provided in these exercises belong to unused domains owned by Microsoft. When you send a message to these addresses, you will receive an error message stating that the message could not be delivered. Delete the error messages when they arrive.

3. In the Options group on the Ribbon, click the Business Card button. The Edit Business Card window is displayed, as shown in Figure 7-1.

4. In the Card Design area in the upper right of the window, verify that Image Left is selected in the *Layout* field and Fit to Edge is selected in the *Image Align* field. This defines the position of the graphic. Currently, the graphic is the default gray bar.

@ The *Bear Side* file is available on the book companion website or in WileyPLUS.

5. Click the Change button. The Add Card Picture dialog box is displayed. Navigate to the data files for this lesson. Click the *Bear Side.jpg* image file and click OK. The bear image is added to the card preview.

6. In the Card Design area, click the *Image Area* field. Change the value to 25%. In the card preview, the image area widens to 25% of the card's width.

7. In the Card Design area, click the Image Align field. In the dropdown list, click Bottom Center. In the card preview, the image is resized and repositioned to appear at the bottom of the card.

8. In the Card Design area, click the Image Align field. In the dropdown list, click Fit to Edge. In the card preview, the image is resized and placed in its original position.

9. In the Fields area, click Business Home Page in the list of fields. Click the Add button. In the dropdown menu, point to Internet Address and then click IM Address. IM Address is added to the list of fields. The *IM Address* field is used for an instant messaging address.

10. With IM Address selected in the list of fields, click the empty field in the Edit area. Key GabeTailspinToys, as shown in Figure 7-2.

Figure 7-2

Modified Edit Business Card window

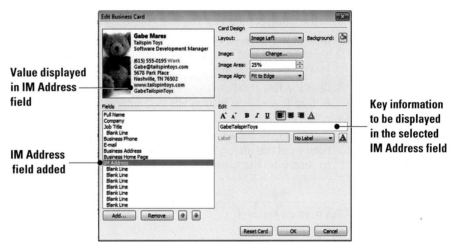

Value displayed in IM Address field

IM Address field added

Key information to be displayed in the selected IM Address field

11. Click OK. The Edit Business Card window is closed. Click the Save & Close button to return to the Contacts window. Gabe's business card is displayed, as shown in Figure 7-3.

Figure 7-3

Modified business card

CERTIFICATION
READY   4.1.1

How do you edit an electronic business card?

PAUSE. LEAVE the Outlook Message window open to use in the next exercise.

Sending an Electronic Business Card

Electronic business cards can be shared with others by simply inserting one or more business cards in a message and clicking the Send button. Users of other e-mail applications can get the contact information from the .vcf files that Outlook automatically creates and attaches to the message when you insert the electronic business cards. In this exercise, you'll insert electronic business cards into an e-mail message and send them along with their .vcf file attachments to a colleague.

STEP BY STEP   **Send an Electronic Business Card**

USE the Gabe Mares contact record.

1. Click the Mail button in the Navigation Pane to display the Mail folder.
2. Click the New E-mail button on the Home tab. The Message window is displayed. By default, the Message tab is selected.

Take Note   Throughout this chapter you will see information that appears in black text within brackets, such as [Press Enter] or [your e-mail address]. The information contained in the brackets is intended to be directions for you rather than something you actually type word for word. It will instruct you to perform an action or substitute text. Do **not** type the actual text that appears within brackets.

3. In the *To* field key [your e-mail address].
4. In the *Subject* field key Business cards attached.
5. Click in the message area. Key I attached the electronic business cards you requested. Press Enter twice to add a bit of space between your text and the business card that you're about to attach.
6. Click the Insert tab. In the Include group, click the Insert Business Card button. A dropdown list is displayed.
7. Click Other Business Cards in the dropdown list. The Insert Business Card window is displayed, as shown in Figure 7-4. Click the Gabe Mares contact. A Preview pane at the bottom of the dialog box shows you an image of the business card you have chosen to send with the message.

Figure 7-4

Insert Business Card window

Click to attach business cards to a message

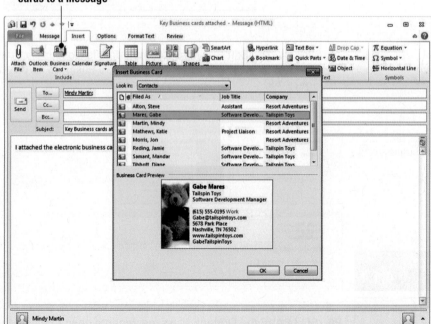

Another Way
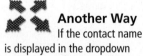
If the contact name is displayed in the dropdown list, you can click the name to insert the electronic business card.

8. With the contact still selected, press Ctrl. This allows you to select multiple contacts. Click the Diane Tibbott contact. Click OK. The electronic business cards are inserted into the message. In the *Attached* field, the contact records are attached as .vcf files, as shown in Figure 7-5.

Figure 7-5

Electronic business cards inserted into a message

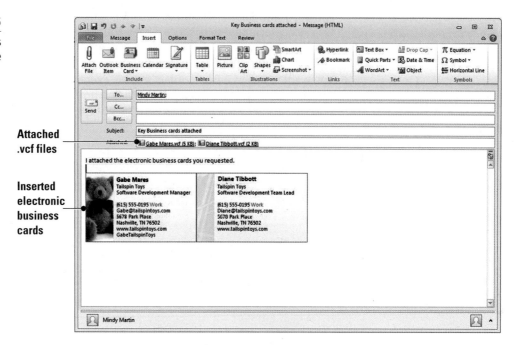

Attached .vcf files

Inserted electronic business cards

9. Click the Send button.

PAUSE. LEAVE Outlook open to use in the next exercise.

Creating a Contact from an Electronic Business Card

When you receive an electronic business card, Outlook allows you to add the contact record to your Contacts list either by using the .vcf file or by right-clicking on the business card itself. All the information on the electronic business card and the card's appearance are saved in your Contacts list. In this exercise, you'll create a contact record based on an electronic business card attached to a received e-mail message.

 Ref   You can find more information on other methods of creating contacts in Lesson 6.

STEP BY STEP   **Create a Contact from an Electronic Business Card**

USE the message you sent in the previous exercise.

1. Click the Mail button in the Navigation Pane to display the mailbox.
2. If the *Business cards attached* message has not arrived yet, click the Send/Receive All Folders button in the Send/Receive group of the Home tab.
3. Click the Key Business cards attached message in the message list to display it in the Reading Pane. The electronic business cards are displayed in the message body.

 Troubleshooting   If the Reading Pane is not visible, click the Reading Pane button in the Layout group of the View tab and select Right.

4. Right-click the Gabe Mares electronic business card in the message body. Click the Add to Outlook Contacts option in the shortcut menu. A Gabe Mares—Contact window is displayed that contains the information from the electronic business card, including the preview image of the card.

5. Click the Save & Close button in the Actions group on the Ribbon. Because you received this contact information at the same e-mail address as was used to send the contact information, the contact record is already in your Contacts window. Therefore, Outlook detects that this is a duplicate contact, and the Duplicate Contact Detected window is displayed. If the contact record was not a duplicate, the contact would be saved with no further action needed.

6. You want to create a new contact for this exercise, so select the Add new contact option at the top of the window. The dialog box changes to show you the information that will be saved in the new contact record, as shown in Figure 7-6.

Figure 7-6

Duplicate Contact Detected window   **Add new contact**

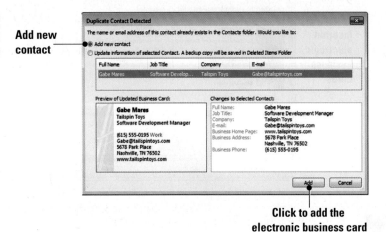

Click to add the electronic business card

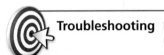 **Troubleshooting**   Normally, when you receive a duplicate record you will use the received information to update the contact in your *Contacts* folder. This exercise simply gives you the scenario for adding a new contact record. You can compare the information in your contact record with the information sent to you in the message. Before you update contact information, be sure that the new data is accurate.

7. Click the Add button at the bottom of the window. The Duplicate Contact Detected window is closed, the contact record is created, and you are returned to the Mail folder.

8. Click the Contacts button in the Navigation Pane to display the Contacts window. Now, you have the original Gabe Mares contact record and the Gabe Mares contact record you created from the electronic business card in the message.

9. In the Contacts window, click the first Gabe Mares contact record and click the Delete button in Home tab. The contact record is moved to the Deleted Items folder. It will not be removed from your computer until the Deleted Items folder is emptied.

PAUSE. LEAVE Outlook open to use in the next exercise.

Using an Electronic Business Card in a Signature

A signature can be added automatically in every message you send. Include your electronic business card in your signature to provide an easy way for the recipient to add the contact to the contacts window. In this exercise, you'll change settings to set an electronic business card as a default digital signature and send an e-mail to test it.

STEP BY STEP | **Use an Electronic Business Card in a Signature**

USE the Gabe Mares electronic business card you modified in a previous exercise.

1. Click the Mail button in the Navigation Pane to display the mailbox.

 Ref

You can find more information on creating signatures in Lesson 2.

2. Click the New E-mail button on the Home tab to open the Message window with the Message tab selected.

3. Click the Signature button in the Include group on the Ribbon. In the dropdown list, click Signatures. The Signatures and Stationery window is displayed.

4. Click the New button to create a new signature. The New Signature dialog box is displayed.

5. To name the new signature, key Gabe into the *Type a name for this signature* field. Click OK. The New Signature dialog box is closed, and Gabe is highlighted in the *Select signature to edit* list box.

6. Click in the empty Edit signature box. Key the following text, pressing Enter to start each new line.

Gabe Mares

Software Development Manager

Tailspin Toys

Gabe@tailspintoys.com

Take Note | Outlook automatically recognizes the e-mail address as a link and formats it as a hyperlink.

7. Click the Business Card button above the Edit Signature box. The Insert Business Card window is displayed (refer to Figure 7-4).

8. Click the Gabe Mares contact record and click OK. The electronic business card is inserted into the signature, as shown in Figure 7-7.

Figure 7-7

Signature containing an electronic business card

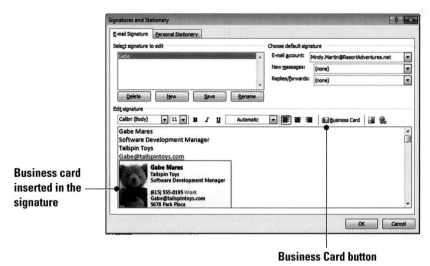

Business card inserted in the signature

Business Card button

9. Click OK to accept your changes and close the Signatures and Stationery window.

10. In the Message window, key [your e-mail address] in the *To* field.

11. In the *Subject* field, key New Signature Test.

12. In the message body, key Testing new signature and press Enter.

13. In the Include group on the Ribbon, click the Signature button and then click Gabe in the dropdown list of signatures that appears. The signature is inserted into the message, as shown in Figure 7-8.

Figure 7-8

Message containing Gabe's signature

Attachment containing information in the business card added automatically

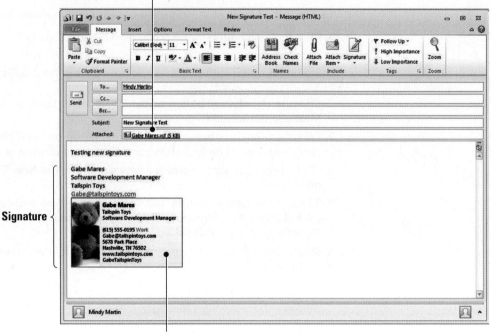

Signature

Electronic business card included in the signature

14. Click the Send button.

PAUSE. LEAVE Outlook open to use in the next exercise.

How do you use an electronic business card as an automatic signature in messages?

Recipients using other e-mail programs might not be able to view the electronic business card or save it as a contact record. However, almost all e-mail programs can read .vcf files. This is why Outlook automatically attaches a .vcf file containing the contact information to messages containing business cards.

Take Note   Remember that for added security some people avoid opening messages with attachments. You can delete the attachment before sending the message. Deleting the attachment doesn't remove the signature from the message, but prevents the recipient's spam filter from deleting your message simply because it has an attachment.

FINDING CONTACT INFORMATION

The Bottom Line   Outlook's search features can help you search your stored contacts for information, so you don't have to rely on your memory. You can use Outlook's Instant Search tool to conduct a quick search, or you can create a custom Search Folder to conduct more detailed searches for contact information as well as other Outlook items, such as messages and Calendar events, related to specific contacts. In this section, you'll use Outlook's search tools to locate messages associated with a contact.

Searching for Contacts

NEW to Office 2010   Outlook 2010 has enhanced the search tools by adding a separate Search Tools tab that contains a variety of tools for filtering the search results. Outlook's improved search and filter tools allow you to use any information in a contact record as the search parameter. For example, you can search for contacts containing text such as Diane, Pittsburgh, or Lead. As you begin keying text into the Instant Search box, Outlook starts searching your contacts list and begins populating the results list with matching contacts as they are found. In this exercise, you'll use Instant Search to find a contact.

STEP BY STEP   **Search for Contacts**

GET READY. LAUNCH Outlook if it is not already running. The contacts used in this
exercise were created in Lesson 6.

1. Click the Contacts button in the Navigation Pane to display the Contacts window.

2. Click in the Instant Search box. The new Search Tools tab appears in the Ribbon.

3. In the Instant Search box, key toy. As you key the search text, Outlook displays all the
   contacts that contain the text *toy* in any of their fields, as shown in Figure 7-9.

Figure 7-9

Search for contacts

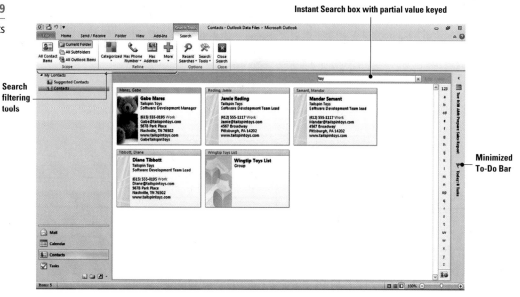

4. Click the More button in the Refine group of the Search Tools tab. A menu of additional
   search fields is displayed, as shown in Figure 7-10.

Figure 7-10

The More Search Criteria
dropdown list

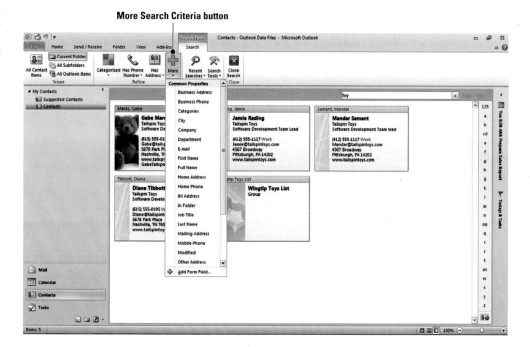

5. Select Business Address from the list. In the *Business Address* field, key Nashville. Outlook refines the results list to show only the two contacts that both contain the word toy and are located in Nashville.

6. Click the Has Address button to open a list of additional filters. Click IM Address. Outlook refines the search results again to find the only one of the contacts that meets the previous search parameters and has an IM address listed, as shown in Figure 7-11.

Figure 7-11

Filtered results list

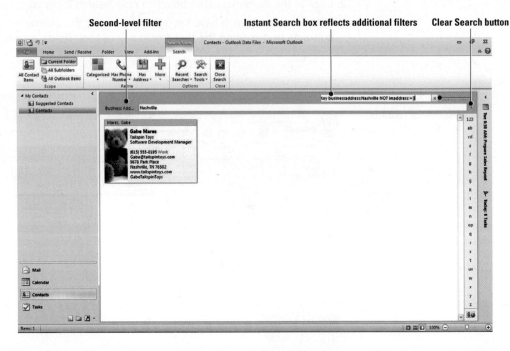

7. Click the Clear Search button next to the Business Address field. Click the Clear Search button next to the original Instant Search box.

PAUSE. LEAVE Outlook open to use in the next exercise.

Your Contacts window currently contains very few contacts. As you add contacts, you can narrow the search results by using the filters on the Search Tools tab.

Searching for Items Related to a Contact

Occasionally, you will want to find all Outlook items related to a contact. For example, you might want to see all the meetings you've had with a sales associate or perhaps all the messages from your boss. Outlook has several easy methods to perform this kind of search. In this exercise, you'll use Outlook's new Instant Search and Filter tool and the People Pane to locate all the Outlook items related to a contact.

STEP BY STEP **Search for Items Related to a Contact**

GET READY. LAUNCH Outlook if it is not already running. The contacts used in this exercise were created in Lesson 6.

1. Click the Contacts button in the Navigation Pane to display the Contacts window. Minimize the To Do Bar.

2. In the Instant Search box, key gabe. Gabe's contact record is displayed.

3. Click the All Outlook Items button in the Scope group of the Search Tools tab. Outlook displays the matching Outlook items. The Gabe Mares contact record and the related messages are displayed, as shown in Figure 7-12.

Figure 7-12

Outlook items related to Gabe

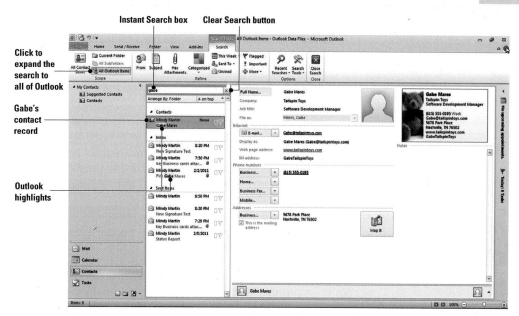

Take Note   Your search results might vary if you deleted any messages sent or received in previous lessons.

4. Click the FW: Gabe Mares message in the results list. Notice that Outlook highlights the term *gabe* wherever it appears in the results list and in the Reading Pane, as shown in Figure 7-13.

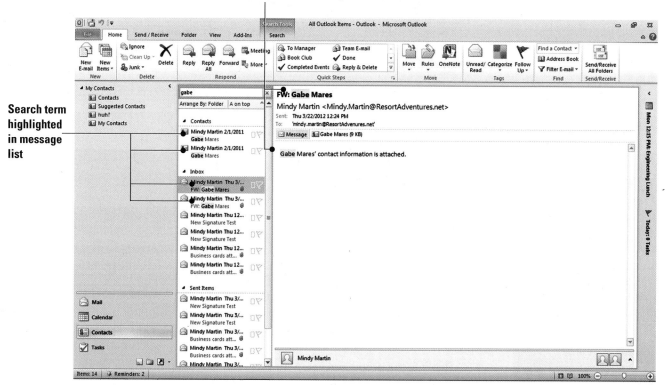

Figure 7-13

Search term is highlighted in the results

5. Click the Clear Search button to clear the search criterion.

6. Click the Contacts button in the Navigation Pane to display the Contacts window. Double-click on Mindy Martin's contact record. Your contact record window is displayed with the People Pane at the bottom.

7. If necessary, click the expand arrow on the minimized People Pane to return it to default view.

8. Click the Mail tab in the People Pane. The results box displays all the messages that you have sent to yourself.

9. Scroll back through the e-mails to locate the FW: Jamie Reding message that you sent to yourself in Lesson 6. Notice that below the FW: Jamie Reding message, you can see the actual name of attachment.

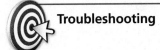 **Troubleshooting** If you do not see this message in your People Pane, choose any other message for this exercise. If not many items are listed it means that either you have Instant Search turned off your computer or that Instant Search has not had an opportunity to finish indexing your account. Because it runs in the background and only when you're logged into your Windows profile, it can take a few days to initially create the search index. Once the initial index is complete, it does a great job of updating.

10. Click the gray expand arrow to the right of the FW: Jamie Reding message line. A dropdown list of actions is displayed, as shown in Figure 7-14. The actions list allows you to perform most mail management actions without having to go to the original message.

Figure 7-14

Finding information related to a contact in the People Pane

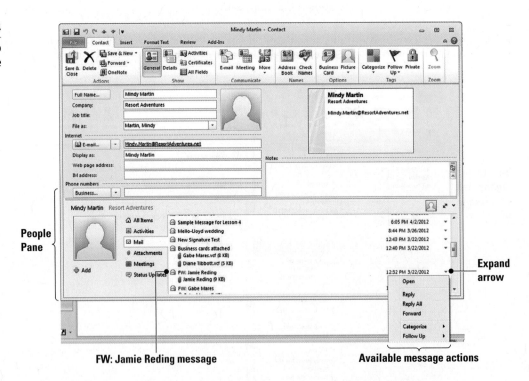

FW: Jamie Reding message

Available message actions

11. Point to Follow Up in the dropdown list. A fly-out list of the Follow Up options appears.

12. Click Reply in the dropdown list. A new RE: Jamie Reding message window is displayed showing the content of the original message.

13. Close the message window without saving or sending. Close your contact record window as well.

PAUSE. LEAVE Outlook open to use in the next exercise.

CERTIFICATION READY 1.3.4

How can you use the People Pane to locate contacts?

Creating a Custom Search Folder

Instant Search quickly finds Outlook items, but it requires you to key the search text every time you want to perform a search. That's all well and good when you need to find a specific item for a one-time need. But there are many times in business where you might need to perform the same search more than once. For example, as an assistant sales manager you might need to submit a weekly status report to your manager that gives her an update on each salesman's progress. Each week you need to search through your messages to locate the progress reports from each of the five salesmen. You can certainly use the Instant Search feature to locate the needed information, but why set up a search each week when you can set it up once and save your search parameters?

In Outlook 2010, **custom Search Folders** are essentially searches saved in a virtual folder. When you create the custom Search Folder with your specific search parameters, Outlook adds a virtual folder to your Navigation Pane under the Search Folders folder. Whenever you click one of these **virtual folders**, you can see all the items that meet the search parameters you specified. Although your search results look like items in a normal Outlook mail folder, the items are actually still stored in their original location (you're seeing a link to the original location). Using virtual folders gives you the convenience of working with items as you would in any folder and the ability to keep the original item in a more appropriate folder based on your mailbox organization. In this exercise, you'll create a custom Search Folder.

STEP BY STEP	**Create a Custom Search Folder**

GET READY. LAUNCH Outlook if it is not already running. The contacts used in this exercise were created in Lesson 6.

1. Click the Mail button in the Navigation Pane to display the mailbox and minimize the To Do Bar.

2. On the Folder tab, click the New Search Folder button to display the New Search Folder dialog box. Scroll to the bottom of the *Select a Search folder* list and click Create a custom Search Folder, as shown in Figure 7-15.

Figure 7-15

New Search Folder window

 Ref

You can learn more about using the built-in Search Folders in Lesson 3.

3. Click the Choose button to display the Custom Search Folder window shown in Figure 7-16.

Figure 7-16

Custom Search Folder window

Key a name for the new Search Folder

Click to specify
search criteria

4. In the *Name* field, key **Messages about Jamie**. When naming a Search Folder, create a name that reflects the search criteria.

5. Click the **Criteria** button to display the Search Folder Criteria window shown in Figure 7-17.

Figure 7-17

Search Folder Criteria window

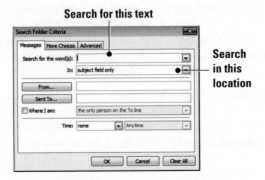

Search for this text

Search in this location

6. In the *Search for the word(s)* field, key **Jamie**. In the *In* field, select **subject field and message body** from the dropdown list. Click **OK** in each window to return to the Mail folder. The new Search Folder and the search results are automatically displayed, as shown in Figure 7-18.

View search result

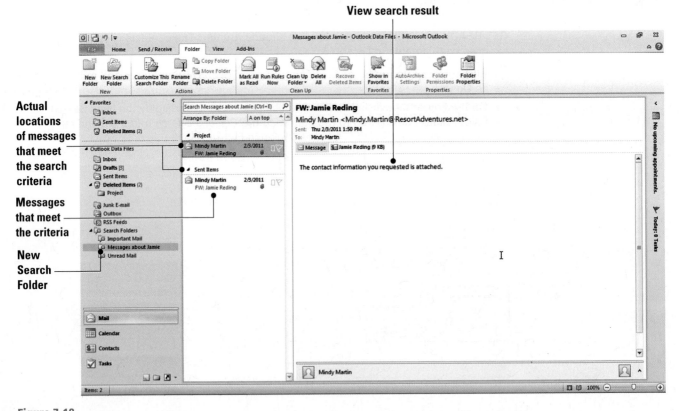

Actual locations of messages that meet the search criteria

Messages that meet the criteria

New Search Folder

Figure 7-18

Search Folder created

PAUSE. LEAVE Outlook open to use in the next exercise.

Take Note   Search Folders are virtual folders. You can delete a Search Folder without deleting the displayed messages because the messages are actually located in other folders. However, because Search Folders let you work with messages as if it were a real folder, if you delete a message within a Search Folder, the original message is really moved into the Deleted Items folder.

CREATING A SECONDARY ADDRESS BOOK

The Bottom Line

Every Contacts folder has its own Outlook **address book** that stores contact information, such as names and e-mail addresses. To keep your personal contacts separate from your business contacts, you can create an additional Contacts folder that has its own address book. For example, it is usually a good idea to keep your personal contacts in a **secondary address book** to keep them separate from the main Contacts list. A secondary address book has all the functionality of the familiar *Contacts* folder. This helps eliminate errors that can occur if you think you're sending a personal e-mail to a friend named Cathy, but you actually send the message to Cathy Reynolds, Regional Sales Manager.

Take Note

Previous versions of Outlook allowed you to create a private address book by creating an Outlook file with the .pab extension. Because the contacts window has more functionality and features than the private address book, Outlook 2010 does not allow you to create or use a personal address book. Instead, you can create a secondary address book.

WileyPLUS Extra! features an online tutorial of this task.

Creating a Secondary Address Book for Personal Contacts

Each Outlook Contacts folder has an associated Outlook address book. In this exercise, you will create a new Contacts folder to hold your secondary address book for personal contacts.

STEP BY STEP   **Create a Secondary Address Book for Personal Contacts**

GET READY. LAUNCH Outlook if it is not already running.

1. Click the Contacts button in the Navigation Pane to display the Contacts window.
2. On the Folders tab, click New Folder in the New group. The Create New Folder window is displayed.
3. In the *Name* field, key Personal Contacts. Because you selected the *Contacts* folder before creating a new folder, Contact Items is already displayed in the *Folder contains* field and the Contacts folder is selected in the *Select where to place the folder* list.
4. Click OK. The Personal Contacts folder is created. The My Contacts heading now contains the following folders: *Contacts, Suggested Contacts,* and the new *Personal Contacts* folders, as shown in Figure 7-19.

Figure 7-19

Personal Contacts folder created

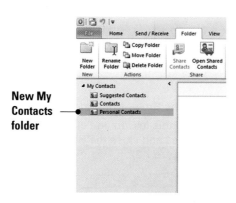

New My Contacts folder

5. Click the Personal Contacts folder in the Folder List. The Personal Contacts window is blank because you don't have any contacts for this folder yet.

PAUSE. LEAVE Outlook open to use in the next exercise.

Importing a Secondary Address Book from a File

Manually keying a large number of contacts can be tedious. It's much easier to import the contact information. When you **import** a file, you bring information into a file from an external source. Most e-mail programs offer the option of exporting your contacts. To bring them into Outlook, you need to be sure you export them into the right file type: .csv (comma-separated value), .txt (tab-delimited text), or .xls (Microsoft Excel 97-2003). In this exercise, you import contact information from a Microsoft Excel file.

Import a Secondary Address Book from a File

USE the My Contacts folder you created in the previous exercise.

1. Click the File tab to open the Backstage view.

2. Click Open in the navigation pane. Click the Import option. The Import and Export Wizard is displayed, as shown in Figure 7-20. Click Import from another program or file, if necessary, in the list of available actions.

Figure 7-20

Import and Export Wizard

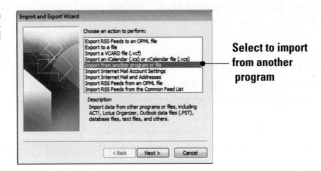

Select to import from another program

3. Click the Next button. In the *Select file type to import from* list box, click Microsoft Excel 97-2003 in the list of available import file types, as shown in Figure 7-21.

Figure 7-21

The Select file type to import from page of the Import and Export window

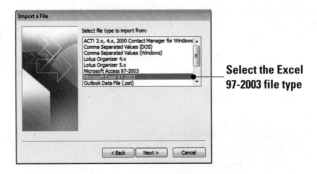

Select the Excel 97-2003 file type

@ The *Source Personal Contacts* file is available on the book companion website or in WileyPLUS.

4. Click the Next button. Click the Browse button. The Browse window is displayed.

5. Navigate to the data files for this lesson and click the *Source Personal Contacts* file. Click OK to apply your choices and close the Browse window to return to the Import a File window, as shown in Figure 7-22.

Figure 7-22

The File to import page of the Import and Export window

Name and location of the source file

6. Back at the Import a File window, click the Next button. *The Select destination folder* list is displayed.

7. Verify that Personal Contacts is selected as the destination folder, as shown in Figure 7-23.

Figure 7-23

The Select destination folder page of the Import and Export window

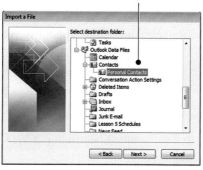

Select the location for the contacts

8. Click the Next button. Click the Finish button. The contacts are imported and displayed in the Personal Contacts folder.

PAUSE. LEAVE Outlook open to use in the next exercise.

 Troubleshooting If you plan to import it using an Excel file, make sure that the file contains only one worksheet and that the area containing the contact data is defined as a range: Contacts.

By default, when you key an address in the *To, Cc,* or *Bcc* field in a new message, the address book displays potential matches from the default *Contacts* folder. If the name is a match, you can click the displayed name to fill the address field.

Alternatively, you click the *To, Cc, Bcc,* or *Address Book* buttons, Outlook displays the Select Names: Contacts window. To work with a different address book, click the *Address Book* down arrow and select the address book you want, as shown in Figure 7-24.

Figure 7-24

The Select Names: Contacts window

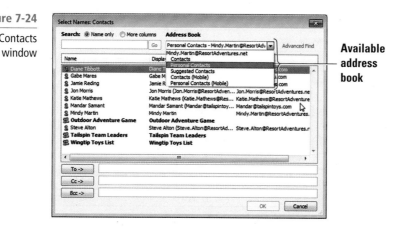

Available address book

If you have contacts stored in social networking sites like LinkedIn or Facebook, you can use Outlook's new Social Connector to sync Outlook to your external sites. This gives you access to the contact information for each of your connections and allows you to keep up with their status updates.

Not only is importing contact information much easier than keying the data into the fields, it also avoids keying errors. One typographical error could result in calling a complete stranger instead of Great-Grandma Mabel on her birthday.

PRINTING CONTACTS AND MULTIPLE CONTACTS

The Bottom Line

In Outlook 2010 it is easy to print a single contact or an entire address book. Outlook can print contacts in five different formats. To print a single contact, select Memo Style. For printing multiple contacts, you can print a list of contact cards, a traditional address book, or a phone listing. You can control the printing settings in Backstage view.

Printing Contacts

In this exercise, you will print a single contact and a phone directory.

STEP BY STEP   **Print Contacts**

GET READY. LAUNCH Outlook if it is not already running.

1. If necessary, select the Jo Berry contact record in the My Contacts folder.
2. Click File to open Backstage view.
3. Click Print in the navigation pane to open the Print Settings page. Notice that the preview pane displays all of the contacts in the My Contacts address book in the Card Style.
4. Click Memo Style. Outlook displays the Jo Berry contact record in the Preview pane, as shown in Figure 7-25. Click Print if you want to print the single contact record using the default printer.

Click to print using the default settings

Click to print a single contact record

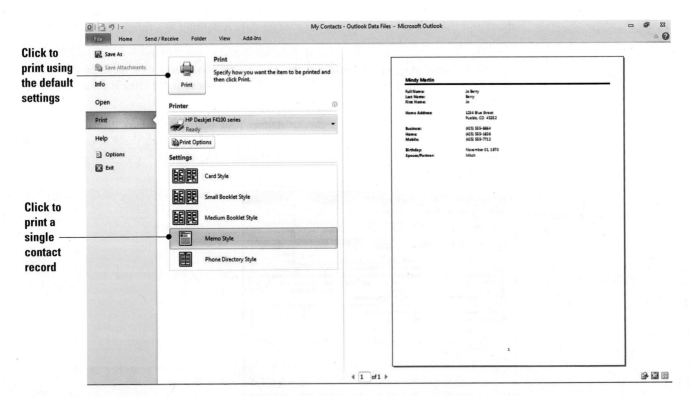

Figure 7-25

A Memo Style contact record

5. Click Phone Directory Style. Outlook displays a preview of the entire phone directory for the My Contacts, as shown in Figure 7-26. Click Print if you want to print a phone directory for all of the contacts in the selected folder using the default printer.

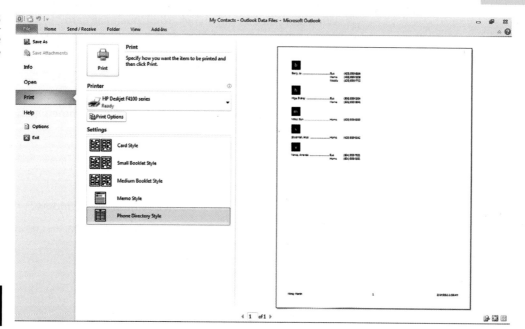

Figure 7-26

The My Contacts folder phone directory

CERTIFICATION
READY   1.5.4

How do you print multiple
contact records?

CLOSE Outlook.

SKILL SUMMARY

In This Lesson You Learned How To:	Exam Objective	Objective Number
Use electronic business cards.	Modify a default business card. Forward a contact. Manage signatures.	4.1.1 4.1.2 3.4.1
Find contact information.	Use the People Pane.	1.3.4
Create a secondary address book.		
Print contacts and multiple contacts.	Print multiple contact records.	1.5.4

Knowledge Assessment

Multiple Choice

Select the best response for the following statements.

1. Where can you store personal contacts in Outlook 2010?
   a. Search Folder
   b. Secondary address book
   c. Private address book
   d. Default address book

2. When is an electronic business card created?
   a. When the electronic business card is viewed
   b. When the electronic business card is modified
   c. When the contact record is created
   d. When the electronic business card is sent with a message

3. What can you do with an electronic business card?

    a. Create a contact record from it

    b. Include it in your signature

    c. Send it as an attachment

    d. All of the above

4. Which Outlook search feature displays results immediately?

    a. Instant Search

    b. Immediate Search

    c. Fast Find

    d. Search Folder

5. How many areas are in the Edit Business Card window?

    a. One

    b. Three

    c. Four

    d. Eight

6. Which folder is a virtual folder?

    a. Secondary Contacts folder

    b. Sent Items folder

    c. Search Folder

    d. Contacts folder

7. How many different styles can you use to print a single contact record?

    a. One

    b. Two

    c. Three

    d. Five

8. Why is a .vcf file automatically attached to a message containing an electronic business card?

    a. The .vcf file contains the graphic used in the electronic business card.

    b. Outlook 2010 requires the .vcf file to create a new contact.

    c. Users of other e-mail applications can use the .vcf file.

    d. The .vcf file contains your signature.

9. What is the default view in the Contacts window?

    a. Address Cards

    b. Phone

    c. Detailed Address Cards

    d. Business Cards

10. Which of the following is an easy way to enter contact information stored in another application?

    a. Key the data

    b. Send the data in an e-mail message

    c. Import

    d. All of the above

Fill in the Blank

Complete the following sentences by writing the correct word or words in the blanks provided.

1. A(n) _____ containing an electronic business card can be added automatically in every message you send.

2. _____ displays search results as they are identified.

3. _____ can contain an image to set them apart from other contact records.

4. The _____ can be used to contain information about personal contacts.

5. The _____ folder contains contact records.

6. You can _____ contact information from an external source.

7. A(n) _____ identifies items in other folders that meet specific criteria.

8. You can use the _____ button to add secondary search criteria.

9. Outlook items are not permanently stored in a(n) _____.

10. The _____ stores names and addresses.

Competency Assessment

Project 7-1: Edit an Electronic Business Card

Diane Tibbott was recently hired by Tailspin Toys. She decided to use a teddy-bear image to brighten up her electronic business card also.

GET READY. LAUNCH Outlook if it is not already running.

1. Display the Contacts window. Click the Contacts folder if necessary.

2. Double-click the Diane Tibbott contact. The Diane Tibbott—Contact window is displayed.

3. In the Options group on the Ribbon, click the Business Card button to display the Edit Business Card window.

@ The *Bear Background* file is available on the book companion website or in WileyPLUS.

4. In the Card Design area in the upper right of the window, select Background Image in the *Layout* field.

5. Click the Change button. The Add Card Picture dialog box is displayed. Navigate to the data files for this lesson. Click the *Bear Background* file and click OK. The bear image is added to the card preview.

6. In the Card Design area, click the Image Align field. Change the value to Fit to Edge.

7. Click Business Phone in the Fields list. Click the Add button. In the dropdown menu, point to Phone and then click Mobile Phone

8. With Mobile Phone selected in the list of fields, click the empty field in the Edit area. Key 6155550197. Click the No Label button and select Right. In the Label box, key Mobile.

9. Click OK to close the Edit Business Card window. Click the Save & Close button to return to the Contacts window.

LEAVE Outlook open for the next project.

Project 7-2: Send an Electronic Business Card

Diane Tibbott wants to stay in touch with her friends at Wingtip Toys. She decided to send her new electronic business card to her former supervisor.

GET READY. LAUNCH Outlook if it is not already running.

1. Display the Mail folder.

2. Click the New E-mail button on the Home tab.

3. Key Molly@wingtiptoys.com in the *To* field of the message window.

4. Key Let's keep in touch! in the *Subject* field

5. Click in the message area. Key the following message: I attached my new electronic business card. Write when you have time. Press Enter.

6. Click the Insert tab. In the Include group, click the Insert Business Card button.

7. Click Diane Tibbott in the dropdown list.

8. Click the Send button.

LEAVE Outlook open for the next project.

Project 7-3: Use an Electronic Business Card in a Signature

Management has decided that every message sent to clients must include an electronic business card. Rather than manually inserting the electronic business card into every message, Diane decided to create a signature containing her new electronic business card.

GET READY. LAUNCH Outlook if it is not already running.

1. Open a new Message window.
2. Click the Signature button on the Ribbon, and then click Signatures in the dropdown list.
3. In the Signatures and Stationery window, click the New button to display the New Signature dialog box.
4. Key Diane into the *Type a name for this signature* field. Click OK.
5. Click the empty Edit signature box. Key in the following:

   Diane Tibbott

   Software Development Team Lead

   Tailspin Toys

   Diane@tailspintoys.com

6. Click the Business Card button above the Edit Signature box to display the Insert Business Card window.
7. Insert Diane Tibbott's electronic business card into the signature.
8. Click OK to close the Signatures and Stationery window and return to the Message window.
9. On the Insert tab, click the Signature button, and then click Diane.
10. **CLOSE** the message without saving or sending it.

LEAVE Outlook open for the next project.

Project 7-4: Create a Custom Search Folder

Diane wants to monitor messages about the team's new software development project. The project has been nicknamed 007 for the fictional character James Bond. All messages about the project must contain "007" in the *Subject* field. Diane decided to create a custom Search Folder to collect messages about the project.

GET READY. LAUNCH Outlook if it is not already running.

1. Click the Mail button in the Navigation Pane to display the Mail folder.
2. From the Inbox, use the tools on the Folder tab to create a New Search Folder button.
3. Create a custom Search Folder called Project 007.
4. Set the Project 007 Search Folder criterion to be the word *007* in the subject field only.
5. Test the new Search Folder by creating a new message that contains the word *007* in the subject field. In the message body, key Testing Search Folder. Click the Send button.
6. After the message arrives, click the Project 007 folder to view its contents. It should contain the 007 message in the Sent Items folder and the 007 message in the Inbox.

LEAVE Outlook open for the next project.

Project 7-5: Create a Secondary Address Book

Diane works for a new company, but she wants to stay in touch with friends she made at Wingtip Toys. Diane decided to create a secondary address book before she imports personal contacts for her friends.

GET READY. LAUNCH Outlook if it is not already running.

1. Display the Contacts window.
2. Create a New Folder.
3. In the *Name* field, key Diane's Contacts. Click OK.

LEAVE Outlook open for the next project.

Project 7-6: Import a Secondary Address Book from a File

After creating the Diane's Contacts folder, Diane can import contact records for her friends at Wingtip Toys.

GET READY. LAUNCH Outlook if it is not already running.

1. Open the Backstage view and select Open in the navigation pane.
2. Click Import to open the Import and Export Wizard.
3. Follow the first two steps of the wizard to import the Microsoft Excel 97-2003 file *Source Diane's Contacts* from the data files for this lesson into the Diane's Contacts folder.
4. Open the Diane's Contacts folder to view the new contacts.
5. Use the Print page in Backstage view to preview of the Card Style.
6. Print the Diane's Contacts folder in Small Address Book style.

CLOSE Outlook.

@ The *Source Diane's Contacts* file is available on the book companion website or in WileyPLUS.

INTERNET READY

Microsoft provides templates for a wide variety of electronic business cards. Sophisticated, casual, fun, and serious designs are available. Go to www.Microsoft.com. Search for electronic business cards. Download a style that appeals to you. Modify the card and use it as your electronic business card.

Workplace *Ready*

USING SEARCH FOLDERS TO TRACK INFORMATION

Sallie Johnson is the hiring manager for Grey-Lawson General Hospital. Although they already have a staff of 250 people, they are in the process of adding on a pediatric specialties wing. This expansion means adding on 100 new employees in a short amount of time. In today's employment environment, most people submit resumes via e-mail or apply on the hospital's website. All of these resumes and applications go straight to her e-mail account. She has already created a rule that sends all e-mails that contains applications or resumes to a Candidates folder, so that they don't clutter up her Inbox.

To help her stay on top of each opening in this rapidly changing environment, Sallie utilizes custom Search Folders. Every time Sallie posts a new job opening, she creates a custom Search Folder. She sets up each Search Folder to look for the specific job opening code in either the subject or body of the message.

At the end of the posting period, she can simply click the Search Folder for the job opening she wants to fill. The virtual folder shows her all the job candidates and any correspondence related to the opening.

Circling Back

Kim Ralls was promoted to Shift Supervisor and transferred to the downtown office at City Power & Light. Although Kim was transferred, her computer and other equipment did not move with her. She needs to set up Outlook 2010 with new rules and contacts to help her manage her new responsibilities. She also needs to update her electronic business card to display her new title and contact information.

Project 1:   Create Mail and Contacts Folders and Import Contacts

Kim starts the process of customizing Outlook 2010 to meet her needs by creating new folders. One mail folder will contain messages about requests for new service. A contact folder will contain Kim's CP & L contacts and a second folder will contain her secondary address book.

Take Note   The folders and contacts you create in this project will be used in Projects 2 and 3.

GET READY. LAUNCH Outlook if it is not already running.

1. Click the Folder tab. In the New group, click the New Folder button. The Create New Folder dialog box is displayed.

2. In the *Name* field, key New Service to identify the new folder. Verify that Mail and Post Items is selected in the *Folder contains* field. If necessary, click Outlook Data Files in the *Select where to place the folder* list. Click OK to create the folder.

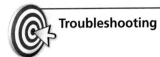

Troubleshooting   For this exercise, you want to select the top-level folder. It's the folder that holds your Inbox, Sent Items folder, and so on. Depending on the settings on your computer and the type of e-mail account you have, this might be called Outlook Data Files, Personal Folders, or simply your e-mail address.

3. Right-click the New Service folder in the Navigation Pane and select New Folder from the shortcut menu. The Create New Folder dialog box is displayed.

4. In the *Name* field, key CP & L to identify the new folder. Select Contact Items in the *Folder contains* field. If necessary, click Contacts in the *Select where to place the folder* list. Click OK to create the folder.

5. Right-click the CP & L folder in the Navigation Pane and select New Folder from the shortcut menu. The Create New Folder dialog box is displayed.

6. In the *Name* field, key CB2 Project 1 to identify the new folder. Select Contact Items in the *Folder contains* field. Click CP & L in the *Select where to place the folder* list. Click OK to create the folder.

7. Click the File tab. Click Open in the Backstage view's navigation pane and select Import. The Import and Export Wizard is displayed.

8. Click Import from another program or file, if necessary, in the list of available actions. Click the Next button. The Browse dialog box is displayed.

9. Click Tab-Separated Values (Windows) in the list of available import file types. Click the Next button. Click the Browse button.

@ The *Kim Ralls Contacts* file is available on the book companion website or in *WileyPLUS*.

10. Navigate to the data files for this lesson and click the *Kim Ralls Contacts* file. Click OK to apply your choices and close the Browse window and return to the Import a File window. Click the Next button.

11. In the *Select destination folder* box, select CB2 Project 1. Click the Next button.

12. Click the Finish button. Click the CB2 Project 1 folder to see that the imported contacts are located there.

13. Select the CB Project 1 folder and click File to open Backstage view.

14. Click Print in the navigation pane to open the Print Settings page. Notice that the preview pane displays all of the contacts in the CB Project 3 address book in the Card Style.

15. Click Phone Directory Style. Select your printer in the Printer area and click Print.

LEAVE Outlook open for the next project.

Project 2: Create Contact Records and a Contact Group

Kim needs to create contact records for herself and the two new Service Technicians in her department. She needs to create a Contact Group containing the Service Technicians in her department.

Take Note   The contacts you create in this project will be used in Project 3.

GET READY. LAUNCH Outlook if it is not already running.

1. Click the Contacts button in the Navigation Pane to display the main Contacts window. If necessary, click the Contacts folders in the Contacts Folder list.
2. Click New Contact on the Home tab to display a blank Contact window.

Take Note   Throughout this chapter you will see information that appears in black text within brackets, such as [Press Enter] or [your e-mail address]. The information contained in the brackets is intended to be directions for you rather than something you actually type word for word. It will instruct you to perform an action or substitute text. Do **not** type the actual text that appears within brackets.

3. Click the *Full Name* field, if necessary. Key Kim Ralls. [Press Tab.]
4. In the *Company* field, key City Power & Light. [Press Tab.]
5. In the *Job title* field, key Shift Supervisor. [Press Tab.]

 Troubleshooting The e-mail addresses provided in these projects belong to unused domains owned by Microsoft. When you send a message to these addresses, you will receive an error message stating that the message could not be delivered. Delete the error messages when they arrive.

6. In the *E-mail* field, key Kim@cpandl.com. [Press Tab.]
7. In the *Web page address* field, key www.cpandl.com.
8. Below the Phone numbers heading, click the *Business* field. Key 2175559821. Outlook formats the number as a phone number.
9. Below the Addresses heading, in the *Business* field, key 324 Main Street. [Press Enter.] Key Springfield, IL 68390. [Press Tab.]
10. In the Actions group on the Ribbon, click the Save & New arrow. In the dropdown list of options, click Contact from Same Company. A new contact record window is displayed containing the same company information as the previous contact.
11. Click the *Full Name* field, if necessary. Key Jay Henningsen. [Press Tab.] Click the *Job title* field. Key New Service Technician. [Press Tab.] Click the *E-mail* field. Key Jay@cpandl.com. [Press Tab.]
12. In the Actions group on the Ribbon, click the Save & New arrow. In the dropdown list of options, click Contact from Same Company. A new contact record window is displayed containing the same company information as the previous contact.
13. Click the *Full Name* field, if necessary. Key Julia Moseley. [Press Tab.] Click the *Job title* field. Key New Service Technician. [Press Tab.] Click the *E-mail* field. Key Julia@cpandl.com. [Press Tab.]
14. In the Actions group on the Ribbon, click the Save & Close button. Close any open contact records.

15. Click the View tab. In the Current View group, click Change View and select List. In the Arrangement group, click Company. The appearance of the Contacts window changes to a simple list of contacts sorted by company name.

16. Click the Home tab. Click the New Contact Group button to display a blank Contact Group window.

17. In the *Name* field, key New Service Technicians.

18. In the Members group of the Contact Group tab, click the Add Members button. Click From Outlook Contacts from the dropdown list that appears. *The Select Members: Contacts* dialog box is displayed.

19. Select the two New Service Technician contact records. Click Members and click OK. Click Save & Close.

20. Select the New Service Technicians Contact Group and drag it to the CP & L folder in the Navigation Pane.

LEAVE Outlook open for the next project.

Project 3: Edit an Electronic Business Card

Now that Kim has created new contact records, she wants to make sure that all the CP & L contacts are located in the CP & L folder. Finally, she wants to dress up her electronic business card so that she can send it out to the Contact Group.

GET READY. USE the Kim Ralls contact record and the Contact Group created in the previous project.

1. If necessary, click the Contacts button in the Navigation Pane to display the Contacts window. If necessary, click the Contacts folder.

2. Double-click the Kim Ralls contact. The Kim Ralls—Contact window is displayed.

3. In the Options group on the Ribbon, click the Business Card button. The Edit Business Card window is displayed.

4. In the *Card Design* area in the upper right of the window, verify that Image Left is selected in the *Layout* field.

5. Also in the *Card Design* area, click the Change button. The Add Card Picture dialog box is displayed. Navigate to the data files for this project. Click the *lights on* file and click OK.

6. In the Card Design area, click the *Image Area* field. Change the value to 25%, if necessary.

7. In the Card Design area, click the *Image Align* field. In the dropdown list, click Fit to Edge.

8. In the Card Design area, click the Background button. The Color dialog box is displayed. Click the Define Custom Colors button and select a medium soft blue shade. Click OK.

9. In the *Fields* area, click E-mail in the list of fields. Click the Bold button.

10. Click OK. The Edit Business Card window is closed. Click Save & Close to save the business card.

11. On the Home tab, click the Forward Contact button in the Share group. Select As a Business Card. A new message window is displayed with Kim's business card attached.

12. In the *To* field, key New Service Technicians. In the Cc field, key [your e-mail address].

13. In the message area, click before the business card and key:

    Here is my new business card. Feel free to forward it to clients as needed. [Press Enter twice.]

    Kim [Press Enter three times.]

14. Click the Send button. The message is moved to the Outbox and sent when the computer is connected to the Internet. Click the Save & Close button to return to the main Contacts window.

15. Click the Instant Search box. Key cpandl. Because this is the domain for the e-mail address you added in Project 1, the three new addresses appear in the results list.

@ The *lights on* file is available on the book companion website or in *WileyPLUS*.

16. Click the All Contact Items button in the Scope group of the Search Tools tab. One more contact record appears in the results list.

17. Select the four contact records and click Move on the Home tab—Action Group. A dropdown list of folders is displayed. Click Other Folders. The Move Items dialog box is displayed.

18. Click the CP & L folder and click OK. The contacts are moved to the CP & L folder but they still remain in the search results list onscreen.

19. Click the Mail button on the Navigation Pane and select the Kim Ralls message. If necessary, click Send/Receive All Folders on the Home tab.

20. Click the Junk button in the Delete Group and select Never Block the Group or Mailing List. Select all the check boxes and click OK.

LEAVE Outlook open for the next project.

Project 4: Manage Your Mailbox

Now that her contacts are in place, Kim decides it's time to manage her mailbox. Kim knows that she will be receiving a lot of messages requesting new service from the Customer Service department. Messages could come from a dozen different Customer Service representatives. However, the *Subject* field for every message contains the words "New Service Request." Kim decided to create a rule moving all of the requests to the New Service folder. After testing the rule, she sets up an archive of the New Service folder.

GET READY. USE the folders, contacts, and message you created in previous exercises. Your computer must be connected to the Internet to test the rule at the end of this project.

1. Click the File tab, then click Manage Rules & Alerts. The Rules and Alerts window is displayed. Turn off all rules except the *Clear categories on mail* rule by deselecting the check boxes.

2. Click the New Rule button. The Rules Wizard window is displayed.

3. In the Stay Organized category, click Move messages with specific words in the subject to a folder.

4. In the Step 2 area, click specific words. The Search Text window is displayed.

5. In the *Specify words or phrases to search for in the subject* field, key New Service Request. Click the Add button. Click OK to close the Search Text window and return to the Rules Wizard window.

6. In the Step 2 area of the Rules Wizard window, click specified to identify the destination folder. The Folder List is displayed in a new Rules and Alerts window.

7. Click the New Service folder, and click OK. The specified destination folder is identified in the Rules Wizard window.

8. Click the Next button twice to continue the Wizard without modifying conditions or actions.

9. Under Select exceptions, click the except if the subject contains specific words check box. Text is added to the rule description at the bottom of the Rules Wizard window.

10. In the rule description area, click specific words. The Search text window is displayed.

11. In the *Specify words or phrases to search for in the subject* field, key RE:. Click the Add button. The RE: text is enclosed by quotation marks and added to the search list for this rule. Click OK to close the Search Text window. The Rules Wizard window is displayed.

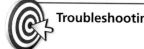 **Troubleshooting** Be sure to include the colon in the specified words or any message subject containing the letters "re" will be an exception.

12. Click the Next button to continue the Wizard. The rule is displayed for your approval. Examine the rule carefully to verify that it is correct. Click the Finish button. The new rule is displayed in the Rules and Alerts window. Click the OK button to close the Rules and Alerts window.

13. On the Home tab, click the New Items button and select E-mail Message to display a new Message window.

14. Address the message to your e-mail address. In the *Subject* field, key New Service Request. In the message area, key Kim. Send the message.

15. Create and send a second message to your e-mail address using RE: New Service Request in the *Subject* field. In the message area, key Kim. Click Send.

16. Click the Send/Receive tab and click Send/Receive All Folders, if necessary, to receive the messages. Verify that the New Service Request message was moved to the New Service folder and the RE: New Service Request message remained in the Inbox.

17. On the Home tab, click Rules and select Manage Rules & Alerts. The Rules and Alerts window is displayed. Turn off all rules except the *Clear categories on mail* rule. Click OK to close the Rules and Alerts window.

18. If necessary, click the Inbox in the Navigation Pane. Click the Instant Search, and key Kim. The message list is replaced with the two messages containing the word *Kim*.

19. Select the two messages that you sent in Project 3 and Project 4 and click More in the Quick Steps gallery. Point to New Quick Step and select Move to folder from the fly-out menu.

20. Click Choose Folder and select New Service. Click Finish. The messages move to the New Service folder.

21. Click the New Service folder and select all the messages in it. Click Unread/Read in the Tags group of the Home tab.

22. Click File tab, click Cleanup Tools and select Archive. In the *Archive this folder and all subfolders* list, select New Service.

23. In the *Archive items older than* box, key tomorrow's date.

24. Click Browse and navigate to your solutions folder. Key CB Project 4_xx (where *xx* is your initials). Click OK to select the archive location. Click OK to close the Archive box and click Yes when prompted to complete the archive.

CLOSE Outlook.

LESSON SKILL MATRIX

Skills	Exam Objective	Objective Number
Creating Appointments		
Setting Appointment Options	Set appointment options. Forward an appointment.	5.1.1 5.1.3
Managing Events		
Printing Appointment Details	Print appointment details.	5.1.2

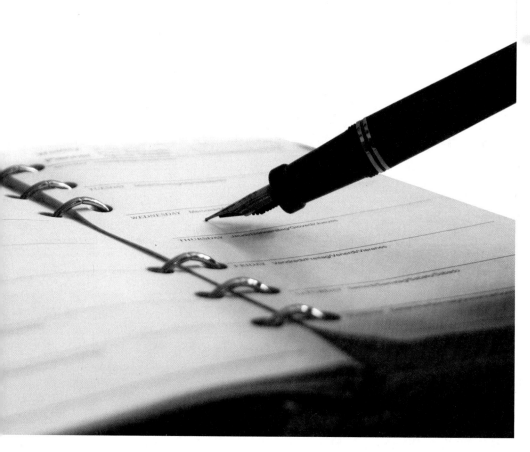

KEY TERMS

- appointment
- banner
- Busy
- event
- Free
- iCalendar
- Out of Office
- private
- recurring appointment
- tasks
- Tentative

As a marketing assistant, Terry Eminhizer knows the value of time. Terry manages her schedule and the schedules of two marketing representatives who are constantly on the road. Setting up travel arrangements, confirming appointments with clients, and generally smoothing out the bumps for the marketing representatives gives them more time to make bigger sales. Time is money. In this lesson, you'll create and manage appointments and events in Outlook.

SOFTWARE ORIENTATION

Microsoft Outlook's Appointment Window

The Appointment window displayed in Figure 8-1 enables you to schedule an appointment or event. Scheduled appointments and events are displayed on your calendar and in your To-Do Bar.

Figure 8-1

Outlook's Appointment window

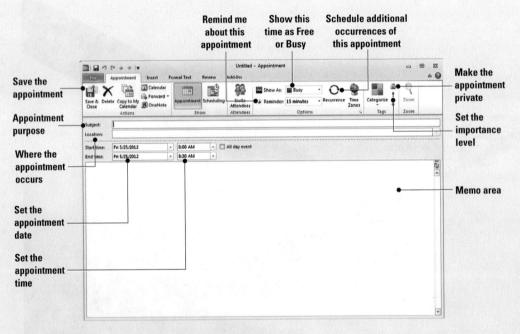

Use the Appointment window to create an appointment or event. Refer to Figure 8-1 as you complete the following exercises.

CREATING APPOINTMENTS

The Bottom Line

An **appointment** is a scheduled activity that does not require sending invitations to other people or resources. An appointment can occur once or occur at regular intervals. In this section, you'll create different kinds of appointments.

Creating a One-Time Appointment

Appointments can involve other people, but they do not require invitations sent through Outlook. Appointments can include activities such as doctor's appointments and picking up your daughter after soccer practice. In this exercise, you'll create a basic one-time appointment.

STEP BY STEP   **Create a One-Time Appointment**

Another Way
You can also select the date in the Appointment window. If the date is displayed in the monthly calendar, it is easier to select the date in the calendar. For appointments that occur several months in the future, it is easier to select the date in the Appointment window.

Another Way
You can key text in the Start time and End time fields rather than a date. Outlook translates the text into a date.

GET READY. Before you begin these steps, be sure to launch Microsoft Outlook.

1. Click the Calendar button in the Navigation Pane to display your Calendar. Click the Month button to display the Month view, if necessary.

2. Click [next Friday's date] on the monthly calendar.

3. On the Home tab, click the New Appointment button. The Appointment window in Figure 8-1 is displayed. The date selected in the monthly calendar is already displayed in the *Start time* and *End time* fields.

4. In the *Subject* field, key Blood Drive.

5. In the *Location* field, key Van in the South parking lot.

6. In the *Start time* fields, click the Start time down arrow. A list of possible starting times appears.

7. Select 2:00 PM. By default, each appointment is 30 minutes long, so the time in the *End time* field changes to 2:30 PM.

8. You need to fill out forms before donating and eat a few cookies after donating, so give yourself a bit more time. Select an *End Time* of 3:00 PM.

9. Click the Save & Close button in the Actions group on the Ribbon. The appointment is displayed on the calendar, as shown in Figure 8-2.

Figure 8-2

The appointment scheduled on the calendar

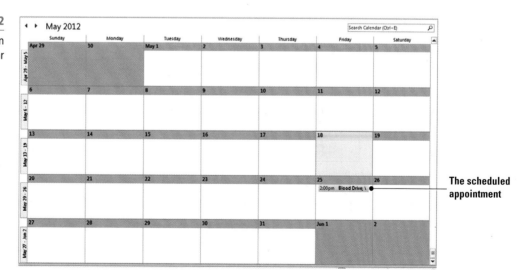

The scheduled appointment

PAUSE. LEAVE the Outlook Message window open to use in the next exercise.

By default, when you select a future date in the calendar, the displayed time of the appointment in the Appointment window will be the start of the workday.

Creating an Appointment from a Message

Sometimes, a message can lead to an appointment. For example, your son's cross-country running coach sends you a message about the awards banquet or you receive a message that a farewell lunch will be held Thursday for a coworker in your department. When you create an appointment from a message you received, the message text is saved automatically in the Appointment window's memo area. This stores the related message with the appointment. In this exercise, you'll simply use an e-mail message to create an appointment.

STEP BY STEP   **Create an Appointment from a Message**

GET READY. Before you begin these steps, be sure to launch Microsoft Outlook.

1. If necessary, click the Calendar button on the Navigation Pane to display the Calendar feature.
2. Click the New Items button in the Home tab. A list of available items is displayed
3. Click E-mail Message in the list to display a new Message window.

Take Note   Throughout this chapter you will see information that appears in black text within brackets, such as [Press Enter], or [next Friday's date]. The information contained in the brackets is intended to be directions for you rather than something you actually type word for word. It will instruct you to perform an action or substitute text. Do **not** type the actual text that appears within brackets.

4. In the *To* field, key [your e-mail address]. In the *Subject* field, key Vice President Duerr visiting Thursday afternoon. In the message area, key Vice President Bernard Duerr is visiting this division on Thursday. An employee meeting will be held in the company cafeteria from 2:00 PM to 4:00 PM. Attendance is mandatory. Click the Send button.
5. Return to your Inbox, if necessary. Click the Send/Receive button if the message has not arrived yet.
6. Click the Vice President Duerr visiting Thursday afternoon message to select it.
7. Click the Move button in the Move group on the Home tab. In the dropdown list, click Other Folder. The Move Items dialog box is displayed, as shown in Figure 8-3.

Figure 8-3

Move Items dialog box

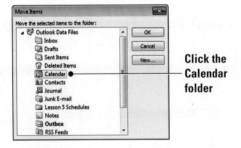

Click the Calendar folder

8. In the Move Items dialog box, click Calendar and then click OK. An Appointment window is opened. The message subject is displayed in the *Subject* field in the Appointment window. A link to the original message is displayed in the Memo area of the Appointment window.
9. Double-click the icon. The original message window is displayed. Close the message window.
10. In the Appointment window, key Company cafeteria into the *Location* field.
11. Key Thursday into the *Start time* field instead of a date. The date of the next available Thursday appears in the Start time date box. Key or select a *Start time* of 2:00 PM.
12. In the *End time* field, key an *End time* of 4:00 PM. The Appointment window should be similar to Figure 8-4.

Figure 8-4

Creating an appointment from
a message

Subject created
automatically from —
message subject

Link to the original
message used to —
create the appointment

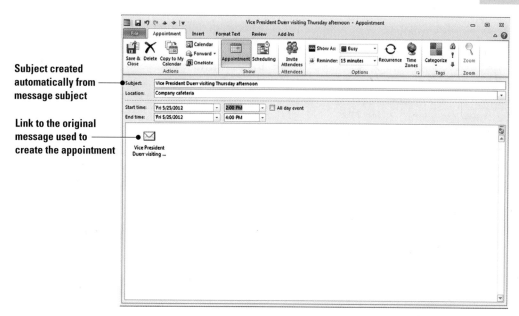

13. Click the Save & Close button in the Actions group on the Ribbon.

14. Click the Calendar button in the Navigation Pane to display the Calendar folder.
   The appointment created from the message is displayed.

PAUSE. LEAVE Outlook open to use in the next exercise.

Creating an Appointment from a Task

Tasks describe activities you have to do. Appointments tell you when activities are performed.
Tasks frequently become appointments when the time to perform a task is scheduled. The task
text is saved automatically in the Appointment window's memo area, storing the information
with the appointment. In this exercise, you'll create an appointment from a task.

STEP BY STEP   **Create an Appointment from a Task**

GET READY. Before you begin these steps, be sure to launch Microsoft Outlook.

1. Click the Calendar button in the Navigation Pane to display the Calendar folder. Click
   the Month button to display the Month view, if necessary.

 Ref   You can find more information on tasks in Lesson 11.

2. Click the View tab. Point to To-Do Bar and then click Normal. The To-Do Bar is
   displayed to the right of the monthly calendar, as shown in Figure 8-5. Your scheduled
   appointments are listed in the To-Do Bar. No tasks are displayed.

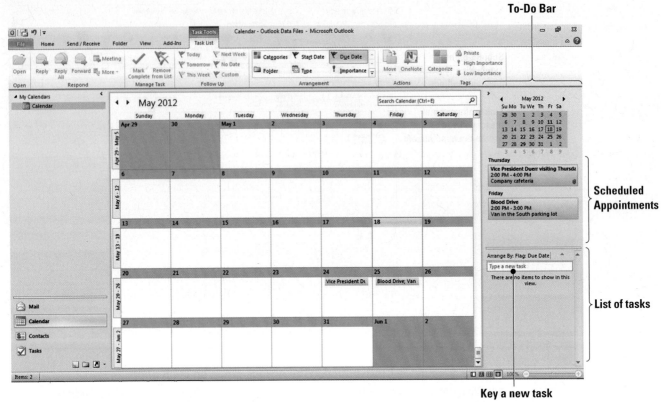

Figure 8-5

To-Do Bar displayed

3. Click the *Type a new task* field, and key Lunch with Vice President Duerr. Press Enter. The task is created.

4. Click the Lunch with Vice President Duerr task. Drag it to Thursday's date on the calendar. You already have an appointment for the employee meeting from 2:00 PM to 4:00 PM for that date.

5. Double-click the Lunch with Vice President Duerr item in the calendar. An Appointment window containing the task information is displayed.

6. Click the All day event check box to clear the check box. The time fields become available.

7. Key a Start time of 12:30 PM and an End time of 1:45 PM. The Appointment window should be similar to Figure 8-6.

Figure 8-6

Creating an appointment from a task

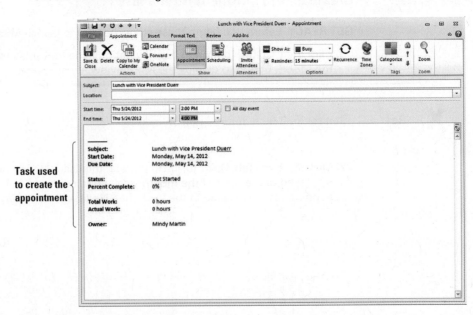

8. Click the Save & Close button in the Actions group on the Ribbon. The appointment created from the task is displayed on the calendar.

PAUSE. LEAVE Outlook open to use in the next exercise.

SETTING APPOINTMENT OPTIONS

The Bottom Line

Creating a basic appointment is one thing, but many appointments don't fit a cookie-cutter mold. For example, you might need to create an appointment that occurs every other Friday, mark an appointment as private, or forward an appointment on to a colleague. You can use Outlook's appointment options to customize the details of each appointment. In this section, you'll set some appointment options to create a recurring private meeting.

Creating and Customizing Appointments

Outlook offers many different kinds of options that you can use to set appointments. Appointment options are located in both the Options and Tags groups on the Appointment tab. The Time Zone option allows you to establish the time zone for an appointment, which can be very helpful when planning appointments with people in multiple time zones. The Show As option allows you to let others know whether you can be disturbed during a meeting. You can set the Reminder tool to give you an alert when an appointment approaches. In this exercise, you'll create an appointment and customize it with tools in the Options group.

STEP BY STEP **Create and Customize an Appointment**

GET READY. Before you begin these steps, be sure to launch Microsoft Outlook.

1. Double-click [next Wednesday's date] on the monthly calendar. A new Appointment window is displayed.

2. In the *Subject* field, key Customizing Appointment Options.

3. In the *Location* field, key Training Center.

4. Click the All day event check box to clear the check box. Key a *Start time* of 1:00 PM and an *End time* of 1:45 PM.

5. Click the Reminder dropdown arrow in the Options group and select 1 hour from the list of available times that appears.

6. Click the Show As down arrow in the Options group and select Tentative.

7. Click the Time Zone button in the Options group on the Ribbon. A new Time Zone box appears next to the Start and End time boxes. The appointment is going to be conducted via a video feed from California, so select Pacific Time from the list, as shown in Figure 8-7.

Figure 8-7

Setting Appointment options

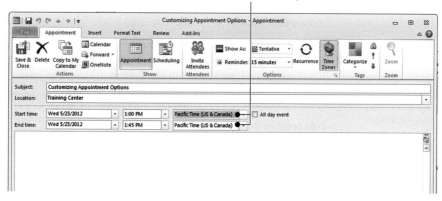

Time Zone boxes

 Ref

You can find more information about using changing time zones and how they affect your calendar in Lesson 11.

8. Click the Save & Close button in the Actions group on the Ribbon. The appointment created from the task is displayed on the calendar.

PAUSE. LEAVE Outlook open to use in the next exercise.

The *Show as* field in the Appointment window determines how the time is displayed on your calendar. When others look at your calendar, this tells them if you are available and how definite your schedule is for a specific activity. You can choose from four options displayed in Table 8-1.

Table 8-1

Show Time as Options

Show As	Description
Free	No activities are scheduled for this time period. You are available.
Busy	An activity is scheduled for this time period. You are not available for other activities.
Tentative	An activity is scheduled for this time period, but the activity might not occur. You might be available for other activities.
Out of Office	You are out of the office.

Scheduling a Recurring Appointment

A **recurring appointment** is an appointment that occurs at regular intervals. Recurring appointments are common in many calendars. Weekly soccer games, monthly lunch dates with an old friend, and semi-annual company dinners are examples of recurring appointments. Recurrences can be scheduled based on daily, weekly, monthly, and yearly intervals. In this exercise, you set a recurring appointment.

STEP BY STEP   **Schedule a Recurring Appointment**

GET READY. Before you begin these steps, be sure to launch Microsoft Outlook.

1. Click the Calendar button in the Navigation Pane to display your Calendar. Click the Month button to display the Month view, if necessary.

2. Double-click the [third Monday of the month] on the monthly calendar. If the third Monday of this month has passed, click the third Monday of next month.

Take Note   In the Month view, double-click the lower part of the square to open a new Untitled—Event window. Double-clicking the top part of the square changes the calendar arrangement to Day view for the selected date.

3. In the *Subject* field, key Engineering Lunch.

4. In the *Location* field, key Conference Room B.

5. Click the All day event check box to clear the check box. Key a *Start time* of 12:15 PM and an *End time* of 1:15 PM.

6. Click the Memo area. Key New techniques and troubleshooting.

7. Click the Recurrence button in the Options group. The Appointment Recurrence dialog box is displayed, as shown in Figure 8-8.

Figure 8-8

Appointment Recurrence window

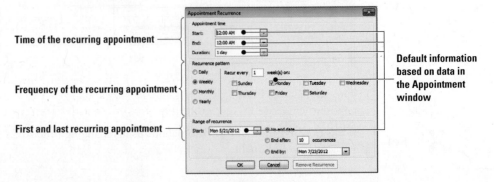

Time of the recurring appointment

Frequency of the recurring appointment

First and last recurring appointment

Default information based on data in the Appointment window

8. In the Appointment Recurrence dialog box, click Monthly in the Recurrence Pattern area. Selecting a different frequency changes the available patterns.

9. On the right side in the Recurrence Pattern area, click the radio button to select The third Monday of every 1 month(s). Because the date of the first recurring appointment was the third Monday of the month, the third Monday of every month is offered as a likely pattern (as is the selected date in each month), as shown in Figure 8-9.

Figure 8-9

Setting the recurrence pattern

Define how frequently the appointment will occur

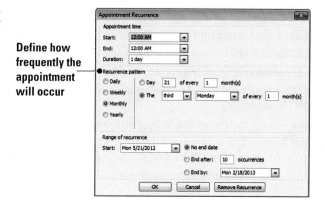

10. Click OK to set the recurrence pattern and return to the Appointment window. The recurrence pattern is displayed in the Appointment window, as shown in Figure 8-10.

Figure 8-10

Recurring appointment

Recurring pattern

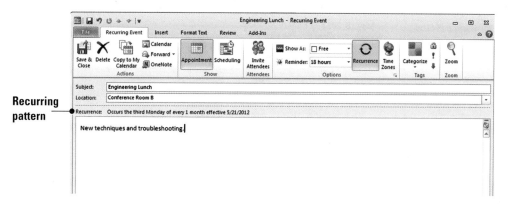

CERTIFICATION READY   5.1.1

How do you create a recurring appointment or event?

11. Click the Save & Close button in the Actions group on the Ribbon. The appointment is displayed on the monthly calendar. Click the Forward button at the top of the monthly calendar to verify that the recurring appointment is displayed in next month's calendar. Click the Back button at the top of the monthly calendar to return to the current month.

PAUSE. LEAVE the Outlook Message window open to use in the next exercise.

Marking an Appointment as Private

If you use your computer in a public place or just don't like the idea of someone looking over your shoulder and seeing the details about your appointments, you can also choose to mark an appointment as **private**. This feature blocks the details of an activity from a casual observer by showing only the subject line in the calendar with a lock icon. In this exercise, you'll mark an appointment as private.

STEP BY STEP   **Mark an Appointment as Private**

GET READY. Before you begin these steps, be sure to launch Microsoft Outlook.

1. Click the Calendar button in the Navigation Pane to display your Calendar. Click the Month button to display the Month view if necessary.

2. Click [next Friday's date] on the monthly calendar. The Blood drive is already scheduled for 2:00 PM on that date.

3. On the Home tab, click the New Appointment button. The Appointment window in Figure 8-1 is displayed. The date selected in the monthly calendar is already displayed in the *Start time* and *End time* fields.

4. In the *Subject* field, key Interview Rebecca Laszlo for receptionist.

5. In the *Location* field, key My office.

6. In the *Start time* field, key or select a time of 4:30 PM. Key or select an End time of 5:00 PM, if necessary.

7. Click the Private button in the Tags group on the Ribbon.

8. Click the Save & Close button in the Actions group on the Ribbon. The appointment is displayed on your monthly calendar.

9. Click [the date of the interview (from step 3)] on the calendar and click Day to display your agenda for the day. Scroll down to see the interview listing. Outlook displays a lock next to the private appointment, as shown in Figure 8-11.

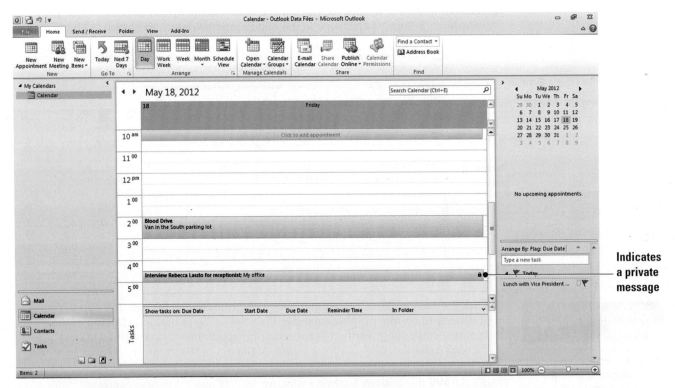

Figure 8-11

A private appointment

PAUSE. LEAVE Outlook open to use in the next exercise.

CERTIFICATION READY 5.1.1

How do you mark an appointment as private?

In the previous exercise, you marked an appointment as Private by clicking the Private button before saving the appointment. You also can open an existing appointment and click the Private button to turn on or off the Private feature for that appointment. Be sure to save the modified appointment after changing the Private status.

Take Note Although marking appointments and events as private hides the details from the casual viewer, it does not ensure privacy. Any person who has Read privileges to your calendar could access the information by a variety of methods.

Forwarding an Appointment

Forwarding an appointment to someone allows you to invite someone to join you or notifies them of your schedule. You can forward an appointment as an attachment using the iCalendar file format. The **iCalendar (.ics)** format is interchangeable between most calendar and e-mail applications, which makes it a versatile tool. When you click on an iCalendar attachment, Outlook automatically adds the appointment to your calendar. In this exercise, you'll forward an appointment as an attachment.

STEP BY STEP **Forward an Appointment**

WileyPLUS Extra! features an online tutorial of this task.

GET READY. Before you begin these steps, be sure to launch Microsoft Outlook.

1. Click the Calendar button in the Navigation Pane to display your Calendar. Click the Month button to display the Month view if necessary.
2. Select the Lunch with Vice President Duerr appointment and click the Forward down arrow. Select Forward as iCalendar. The FW: Lunch with Vice President Duerr message window is displayed with the appointment attached as an .ics file.
3. In the *To* field, key [your e-mail address].
4. In the message area, key Come and join us at McCarty's.
5. Right-click the .ics file and click Save As from the shortcut menu.
6. Save the file to the location where you store your solution files. Click Save.

Troubleshooting It is important to save the file to a location that both you and the recipient can access. If you are on the same server, you can save it there. If not, you might try a website.

7. Click in the bottom of the message area. Click the Insert tab and click Picture. Navigate to the data files for this lesson. Click the iCalendar file and click Open. Outlook's stock iCalendar image is added to the message, as shown in Figure 8-12.

Figure 8-12

Sending an appointment as an attachment

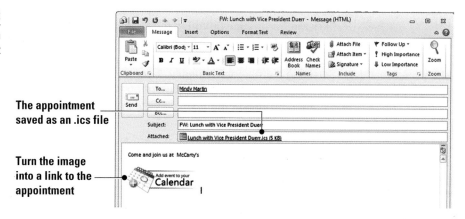

The appointment saved as an .ics file

Turn the image into a link to the appointment

8. Right-click the image and select Hyperlink. The Insert Hyperlink dialog box is displayed, as shown in Figure 8-13.
9. Select Existing File or Web Page, then use the Look In directory to navigate to the solution folder where you stored the appointment. Select the appointment and click OK.

Figure 8-13

Insert Hyperlink dialog box

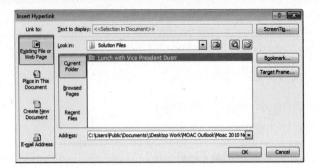

How do you send an appointment as an iCalendar attachment?

The Bottom Line

10. Click Send. The recipient can open the appointment from the attachment or the link.

PAUSE. LEAVE Outlook open to use in the next exercise.

CREATING AN EVENT

An **event** is an activity that lasts one or more days. In your calendar, an event is displayed as a **banner** text prominently displayed at the top of the day window that indicates an activity is going to require the entire day. For scheduling purposes, an event is displayed as free time, meaning that you are still available for appointments. In this exercise, you'll create an event in Outlook 2010.

STEP BY STEP **Create an Event**

GET READY. Before you begin these steps, be sure to launch Microsoft Outlook.

1. Click the Calendar button in the Navigation Pane to display your Calendar. Click the Month button to display the Month view, if necessary.

2. On the Home tab, click the New Appointment button. The Appointment window in is displayed (refer to Figure 8-1).

3. In the *Subject* field, key Anniversary.

4. In the *Start time* field, key the date of your anniversary or a family member's anniversary.

5. Click the All day event check box to select the option. The time fields are dimmed.

6. Click the Private button in the Options group on the Ribbon.

7. Click the Recurrence button in the Options group on the Ribbon. The Appointment Recurrence window is displayed.

8. In the Appointment Recurrence window, click Yearly in the *Recurrence pattern* area. Selecting a different frequency changes the patterns available for selection on the right side in the Recurrence pattern area.

9. On the right side in the *Recurrence pattern* area, click the radio button to select On [month] [date].

Another Way

The methods of creating new appointments from messages or tasks that you performed in the earlier exercises in this lesson can also be used to create events.

10. Click OK to set the recurrence pattern and return to the Appointment window. The recurrence pattern is displayed in the Appointment window.

11. Click the Reminder dropdown list arrow. Click the 1 week option, to schedule Outlook to remind you one week in advance of the scheduled event.

12. Click the Save & Close button in the Actions group on the Ribbon. The appointment is added to your calendar.

13. Click the Forward button at the top of the monthly calendar to verify that the recurring event is displayed on the correct date. Click the Back button at the top of the monthly calendar to return to the current month.

PAUSE. LEAVE Outlook open to use in the next exercise.

PRINTING APPOINTMENT DETAILS

The Bottom Line

In Outlook 2010 it is easy to print out the details about an appointment or even print out a calendar. The Memo Style format allows you to print the selected appointment. You can use settings in the Print Options dialog box to select the print style and the range of dates to include.

Printing Appointment Details

In this section, you will print the details about one of your appointments.

STEP BY STEP   **Print Appointment Details**

GET READY. Before you begin these steps, be sure to launch Microsoft Outlook.

1. Click the Calendar button in the Navigation Pane to display your Calendar. Click the Month button to display the Month view, if necessary.

2. Click File to open Backstage view and click Print in the navigation pane to open the print settings page.

3. Click the Print Options button. The Print dialog box is displayed, as shown in Figure 8-14.

Figure 8-14

Print dialog box

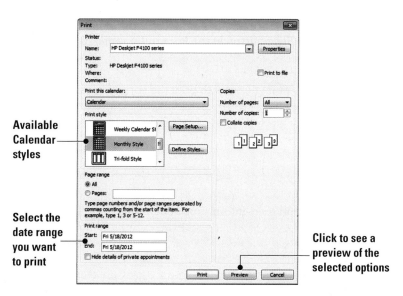

Available Calendar styles

Select the date range you want to print

Click to see a preview of the selected options

4. In the *Print Style* area, click Calendar Details Style.

5. In the *Start box* of the Print range area, key [next Friday's date].

6. In the *End* box, key [next Friday's date]. Click the Preview button. The Print settings page of Backstage view is displayed showing a preview of the new settings, as shown in Figure 8-15.

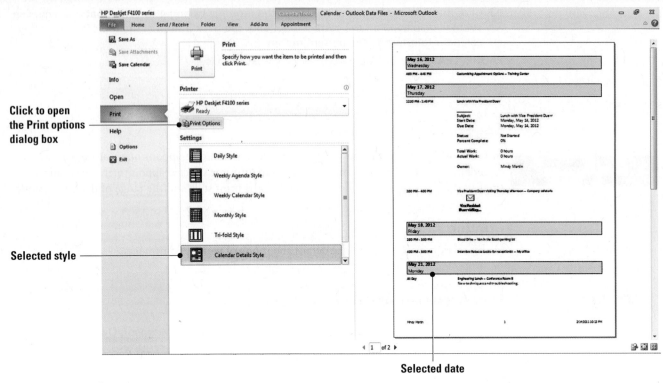

Click to open the Print options dialog box

Selected style

Selected date

Figure 8-15

Print preview of next Friday's schedule

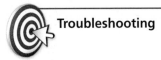

Troubleshooting Notice that all the appointments for the week appear on the preview. Although you selected a specific date, the default for this style is to print the entire week. You can click the Define Style button in the Print options dialog box to edit the default style.

7. Click **Print** if you want to print the contact record using the default printer.

CLOSE Outlook.

CERTIFICATION READY   5.1.2

How do you print an appointment's details?

 Ref   You can find more information about using the Calendar folder in Lesson 10.

SKILL SUMMARY

In This Lesson You Learned How To:	Exam Objective	Objective Number
Create appointments		
Set appointment options	Set appointment options.	5.1.1
	Forward an appointment.	5.1.3
Manage events		
Print appointment details	Print appointment details.	5.1.2

Knowledge Assessment

Multiple Choice

Select the letter beside the term that best completes each of the following statements.

1. A _____ appointment is one that occurs at regular intervals.
   a. recurring
   b. regular
   c. routine
   d. repeating

2. No activities are scheduled for a(n) _____ time period.
   a. Tentative
   b. Open
   c. Free
   d. Available

3. An activity that lasts one or more days is referred to as a(n) _____.
   a. extended activity
   b. session
   c. event
   d. All of the above

4. In Outlook, an activity that has to be performed is a(n) _____.
   a. duty
   b. task
   c. event
   d. chore

5. A(n) _____ is a scheduled activity that does not require sending invitations to other people or resources.
   a. private meeting
   b. solo meeting
   c. closed event
   d. appointment

6. The _____ feature protects the details of an activity from a casual observer.
   a. private
   b. secure
   c. encrypted
   d. lock

7. The _____ contains an option to print appointments from selected dates.
   a. Appointment Options dialog box
   b. Print Options dialog box
   c. Edit Settings box
   d. Layout dialog box

8. The _____ setting indicates that an activity is scheduled for this time period, but the activity might not occur.
   a. Show As: Possible
   b. Show As: Free
   c. Show As: Saved
   d. Show As: Tentative

9. A(n) _____ is text displayed at the top of a day to indicate an event.

    a. opener

    b. header

    c. flag

    d. banner

10. The _____ enables you to create a schedule.

    a. calendar

    b. appointment book

    c. weekly organizer

    d. ledger

True/False

Circle T if the statement is true or F if the statement is false.

T   F   1. A task cannot be used to create an appointment unless the task is private.

T   F   2. Marking an appointment as private ensures that users who can view your calendar cannot view the details of the private appointment.

T   F   3. Appointments require invitations sent through Outlook.

T   F   4. By default, each appointment is one hour long.

T   F   5. An event is displayed as a banner in your calendar.

T   F   6. You are not available for other activities when your time is displayed as Busy.

T   F   7. You can key text in the *Start time* and *End time* fields rather than a date.

T   F   8. Use the Appointment window to print an event.

T   F   9. A message is deleted automatically when it is used to create an appointment.

T   F   10. Recurrences can be scheduled based on daily, weekly, monthly, and yearly intervals.

Competency Assessment

Project 8-1: Schedule Vacation

Your boss has finally approved your vacation request for July. Now that it's official, it's time to add your vacation to the calendar.

GET READY. LAUNCH Outlook if it is not already running.

1. Click the Calendar button in the Navigation Pane to display the Calendar folder.

2. On the Home tab, click the New Appointment button. The Appointment window is displayed.

3. In the *Subject* field, key Vacation.

4. In the *Start time* field, key the [date of the first day] of your vacation.

5. In the *End time* field, key the [date of the last day] of your vacation.

6. Click the All day event check box to select the option. The time fields are dimmed.

7. Click the Save & Close button in the Actions group on the Ribbon. The appointment is added to your calendar.

LEAVE Outlook open for the next project.

Project 8-2: Create a One-Time Appointment

You have been selected to create a presentation about a new product your company will sell in the coming year. You will deliver the presentation at a company dinner on Wednesday. Schedule the time to prepare the presentation.

1. Click the Calendar button in the Navigation Pane to display the Calendar folder.

2. Click [next Monday's date] on the monthly calendar.

3. On the Home tab, click the New Appointment button. The Appointment window is displayed.

4. In the *Subject* field, key Prepare new product presentation.

5. In the *Start time* fields, key or select the time of 9:30 AM. Key or select the *End time* of 2:00 PM.

6. Click the Save & Close button in the Actions group on the Ribbon. The appointment is added to the calendar.

LEAVE Outlook open for the next project.

Proficiency Assessment

Project 8-3: Schedule a Recurring Appointment

Every week, you collect sales information to track the difference between sales goals and actual sales. Create a recurring appointment every Monday to gather the information and post the sales information for the managers to review.

GET READY. LAUNCH Outlook if it is not already running.

1. Click the Calendar button in the Navigation Pane to display the Calendar folder.

2. Click [next Tuesday's date] on the monthly calendar.

3. On the Home tab, click the New Appointment button. The Appointment window is displayed.

4. In the *Subject* field, key Prepare Sales Report.

5. In the *Start time* field, key or select 8:30 AM. Key or select an *End time* of 9:30 AM.

6. Click the Recurrence button in the Options group on the Ribbon. The Appointment Recurrence dialog box is displayed.

7. Click OK to accept the recurrence pattern and return to the Appointment window.

8. Click the Save & Close button in the Actions group on the Ribbon. The appointment is added to the calendar.

LEAVE Outlook open for the next project.

Project 8-4: Create an Appointment from a Message

A friend sent you a message about a concert in August. Create an appointment from the message.

GET READY. LAUNCH Outlook if it is not already running.

1. If necessary, click the Mail button in the Navigation Pane to display the Mail folder.

2. Click the New E-mail button on the Home tab to display the Message window.

3. In the *To* field, key [your e-mail address]. In the *Subject* field, key Concert! In the message area, key [the name of your favorite musical performer] is coming to [the name of the local concert hall]! Mark August 10 on your calendar! I've already bought our tickets! Click the Send button.

4. Return to your Inbox, if necessary. Click the Send/Receive button if the message has not arrived yet.

5. Double-click the Concert message to open it.

6. Click the Move to Folder button in the Actions group. In the dropdown list, click Other Folder. The Move Items dialog box is displayed.

7. In the Move Items dialog box, click Calendar, and then click OK. An Appointment window is opened.

8. Key August 10 in the *Start time* field. Key or select 7:00 PM.

9. Key or select an *End time* of 11:00 PM.

10. Click the Save & Close button in the Actions group on the Ribbon.

LEAVE Outlook open for the next project.

Project 8-5: Create and Print an Appointment from a Task

Last week, a coworker asked you to review a new marketing presentation. He finished the presentation yesterday. Turn the task into an appointment to review the presentation tomorrow after lunch.

GET READY. LAUNCH Outlook if it is not already running.

1. Display the *To-Do Bar*, if necessary.
2. Click the *Type a new task* field, and key Review presentation for Gary Schare. Press Enter. The task is created.
3. Click the Review presentation for Gary Schare task. Drag it to [tomorrow's date] on the calendar.
4. Double-click the Review presentation for Gary Schare item in the calendar. An Appointment window is displayed.
5. Click the All day event check box to clear the check box. The time fields become available.
6. Key or select a *Start time* of 3:30 PM and an *End time* of 5:00 PM.
7. Click the Save & Close button in the Actions group on the Ribbon. The appointment is added to the calendar.
8. Click the File tab and select Print in the Navigation Pane.
9. Click Memo Style in the Settings area and click Print.

LEAVE Outlook open for the next project.

Project 8-6: Mark an Appointment as Private

In Project 8-4, you created an appointment for the concert. Your taste in music might not be appreciated by everyone who views your calendar. Make the appointment private.

GET READY. LAUNCH Outlook if it is not already running.

1. Click the Calendar button in the Navigation Pane to display the Calendar folder.
2. Display August in the calendar.
3. Double-click the Concert appointment to open it.
4. Click the Private button in the Options group.
5. Click the Save & Close button in the Actions group. The private appointment is added to the calendar.

CLOSE Outlook.

INTERNET READY

Use the Internet to find some local events that you would like to attend. A local sports game or a concert performed by your favorite artist could be fun. Schedule the activities in your calendar.

LESSON SKILL MATRIX

Skills	Exam Objective	Objective Number
Creating a Meeting Request	Send a meeting to a contact group.	**4.2.6**
	Schedule a meeting with a message sender.	**5.1.4**
	Set response options.	**5.2.1**
Responding to a Meeting Request	Propose a new time for a meeting.	**5.2.4**
Managing a Meeting		
Updating a Meeting Request	Update a meeting request.	**5.2.2**
	Cancel a meeting or invitation.	**5.2.3**
Managing a Recurring Meeting		

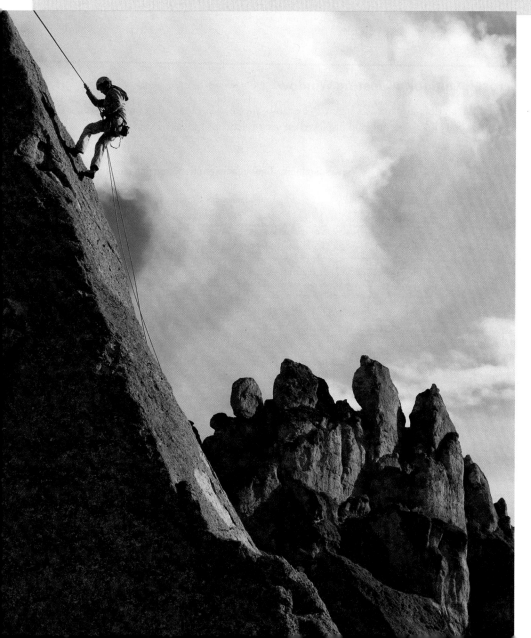

KEY TERMS

- **cancel**
- **mandatory attendee**
- **meeting**
- **meeting organizer**
- **meeting request**
- **occurrence**
- **optional attendee**
- **recurring meeting**
- **resource**

Tailspin Toys has been working with Resort Adventures on a new adventure sports game. The project is scheduled to move into its final phase next month. Gabe Mares, Software Development Manager for Tailspin Toys, just finished reviewing the latest bug reports for Project Snow. Unfortunately, the list is much longer than it should be at this stage in the software development cycle. If the problems don't get resolved quickly, they won't be able to meet their deadline. It is obviously time to call a meeting to identify the reason for the long list of problems and determine how the problems could be resolved to meet the project deadlines. Outlook's Calendar feature is a great tool for managing your meetings because of the flexibility and control it gives you. You can use Outlook to invite guest to a meeting, schedule your resources, and check the availability of attendees. In this lesson, you'll work on all the different aspects of using meetings in the Outlook calendar. You'll create, modify, and cancel meetings. You'll also respond to meetings set by others.

SOFTWARE ORIENTATION

Microsoft Outlook's Meeting Window

The Meeting window displayed in Figure 9-1 enables you to create a meeting involving other people or resources. Scheduled meetings are displayed on your calendar.

Figure 9-1

Outlook's Meeting window

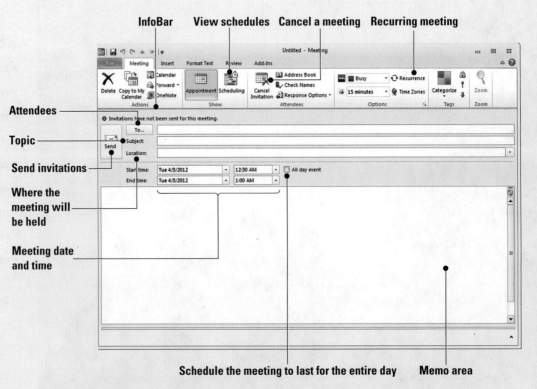

InfoBar   View schedules   Cancel a meeting   Recurring meeting

Attendees

Topic

Send invitations

Where the meeting will be held

Meeting date and time

Schedule the meeting to last for the entire day   Memo area

Use the Meeting window to create a meeting. Refer to Figure 9-1 as you complete the following exercises.

CREATING A MEETING REQUEST

The Bottom Line

In Outlook, a **meeting** is a scheduled appointment that requires sending invitations to other people or resources. A **resource** is an item or a location that can be invited to a meeting. Therefore, Outlook's Meeting window, shown in Figure 9-1, is very similar to the Appointment window. However, the Meeting window also includes the *To* field to invite attendees and the *Send* button to send the invitations. A meeting can occur once or at regular intervals.

 Ref   For more information about appointments, refer to Lesson 8.

Creating a One-Time Meeting

Meeting a goal often requires more than one person. Working with others to accomplish a goal usually requires meetings. Use Outlook to start planning a good meeting by selecting the right time, the right place, and the right people to accomplish the goal. A **meeting request** is an Outlook item that creates a meeting and invites attendees. In this exercise, you will start the process of creating a one-time meeting. In this exercise, you'll create a single meeting.

STEP BY STEP   **Create a One-Time Meeting**

GET READY. LAUNCH Outlook if it is not already running.

1. Click the Calendar button in the Navigation Pane to display the Calendar window.
2. Use the Date Navigator in the Navigation Pane to select [the third Monday of April].

WileyPLUS Extra! features an online tutorial of this task.

 Ref   You can find more information on the Calendar folder in Lesson 10.

 Troubleshooting   If you completed Lesson 8, a recurring appointment for the Engineering Lunch is scheduled for 12:15 PM to 1:15 PM on the third Monday of every month. If you did not complete Lesson 8, the busy times shown on your schedule will differ.

 Another Way   You can schedule a meeting from within the Mail and Contact features as well. Hover over a contact's name and click View More Options from the Contact Card. Select Schedule a Meeting from the option's dropdown menu.

3. On the Home tab, click New Meeting in the New group. The Meeting window shown in Figure 9-1 is displayed. Outlook selects a default time for the meeting and displays it adjacent to the existing 8:30 AM meeting.
4. Click the *Subject* field and key Discuss Annual Convention. In the *Location* field, key Conference Room A.

 Ref   You can find more information on scheduling meeting locations later in this lesson.

PAUSE. LEAVE the Meeting window open to use in the next exercise.

Inviting Mandatory and Optional Attendees

A **mandatory attendee** is a person who must attend the meeting. An **optional attendee** is a person who should attend the meeting, but whose presence is not required. When planning a meeting, you should always invite at least one mandatory attendee. If a mandatory attendee is not needed to accomplish a goal at the meeting, you might not need a meeting at all. When you select a meeting time, choose a time slot when all mandatory attendees are available. It is helpful to use the message area to provide information about the meeting, including an agenda. In this exercise, you will select the right people to make this meeting a success. You will add both a mandatory attendee and an optional attendee and write a brief note to the attendees.

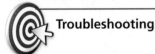 **STEP BY STEP**   **Invite Mandatory and Optional Attendees**

Troubleshooting When creating messages you must send and receive the requests and responses from two different e-mail accounts. So, for the exercises in this lesson, you will need to either work with a friend or coworker or have access to a separate e-mail account.

GET READY. USE the meeting request you began in the preceding exercise. The mandatory attendee used in this exercise must have a different active e-mail account from you and be able to respond to your meeting invitation.

1. Click the Scheduling Assistant (or Scheduling) ibutton in the Show group on the Ribbon. Scheduling information is displayed, as shown in Figure 9-2.

Figure 9-2

Scheduling information

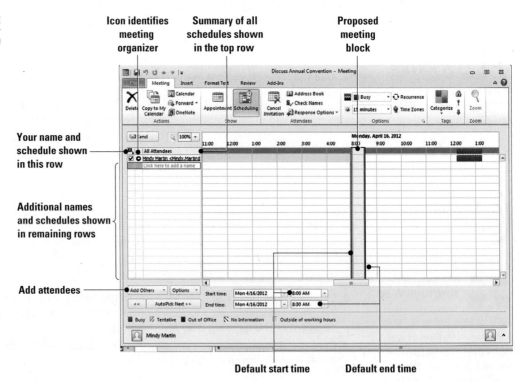

Troubleshooting If you are using Microsoft Exchange, the Scheduling button is called Scheduling Assistant and should include free/busy information for your contacts.

2. Click Add Others and then click Add from Address Book from the dropdown list that appears. The Select Attendees and Resources window appears, as shown in Figure 9-3.

Figure 9-3

Select Attendees and
Resources: Contacts window

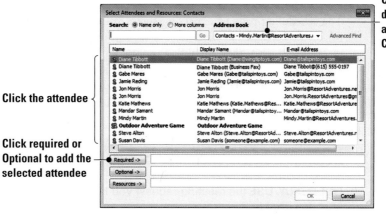

**Change address if
desired attendees
are in a different
Contacts folder**

Click the attendee

**Click required or
Optional to add the
selected attendee**

Another Way
If the person who
will respond to your invitation
is not in the address book, click
the *Click here to add a name*
text in the Meeting window.
Key the desired e-mail address.
Verify that the icon next to
the keyed name is *Required
Attendee*.

3. In the Search box, key [the name of the person or account that is acting as your mandatory attendee] for this lesson.

Troubleshooting If you have not sent messages to your mandatory attendee before now, create a contact record for the new user before completing this exercise, or key the new user's e-mail address directly into the *To* field.

4. Click [the name of your attendee] from the results list, then click Required to indicate that their attendance is mandatory. In this example, Mindy's mandatory attendee is Sara James.

5. Click Gabe Mares' contact information. Click the Optional button to indicate that his attendance is optional. Click OK to return to the Meeting window's Scheduling page. Your mandatory attendee and Gabe have been added to the list of attendees, as shown in Figure 9-4.

Figure 9-4

Attendees displayed

Summary row **Attendees' schedules**

Your schedule

**Icons identify
attendees as
mandatory or
optional**

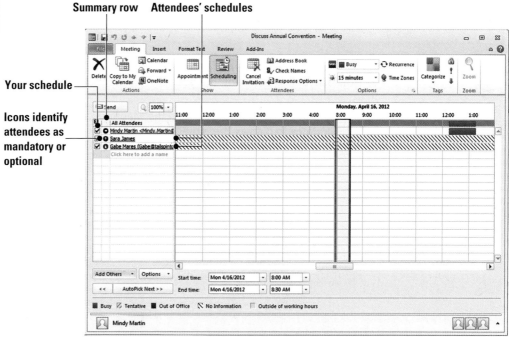

Another Way
You can also attach
documents to the invitation
before sending it. To attach
documents, click the Insert
tab and click the Attach File
button in the Include group on
the Ribbon.

6. Click the Appointment button in the Show group. In the message body, key: It's time to start planning for our annual convention. Bring the comments from last year's convention and we'll create our project plan during the meeting. Gabe, I hope you can join us. Press Enter twice and sign with your name.

PAUSE. Leave the meeting window open to use in the next exercise.

Determining When Attendees Can Meet

The scheduling page of a meeting shows your schedule for the selected day. If you are working on a Microsoft Exchange network, you can see when your attendees are free to attend your meeting and when they are busy. Ideally, you will be able to view this information for all of the attendees, but if you are inviting people outside of your Microsoft Exchange network, you will not have this information. In this exercise, you will examine the available scheduling information for the people you want to invite to the meeting, manually select a meeting time, and then let Outlook select a time for the meeting.

STEP BY STEP | **Determine When Attendees Can Meet**

GET READY. USE the meeting request you began in a previous exercise. The mandatory attendee used in this exercise must have an active e-mail account and be able to respond to your meeting invitation.

Take Note | The directions below require that you are operating on a Microsoft Exchange network. If you are not using Microsoft Exchange, take note of the Troubleshooting alerts throughout this exercise.

1. In the *Start time* field, key or select 9:00 AM. Notice that the green and red vertical bars indicating the start and end time for the meeting moved to enclose the 9:00 AM to 9:30 AM time slot.

 Ref | You can find more information on sharing calendars in Lesson 10.

2. Click the red vertical line and drag it to the right so that the bars enclose the 9:00 AM to 10:00 AM time slot. Notice that the *End time* field changed to 10:00 AM.

3. Change the *Start time* field to 1:00 PM and change the *End time* field to 2:00 PM, if necessary. The green and red vertical lines move. The meeting time overlaps your scheduled appointment.

4. The Scheduling Assistant populates Meeting Suggestions pane with the best times available for all attendees to meet on your preferred date.

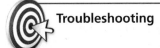 **Troubleshooting** If you invite someone not on your Microsoft Exchange network, you will see the name on the Scheduling Assistant, but you will not see their schedule.

5. Click on 11:00 AM–12:00 AM in the Meeting Suggestions pane and the schedule grid updates to display the attendees' availability at that time, as shown in Figure 9-5.

Figure 9-5

Updated schedule grid

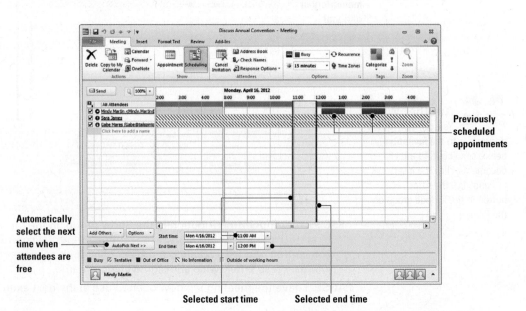

Automatically select the next time when attendees are free

Previously scheduled appointments

Selected start time   Selected end time

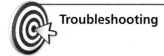 **Troubleshooting** If you are not using Microsoft Exchange, you will see an AutoPick Next button on the bottom left of the schedule grid. As with the Meeting Suggestions pane, the AutoPick Next button adjusts the schedule grid to show attendees' availability. Press the back arrow button (to the left of the AutoPick Next button) twice to jump back to 11:00 AM.

6. Click **Appointments** from the Show group on the Meeting tab to return to the Meeting window. The *To* field is automatically filled with the attendees' e-mail addresses, and the *Start time* and *End time* fields have been updated. Your Meeting window should resemble Figure 9-6.

Figure 9-6

Updated Meeting window

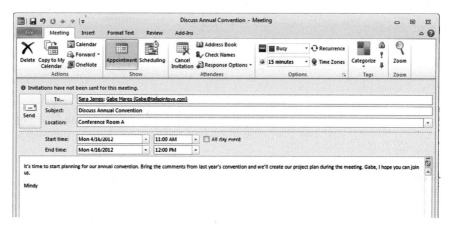

7. Click the **Send** button.

PAUSE. LEAVE Outlook open to use in the next exercise.

Sending a Meeting to a Contact Group

In Lesson 6, you discovered that creating a contact group is an efficient way to send frequent e-mails to a group of people. You also can use your contact groups to invite several people to your meeting at one time. In this exercise, you will send a meeting request to the contact group you created in Lesson 6.

STEP BY STEP **Send a Meeting to a Contact Group**

GET READY. USE the Tailspin Team Leaders Contact Group you created in Lesson 6.

1. Click the **Calendar** button in the Navigation Pane to display the Calendar window.
2. Use the Date Navigator in the Navigation Pane to select [the third Monday of April].
3. On the Home tab, click **New Meeting** in the New group. The Meeting window shown in Figure 9-1 is displayed.
4. Click the *Subject* field and key **First Weekly Meeting**. In the *Location* field, key **Conference Room A**.
5. In the Meeting window, click the **To** button to open the Address Book. Select the **Tailspin Team Leaders Contact Group** you created in Lesson 6 and click the **Required** button to indicate that their attendance is mandatory.
6. Click **OK** to return to the Meeting window's Scheduling page. Click the **plus sign** in front of the contact group name. The Expand List dialog box is displayed asking if you want to replace the Contact Group name with the names of the individual members, as shown in Figure 9-7.

Figure 9-7

Expand List dialog box

Contact Group

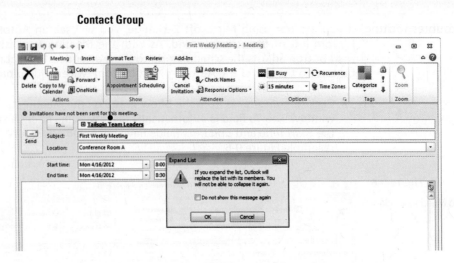

7. Click **OK** to close the dialog box and return to the Meeting window. The *To* field now shows the name of each of the Contact Group's members, as shown in Figure 9-8.

Figure 9-8

Meeting invitation to Contact Group

Expanded Contact Group attendees

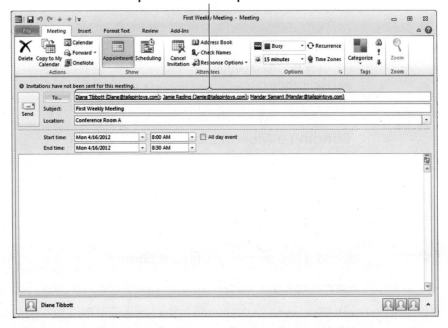

8. Change the *Start time* field to **2:00 PM** and change the *End time* field to **3:00 PM**, if necessary.

9. In the message body, key **Agenda: Create project plan**. Press **Enter**. **Assign project roles**. Press **Enter** twice and sign with [your name].

10. Click **Send**.

PAUSE. LEAVE Outlook open to use in the next exercise.

CERTIFICATION
READY **4.2.6**

How do you send a meeting request to a contact group?

Creating a Meeting from a Message

Sometimes, a message can lead to a meeting. For example, when Gabe received the bug report in the weekly status update memo about Project Snow, he realized that there was a problem that needed to be addressed face-to-face in order to get to the bottom of it. When you create a meeting from a message you received, the message text is saved automatically in the Meeting Request window's message area. In this exercise, you'll reply to a message with a meeting request.

STEP BY STEP   **Create a Meeting from a Message**

GET READY. USE the Diane Tibbott contact record you created in Lesson 6.

1. From the Calendar folder, click the New Items button in the Home tab. A list of available items is displayed

2. Click E-mail Message in the list to display a new Message window.

3. In the *To* field, key [the e-mail address of the person or account that is acting as your mandatory attendee] for this lesson.

4. In the *Subject* field, key Latest bug report issues. In the message area, key Unfortunately, this week's bug report doesn't show much progress. We are still experiencing 20 glitches per unit. The cause is still unknown. Will send you the particulars later today. Click the Send button.

5. Return to your Inbox, if necessary. Click the Send/Receive All Folders button if the message has not arrived yet.

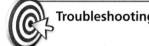

Troubleshooting If you are not working with a friend or coworker on this lesson, switch to the mandatory attendee account that you are using.

6. In the mandatory attendee account, click the Latest bug report issues message. Click the Reply with Meeting button in the Respond group on the Home tab. The *Latest bug report issues—Meeting* request window is displayed with the contents of the original message, as shown in Figure 9-9.

Reply with a
Meeting button

Address
Book

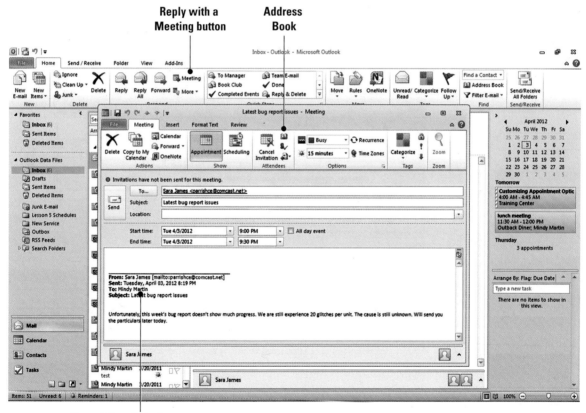

Text of the original message

Figure 9-9

Replying to a message with a
meeting request

7. In the Meeting window, key Design Center 2 into the *Location* field.

8. Key Wednesday into the *Start time* field instead of a date. Key or select a start time of 9:00 AM.

9. In the *End time* field, key 11:00 AM.

CERTIFICATION
READY   5.1.4

How do you schedule a
meeting with a message
sender?

10. Click High Importance in the Tags group.

11. Click the Address Book button in the Attendees group. Select Diane Tibbott, Jamie Reding, and Mandar Samant from the address book. Click Required and click OK.

PAUSE. LEAVE Outlook open to use in the next exercise.

Setting Response Options for a Meeting Request

By default, when you create a meeting in Outlook, there are two response options selected: Request Responses and Allow New Time Proposals. The Request Responses option adds response buttons to the meeting request. These buttons allow attendees to respond to the request letting you know whether they will attend. The Allow New Time Proposals option allows recipients to propose a different time to hold the meeting. As the meeting organizer, you still have final say about the meeting time; you also can choose to turn off one or both options. In this exercise, you'll reply to a message with a meeting request, but will not give anyone the option of changing the meeting time.

STEP BY STEP   **Set Response Options for a Meeting Request**

GET READY. USE the meeting request you starting in the preceding exercise.

1. In the *Latest bug report issues—Meeting* window, click the message area. Key This continuing problem is unacceptable. Bring all your data to this meeting. No one leaves until we have some answers.

2. In the Attendees group, click the Response Options button. A dropdown list is displayed, as shown in Figure 9-10.

Figure 9-10

Setting Response options

Response Options

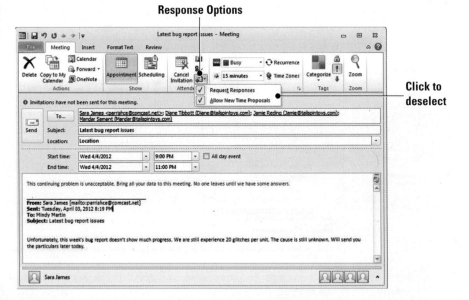

Click to deselect

CERTIFICATION
READY   5.2.1

How do you set response
options when creating a
message?

3. Click the Allow New Time Proposals option to deselect it.

4. Click Send. The meeting request is sent to your attendees and the meeting is added to your calendar.

PAUSE. LEAVE Outlook open to use in the next exercise.

RESPONDING TO A MEETING REQUEST

The Bottom Line

When you are invited to a meeting, you receive a meeting request in your Inbox. The meeting request can contain up to five options at the top of the message depending on the response options set by the meeting organizer. These meeting response options are used to let the meeting organizer know whether to expect you at the meeting, as shown in Table 9-1.

Table 9-1

Meeting Response Options

Detail Level	Description
Accept	Indicates that you have accepted the invitation and marks your calendar as busy.
Decline	Indicates that you will not attend the meeting and leaves your calendar free at the requested time.
Tentative	Indicates that you *might* attend the meeting, but does not commit you. Your calendar is marked as tentative with diagonal stripes.
Propose New Time	Indicates that you *might* be able to attend the meeting if the organizer were to change the time of the meeting to something that better fits your schedule.
Please Respond	Allows you to ask a question of the meeting organizer, perhaps asking for clarification, without accepting or declining the actual invitation. This link appears in the InfoBar, not at the top of the message.

Responding to a Meeting Request

Response options are set by the meeting organizer. The invitee must choose one of these options to let the meeting organizer know that invitee's intentions. In this exercise, you will tentatively accept a meeting invitation.

STEP BY STEP **Respond to a Meeting Request**

GET READY. LAUNCH Outlook if it is not already running and complete the previous exercises. The mandatory attendee used in this exercise must have a different active e-mail account from yours and be able to respond to your meeting invitation.

1. In the mandatory attendee's account, click the Mail button in the Navigation Pane to display the Mail folder, if necessary.
2. Locate the Discuss Annual Convention message in the message list. If it has not arrived, click the Send/Receive All Folders button on the Home tab. The Discuss Annual Convention message is identified in the message list by the Meeting icon, shown in Figure 9-9, which resembles the New Meeting button on the Calendar's Home tab.
3. Click the Discuss Annual Convention message in the message list. The message is displayed in the Preview pane, as shown in Figure 9-11.

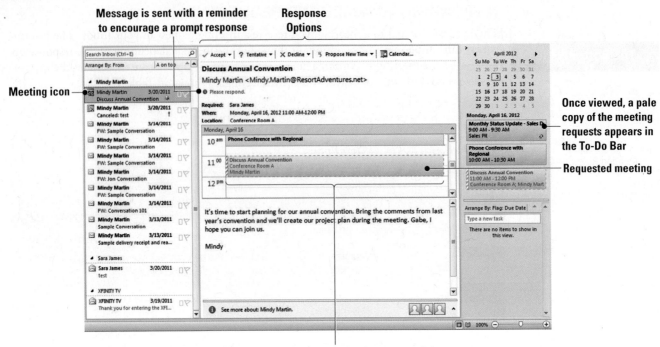

Message is sent with a reminder to encourage a prompt response

Response Options

Meeting icon

Once viewed, a pale copy of the meeting requests appears in the To-Do Bar

Requested meeting

Preview of your schedule for the requested time

Figure 9-11

Previewing a meeting request in the Reading Pane

4. Click the Tentative button. A dropdown list of options is displayed offering you the options to send your response now, add a comment before sending the response, or choose to not send a response, as shown in Figure 9-12.

Figure 9-12

Sending a Tentative response to a meeting request

Tentative response options

Click to send the default tentative response

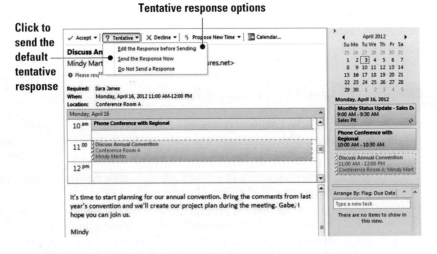

Another Way
You can also right-click on a meeting request in the message list to access the different response options.

5. Click the Send the Response Now option. Click OK. The meeting request is removed from your Inbox, and the meeting is added to your calendar.

LEAVE Outlook open to use in the next exercise.

Proposing a New Time for a Meeting

Meeting times are set by the **meeting organizer**, the person who creates the meeting and sends meeting invitations. In most cases, when a meeting invitation is received, an attendee can suggest a different time for the meeting that better fits the attendee's schedule as long as the organizer has enabled the setting on the meeting invitation. In this exercise, you will propose a new meeting time for a meeting invitation.

STEP BY STEP   **Propose a New Time for a Meeting**

GET READY. Before you begin these steps, complete the previous exercises. The mandatory attendee used in this exercise must have a different active e-mail account from yours and be able to respond to your meeting invitation.

1. In the mandatory attendee's account, click the Mail button in the Navigation Pane to display the Mail feature, if necessary.

2. Click the Deleted Items folder and locate the Discuss Annual Convention message. Because you already responded *Tentatively* to the meeting request, the message has been moved to the Deleted Items folder.

3. Double-click the Discuss Annual Convention deleted meeting request. The Discuss Annual Convention—Meeting window is displayed. Notice that the InfoBar reminds you that you have already responded to this request using the *Tentatively* option, as shown in Figure 9-13.

Figure 9-13

Discuss Annual Convention—
Message window

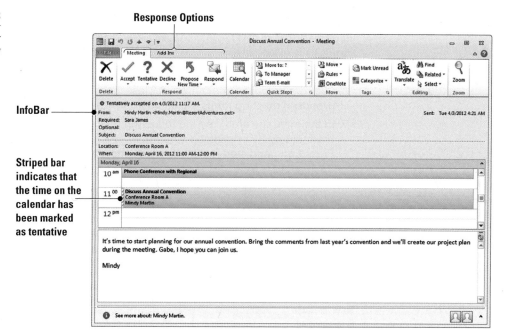

4. Click the Propose New Time button at the top of the message. The Propose New Time window is displayed, as shown in Figure 9-14. The meeting time is indicated with as a yellow bar.

Figure 9-14

Propose New Time: Discuss
Annual Convention window

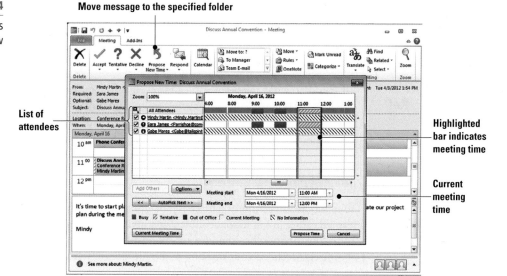

5. Verify that 11:00 is in the *Start time* field. Click the *End time* field. Key **12:30 PM**. The red line indicating the meeting's end time has moved to 12:30, as shown in Figure 9-15.

Figure 9-15

Proposing a new meeting time

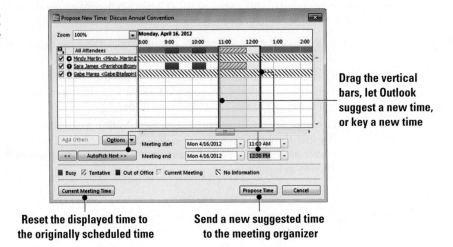

Drag the vertical bars, let Outlook suggest a new time, or key a new time

Reset the displayed time to the originally scheduled time

Send a new suggested time to the meeting organizer

6. Click the Propose Time button. A Message window is displayed. Both the current and proposed meeting times are listed above the message area.

7. In the message area, key the following message. Let's add 30 minutes and conclude the meeting by offering a sampling of foods available for the convention luncheon. Press Enter and sign [your name], as shown in Figure 9-16.

Figure 9-16

Updated meeting request

Send the message

Time sent by the meeting organizer

Time attendee is suggesting

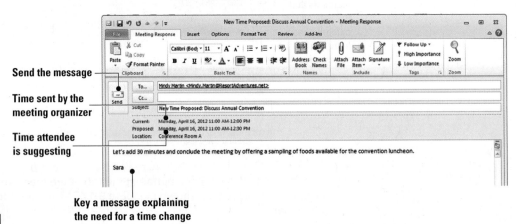

Key a message explaining the need for a time change

8. Click the Send button.

PAUSE. Switch to your e-mail account, if necessary. If someone else is responding to the invitation, **LEAVE** Outlook open to use in the next exercise.

 Ref

If you share your calendar, you can prevent some message exchanges regarding meeting times by keeping your free and busy times up to date in your calendar. For more information about sharing calendars, see Lesson 10.

MANAGING A MEETING

Your job as a meeting organizer is not done once you've sent your meeting invitation. As you learned earlier in this lesson, contacts you invited can respond to that invitation in one of five ways. You'd look pretty silly attending a meeting all by yourself because you neglected to notice that everyone else declined your meeting request. Outlook tracks meeting responses for every meeting.

Tracking Responses to a Meeting Request

When an attendee responds to your meeting invitation, you receive a message. If the attendee included comments in the response, the comments are contained in the message. The responses are stored in the meeting information in your calendar. So, you can just open the Meeting window to view a summary of the responses. In this exercise, you will learn how to track responses.

STEP BY STEP **Track Responses to a Meeting Request**

GET READY. Before you begin these steps, complete the previous exercises. The mandatory attendee used in this exercise must have a different active e-mail account from yours and be able to respond to your meeting invitation.

1. In your account, click the Mail button in the Navigation Pane to display the mailbox, if necessary. If the *Tentative: Discuss Annual Convention* message has not arrived, click the Send/Receive button.

2. Click the Tentative: Discuss Annual Convention message in the message list to preview it in the Reading Pane, as shown in Figure 9-17.

Figure 9-17

Message tentatively accepting the meeting invitation

Response to meeting invitation

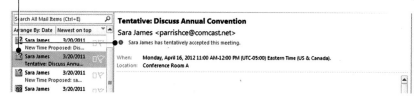

3. Click the Calendar button in the Navigation Pane to display the Calendar folder. Click the Month button to display the Month view, if necessary.

4. Double-click the Discuss Annual Convention meeting item on the calendar. The Discuss Annual Conference—Meeting window is displayed, as shown in Figure 9-18. The InfoBar contains a summary of the responses received.

Figure 9-18

Summary of responses received

Tracking button

Summary of responses received

5. Click the Tracking button on the Meeting tab. Detailed tracking information is displayed, as shown in Figure 9-19. You can see at a glance which attendees have responded.

Figure 9-19

Detailed tracking information

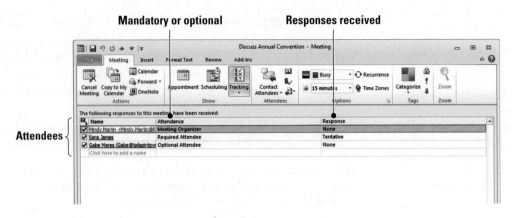

6. Close the Meeting window without saving changes.

PAUSE. LEAVE Outlook open for the next exercise.

Accepting a Proposed New Meeting Time

By default, anyone invited to the meeting can suggest a new date and time for the meeting. However, the meeting organizer has the final word on setting the meeting time. When an attendee proposes a new meeting time, the meeting organizer must evaluate the proposed time and accept or decline the proposal.

When the meeting time is changed, you need to click the Send Update or Send button to send an update message to your attendees notifying them of the new time. They must accept or decline the meeting again, as they did for the initial invitation. In this exercise, you accept a new meeting time proposed by an attendee.

STEP BY STEP   **Accept a Proposed New Meeting Time**

GET READY. Before you begin these steps, complete the previous exercises. The mandatory attendee used in this exercise must have a different active e-mail account from yours and be able to respond to your meeting invitation.

Troubleshooting More than one of your invitees could propose a new time for the meeting. You may choose any of the New Time Proposed e-mails to complete this exercise.

1. In your account, click the Calendar button in the Navigation Pane to display the Calendar window, if necessary.
2. Click April 16 on the Date Navigator and double-click the Discuss Annual Convention meeting item on the calendar. The Discuss Annual Conference—Meeting window is displayed
3. Click the Scheduling Assistant (or Scheduling) button in the Show group on the Ribbon. All proposed times appear in the scheduling grid so that you can see how each time affects the mandatory attendees, as shown in Figure 9-20.

Troubleshooting If you are using Microsoft Exchange, the Scheduling button is called Scheduling Assistant.

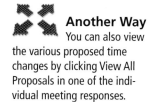

Another Way
You can also view the various proposed time changes by clicking View All Proposals in one of the individual meeting responses.

Figure 9-20

Proposed time shown in Scheduling view

4. Click [the extended time that you proposed]. The schedule changes to show how the new time will affect the attendees; it looks as if you'll have a conflict, as shown in Figure 9-20. You'll need to modify the times for one of the meetings.

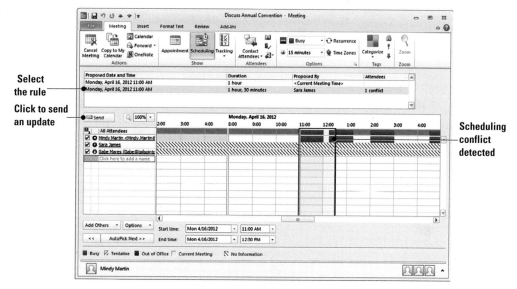

5. On the Meeting tab, click Contact Attendees in the Attendees group and select Reply to All with E-mail from the dropdown menu.

6. A message window opens. In the message body, key: Jon had a great suggestion that we take advantage of the scheduled meeting to sample some of the food we will provide at the luncheon. I'm adding time at the end of this meeting for that purpose. Press Enter twice and sign your name.

7. On the Meeting tab, click the Scheduling Assistant (or Scheduling) button in the Show group and press the Send button above the scheduling grid.

PAUSE. LEAVE Outlook open to use in the next exercise.

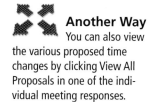

Another Way
You can accept or reject proposals in the individual meeting responses by selecting each one from the Inbox.

UPDATING A MEETING REQUEST

The Bottom Line

Whenever you are trying to get a group of people to sit at the same table at the same time, problems can emerge. One person will go out of town on an emergency business trip. Another person has to attend a meeting with a higher priority. Necessary audio-visual equipment has been shipped to a trade show. The list of potential problems is endless. Modifying a meeting and updating the attendees is a simple task in Outlook.

Changing a Meeting Time

The most common modifications to a meeting are changing the time and the location of a meeting. In the previous exercise, you modified the meeting time because of a proposed change by one of the attendees. In this exercise, you will make the change yourself and send an update to the attendees. Because this is a change to the meeting time, attendees will need to respond to the meeting invitation again.

STEP BY STEP | **Change a Meeting Time**

GET READY. Before you begin these steps, complete the previous exercises. The mandatory attendee used in this exercise must have a different active e-mail account from yours and be able to respond to your meeting invitation.

1. In your account, click the Calendar button in the Navigation Pane to display the Calendar folder. Click the Month button to display the Month view, if necessary.
2. Use the Date Navigator to select the month of April.
3. Double-click the Discuss Annual Convention meeting item on the calendar. The Discuss Annual Conference—Meeting window is displayed, as shown in Figure 9-9.
4. Click the *Start time* field. Key Tuesday. Press Enter. The *End time* field automatically changes to match.
5. In the message area, key Sorry guys, we've been bumped out of Conference Room A. The next availability isn't until Tuesday. Press Enter and key [your name]. Compare your Meeting window to Figure 9-21.

Figure 9-21

Updated Meeting window

Send update to attendees

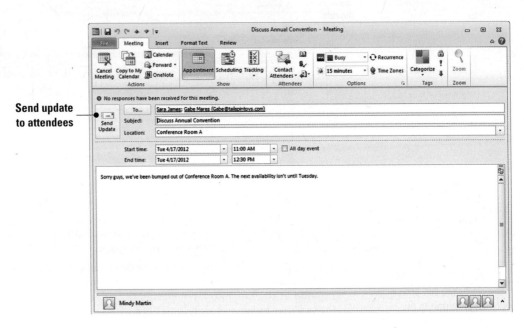

6. Click the Send Update button below the InfoBar to send the modified time information to the attendees.

PAUSE. Switch to the mandatory attendee's account, if necessary. If someone else is responding to the invitation, **LEAVE** Outlook open to use in the next exercise.

Scheduling a Meeting Resource

Scheduling meeting resources is a great way to keep track of who needs to use each piece of equipment. Resources can include cars, presentation equipment, and conference rooms. You can invite a resource to a meeting just as you invite attendees. A resource has its own mailbox and maintains its own schedule. It accepts invitations for free times and updates its calendar. It declines invitations if the requested time is already scheduled.

Scheduling resources ensures that meetings aren't scheduled at the same time in different locations that both require the same equipment. For example, let's say the human resources department is planning to show a DVD during a new-hire meeting in Conference Room A at 2:00 PM. Meanwhile, the Sales Department has a training DVD that they are planning to use in the Sales Pit during their meeting at 1:30 PM. At first glance they looked at room availability and the schedule of the attendees and saw no conflicts. If they schedule the DVD equipment as a resource, they would realize that the DVD equipment will be in the Sales training meeting from 1:30 to 3:00 PM. It won't be available for the new-hire meeting. In this exercise, you will create a new meeting and add a slide projector resource that is essential to the meeting.

STEP BY STEP   **Schedule a Meeting Resource**

GET READY. LAUNCH Outlook if it is not already running.

Troubleshooting Scheduling a resource requires Microsoft Exchange and a resource with a separate mailbox.

1. In the mandatory attendee's account, click the Calendar button in the Navigation Pane to display the Calendar folder.

2. On the Home tab, click New Meeting in the New group. The Meeting window shown in Figure 9-1 is displayed.

3. Click the *Subject* field and key Project Presentation Review. In the *Location* field, key Dept Room 62.

4. Click the Scheduling Assistant (or Scheduling) button in the Show group on the Ribbon. Scheduling information is displayed.

5. Change the *Start time* field to 9:00 AM and change the *End time* field to 10:00 AM. The green and red vertical lines move.

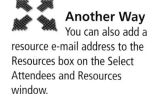

Another Way
You can also add a resource e-mail address to the Resources box on the Select Attendees and Resources window.

6. Click Add Others, and then click Add from Address Book. The Select Attendees and Resources window is displayed, as shown in Figure 9-3.

7. Click Diane Tibbott and click Required. Click OK to return to the Meeting window.

8. In the scheduling grid, click the Click here to add a name text in the Meeting window. Key AV01@tailspintoys.com and the box just to the left of the e-mail address. A dropdown list of attendee types appears, as shown in Figure 9-22.

Click to open attendee options

Select the Resource option

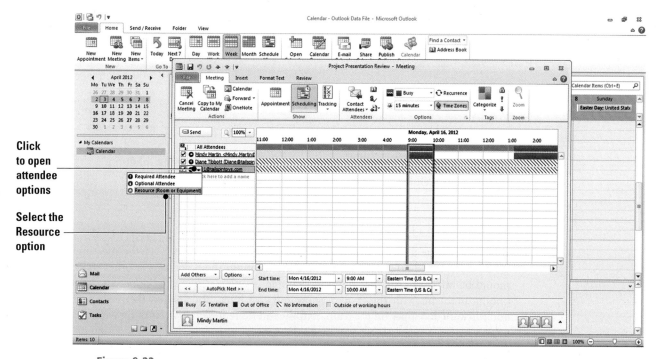

Figure 9-22

Scheduling a resource

Another Way
Even without Microsoft Exchange, you can create your own contact records for the resources you use. This enables you to select the resource from a secondary address book instead of keying the name each time you create a meeting.

9. Although there is a Resource (Room or Equipment) option, the projector is essential for the success of the meeting. Click Required Attendee to invite a slide projector to your meeting with Diane.

10. Click the icon next to the keyed address and select Resource (Room or Equipment.) A dialog box will be displayed asking if you want to change the location to AV01. Click No.

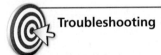

Troubleshooting If the location of a meeting is scheduled as a resource and the room is not available for any of the recurring meetings, you will not be able to schedule the recurrent meeting. You will learn more about scheduling resources later in this lesson.

11. Click the Appointment button in the Show group on the Ribbon.

12. Compare your Meeting window to Figure 9-23.

Resource invited

Figure 9-23

Meeting window with resource added

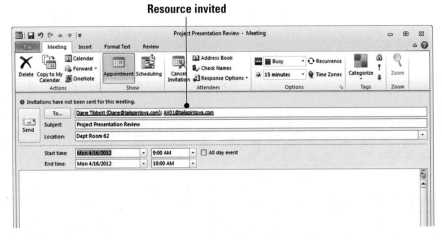

13. Click the Send button. Your calendar is updated to display the meeting.

PAUSE. LEAVE Outlook open to use in the next exercise.

Adding and Updating a New Attendee

When you create a meeting, you select the attendees needed to meet the meeting's objective. When the selected attendees learn about the meeting, they can suggest other individuals who should be invited to the meeting. For example, say that you created a meeting about the continuing problems with the Project Snow software bugs. You invited the project manager, the lead software developer on the team, and the service representative working with the client. The project manager suggests that you invite the concept artist who has been working on the project as well. In this exercise, you will add an attendee to a scheduled meeting and send an updated meeting request only to the new attendee.

STEP BY STEP **Add and Update a New Attendee**

GET READY. USE the meeting request you sent in the preceding exercise.

1. In your account, click the Calendar button in the Navigation Pane to display the Calendar folder. Click the Month button to display the Month view, if necessary.

2. Use the Date Navigator to select the month of April.

3. Double-click the Project Presentation Review meeting item on the calendar. The Project Presentation Review—Meeting window is displayed, as shown in Figure 9-23.

4. Click the Scheduling Assistant (or Scheduling) button in the Show group on the Ribbon. Click the Add Attendees button below the scheduling grid. The Select Attendees and Resources: Contacts window is displayed. The mandatory attendee and the projector are already displayed in the fields.

5. Click the Jamie Reding contact record to add that person as an attendee and click the Optional button. Click OK to return to the Meeting window.

6. Click the Send button. Outlook recognizes that the list of attendees has changed and displays the Send Update to Attendees dialog box shown in Figure 9-24.

Figure 9-24

Send Updates to Attendees dialog box

CERTIFICATION READY 5.2.2

How do you update a meeting request?

7. Click OK to only send the message to the added attendee. The updated meeting information is sent to Jamie Reding.

PAUSE. LEAVE Outlook open to use in the next exercise.

Cancelling a Meeting or Invitation

Regardless of how much planning went into creating a meeting, some meetings are **cancelled**. Reasons for cancelling a meeting are varied. For example, mandatory attendees could become unavailable or issues are resolved before the scheduled meeting occurs. When you cancel a meeting, it is deleted from your calendar and the attendees are notified. Cancellation notices are saved in your Sent Items folder in case you need to track cancelled meetings or keep a record of the reason a meeting was cancelled. In this exercise, you will cancel a meeting and send a cancellation notice to the attendees.

STEP BY STEP   **Cancel a Meeting or Invitation**

GET READY. LAUNCH Outlook if it is not already running.

Before you begin these steps, complete the previous exercises.

1. Click the Calendar button in the Navigation Pane to display the Calendar folder. Click the Month button to display the Month view, if necessary. Use the Date Navigator to select the month of April.

2. Double-click the Discuss Annual Convention meeting item on the calendar. The Discuss Annual Convention—Meeting window is displayed.

3. On the Meeting tab, click Cancel Meeting in the Actions group. The InfoBar changes to let you know that the cancellation has not been sent yet.

4. Click the message body. Delete any existing text and key the following message: This meeting was cancelled because Sara had an emergency appendectomy earlier today. She is recovering at Mountain View Hospital and we expect her to return to the office next week. We'll reschedule the meeting after she returns. Press Enter and sign your name. Compare your Meeting window to Figure 9-25.

Figure 9-25

Cancelling a meeting

Click to move the cancellation to the Calendar

Click to send the cancellation to attendees

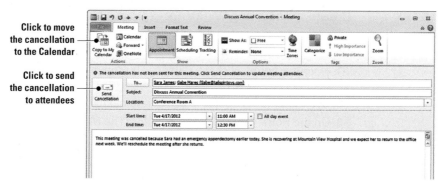

5. Click the Send Cancellation button. The message is sent and the meeting is removed from your calendar.

PAUSE. LEAVE Outlook open to use in the next exercise.

In the attendee's mailbox, the cancellation notice is automatically assigned a High Importance. The attendee opens the message and clicks the Remove from Calendar button in the Respond group. The attendee's calendar is updated, as shown in Figure 9-26.

Figure 9-26

Cancelled meeting in the message list

Click to delete meeting from your schedule

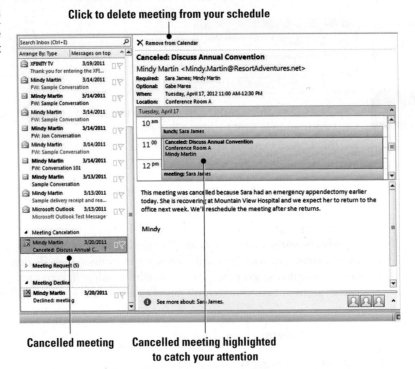

Cancelled meeting   **Cancelled meeting highlighted to catch your attention**

MANAGING A RECURRING MEETING

The Bottom Line

A **recurring meeting** is a meeting that occurs at regular intervals. The meeting always has the same attendees, location, and purpose. The interval could be a number of days, weeks, or months. For example, status meetings commonly occur at weekly or monthly intervals.

Creating a Recurring Meeting

The process of creating a recurring meeting is very similar to creating a one-time meeting. The only difference is setting the recurrence pattern. In this exercise, you will create a recurring meeting. The attendees will meet every Friday morning to review the status of their active projects.

STEP BY STEP   **Create a Recurring Meeting**

GET READY. LAUNCH Outlook if it is not already running.

1. In your account, click the Calendar button in the Navigation Pane to display the Calendar window.

2. Use the Date Navigator to select [the next Friday].

3. On the Home tab, click New Meeting. The Meeting window shown in Figure 9-1 is displayed.

4. Click the *Subject* field and key Project Status. In the *Location* field, key Dept Room 62.

5. Click the Scheduling Assistant (or Scheduling) button in the Show group on the Ribbon.

6. Click the Add Others button and click Add from Address Book. The Select Attendees and Resources window is displayed.

7. Press Ctrl while clicking the four Tailspin Toys employees. Click Required. Click OK to return to the Meeting window.

8. Change the *Start time* field to 9:00 AM and change the *End time* field to 10:00 AM, if necessary. The green and red vertical lines move.

9. Click the Recurrence button in the Options group on the Ribbon. The Appointment Recurrence window is displayed, as shown in Figure 9-27.

Figure 9-27

Appointment Recurrence window

Time of the recurring appointment

Frequency of the recurring appointment

First and last recurring appointment

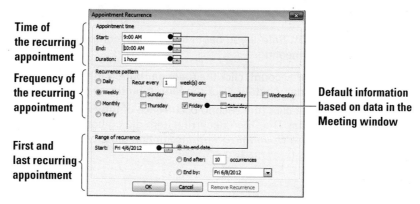

Default information based on data in the Meeting window

10. By default, Outlook assumes a weekly recurrence pattern on the same day you originally suggested, Friday. In this case, the pattern is correct. The Project Status meeting will be held every Friday. Click OK to accept the recurrence pattern and return to the meeting window.

11. Click the Appointment button in the Show group on the Ribbon. The *To* field is automatically filled with the attendees' e-mail addresses, as shown in Figure 9-28. The recurrence pattern is listed in the information bar under the *Location* field. In this case, the meeting recurrence pattern is *Occurs every Friday effective 4/6/12*.

Figure 9-28

Meeting request for a recurring meeting

InfoBar

Attendees

Topic

Meeting date, time, and recurrence pattern

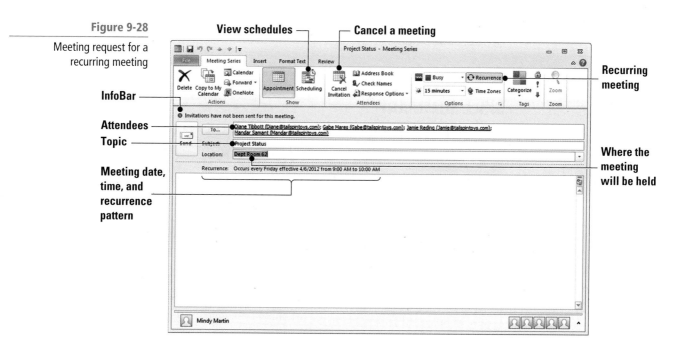

View schedules

Cancel a meeting

Recurring meeting

Where the meeting will be held

12. Click the Send button. Your calendar is updated, and the 9:00 AM to 10:00 AM time slot is displayed as busy for every Friday.

PAUSE. LEAVE Outlook open to use in the next exercise.

Changing One Occurrence of a Recurring Meeting

A single meeting in a series of recurring meetings is an **occurrence**. When a recurring meeting is held regularly for a long period of time, an occurrence will eventually conflict with some other event. At any time, you can change the date, time, and location of a single occurrence without affecting the other occurrences. When you change one occurrence, your calendar is updated and updates are sent to the attendees. In this exercise, you will change the time of one meeting in a series of recurring meetings.

STEP BY STEP   **Change One Occurrence of a Recurring Meeting**

GET READY. Before you begin these steps, complete the previous exercise to create the recurring meeting.

1. In your account, click the Calendar button in the Navigation Pane to display the Calendar window. Click the Month button to display the Month view, if necessary.

2. Double-click [the second occurrence of the *Project Status*] meeting item on the calendar. The Open Recurring Item dialog box is displayed, as shown in Figure 9-29, with the *Open this occurrence* option already selected.

Figure 9-29

Open Recurring Item dialog box

3. Click OK to open the single occurrence. The Project Status—Meeting window is displayed. The meeting information applies to the single occurrence only.

4. Click the *Start time* field. Key or select 10:00 AM and press Enter. The *End time* field automatically changes to 11:00 AM. Click the Send Update button. In your calendar, the single occurrence is modified to show the new time. The other occurrences are not changed.

PAUSE. CLOSE Outlook.

SKILL SUMMARY

In This Lesson You Learned How To:	Exam Objective	Objective Number
Create a meeting request.	Send a meeting to a contact group.	4.2.6
	Schedule a meeting with a message sender.	5.1.4
	Set response options.	5.2.1
Respond to a meeting request.	Propose a new time for a meeting.	5.2.4
Managing a meeting.		
Updating a meeting request.	Update a meeting request.	5.2.2
	Cancel a meeting or invitation.	5.2.3
Managing a recurring meeting.		

Matching

Match the term with its definition.

    a. cancel

    b. scheduling grid

    c. mandatory attendee

    d. meeting

    e. meeting organizer

    f. meeting request

    g. occurrence

    h. optional attendee

    i. recurring meeting

    j. resource

  1. A person who should attend the meeting, but whose presence is not required.

  2. A single meeting in a series of recurring meetings.

  3. An item or a location that can be invited to a meeting.

  4. Displays scheduling information for all attendees.

  5. A meeting that occurs at regular intervals.

  6. A person who must attend the meeting.

  7. Delete a meeting.

  8. A scheduled activity that requires sending invitations to other people or resources.

  9. The person who creates the meeting and sends meeting invitations.

  10. The Outlook item that creates the meeting and invites attendees.

True/False

Circle T if the statement is true or F if the statement is false.

T F   **1.** Outlook's Meeting window is exactly like the Appointment window.

T F   **2.** When an attendee accepts a meeting request, the attendee's schedule displays the meeting time as tentative.

T F   **3.** Only people or resources in your address book can be invited to a meeting.

T F   **4.** Any attendee can propose a new meeting time.

T F   **5.** When you add an attendee, you can send updated information to only the new attendee.

T F   **6.** A recurring meeting can occur only 10 times.

T F   **7.** Every meeting should have at least one mandatory attendee.

T F   **8.** To be scheduled, a resource must have its own mailbox.

T F   **9.** Your calendar is updated when you send a meeting request.

T F **10.** Any attendee can cancel a meeting.

Project 9-1: Create a One-Time Meeting

It's time to launch a new project at Tailspin Toys. Gather the team leaders in a meeting to divide the duties.

GET READY. LAUNCH Outlook if it is not already running.

  1. Click the Calendar button in the Navigation Pane to display the Calendar folder.

  2. Use the Date Navigator to select [next Thursday's date].

3. On the Home tab, click New Meeting in the New group. The Meeting window opens.

4. Click the *Subject* field and key Decoder: Project Launch. In the *Location* field, key Dept Room 62.

5. Click the Scheduling Assistant (or Scheduling) button in the Show group on the Ribbon.

6. Click the Add Others button and click Add from Address Book. The Select Attendees and Resources window is displayed.

7. Click Jamie Reding's contact information and click the Required button. Click Mandar Samant's contact information and click the Optional button. Click OK to return to the Meeting window.

8. Change the *End time* value so the meeting is one hour long. Use the Meeting Suggestions or the AutoPick Next button to select an open time for the meeting.

9. Click the Appointment button in the Show group on the Ribbon. The *To* field is automatically filled with the attendees' e-mail addresses and the *Start time* and *End time* fields are filled.

10. Click the Send button. Your calendar is updated, and the time slot is displayed as busy.

LEAVE Outlook open for the next project.

Project 9-2: Create a Recurring Meeting

After the Decoder project is launched, set up a recurring meeting to monitor the project's status.

GET READY. Before you begin these steps, complete the previous exercises.

1. Click the Calendar button in the Navigation Pane to display the Calendar folder.

2. Use the Date Navigator to select [the Thursday following the *Decoder: Project Launch* item].

3. On the Home tab, click New Meeting. The Meeting window is displayed.

4. Click the Subject field and key Decoder: Project Status. In the *Location* field, key Dept Room 62.

5. Click the Scheduling Assistant (or Scheduling) button in the Show group on the Ribbon.

6. Click the Add Others button and click Add from Address Book. The Select Attendees and Resources window is displayed.

7. Click Jamie Reding's contact information and click the Required button. Click Mandar Samant's contact information and click the Required button. Click OK to return to the Meeting window.

8. Change the *Start time* field to 10:00 AM and change the *End time* field to 11:00 AM, if necessary. The green and red vertical lines move to enclose the specified time slot.

9. Click the Recurrence button in the Options group on the Ribbon. The Appointment Recurrence window is displayed.

10. Click OK to accept the weekly recurrence pattern and return to the meeting window.

11. Click the Appointment button in the Show group on the Ribbon. The *To* field is automatically filled with the attendees' e-mail addresses, and the recurrence pattern is displayed.

12. Click the Send button. Your calendar is updated and the 10:00 AM to 11:00 AM time slot is displayed as busy for every Thursday

LEAVE Outlook open for the next project.

Proficiency Assessment

Project 9-3: Add an Attendee to a Recurring Meeting

Diane Tibbott has been assigned to the Decoder project. Add her as an attendee to the recurring Decoder project status meeting.

GET READY. Before you begin these steps, complete the previous exercises. The mandatory attendee used in this exercise must have a different active e-mail account from yours and be able to respond to your meeting invitation.

1. Click the Calendar button in the Navigation Pane to display the Calendar folder.

2. Double-click the first Decoder: Project Status meeting. The Open Recurring Item dialog box is displayed.

3. Click the Open the Series option and click OK.

4. Click the Scheduling Assistant (or Scheduling) button in the Show group on the Ribbon. Scheduling information for the attendees is displayed.

5. Click the Add Others button and click Add from Address Book. The Select Attendees and Resources window is displayed.

6. In the *Required* field, key [the e-mail address of the person or account that is acting as your mandatory attendee] for this lesson.

7. Click OK to return to the Meeting window.

8. Click the Send button. The Send Update to Attendees dialog box is displayed.

9. Click OK. The updated meeting information is sent to Diane Tibbott and no one else.

LEAVE Outlook open for the next project.

Project 9-4: Propose a New Meeting Time

Diane is currently assigned to the TopHat project; it is coming to a close and it takes priority over the Decoder project. To be able to participate in both meetings, Diane asked you to hold the Decoder: Project Status meeting later in the day.

GET READY. Before you begin these steps, complete the previous exercises. The mandatory attendee used in this exercise must have a different active e-mail account from yours and be able to respond to your meeting invitation.

1. In the mandatory attendee's account, click the Decoder: Project Status meeting request in the message list.

2. In the Reading Pane, click Propose New Time. In the Propose New Time dialog box that appears, propose a new start time of 1:00 PM.

3. Verify that 2:00 PM is the time in the *End* field and click OK. The dialog box closes and a New Proposed Time: Message window is displayed.

4. In the message area, key [a note asking for the change in schedule].

5. Click the Send button.

LEAVE Outlook open for the next project.

Mastery Assessment

Project 9-5: Change an Occurrence of a Recurring Meeting

The TopHat project plans to camp in your meeting room for a week of intensive testing. Change the location of the first Decoder: Project Status meeting.

GET READY. LAUNCH Outlook if it is not already running.

1. Open the first Decoder: Project Status meeting in the Calendar. The Open Recurring Item dialog box is displayed.

2. Open just this occurrence of the meeting.

3. Change the location to Dept Room 50.

4. Send an update to all attendees.

LEAVE Outlook open for the next project.

Project 9-6: Cancel a Meeting

The upper management at Tailspin Toys has changed. New leadership brings new priorities. The Decoder project has been cancelled. Cancel the Decoder project launch meeting and the recurring project status meeting.

GET READY. LAUNCH Outlook if it is not already running.

1. Open the first Decoder: Project Status meeting in the Calendar. The Open Recurring Item dialog box is displayed.

2. Open the series of meetings and cancel the meeting.

3. Send a meeting cancellation notice to the attendees explaining the reason for the cancellation.

CLOSE Outlook.

INTERNET READY

Your coworkers might not work in your office. Between telecommuting and traveling to client locations, you might find that several attendees do not attend meetings in person. Use the Internet to investigate meeting methods that can be used when all of the attendees are not in the same location.

LESSON SKILL MATRIX

Skills	Exam Objective	Objective Number
Setting Calendar Options	Set calendar options. Change the calendar color.	1.1.3 5.3.2
Sharing Your Calendar		
Working with Multiple Calendars	Display or hide calendars. Create a calendar group. Arrange the calendar view.	5.3.3 5.3.4 5.3.1
Printing Calendars	Print calendars.	1.5.2

KEY TERMS

- calendar group
- Internet Calendar Subscription
- Microsoft Outlook Calendar Sharing Service
- Overlay mode
- Overlay stack
- Side-by-side mode
- Time zone
- Coordinated Universal Time (UTC)
- view
- work week

Mindy is a co-owner of Resort Adventures. Mindy and her partner, Jon, work different hours so that an owner is on the premises as much as possible. Their work schedules overlap for several hours a day and they come into the office for meetings or extra hours on busy days when necessary. It's a good thing Outlook lets Mindy modify the Calendar to reflect her unusual work schedule. In this lesson you'll customize your main Outlook calendar, create and work with a secondary calendar, share calendars, and print them.

SOFTWARE ORIENTATION

Outlook Options Dialog Box

You can customize the Outlook calendar to make it fit your needs or work patterns using the Outlook Options dialog box shown in Figure 10-1. Access these calendar options from the Backstage view, then select or modify specific settings.

Figure 10-1

Outlook Options window

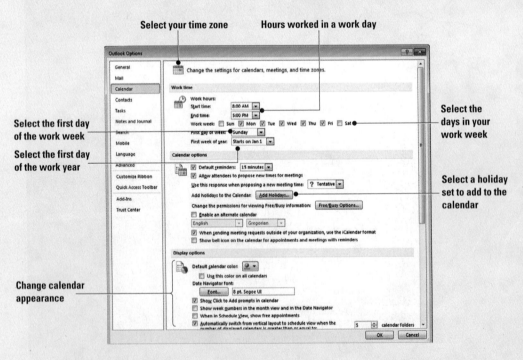

SETTING CALENDAR OPTIONS

The Bottom Line

To make your calendar more useful, you can customize it in several ways. You can define your work week, display the time zones you use regularly, set your own time zone, and add holidays to the calendar.

Defining Your Work Week

Your **work week** is the hours or days you work in a calendar week. The most common work week is 8:00 AM to 5:00 PM Monday through Friday. Your work week may differ. In this exercise, you will define your work week as Tuesday through Saturday from 6:00 AM to 3:00 PM, since you don't work on Sunday and Monday.

STEP BY STEP   **Define Your Work Week**

GET READY. LAUNCH Outlook if it is not already running.

1. On the File tab, click Options. The Outlook Options window is displayed.
2. Click Calendar in the navigation pane. The calendar options are displayed as in Figure 10-1.
3. In the Work Time section of the dialog box, click the Mon check box to deselect it and remove Monday from your work week.
4. Click the Sat check box to add Saturday to your work week.
5. Click the *Start time* field. Key or select 6:00 AM. Click the *End time* field. Key or select 3:00 PM.
6. In the *First day of the week* field, select Tuesday as the start of your work week. Compare your work time calendar options to Figure 10-2.

CERTIFICATION READY   **1.1.3**

How do you define your calendar's work week?

Figure 10-2

Work week defined

Work Week options

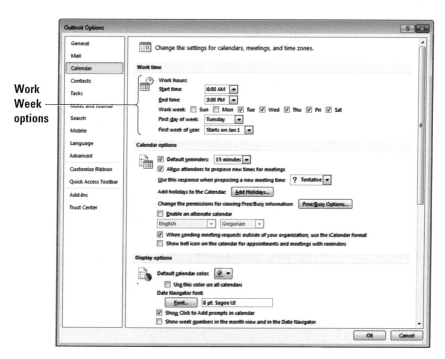

7. Click OK to save the modified work week. Click the Calendar button on the Navigation Pane to display the Calendar window.
8. On the Home tab, click Week from the Arrangement group to see how the modified work week affects your calendar. Note that Saturday is now a workday and Monday and Sunday are shaded to indicate that they are not workdays, as shown in Figure 10-3.

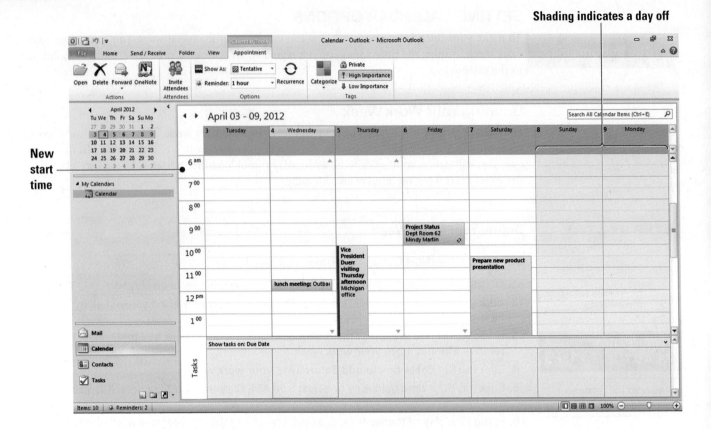

Figure 10-3

Modified Work Week view

PAUSE. LEAVE Outlook open to use in the next exercise.

Changing Your Time Zone

A **time zone** is a geographic location using the same standard time. In Microsoft Outlook, time zones are defined in terms of the difference between their local time and **Coordinated Universal Time**, or UTC, the time standard based on International Atomic Time. If you move, transfer to another office, or remain onsite at a client's office for several weeks, you can change the time zone in your calendar. If you frequently travel and stay in a different time zone for any length of time, changing the time zone to match the local time will help ensure that you don't miss any appointments. In this exercise, you will temporarily change your local time zone.

STEP BY STEP   **Change Your Time Zone**

GET READY. LAUNCH Outlook if it is not already running.

1. On the File tab, click Options. The Outlook Options window is displayed.
2. Click Calendar in the navigation pane. The calendar options are displayed as in Figure 10-1.
3. Scroll down to see additional calendar options, as shown in Figure 10-4.

Figure 10-4

Time Zone options

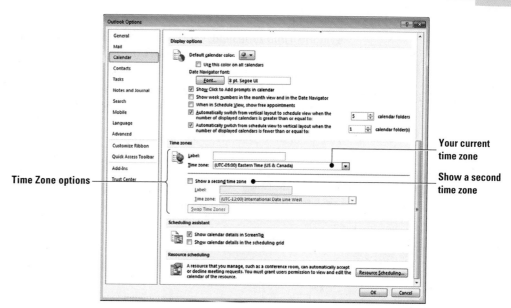

Time Zone options

4. In the *Time Zone* field, select [a time zone that differs from your current time zone by several hours].

5. In the *Label* field, key Training Site.

6. Click OK to save the changes.

7. On the Home tab, click Week from the Arrangement group to see how the modified time zone affects your calendar. The times of any set appointments and meetings will have been adjusted.

8. On the File tab, click Options.

9. Click Calendar to see the calendar options.

10. Scroll down to see the *Time Zone* field, select [your own time zone] from the list.

11. In the *Label* field, key Home.

12. Click OK to save the changes.

13. On the Home tab, click Week from the Arrangement group to verify that your changes have taken affect.

PAUSE. LEAVE Outlook open to use in the next exercise.

CERTIFICATION
READY   1.1.3

How do you change your time zone?

Displaying Multiple Time Zones

Depending on your business, family, and friends, you may communicate frequently with one or more businesses or individuals in a different time zone. To easily agree on times for meetings and phone calls, it can be useful to display other time zones in your calendar. You don't want to miss talking to an important client by calling after business hours. In this exercise, you will add a second time zone to your calendar.

STEP BY STEP   **Display Multiple Time Zones**

CERTIFICATION
READY   1.1.3

How do you display a calendar with multiple time zones?

GET READY. LAUNCH Outlook if it is not already running.

1. On the File tab, click Options. The Outlook Options window is displayed.

2. Click Calendar in the navigation pane. The calendar options are displayed as in Figure 10-1.

3. Scroll down to see the time zone options. Click the Show a second time zone check box.

4. In the *Label* field, key Kathmandu.

5. In the *Time zone* field, select (UTC+05:45) Kathmandu. (Kathmandu Time is five hours and 45 minutes different from UTC.)

6. Click OK to save the changes.

7. On the Home tab, click Week from the Arrangement group to verify how the change affects your calendar. Compare your calendar to the one in Figure 10-5.

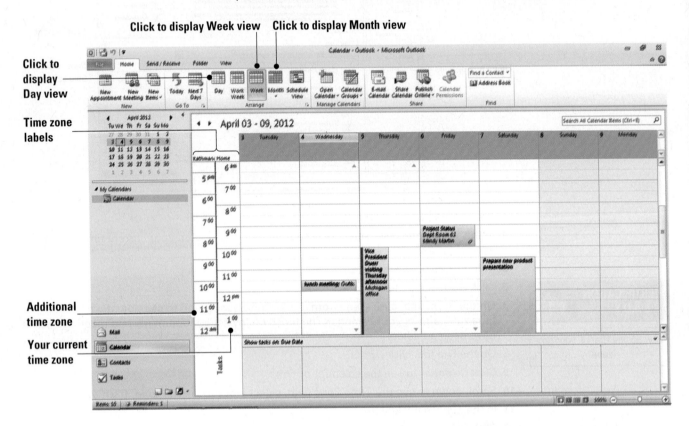

Figure 10-5

Calendar with two time zones

8. On the File tab, click Options. Click Calendar to see the calendar options.

9. Scroll down to see the time zone options. Click the Show a second time zone check box to deselect it.

PAUSE. LEAVE Outlook open to use in the next exercise.

Adding Holidays to the Calendar

Holidays are classified as all-day events. In your calendar, a holiday is displayed as a banner at the top of the day. When you install Outlook, holidays are not placed on your calendar. Outlook provides standard sets of holidays based on individual country traditions. Separate sets of some religious holidays are also available. In this exercise, you will add the official government holidays for your location.

STEP BY STEP   **Add Holidays to the Calendar**

**CERTIFICATION
READY   1.1.3**

How do you add holidays to
your calendar?

GET READY. LAUNCH Outlook if it is not already running.

1. On the File tab, click Options. The Outlook Options window is displayed.

2. Click Calendar in the navigation pane. The calendar options are displayed as in Figure 10-1.

3. Under the Calendar options group, click Add Holidays.

4. Click [the check box next to the country or region's holiday set that you want to add], as shown in Figure 10-6. By default, your country or region is already selected.

Figure 10-6

Add Holidays to Calendar window

Figure 10-6

Add Holidays to Calendar window

Take Note   If you frequently do business with someone from another country, you might consider adding their holiday set to your calendar as well.

5. Click OK. A small window is displayed while the holidays are added to your calendar. When the holidays are added, a message is displayed telling you that the holidays were added. Click OK.

Troubleshooting   If you try to add the same holiday set again, you will see duplicate holiday and event entries in your calendar. Outlook will display a warning message before adding these holidays a second time.

6. Click OK to save the change and close the Add Holidays to Calendar dialog box.

7. On the Home tab, click Month in the Arrangement group to display the Month view. If necessary, click the Forward or Back button to view a month containing a holiday. Click the Forward or Back button to return to the current month, as shown in Figure 10-7.

Figure 10-7

Holidays added to the Calendar

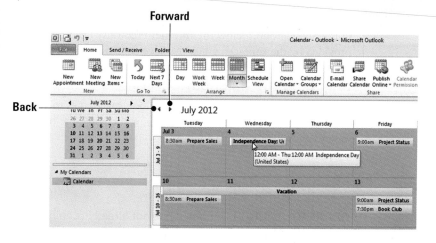

PAUSE. LEAVE Outlook open to use in the next exercise.

Configuring Your Free/Busy Settings

Your free/busy information is used by people sending meeting requests to determine if you are available for meetings. If your company uses Microsoft Exchange software, free/busy times are automatically shared with others on your network and this information is available through the Calendar. You can configure the Free/Busy settings to specify the number of months' worth of free/busy information you want to share and the frequency at which the information is updated. In this exercise, you will configure your own free/busy settings to aid others in inviting you to scheduled meetings.

Ref   You can find more information on creating meetings in Lesson 9.

STEP BY STEP   **Configure Your Free/Busy Settings**

GET READY. LAUNCH Outlook if it is not already running.

1. On the File tab, click Options. The Outlook Options window is displayed.
2. Click Calendar in the navigation pane. The calendar options are displayed as in Figure 10-1.
3. Under the Calendar options group, click the Free/Busy Options button. The Free/Busy Options window is displayed, as shown in Figure 10-8. By default, two months of free/busy time are already selected.

Figure 10-8

Free/Busy Options window

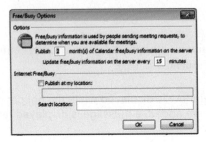

4. In the *Publish* field, key 1 to change the numbers of months ahead of the current date that your free/busy information is available to other network users.
5. In the *Update free/busy information on the server* field, key 30 to reduce the frequency with which your information is updated on the Microsoft Exchange server.
6. Click OK in the Free/Busy Options window and the Outlook Options window to return to the Calendar folder.

PAUSE. LEAVE Outlook open to use in the next exercise.

**CERTIFICATION
READY   1.1.3**

How do you configure free/busy settings?

You can also access the free/busy information for contacts outside of your network. To view a contact's free/busy information, you can ask them for the URL where the free/busy information is stored. Once you receive their information, open their contact record and click Details in the Show group. Below the Internet Free-Busy heading, in the *Address* field key [the location provided by the contact]. Click the Save & Close button on the Ribbon.

Changing the Calendar Color

Another way of customizing your Outlook calendar is to change the background color for the calendar grid itself. In this exercise, you will change the background color for your main Outlook calendar.

STEP BY STEP   **Change the Calendar Color**

GET READY. LAUNCH Outlook if it is not already running.

Another Way
You can also set Calendar color using the Color button on the View tab.

1. On the File tab, click Options. The Outlook Options dialog box is displayed.
2. Click Calendar. The calendar options are displayed as in Figure 10-1.
3. In the Display options area, click the Default calendar color drop-down arrow and select the color you want.

Take Note   The *Use this color on all calendars* check box will apply this same background color to your custom and shared calendars as well.

**CERTIFICATION
READY   5.3.2**

How do you change the calendar color?

4. Click OK to save the changes.
5. On the Home tab, click Month in the Arrangement group to display the Month view.
6. Click the View tab. Click the Color button in the Color group. Notice that the new Automatic Color matches the color you selected in the Outlook Options dialog box.

PAUSE. LEAVE Outlook open to use in the next exercise.

Take Note   If desired, go back to the Outlook Options dialog box, click the Default calendar color drop-down arrow, and choose the default blue color to restore the original calendar appearance.

SHARING YOUR CALENDAR

The Bottom Line   When you work with others, sharing your schedule makes it easier to arrange meetings, determine deadlines, and set realistic goals. Regardless of the type of e-mail account you use, you can share your calendar with others. You can share calendar information through a company server using Microsoft Exchange or share your calendar using the Internet.

Sharing Your Calendar with Other Network Users

By default, the free/busy details of your Calendar are already shared with everyone on your Exchange network. But, you can also use Share Calendar to allow members of your Exchange Server network to see additional details and make edits to your calendar. You decide who can see your calendar and exactly what level of detail you want to share. In this exercise, you will share your calendar with to another user.

STEP BY STEP   **Share Your Calendar with Other Network Users**

GET READY. LAUNCH Outlook if it is not already running.

This exercise requires a Microsoft Exchange account.

Troubleshooting If the Share Calendar button is gray on the Share group of the Home tab, you do not have a Microsoft Exchange account configured. If this is the case, you cannot complete this exercise.

1. If necessary, click the Calendar button in the Navigation Pane to display the Calendar window.
2. On the Home tab, click Share Calendar in the Share group.
3. In the *To* field, key [the name of the individual who will view your calendar].
4. Click the Request Permission To View Recipient's Calendar check box.

Troubleshooting If you clicked Share Calendar but don't see the *Request permission to view recipient's Calendar,* you do not have the Microsoft Exchange account described here. Once you've published a calendar to the Internet, the Share Calendar button changes to display a message window that you can use to send the URL of your published calendar. See more details in the next couple of exercises.

5. In the *Details* field, select Limited Details.
6. Click the Send button. A dialog box is displayed. Click OK to confirm the information. A message is sent to the person you're sharing your calendar with, notifying them that they can now open and view your calendar.

PAUSE. LEAVE Outlook open to use in the next exercise.

    Ref   You can find information about viewing another network user's calendar in the "Viewing Another Network User's Calendar" section later in this lesson.

Sending Calendar Information via E-mail

If you don't have a Microsoft Exchange Server, you might find it useful to share your calendar information to help with trying to schedule a meetings or events. When you share a calendar with someone, they will be able to see when you are available. In Outlook 2010, you can send a copy of your calendar to anyone using an e-mail message. You select the date range you want to include and the level of detail to share, as shown in Table 10-1. In this exercise, you'll send a calendar to a friend or coworker via e-mail.

Table 10-1

Calendar Details Options

Detail Level	Description
Availability only	Time is displayed as free, busy, tentative, or out of office. This is enough information for scheduling purposes.
Limited details	The attached calendar includes availability information and the subjects of all calendar items.
Full details	The attached calendar includes availability information and the complete details of all calendar items.

STEP BY STEP   **Send Calendar Information via E-mail**

GET READY. LAUNCH Outlook if it is not already running.

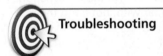

Another Way
If you have more than one calendar, you can specify your alternate calendar's name here.

1. If necessary, click the Calendar button in the Navigation Pane to display your Calendar.
2. On the Home tab, click the E-mail Calendar button in the Share group. An untitled message window is displayed along with the Send a Calendar via E-mail dialog box.
3. In the *Calendar* field, select Calendar, if necessary.
4. Click the Show button in the Advanced area to display more options, as shown in Figure 10-9.

Figure 10-9

Send a Calendar via E-mail window

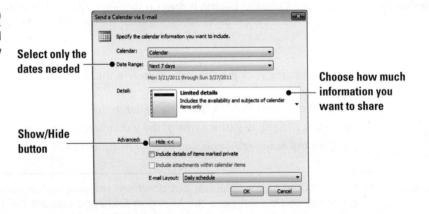

Select only the dates needed

Choose how much information you want to share

Show/Hide button

5. In the *Date Range* field, select Next 30 days.
6. In the *Detail* field, select Limited details.
7. In the *E-mail Layout* field, select List of events.

Troubleshooting   Be sure to select the smallest date range necessary for the recipient's needs. Every added day increases the size of the message. Many e-mail servers restrict the size of messages that can be received. If the date range is too large or if you included unnecessary details, the message might be too large for the recipient to receive.

8. Click OK. A new Outlook Message window is displayed with the calendar information included in the body of the message.
9. In the *To* field, key [the e-mail address of a friend or coworker]. In the *Cc* field, key [your e-mail address].
10. In the message body above the calendar details, key Susan, [press Enter] As you can see from the details below, my week is pretty open. Find a time that works for you and I'll add it to my calendar as well. [Press Enter twice.] Mindy.

11. Compare your message to Figure 10-10. Scroll down the message body if necessary to view the data in the message.

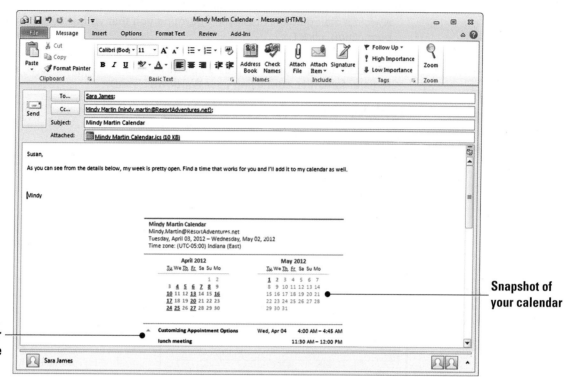

A list of items in your calendar for the selected time

Snapshot of your calendar

Figure 10-10

Sharing a calendar via e-mail

Take Note   Calendars sent in this manner are a snapshot of your calendar details, so the calendar information will not be automatically updated.

12. Click Send to return to your Calendar.

PAUSE. LEAVE Outlook open to use in the next exercise.

Registering for Microsoft Outlook Calendar Sharing

Sharing calendar information via e-mail works best for sharing specific information over a short term. However, in certain circumstances, you might find that you need to share calendar information more frequently and want to ensure that your calendar is automatically updated. For example, a sales manager can create a calendar of scheduled sales calls that needs to be distributed to the sales team. In this instance, the manager can publish the calendar to Office.com. Each salesman can access the calendar to see the most accurate information about the week's meetings. By registering for **Microsoft Outlook Calendar Sharing Service,** you can share your calendar at Office.com. In this exercise, you'll register for Microsoft Outlook Calendar Sharing.

STEP BY STEP   **Register for Microsoft Outlook Calendar Sharing**

GET READY. LAUNCH Outlook if it is not already running and connect to the Internet before you begin these steps. You must also have a Windows Live account to publish your calendar to Office.com.

Troubleshooting   If you are logged in to a secure Microsoft Exchange network, your Administrator may block this feature. Ask about any alternate methods for sharing calendar information outside your network.

1. If necessary, click the Calendar button in the Navigation Pane to display the Calendar. If necessary, select your calendar.

2. Click the Publish Online button in the Share group and then click Publish to Office. com. If a dialog box is displayed informing you that you will view pages over a secure connection, click OK.

3. If this is the first time you have used the Outlook Calendar Publishing Service, the Office.com Registration window appears, as shown in Figure 10-11, so that you can register for Office.com using your Windows Live ID.

Figure 10-11

Office.com Registration— Calendar Sharing Overview window

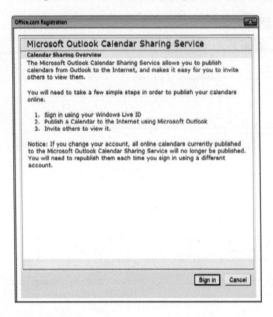

Troubleshooting If the Publish Calendar to Office.com dialog box, shown later in Figure 10-15, is displayed instead, it means that the registration process is already complete. Leave the dialog box open and proceed to the next exercise.

4. Click Sign In. The Microsoft Outlook Calendar Sharing window is displayed, as shown in Figure 10-12.

Figure 10-12

Office.com Registration—Sign in to Office.com window

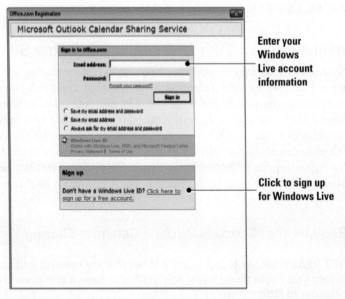

5. In the *E-mail address* field, key [your Windows Live ID e-mail address].

Take Note If you are sharing your calendar information on Office.com as a business tool, then consider the Windows Live ID display name as a reflection of your business. The display name is visible to anyone with whom you share your calendar. If your existing display name has personal meaning but is not business appropriate, you should create a second account for business use.

6. In the *Password* field, key [your Windows Live password]. Click Sign In. The Legal Agreements page for the Microsoft Outlook Calendar Sharing Service is displayed, as shown in Figure 10-13.

Figure 10-13

Office.com Registration—Legal Agreements window

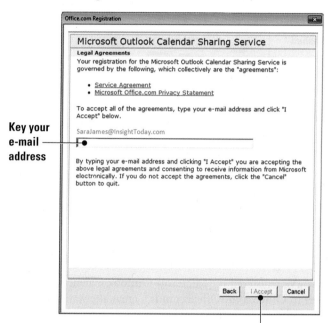

Key your e-mail address

Click when the button becomes active

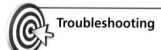 **Troubleshooting** If you do not have a Windows Live ID, consider getting one. This free account can be used to access a number of additional Windows and Office features. To sign up for a Windows Live account, click the *Click here to sign up for a free account* link.

7. In the box below your e-mail address, key [your e-mail address] for verification purposes. When you finish keying your e-mail address, the I Accept button becomes available.

8. Click the I Accept button. The final page of the Microsoft Outlook Calendar Sharing Service is displayed, as shown in Figure 10-14.

Figure 10-14

Office.com Registration—Sign In Complete window

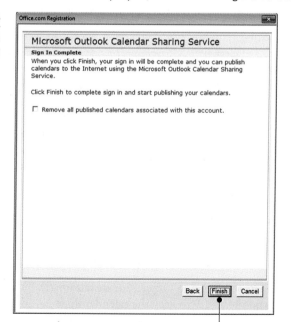

Click to complete the registration

9. At the Sign In Complete page, click Finish. The Publish Calendar to Office.com dialog box is displayed, as shown in Figure 10-15.

Figure 10-15

The Publish Calendar to Office. com window

Calendar to be published

Time Period to be published

Detail level to be published

Limit the users who can view your calendar

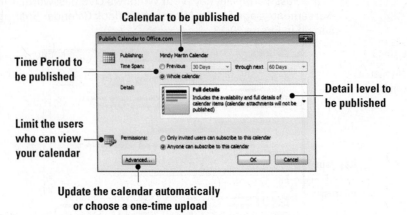

Update the calendar automatically or choose a one-time upload

PAUSE. **LEAVE** Outlook the Publish Calendar to Office.com dialog box open to use in the next exercise.

Publishing Calendar Information to Office.com

Once you've registered for Microsoft Outlook Calendar Sharing Service, you can publish your calendar to Office.com. Office.com is a great alternative for users who do not have a company server or who want to share calendar information with people who are not members of their Exchange Server network. When you publish a calendar to Office.com, you can control the amount of calendar information published and limit the number of people who can view your calendar. By default, the calendar information on Office.com is updated every 30 minutes. This means that the people you've shared the published calendar with will always have the most up-to-date information. In this exercise, you'll publish a calendar to Office.com.

STEP BY STEP | **Publish Calendar Information to Office.com**

GET READY. LAUNCH Outlook if it is not already running.

Before you begin these steps, you must have a Windows Live ID, be connected to the Internet, and be registered for Microsoft Outlook Calendar Sharing service at Office.com.

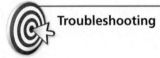 **Troubleshooting** If you are logged into a secure Microsoft Exchange network, your Administrator may block this feature. Ask about any alternate methods for sharing calendar information outside your network.

1. If necessary, click the Calendar button in the Navigation Pane to display the Calendar. If necessary, select your calendar and click the Publish Online button in the Share group; then click Publish to Office.com to open the Publish Calendar to Office.com dialog box shown in Figure 10-15.
2. In the *Time Span* field, select the Whole calendar option.
3. In the *Detail* field, select Full details.
4. In the *Permissions* field, click the Only invited users can subscribe to this calendar option.

Take Note

By default, calendars published to Office.com are automatically updated every 30 minutes. For this exercise, it is not necessary to keep the calendar updated, so you will choose the Single Upload option in the Advanced settings.

5. Click the Advanced button. The Published Calendar Settings window is displayed, as shown in Figure 10-16.

The Published Calendar Settings window

6. Select the Single Upload: Updates will not be uploaded option. Click OK to close the Published Calendar Settings window and return to the Publish Calendar to Office.com dialog box.

7. Click OK to publish your calendar. Key your password again, if necessary. When the upload is complete, the Send a Sharing Invitation window is displayed, as shown in Figure 10-17.

Figure 10-17

Send a Sharing Invitation window

8. Click Yes. A Share window resembling an Outlook Message window is displayed, as shown in Figure 10-18.

Figure 10-18

A Share window

Calendar to be published

Calendar location

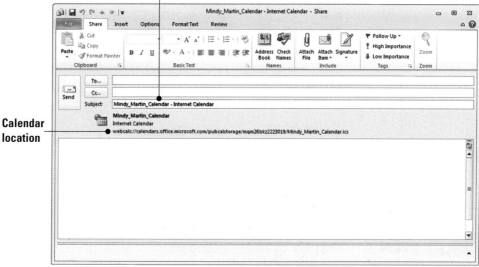

9. In the *To* field, key [your e-mail address]. Click the Send button. The invitation is sent.

Take Note   To view your calendar, the invited individual must also have a Windows Live ID.

PAUSE. LEAVE Outlook open to use in the next exercise.

WORKING WITH MULTIPLE CALENDARS

The Bottom Line

Keeping multiple calendars is a great way to stay organized and keep your personal information private. Outlook makes it easy to create custom calendars. You can also share calendars with others and subscribe to calendars via the Internet. Use the Outlook tools to hide and display multiple calendars and to view them in different combinations and arrangements.

Creating a Custom Calendar

Many times your work involves participation in a number of project teams. Project teams have their own set of meetings, deadlines, and tasks. In this exercise, you will create a new calendar for managing the details of a project dedicated to Resort Adventures' anniversary celebration party.

STEP BY STEP **Create a Custom Calendar**

GET READY. LAUNCH Outlook if it is not already running.

Another Way
You can create, delete, or rename a custom calendar by selecting those options in the right-click shortcut menu in the Navigation Pane.

1. On the Folder tab, click New Calendar in the New group. The Create New Folder dialog box is displayed.
2. In the *Name* field, key Anniversary Celebration.
3. In the *Select where to place the folder* field, select Calendar.
4. Click OK to close the dialog box.
5. The new Anniversary Celebration calendar appears in the Navigation Pane under the My Calendars heading, as shown in Figure 10-19.

Figure 10-19

Creating a new calendar

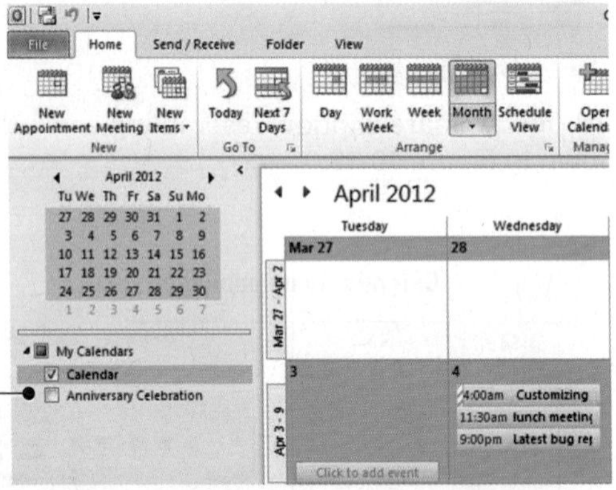

New Anniversary calendar

PAUSE. LEAVE Outlook open to use in the next exercise.

Displaying or Hiding Calendars

Now that you have more than one calendar to view, you will need a way to make sure that you know which calendar you are viewing at any given time. In this exercise, you will learn how to display and hide the calendars. Specifically, you will display calendars in **side-by-side** view, which means the calendars will appear beside each other in the Outlook window.

STEP BY STEP **Display or Hide Calendars**

GET READY. LAUNCH Outlook if it is not already running.

You must first complete the previous exercises.

1. If necessary, click the Calendar button in the Navigation Pane to display the Calendar window.
2. If necessary, click [the check boxes next to both your main Outlook calendar and the Anniversary Celebration calendar].
3. Both calendars appear side by side, as shown in Figure 10-20.

Both calendars are visible

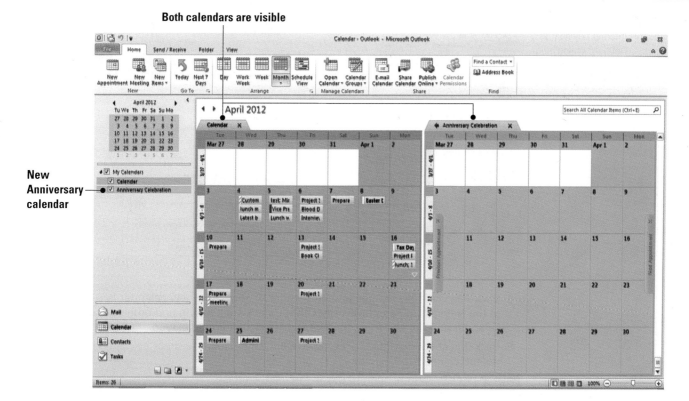

Figure 10-20

Side-by-side calendars

4. Click the check box next to the Anniversary Celebration calendar in the Navigation Pane to clear the check box. The second calendar is now hidden from view.

PAUSE. LEAVE Outlook open to use in the next exercise.

CERTIFICATION READY   5.3.3

How do you display or hide calendars?

Viewing Calendar Shared via E-mail

In the previous section, you learned several ways to share your calendar with others. Now, you will learn how to view shared calendars. In a previous exercise, you shared a calendar via e-mail. As you saw during the exercise, a snapshot of the shared calendar appeared at the bottom of the e-mail message. In addition to the image of the calendar, the message included a calendar attachment. You can open this calendar file and use it to view the sender's free/busy information when scheduling meetings. In this exercise, you'll view a calendar shared by e-mail.

STEP BY STEP   **View Calendar Shared via E-mail**

GET READY. LAUNCH Outlook if it is not already running.

For this exercise you need to have completed the Send Calendar Information via E-mail exercise earlier in this lesson.

1. If necessary, click the Mail button in the Navigation Pane to display the mailbox.

2. In the message list, click [a sharing invitation] sent to you by a friend or coworker. If you do not have one, locate the sharing invitation that you copied yourself on in the Send Calendar Information via E-mail exercise. The message is previewed in the Reading Pane.

3. Click the Open this Calendar button at the top of the Reading Pane. The Add this Internet Calendar to Outlook? dialog box is displayed, as shown in Figure 10-21.

Figure 10-21

Add this Internet Calendar to Outlook? dialog box

Open this Calendar button

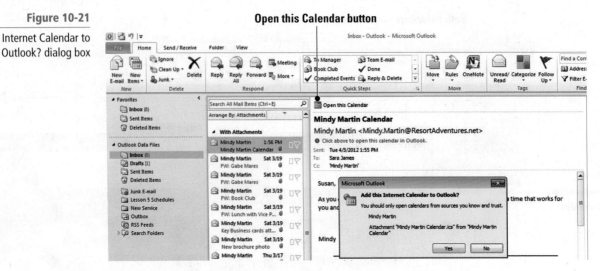

4. Click **Yes**. Outlook changes to the Calendar window. The new calendar has been added to the Navigation Pane under the Other Calendars heading and both your default calendar and the one that you received via e-mail are displayed.

5. Click [the check box next to the new calendar] to clear the check box and view the default calendar on its own.

PAUSE. LEAVE Outlook open to use in the next exercise.

Viewing Another Network User's Calendar

In the previous section, you learned to share calendars with other users on your Microsoft Exchange network. Now, you will learn how to view the calendars that members of your Exchange network share with you. To view someone's calendar, you must have permission. After permission is granted, you can create a link to the shared calendar that will be stored in your Navigation Pane. In this exercise, you'll view a network user's calendar.

STEP BY STEP **View Another Network User's Calendar**

GET READY. LAUNCH Outlook if it is not already running.

This exercise requires a Microsoft Exchange account.

 Troubleshooting If you do not have a Microsoft Exchange account configured, you cannot complete this exercise.

1. If necessary, click the Calendar button in the Navigation Pane to display the Calendar window.

2. On the Home tab, click the Open Calendar button on the Manage Calendars group.

3. Select Open Shared Calendar from the drop-down menu.

4. In the Name field, key [the calendar owner's name]. Click OK. The shared calendar is displayed next to your calendar, and the new calendar has been added to the Navigation Pane under the Shared Calendars heading.

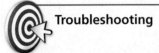 **Troubleshooting** If you do not have permission to view the calendar, Outlook will prompt you to request permission. If you agree to request permission, a sharing request addressed to the user is displayed. Send the request to obtain permission to view the calendar. You'll receive a message notifying you when the owner has agreed to share.

5. Click [the check box next to your default calendar] to clear the check box and view the new shared calendar on its own.

PAUSE. LEAVE Outlook open to use in the next exercise.

Subscribing to an Internet Calendar

An **Internet Calendar Subscription** is a downloaded calendar that is automatically updated. You can use an invitation, like the one that you created earlier in this lesson, to subscribe to an Internet calendar. You can search one of several websites that host Internet calendars, such as Office.com or iCalShare.com. In this exercise, you will subscribe to the published calendar you received earlier in the lesson and a public calendar.

STEP BY STEP   **Subscribe to an Internet Calendar**

GET READY. LAUNCH Outlook if it is not already running.

This exercise requires Internet access.

1. If necessary, click the Mail button in the Navigation Pane to display the mailbox. Click [the check box next to your default calendar] if necessary to display it.

2. In the message list, click [a sharing invitation sent to you by a friend or coworker]. The message is previewed in the Reading Pane.

Take Note   If you didn't receive an invitation from someone else, locate the sharing invitation that you copied yourself on in the Publish Calendar Information to Office.com exercise.

3. Click the Subscribe to this Calendar button on the top of the Reading Pane. The Add this Internet Calendar to Outlook and Subscribe to Updates? dialog box is displayed, as shown in Figure 10-22.

Figure 10-22

The *Add this Internet Calendar to Outlook and Subscribe to Updates?* dialog box

Click to create a permanent link to this calendar

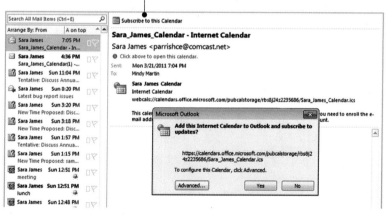

4. Click Yes. The new calendar has been added to the Navigation Pane under the Shared Calendars heading.

5. Click [the check box next to your default calendar] to clear the check box and view the new shared calendar on its own.

6. In the Navigation Pane, click [the default calendar's check box] and deselect [any other calendars].

PAUSE. LEAVE Outlook open to use in the next exercise.

Using Overlay Mode to View Multiple Calendars

You have seen how multiple calendars in Outlook can be viewed side by side, but you can also use Outlook's **overlay mode** to view a merged version of the calendars on top of each other. Color coding helps you determine which calendar holds scheduled items that appear in the merged view. Several calendars displayed in overlay mode are called an **overlay stack**. In this exercise, you will use the overlay mode to find free time that is common to all the displayed calendars.

Use Overlay Mode to View Multiple Calendars

GET READY. LAUNCH Outlook if it is not already running and complete the previous exercises first.

1. If necessary, click the Calendar button in the Navigation Pane to display the Calendar window.

2. Click [the check box next to the Anniversary Celebration calendar] to select it. The Anniversary Celebration calendar appears next to the default calendar.

3. Point to the date a week from Friday in the Anniversary Celebration calendar. When the *Click To Add Event* box appears, click it and key Planning session.

4. Click [the check box next to one of the calendars under the Shared Calendars heading]. All three calendars are now visible in the Side-by-Side mode, as shown in Figure 10-23.

View in Overlay Mode toggle button

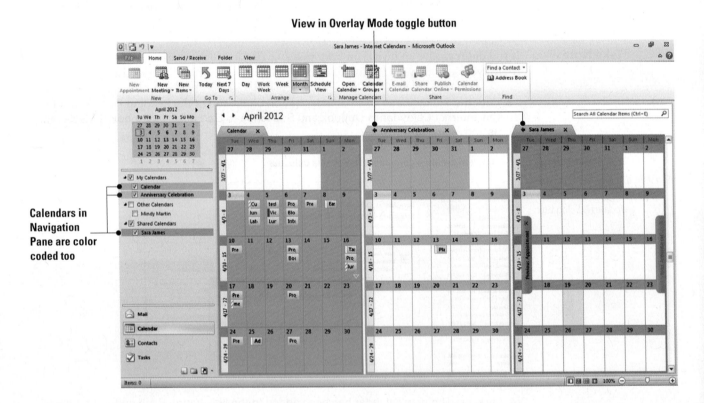

Calendars in Navigation Pane are color coded too

Figure 10-23

Viewing multiple calendars

5. On the Anniversary Celebration calendar, click the View in Overlay Mode toggle button, which is the small right arrow next to the calendar's name. The Anniversary Celebration calendar slides over on top of the default calendar.

6. Click the View in Overlay Mode toggle button on the shared calendar. The calendars will be displayed in an overlay stack, as shown in Figure 10-24.

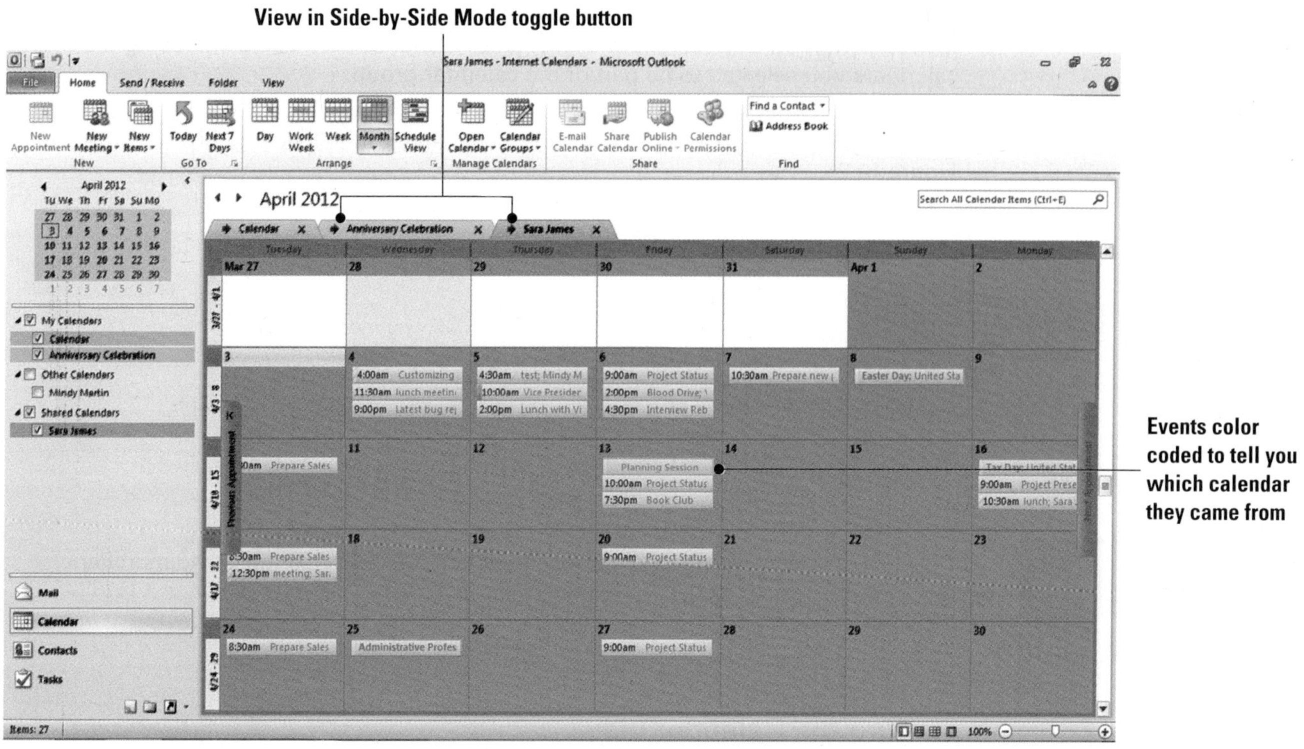

View in Side-by-Side Mode toggle button

Figure 10-24

Calendars in an overlay stack

Events color coded to tell you which calendar they came from

7. Click [the check box next to the shared calendar's name] to clear the check box.

8. Click the View in Side-by-Side Mode toggle button again to return to the Side-by-Side mode.

9. Click [the check box next to the Anniversary Celebration calendar] to clear the check box.

PAUSE. LEAVE Outlook open to use in the next exercise.

Creating a Calendar Group

NEW to Office 2010

If you have several calendars that you frequently view together, for instance, your main calendar and those of your project's team members, you may find it helpful to create a calendar group. A **calendar group** adds a heading to the Navigation Pane in the Calendar and allows you to view all calendars with the group at one time. In this exercise, you'll create a calendar group.

STEP BY STEP

Create a Calendar Group

Another Way
You can use Out-look's Address Book to create a new calendar group. Select Create a New Calendar Group from the Calendar Groups dropdown menu and give the group a name, then use the Address Book button to add group members.

GET READY. LAUNCH Outlook if it is not already running and complete the previous exercises first.

1. If necessary, click the Calendar button in the Navigation Pane to display the Calendar window.

2. Click [the check box next to the Anniversary Celebration calendar].

3. Click [the check box next to one of the calendars under the Shared Calendars heading].

4. On the Home tab, click Calendar Groups from the Manage Calendars group.

5. Select Save as New Calendar Group from the drop-down menu. The Create New Calendar Group dialog box is displayed, as shown in Figure 10-25.

Figure 10-25

Create New Calendar Group dialog box

6. In the *Name* field, key My Team Members and then click OK. A new heading called My Team Members appears in the Navigation Pane. Under this new heading are the calendars you selected to be part of the calendar group.

7. In the Navigation Pane, drag another calendar from the Navigation Pane to the My Team Members group to add a copy of that calendar to this new group, as shown in Figure 10-26.

Figure 10-26

Calendar group in the Navigation Pane

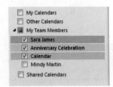

8. Deselect [all the calendars except for the default Calendar] in the Navigation Pane.

PAUSE. LEAVE Outlook open to use in the next exercise.

Arranging the Calendar View

NEW to Office 2010

In the Outlook Calendar, a **view** is a specific layout for the calendar details. By default, the Calendar displays appointments, meetings, and events for the current day with the Daily Task List visible below. Table 10-2 describes how the layout changes as each of the four View buttons on the status bar is selected. In addition, Outlook provides a number of ways to quickly change the calendar display using the buttons on the Arrangement group of the Home tab. In this exercise, you will explore the other views available in the Calendar.

Table 10-2

Calendar View Buttons

View name	Description
Normal	This view displays the Calendar with the Daily Task List below it.
Calendar and Tasks	Like the Normal view, this view displays the Calendar and the Daily Task List, but the Navigation Pane is minimized to allow more room for the Calendar display.
Calendar Only	The Navigation Pane is still minimized in this view and the Daily Task List is not displayed.
Classic	All three elements are visible in this view, but the Daily Task List is displayed to the right of the Calendar, instead of below it.

STEP BY STEP   **Arrange the Calendar View**

GET READY. LAUNCH Outlook if it is not already running.

1. If necessary, click the Calendar button in the Navigation Pane to display the Calendar folder.

2. Use the Date Navigator to select [the Monday in the second week of April].

3. If necessary, click the Normal View button on the status bar. This is Outlook's default Calendar view.

4. On the Home tab, select Work Week in the Arrangement group. Notice that the view now reflects the Tuesday through Saturday schedule you established earlier in this lesson. Your calendar view should be similar to that in Figure 10-27.

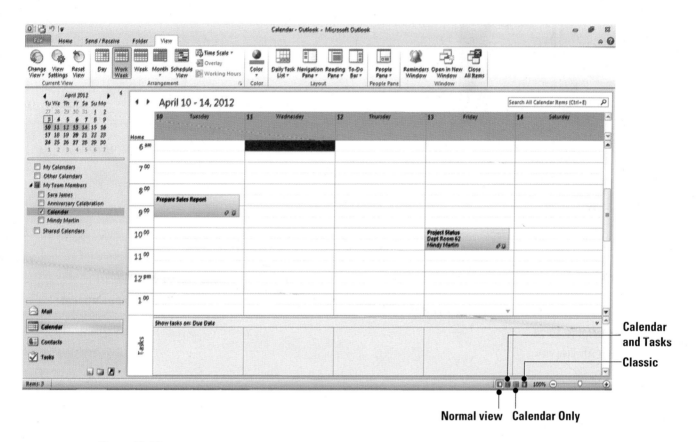

Calendar and Tasks

Classic

Normal view   Calendar Only

Figure 10-27

Calendar in Work Week View

5. On the Home tab, select Week in the Arrangement group. Notice that the full week is displayed from Sunday through Saturday.

6. On the Home tab, select Next 7 Days in the Arrangement group. Notice that you can see seven calendars days beginning with the current date.

7. On the Home tab, select Month in the Arrangement group. Notice that you can see the entire month of April in this view.

8. In the Navigation Pane, click [the check box next to a shared calendar].

NEW to Office 2010

9. On the Home tab, select Schedule View in the Arrangement group. Notice that both calendars are now stacked vertically with the time appearing along the top, as shown in Figure 10-28. Notice that appointments and time marked as busy on the calendar appear as solid blocks of time.

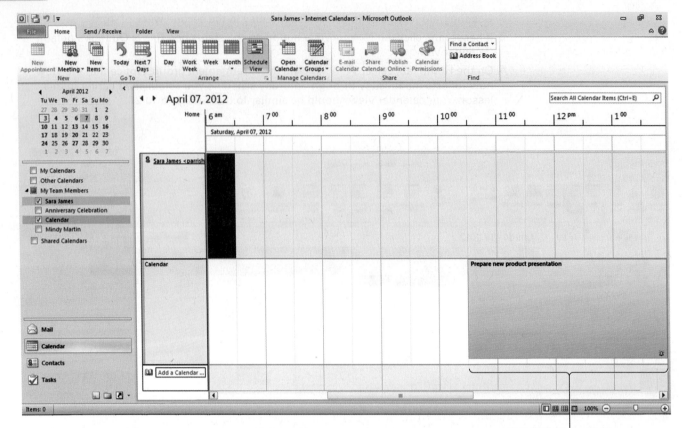

Scheduled appointment

Figure 10-28

Calendar in Schedule View

10. Deselect [the shared calendar] in the Navigation Pane.

PAUSE. LEAVE Outlook open to use in the next exercise.

PRINTING CALENDARS

You may find it handy to take a copy of your Outlook calendar with you to meetings, or any time you need to be away from your computer. Printing the calendar to produce a hard copy is one way to create a portable version of your Outlook calendar.

Printing Calendar

Outlook provides several different printing options for the calendar, as shown in Table 10-3. In this exercise, you'll print a weekly agenda.

Table 10-3

Calendar Printing Options

Print Style	Description
Daily Style	This option prints the calendar details for a single day, including a Daily Task List. This style will print only the work hours you have defined.
Weekly Agenda Style	This option prints the calendar items on a page that looks similar to a day planner.
Weekly Calendar Style	This option prints the calendar items on a page that look similar to the Weekly Calendar view.
Monthly Style	This option prints your calendar items on a single sheet that resembles a monthly calendar.
Tri-Fold Style	This option prints your calendar items in three columns: your hourly appointments on the left, your Daily Task List in the center, and a weekly summary on the right.
Calendar Details Style	This option prints the full details of your calendar items vertically on the page, grouped by day.
Memo Style	This option prints the full details of your calendar items, including any attachments.

STEP BY STEP   **Print Calendar**

GET READY. LAUNCH Outlook if it is not already running.

1. If necessary, click the Calendar button in the Navigation Pane to display the Calendar window.
2. Use the Date Navigator to select [the second week of April].
3. On the File tab, click Print.
4. In the *Printer* field, select [your printer] from the drop-down menu.
5. In the *Settings* field, click Weekly Agenda Style. A preview of your printed page appears in the Preview pane, as shown in Figure 10-29.

Figure 10-29

Weekly Agenda Style in Print Preview

Calendar print formats

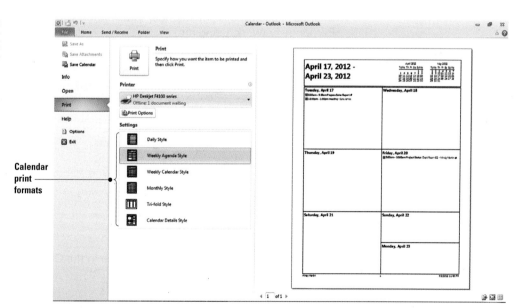

6. Click **Print** to send your calendar to the printer.

PAUSE. LEAVE Outlook open to use in the next exercise.

CERTIFICATION
READY   1.5.2

How do you print a calendar?

SKILL SUMMARY

In This Lesson You Learned How To:	Exam Objective	Objective Number
Set calendar options.	Set Calendar options.	1.1.3
	Change the calendar color.	5.3.2
Share your calendar.		
Work with multiple calendars.	Display or hide calendars.	5.3.3
	Create a calendar group.	5.3.4
	Arrange the calendar view.	5.3.1
Print calendars.	Print calendars.	1.5.2

Knowledge Assessment

Fill in the Blank

Complete the following sentences by writing the correct word or words in the blanks provided.

1. Many people do not work on _____.
2. A common _____ is Monday through Friday.
3. A downloaded calendar that is automatically updated is a(n) _____.
4. Your _____ is based on your location.
5. _____ mode displays calendars on top of one another.
6. A _____ calendar tracks details for specific projects separate from your default calendar.
7. Share a snapshot of your calendar information with someone not on your Microsoft Exchange network, using a(n) _____.
8. In _____ mode, calendars are displayed next to each other.
9. Time zones are defined by the difference between local time and _____.
10. Several calendars displayed in overlay mode are known as a(n) _____.

Multiple Choice

Select the best response for the following statements.

1. What is the most common work week?
   a. Sunday through Saturday
   b. Saturday and Sunday
   c. Monday through Saturday
   d. Monday through Friday
2. Which of the following is not customizable in the Outlook Options?
   a. Calendar color
   b. Custom Calendars
   c. Time zones
   d. Holidays

3. Your time zone is determined by your distance from
   a. the North Pole.
   b. UTC.
   c. Boston.
   d. the Pacific Ocean.

4. In Outlook, holidays are classified as
   a. weekends.
   b. appointments.
   c. all-day events.
   d. vacations.

5. What is automatically shared with other users on a Microsoft Exchange server?
   a. Free/busy times
   b. E-mail
   c. Internet Calendar Subscriptions
   d. Holiday sets

6. What does a Sharing invitation e-mail invite the recipient to share?
   a. Your calendar details
   b. Your Outlook options
   c. Your Inbox
   d. Your free/busy information

7. What does another user on your network need in order to view your calendar?
   a. Your e-mail address
   b. A POP3 account
   c. Your IP address
   d. Your permission

8. When you share your calendar, how much detail is needed for scheduling purposes?
   a. Availability only
   b. Limited details
   c. Full details
   d. Complete calendar

9. What site does Microsoft offer for publishing Internet calendars?
   a. Microsoft Internet Calendars (MIC)
   b. Shared Calendars
   c. Microsoft My Calendar
   d. Office.com

10. What is an advantage of subscribing to an Internet calendar?
   a. Internet calendars are fun.
   b. Internet calendars are automatically updated.
   c. Internet calendars always contain useful information.
   d. All of the above.

Competency Assessment

Project 10-1: Define a Work Week

Sharon Salavaria works at a trendy restaurant in downtown Boston. The restaurant opens at 4:00 PM, stays open for late diners, and closes at 11:00 PM. This fashionable restaurant earned a culinary award for its fine cuisine—on the four days a week that it is open. Not surprisingly, it is difficult to get a table during its limited hours. Modify your calendar to match Sharon's work week.

GET READY. LAUNCH Outlook if it is not already running.

1. On the File tab, click Options.
2. Click Calendar to display the Calendar options.
3. Select the Sun check box to add Sunday to the work week.
4. Click the Thu and Fri check boxes to clear the check boxes, removing them from the work week. The restaurant is open Sunday through Wednesday only.
5. Click the *Start time* field. Key or select 3:00 PM. Click the *End time* field. Key or select 11:00 PM.
6. Click OK to save the modified work week.

PAUSE. LEAVE Outlook open to use in the next exercise.

Project 10-2: Change Your Time Zone

Arthur Yasinki has been the top salesperson at his company for the last six years. His record is amazing because he lives in Florida, but his two biggest clients are located in London and San Francisco. He displays San Francisco as his current time zone and London as his additional time zone. You'll set up the additional time zone in the next project. In this project, change your current time zone to match San Francisco's time zone. If you live in the Pacific time zone, change your current time zone to the Central time zone and change the label name to South Dakota.

GET READY. LAUNCH Outlook if it is not already running.

1. On the File tab, click Options.
2. Click Calendar to display the calendar options.
3. In the *Time Zone* field, select (GMT-08:00) Pacific Time (US & Canada); Tijuana. (If you live in the Pacific time zone, change your current time zone to the Central time zone.)
4. In the *Label* field, key San Francisco. (If you live in the Pacific time zone, change the label name to South Dakota.)
5. Click OK to save the changes.

PAUSE. LEAVE Outlook open to use in the next exercise.

Proficiency Assessment

Project 10-3: Display Multiple Time Zones

If you ask Arthur Yasinki for the key to his success in sales, he'll laugh and respond, "It's location, location, location." Because this phrase usually refers to brick-and-mortar stores or real estate, it might be difficult to understand his answer. When you look at his calendar, it becomes clear. Arthur spends about 200 days of every year away from home at client sites. It's no wonder that he doesn't display the time zone where he lives. In this project, add the time zone for London to your calendar display.

GET READY. LAUNCH Outlook if it is not already running.

1. Open Backstage and display the Calendar options.
2. Scroll down to see the time zone options. Click the Show a second time zone check box.
3. In the *Label* field, key London.
4. In the *Time zone* field, select (UTC) Universal Coordinated Time; Dublin, Edinburgh, Lisbon, London.
5. Click OK to save the changes.

LEAVE Outlook open for the next project.

Project 10-4: Send Calendar Information via E-mail

Once a week Arthur Yasinki sends a copy of his schedule to the department's administrative assistant. Without access to his calendar information, the department would have a hard time finding Arthur on a map.

GET READY. LAUNCH Outlook if it is not already running.

1. If necessary, display your Calendar.
2. On the Home tab, click the E-mail Calendar button in the Share group to display the Send a Calendar via E-mail window.
3. In the *Calendar* field, select Calendar, if necessary.
4. In the *Date Range* field, select Next 7 days.
5. In the *Detail* field, select Full details.
6. In the *E-mail Layout* field, select List of events.
7. Click OK. A new Outlook Message window is displayed with the calendar information included in the body of the message.
8. In the *To* field, key [your e-mail address].
9. Scroll down the message body, if necessary, to view the data in the message. Click Send.

LEAVE Outlook open for the next project.

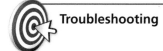

Mastery Assessment

Project 10-5: Publish Calendar to Office.com

Arthur Yasinki and the department's administrative assistant are trying Outlook Internet sharing features. Arthur is publishing his calendar to Office.com. The administrative assistant will subscribe to Arthur's calendar. In this project, publish your calendar to Office.com.

Troubleshooting   If you are logged in to a secure Microsoft Exchange network, your Administrator may block this feature. Ask about any alternate methods for sharing calendar information outside your network.

GET READY. LAUNCH Outlook if it is not already running.

You must also have a Windows Live account to publish your calendar to Office.com.

1. If necessary, open your Calendar window
2. Click the Publish Online button in the Share group and then click Publish to Office.com. Click OK, if necessary, to view pages over a secure connection.
3. Set the options to publish limited details about the next week of your calendar.
4. Click the Only invited users can subscribe to this calendar option and click OK.
5. If necessary, log in to Windows Live and indicate that you want to send a sharing invitation.
6. Send the invitation to yourself and a friend or coworker.

LEAVE Outlook open for the next project.

Project 10-6: Subscribe to an Internet Calendar

The department's administrative assistant is looking forward to subscribing to Arthur Yasinki's published calendar. Arthur's calendar information will be up to date and easy to access.

GET READY. LAUNCH Outlook if it is not already running.

This exercise requires Internet access.

1. If necessary, open your Inbox and click the Send/Receive All Folders button.
2. Open [the new Share message you received from a friend or coworker] (if you did not work with a friend or coworker, open the one you sent to yourself).
3. Choose to subscribe to the new calendar.

4. If necessary, sign in to Windows Live to download and display the calendar.

5. Close the Share message and deselect the new calendar.

6. To clean up after completing these projects, configure the work week to match your own schedule, set the time zone to match your location, and delete any calendar subscriptions displayed in the Navigation Pane for the Calendar folder.

CLOSE Outlook.

INTERNET READY

Search the Internet for one of several websites that host Internet calendars, such as iCalShare.com. Browse through the different types of calendars available. Select one and subscribe.

Workplace *Ready*

SHARING SCHEDULES

The number of telecommuters and freelance workers is growing all the time. New tools and technology make it easier to share information with workers in the next cubicle, the next state, or the next country.

Large corporations with remote workers can purchase standard software packages or provide customized software and security features that enable those workers to log in and access all the features of the company's network regardless of the workers' locations. Some of these features are out of reach for smaller businesses or not feasible for large corporations with only a handful of telecommuters.

That doesn't mean that smaller companies that utilize a lot of telecommuters and freelance workers do not have deadlines or that scheduling isn't necessary. Whether your employee is wearing a pinstriped suit in the boardroom at 8:00 AM or fuzzy slippers in a home office at 11:00 PM, deadlines are critical. Consider publishing schedules to Office Online. Workers can subscribe to a master schedule that tracks progress as a project is completed.

If you publish a calendar to Office Online, consider these tips:

- Keep the calendar up to date. Old information doesn't help anyone.
- Send a Share message to all project members inviting them to view the calendar. They can't meet deadlines they don't know about.
- Provide the right amount of information. Too much information can be confusing. Too little information can be useless.

The Baldwin Museum of Science is planning a major event this coming August 31. Ajay Manchepalli, the Director of Special Exhibits, has worked tirelessly to arrange an exhibit of Egyptian antiquities. In a small town like Sun Ridge, Wisconsin, this is a major coup. As the plan for the event develops, Ajay must schedule a whirlwind of appointments and meetings leading up to the big event.

Project 1: Modify Your Calendar

Ajay immediately adds the event to his calendar and adds his first task: update the museum's insurance plan to cover the event. Ajay will be making several calls to antiquities experts and officials in Egypt every day. Since Egypt is seven hours ahead of Wisconsin, he has decided to modify his work schedule so that he is available during the day in both Egypt and Wisconsin. Ajay also wants to share Outlook calendars with Fadi Mohammed, the Egyptian museum director. Modify your calendar events to match Ajay's and change your work week to match his schedule, and then display Egypt's time zone so that Ajay is always aware of the time when he calls Egypt. Share your calendar with a friend or classmate to match Ajay's actions.

GET READY. LAUNCH Outlook if it is not already running.

1. Click the Calendar button in the Navigation Pane to display the Calendar. Click the Month button to display the Month view, if necessary.
2. On the Home tab, click New Appointment.
3. In the *Subject* field, key Egypt: Sands of Mystery Exhibit.
4. In the *Start time* field, select August 31.
5. Click the All day event check box to select the option. The time fields are dimmed.
6. Click the Save & Close button in the Actions group on the Ribbon. The event has been added to your calendar.
7. Click the View tab. Point to To-Do Bar and then click Normal. The To-Do Bar is displayed to the right of the monthly calendar.
8. Click the Type a new task field, and key Update insurance for Sands of Mystery exhibit. Press Enter. The task is created.
9. On the File tab, click Options.
10. Click Calendar.
11. In the Work time group, click the Start time field. Key or select 5:00 AM. Click the End time field. Key or select 3:00 PM.
12. Scroll down to see the time zone options.
13. In the *Time Zone* field, select (UTC-06:00) Central Time (US & Canada).
14. In the *Label* field, key Wisconsin.
15. Click the Show a second time zone check box.
16. In the *Label* field, key Egypt.
17. In the *Time Zone* field, select (UTC+02:00) Cairo.
18. Click OK to save the changes return to the Calendar folder.
19. Click the Day button to display the Day view. Note that both time zones are displayed and the calendar displays the new working hours.
20. Click the Publish Online button in the Share group and then click Publish to Office. com. If a dialog box is displayed informing you that you will view pages over a secure connection, click OK.
21. In the *Time Span* field, select the Whole calendar option.
22. In the *Detail* field, select Limited details.
23. In the *Permissions* field, click the Only invited users can subscribe to this calendar option.

24. Click OK to publish your calendar. Key your password again, if necessary. When the upload is complete, the Send a Sharing Invitation window is displayed.

25. Click Yes. A Share window resembling an Outlook Message window is displayed.

26. In the *To* field, key [the e-mail address for a friend or classmate]. Click the Send button. The invitation is sent.

27. Click the Mail button in the Navigation Pane to display the Inbox.

28. Click the calendar sharing invitation message, select the URL, and then press Ctrl+C to copy to the Windows clipboard and close the message.

29. Sign into the Microsoft calendar sharing website (http://www.calendar.live.com/calendar/calendar.aspx) using your Windows Live ID.

30. On your Calendar page, click Subscribe, and then click Subscribe to a public calendar.

31. In the *Calendar URL* box press Ctrl+V to paste the URL that you copied in step 28. Remember to change the beginning of the URL from webcals:// to webcal://, removing the letter s.

32. In the Calendar name box, enter the name of the person whose calendar you subscribe to.

33. Click Subscribe to calendar. The calendar appears on your Windows Live Calendar page.

LEAVE Outlook open for the next project.

Project 2: Schedule and Print Appointments

The Egypt: Sands of Mystery exhibit is scheduled for the month of August next year. Ajay has several appointments scheduled for next week, but his first is a meeting with the insurance agent on Monday. Add the appointment to your calendar and print the details to take with you on a tour of the facilities with the agent.

GET READY. LAUNCH Outlook if it is not already running. Complete the previous project.

1. Click the View tab. Point to To-Do Bar and then click Normal. The To-Do Bar is displayed to the right of the monthly calendar.

2. Click the Update insurance for Sands of Mystery exhibit task. Drag it to Monday's date on the calendar. Your insurance agent, Susan Dryer, has requested that you schedule a couple of hours after lunch to tour the facilities with her.

3. In the *Subject* field, key Susan Dryer- Insurance for Sands of Mystery to change the subject line for the appointment.

4. In the *Location* field, key Here. Susan will come to Ajay's office.

5. Key a Start time of 12:30 PM and an End time of 2:30 PM.

6. In the message body, key: Remember to talk to Susan about obtaining security guards for all of the entrances and exits, our plan to upgrade the current alarm system, and transportation insurance while the exhibit is in transit.

7. Click the Save & Close button in the Actions group on the Ribbon.

8. Click the Calendar button in the Navigation Pane to display the Calendar folder. Click the Month button to display the Month view, if necessary.

9. Click the Reminder drop arrow in the Options group and select 1 hour from the list of available times that appears.

10. Click the Show As down arrow in the Options group and select Busy to update your availability.

11. Click the File tab to open Backstage view and click Print in the navigation pane to open the Print settings page.

12. Click the Print Options button.

13. In the Print Style area, click Calendar Details Style.

14. In the *Start* box of the Print range area, select [Monday's date].

15. In the *End* box, select [Monday's date].

16. Click Print if you want to print the contact record using the default printer.

LEAVE Outlook open for the next project.

Project 3: Schedule a Recurring Meeting

Every Friday, Ajay holds a brief status meeting to update the museum director and any interested staff members. Ajay will need to use the video conferencing resource so that the Egyptian team can participate. Ajay's family has had trouble adjusting to his new schedule and has asked that he print his calendar each week so they know when to expect him at home. Schedule a recurring meeting with a friend or coworker to match Ajay's schedule and print your calendar.

Troubleshooting The e-mail addresses provided in these exercises belong to unused domains owned by Microsoft. When you send a message to these addresses, you will receive an error message stating that the message could not be delivered. Delete the error messages when they arrive.

GET READY. LAUNCH Outlook if it is not already running. Complete the previous project.

1. In your account, click the Calendar button in the Navigation Pane to display the Calendar folder.

2. Use the Date Navigator to select the next Friday.

3. On the Home tab, click New Meeting. The Meeting window is displayed.

4. Click the *Subject* field and key Sands of Mystery Status. In the *Location* field, key videoconf@baldwinmuseumofscience.com to invite the resource to your meeting.

5. Change the *Start time* field to 9:00 PM and change the *End time* field to 9:30 PM, if necessary. The green and red vertical lines move.

6. Click Scheduling Assistant or Scheduling button in the Show group on the Ribbon.

7. Click the Click here to add a name text below your name. Key Steve@ baldwinmuseumofscience.com. Press Enter. Steve is the director, so click the icon next to his name and select Required Attendee.

8. Click the Click here to add a name text on the next line. Key Fadimohammed@ egyptianantiquities.eg. Press Enter. Click the icon next to Fadi's name and select Required Attendee.

9. Click the Click here to add a name text on the next line. Key [your own e-mail address] and select Optional Attendee.

10. Click the Recurrence button in the Options group on the Ribbon. The Appointment Recurrence window is displayed.

11. Click OK to accept the recurrence pattern and return to the meeting window.

12. Click the Appointment button in the Show group on the Ribbon. The *To* field is automatically filled with the attendees' e-mail addresses, and the recurrence pattern is displayed.

13. Click the Send button. Your calendar is updated, and the 9:00 PM to 9:30 PM time slot is displayed as busy for every Friday.

14. Click the Mail button in the Navigation Pane to display the Mail folder.

15. If the Sands of Mystery Status message has not arrived, click the Send/Receive button.

16. Click the Sands of Mystery Status message in the message list. The message is displayed in the Preview pane.

17. Click the Propose New Time button at the top of the message. The Propose New Time window is displayed.

18. In the *Start time* field, select 9:00 AM. In the *End time* field, select 9:30 AM, if necessary. Click the Propose Time button. A Message window is displayed.

19. In the message area, key the following message. Looks like you might have made a typing error in this meeting invite. 9:00 PM is midnight in Egypt! Press Enter and type [your name].

20. Click the Send button.

21. In your account, click the Mail button in the Navigation Pane to display the Mail folder, if necessary.

22. If the New Time Proposed: Sands of Mystery Status message has not arrived, click the Send/Receive button.

23. Click the New Time Proposed: Sands of Mystery Status message in the message list. The message is displayed in the Reading Pane.

24. Click the View All Proposals button on the Meeting Response tab. All proposed times appear in the scheduling grid so that you can see how each time affects the mandatory attendees.

25. Select 9:00 AM proposed time.

26. On the Meeting tab, click Contact Attendees in the Attendees group and select Reply to All with E-mail from the dropdown menu.

27. A message window opens. In the message body, key: Looks like the change in my sleep patterns has affected me this week. I'm updating the meeting so that it is scheduled during work hours. [Press Enter twice] and type [your name].

28. On the Meeting tab, click Scheduling Assistant or Scheduling and click the Send button above the scheduling grid.

29. Click the Calendar button in the Navigation Pane to display the Calendar folder. Click the Month button to display the Month view, if necessary.

30. To clean up Outlook after completing these projects, configure the work week to match your schedule, set the time zone to match your schedule, and remove the second time zone, the appointments, events, and recurring meeting scheduled during this project.

CLOSE Outlook.

LESSON SKILL MATRIX

Skills	Exam Objective	Objective Number
Creating New Tasks	Create a task.	6.1.1
Working with Task Options	Set Tasks options.	1.1.4
	Use Current view.	6.1.9
Managing and Completing a Task	Update an assigned task.	6.1.8
	Manage task details.	6.1.2
	Mark a task as complete.	6.1.4
	Move or copy a task to another folder.	6.1.5
	Print tasks.	1.5.5
Working with Assigned Tasks	Assign a task to another Outlook user.	6.1.6
	Accept or decline a task assignment.	6.1.7
	Send a status report.	6.1.3

KEY TERMS

- assign
- complete
- Deferred
- In Progress
- owner
- recurring task
- task
- task request
- to-do item

Developing and releasing a new product are complicated processes that can take months or years to complete. Ruth Ann Ellerbrock knows this from firsthand experience. She has managed the product development team at Tailspin Toys, releasing three new products in five years. Ruth Ann and her team use the Tasks folder to track the multitude of tasks required to accomplish the goal of releasing solid, marketable new products. In this lesson, you'll create, modify, move, and print tasks and to-do items. You'll also assign a task to someone else, respond to a task request, and update the status of a task.

SOFTWARE ORIENTATION

Microsoft Outlook's Task Window

Create and modify your tasks in the Task window shown in Figure 11-1. Use the Task window to create and track tasks that you are managing or performing. Keep your task information readily available in one location.

Figure 11-1

Outlook's Task window

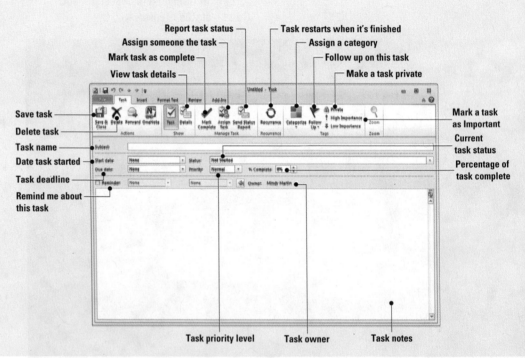

CREATING NEW TASKS

The Bottom Line

A **task** is an Outlook item that you create. It usually has a due date and can be tracked from creation to completion. When any task is created, it is automatically flagged for follow-up. Any Outlook item that can be flagged for follow-up, including messages and contacts, is called a **to-do item**. Thus, creating a task also creates a to-do item.

Creating a One-Time Task

You create a one-time task to track your progress on a task that only needs to be completed once. For example, you would create a one-time task to register for a specific trade show. Once you have registered for the trade show, the task is complete—you don't need to return to the task every week or every month. In this exercise, you will create a one-time task.

STEP BY STEP   **Create a One-Time Task**

GET READY. Before you begin these steps, be sure to launch Microsoft Outlook.

1. If necessary, click the Tasks button in the Navigation Pane to display the Tasks folder, as shown in Figure 11-2.

Figure 11-2

The Tasks folder

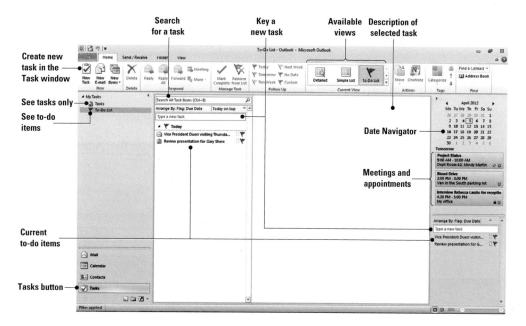

Troubleshooting Depending on the exercises you completed in previous lessons, you might already have some items displayed in the To-Do List.

2. In the *Type a new task* field, key Sample. The new Sample task appears in the To-Do list.

Another Way
In every Outlook folder, you can create a new task by selecting Task in the New Items dropdown menu or by pressing Ctrl+Shift+K.

3. Click New Task on the Home tab. A Task window is displayed, as shown in Figure 11-1.
4. In the *Subject* field, key Create marketing brochure.
5. In the *Due date* field, key or select [the date five weeks from today].
6. In the *Priority* field, select Low.
7. In the task note area, key Photographer's name is Ann Beebe.
8. Compare your Task window to Figure 11-3.

Figure 11-3

Creating a new task

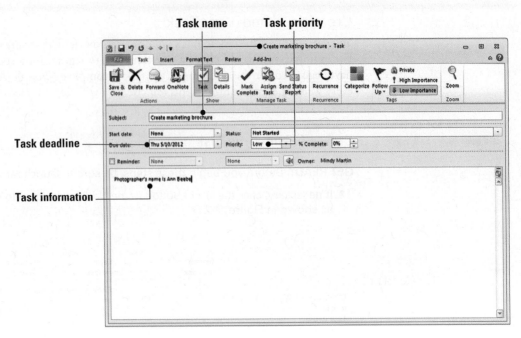

Task name Task priority

Task deadline

Task information

9. Click Save & Close in the Actions group on the Ribbon. The new task is displayed at the bottom of the To-Do Bar.

10. Click the Arrange By: tab in the To-Do Bar. A list of options is displayed, as shown in Figure 11-4.

Figure 11-4

Arranging tasks in the To-Do Bar

Arrange By tab

Click to group items by date

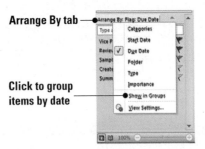

11. If necessary, click the Show in Groups option to select it. The to-do items in the To-Do Bar are grouped by date, as shown in Figure 11-5.

Figure 11-5

Task list grouped by date

New tasks created

CERTIFICATION READY   6.1.1

How do you create a one-time task?

PAUSE. LEAVE Outlook open to use in the next exercise.

Creating a Recurring Task

A **recurring task** is a task that must be completed at regular intervals. Common recurring tasks include creating a weekly status report or turning in your travel receipt to the accounting department every month. When you mark a recurring task as complete, the task is automatically re-created with the next due date displayed. In this exercise, you will create a recurring task that starts in January and ends after six months. Frequently, start and end dates coincide with project deadlines.

STEP BY STEP   Create a Recurring Task

 Ref   You can find more information on completing a task later in this lesson.

GET READY. Before you begin these steps, be sure to launch Microsoft Outlook.

1. If necessary, click the Tasks button in the Navigation Pane to display the Tasks folder.
2. Click New Task on the Home tab. A Task window is displayed as shown in Figure 11-1.
3. In the *Subject* field, key Summarize team's progress on Vault project.
4. In the *Start date* field, select [the second Monday in January of next year].
5. Click the Recurrence button in the Options group on the Ribbon. The Task Recurrence window is displayed, as shown in Figure 11-6.

Figure 11-6

Task Recurrence window

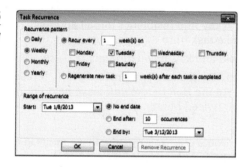

6. Select the Monthly option in the *Recurrence pattern* field.
7. Click the End by radio button and key or select [the second Monday in July]. This ends the recurring task in six months.
8. Click OK to return to the Task window.
9. Compare your Task window to Figure 11-7. Depending on the current date, the number of days before the first deadline will differ.

Figure 11-7

Creating a new recurring task

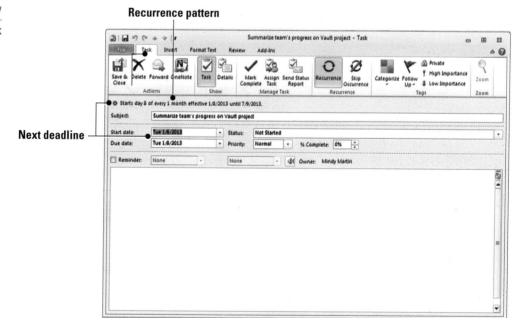

10. Click Save & Close in the Actions group on the Ribbon.
11. Examine your To-Do List. The new task is displayed below a heading. The heading title depends on the amount of time between today's date and the first deadline.

PAUSE. LEAVE Outlook open to use in the next exercise.

CERTIFICATION READY   6.1.1

How do you create recurring tasks?

Creating a Task from a Message

E-mail messages are used to convey a variety of information. Sometimes, a message contains information about tasks that must be performed. To save time in data entry and keep a record of the original e-mail message with the task, you can use the message to create a tracked task. In this exercise, you will create a task from a message.

STEP BY STEP   **Create a Task from a Message**

GET READY. Before you begin these steps, be sure to launch Microsoft Outlook. This exercise requires exchanging messages with another Outlook user with an active e-mail account who can respond to a message or who has the ability to access and use another user's Outlook profile.

1. Click New E-mail on the Home tab to display a Message window.
2. Click the *To* field and key [the recipient's e-mail address]. The recipient is the Outlook user who will create a task from this message.
3. Click the *Subject* field and key Travel Itinerary.
4. In the message area, key the following message: Hi, [Press Enter] Please give a copy of your itinerary to Arlene Huff before you leave next Friday. [Press Enter twice.] Thanks. [Press Enter twice.] Mindy.

Take Note   Throughout this chapter you will see information that appears in black text within brackets, such as [Press Enter], or [next Friday's date]. The information contained in the brackets is intended to be directions for you rather than something you actually type word for word. It will instruct you to perform an action or substitute text. Do **not** type the actual text that appears within brackets.

5. Click the Send button to send the message.
6. In the recipient's account, click Send/Receive All Folders if the Travel Itinerary message has not arrived.
7. Click the Travel Itinerary message in the message list. Drag it to the Tasks button on the Navigation Pane and drop it there. A Task window containing information from the message is automatically opened, as shown in Figure 11-8.

Figure 11-8

Task window showing Travel Itinerary message

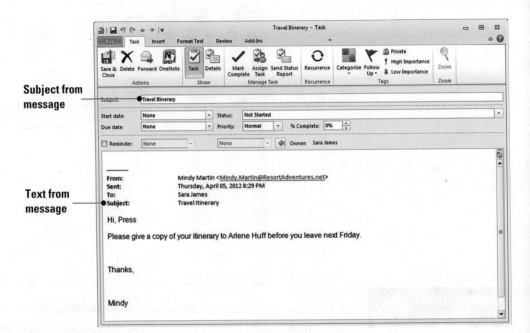

8. In the Task window, click the *Due date* field. Key or select [next Friday's date].

9. Click Save & Close in the Actions group on the Ribbon.

10. Click Tasks in the Navigation Pane to display the Tasks folder. Examine your To-Do List. The new task is displayed below the Later heading.

PAUSE. CLOSE the recipient's Outlook account and return to your own if necessary. If you exchanged tasks with another user so that you received the task in your mailbox, leave Outlook open to use in the next exercise.

<table>
<tr><td>

CERTIFICATION READY   **6.1.1**

How do you create a task from a message?
</td></tr>
</table>

WORKING WITH TASK OPTIONS

The Bottom Line

In this section, you will learn how to set the default task options and use Outlook's views to find the one that best meets your working style.

Setting Task Options

To make creating tasks more efficient, you can customize the default options in several ways. You can set the color for the overdue and completed flags, specify the amount of time you need reminders, and decide whether or not to keep copies of items you assign to someone else. In this exercise, you will set your working hours and change the Task Quick Click option.

 Ref

You can find more information on assigning tasks to others later in this lesson.

STEP BY STEP   **Set Task Options**

GET READY. Before you begin these steps, be sure to launch Microsoft Outlook.

1. On the File tab, click Options. The Outlook Options dialog box opens.

2. Click Tasks in the Navigation Pane. The Outlook Options window displays Task options, as shown in Figure 11-9.

Figure 11-9

Outlook's Tasks options

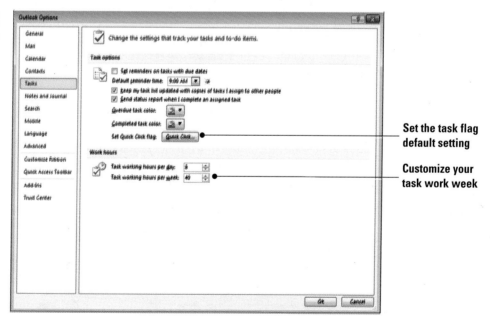

Set the task flag default setting

Customize your task work week

3. Under the *Task options* group, click the Quick Click button. The Set Quick Click window opens.

4. From the drop-down menu, select Tomorrow. Click OK. The next time you want to flag a Mail message or a contact, click the flag column to have Outlook set the due date to Tomorrow.

5. In the *Work hours* group, key or select 4 in the *Task working hours per day* field to indicate that you work only four hours a day on tasks.

CERTIFICATION
READY 1.1.4

How do you set task options?

6. In the *Task working hours per week* field, key or select 20.

7. Click OK.

PAUSE. LEAVE Outlook open to use in the next exercise.

Working with Task Views

To see information about your tasks that have been marked as complete, click the Completed Tasks view in the Navigation Pane. Table 11-1 lists and describes Outlook's Task views, which you will learn to use in this exercise.

Table 11-1

Task Views

Views	Description
Detailed	Similar in appearance to the Simple List, this view also includes the status, percent complete, and category of your tasks, complete or active.
Simple List	This view shows the subject and due date only for all tasks, completed or not.
To-Do List	This view includes not only your active tasks, but all other To-Do items, such as messages and contacts that you have flagged for follow-up.
Prioritized	This view shows your active tasks sorted by the Priority field. Tasks at the top have a High priority.
Active	This view shows only the tasks that you have not yet marked as completed.
Completed	This view shows only the tasks that you have marked as completed.
Today	This view shows all tasks due today.
Next 7 Days	This view shows all tasks due within the next seven days.
Overdue	This view shows all tasks that are currently overdue.
Assigned	This view shows all tasks that were assigned to you, or that you have assigned to someone else.
Server Tasks	If you are operating on a Microsoft Exchange network and using SharePoint 2010, this Outlook views shows all tasks created and tracked through SharePoint.

STEP BY STEP **Work with Task Views**

GET READY. Before you begin these steps, be sure to launch Microsoft Outlook.

1. If necessary, click the Tasks button in the Navigation Pane to display the To-Do List.

2. Click the More button in the Current View group. The Current View gallery is displayed, as shown in Figure 11-10.

Figure 11-10

The Current View gallery

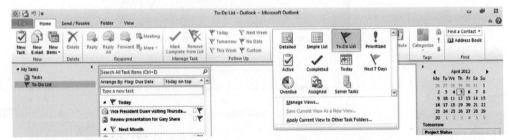

3. Select Detailed. The Tasks view changes to show all the details about the tasks in your To-Do List.

4. Repeat Step 2 for each of the views on the Change View dropdown menu. Take note of how the task list changes in each view.

5. Because tasks have due dates, you also can view your tasks in the Calendar. Click the Calendar button in the Navigation Pane.

6. Click the Calendar and Tasks button in the status bar. If necessary, click Week from the Arrangement group on the View tab. The Daily Task List appears at the bottom of the window, as shown in Figure 11-11.

Figure 11-11

Viewing the Task list in Calendar

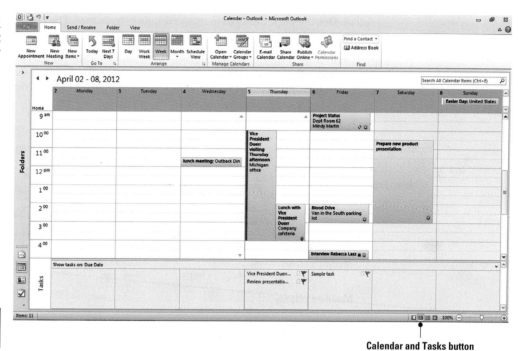

Calendar and Tasks button

CERTIFICATION READY   6.1.9

How do you use Current view in looking at tasks?

PAUSE. LEAVE Outlook open to use in the next exercise.

MANAGING AND COMPLETING A TASK

The Bottom Line

After a task is created, you may have to modify the task by setting its priority as High, Low, or Normal. You also can change a task's status and update the amount of the task that has been completed. You can also mark a task as private, keeping the details hidden from other users.

Updating a Task

Tracking the status of a task includes modifying the task's status and percentage complete each time you work on it. The Status and % Complete fields work together to define your progress, as shown in Table 11-2. In this exercise, you will update an existing task.

Table 11-2

Task Status

Status	% Complete	Description
Not Started	0	The Not Started status indicates that work on the task has not yet begun.
In Progress	1–99	The **In Progress** status indicates that work on the task has started.
Complete	100	The Complete status indicates that all work on this task is finished. When you finish a task, mark it as **Complete**.
Waiting on Someone Else	0–99	The Waiting on Someone Else status indicates that your progress on the task has been postponed until you receive something (e.g., confirmation on a detail, a hard copy in the mail) from someone else.
Deferred	0–99	The **Deferred** status indicates that the task has been postponed without changing the deadline or the percentage complete.

Update a Task

GET READY. Before you begin these steps, you must have launched Microsoft Outlook and completed the first exercise in this lesson.

1. If necessary, click the Tasks button in the Navigation Pane to display the Tasks folder.
2. Double-click the Create marketing brochure task. The task is opened in a Task window.
3. Click the *Status* field. Select In Progress to indicate that you have started work.
4. In the *Priority* field, select High to reflect its importance relative to other tasks. You know that your company cannot launch the Big Blue product line without your marketing brochure, so you will need to start work on it right away.
5. Compare your Task window to Figure 11-12.

Figure 11-12

Task window showing updated task

Modified percentage completed

Modified status

Modified priority

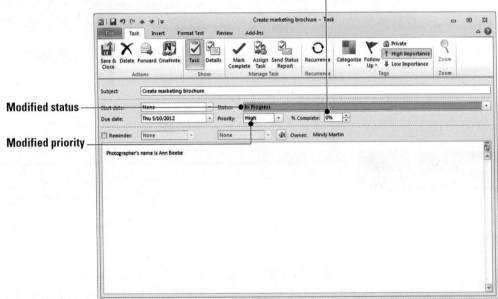

6. Click the Save & Close button in the Actions group on the Ribbon.
7. Halfway through your work on the brochure, your manager stops by your desk to let you know that the release date for Big Blue has been delayed. You decide to change the status of your task to Deferred and move on to something else. Double-click the Create marketing brochure task. The task is opened in a Task window.
8. Click the *Status* field and select Deferred.
9. Click the *% Complete* field and key or select 50%.
10. In the task note area, key the additional text: Filename is My Documents/ BigBluebrochure.docx.
11. Compare your Task window to Figure 11-13. Click Save & Close in the Actions group on the Ribbon.

Figure 11-13

Deferring a task

Modified percentage completed

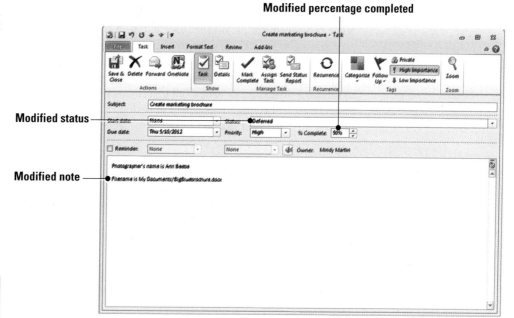

Modified status

Modified note

CERTIFICATION
READY 6.1.8

How do you update an assigned task?

PAUSE. LEAVE Outlook open to use in the next exercise.

Making a Task Private

NEW to Office 2010

To make it easier to work with tasks, you can use the new Task Tools Task List tab. The Task Tools Task List tab contains options for changing the arrangement of the tasks, moving task items to other folders and applying tags to tasks.

Like appointments and meetings, you can tag a task as private. This protects the details of the task from casual observers on your network. Without permission to access your account, the details of any private task will not be visible to them. In your account, your private tasks do not look different from any other task until you open the task. Once opened, the Private button in the Options group on the Ribbon will be highlighted. In this exercise, you will mark the marketing brochure as a private task.

STEP BY STEP | **Make a Task Private**

GET READY. Before you begin these steps, you must have launched Microsoft Outlook and completed the previous exercise.

1. If necessary, click the Tasks button in the Navigation Pane to display the Tasks folder.
2. Click the Create marketing brochure task. The Task Tools Task List tab is displayed on the Ribbon, as shown in Figure 11-14.

Figure 11-14

Task Tools Task List tab

Mark a task as Private

3. Click the Private button in the Tags group. The task is classified as private.

PAUSE. LEAVE Outlook open to use in the next exercise.

Managing Task Details

Some tasks seem simple on the surface, but in the end, you find that you expended a lot of energy driving to your client's site to complete them. If you are one of the millions of people who use Outlook to track project tasks, you might find that keeping track of details like time, billing, and mileage information for your tasks is an essential part of your business. When it comes time to submit a time sheet or issue a bill to a client, you can retrieve the information from your Tasks folder instead of trying to keep it all in your head. In this exercise, you will add details, as shown in Table 11-3, to your existing tasks.

Table 11-3

Task Details Fields

Format	Description
Total work	Use this field to track the total amount of work spent for the task or client. You may want to track the number of days or weeks, as opposed to hours.
Actual work	This field tracks the actual number of hours and minutes spent on a given task.
Company	Key the client's name in this field. If you don't work with outside clients, you could enter the project manager's name or the project name used on your timecard.
Mileage	Key information about mileage, gas prices, and the purpose of the trip.
Billing information	Use this field to track your billing rate or any discounts you might have offered.

STEP BY STEP | **Manage Task Details**

GET READY. LAUNCH Microsoft Outlook if it is not already running.

1. If necessary, click the Tasks button in the Navigation Pane to display the Tasks folder.
2. Double-click the Create marketing brochure task. The task is opened in a Task window.
3. Click Details in the Show group. The details fields are displayed in the Task window, as shown in Figure 11-15.

Figure 11-15

Viewing Task details

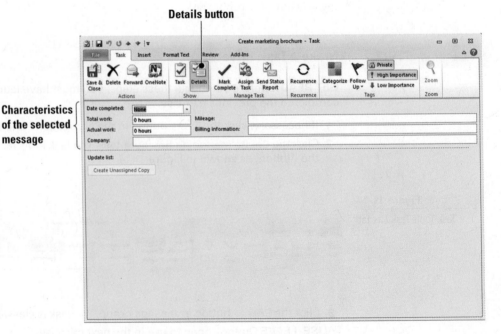

4. In the *Company* field, key Big Blue merger, the company's code name for its new product line.

CERTIFICATION READY 6.1.2

How do you manage task details?

5. In the *Actual work* field, key 23 hours to indicate that you've already worked on the project for 23 hours.

6. Click Save & Close.

PAUSE. LEAVE Outlook open to use in the next exercise.

Marking a Task as Complete

When you finish a task, you will need to mark the task as complete. Completed tasks are not displayed on your To-Do List, but are visible on the Completed Tasks view. As your list of completed tasks grows over time, the Completed Tasks view becomes a record of the tasks you have accomplished.

In this exercise, you will mark a task as complete.

STEP BY STEP **Mark a Task as Complete**

GET READY. LAUNCH Microsoft Outlook if it is not already running. Before you begin these steps, be sure to complete the first exercise in this lesson.

Another Way
You can also mark a task as complete by opening a task window and clicking Mark Complete in the Ribbon.

1. If necessary, click the Tasks button in the Navigation Pane to display the Tasks folder.

2. Click the Create marketing brochure task in the To-Do Bar. The Task Tools Task List tab is displayed in the Ribbon.

3. Click the Mark Complete button in the Manage Task group on the Ribbon. The task is moved to the Completed Tasks list so it is no longer displayed on your To-Do List.

4. Click the Home tab. In the Current View gallery, click the Completed Tasks button to view all of your completed tasks, as shown in Figure 11-16.

Figure 11-16

Viewing Completed Tasks details

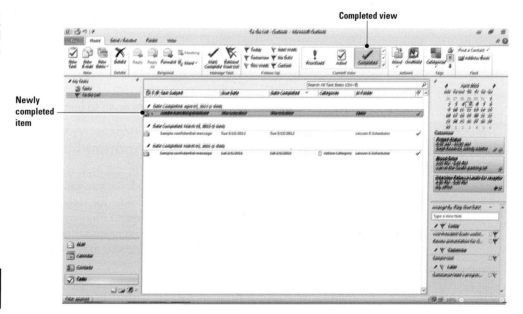

CERTIFICATION READY 6.1.4

How do you mark a task as complete?

PAUSE. LEAVE Outlook open to use in the next exercise.

Searching for Tasks

Outlook's Instant Search feature makes it simple to find a task quickly, even those stored in the Mail folders. Instant Search can match your search terms with any text, including text in the Task window fields, the notes area, and the Task Details. You can also use Outlook's new Search Tools tab to filter your search results to find the task you need.

In this exercise, you will use Instant Search to locate specific tasks in any folder.

STEP BY STEP   **Search for Tasks**

GET READY. Before you begin these steps, launch Microsoft Outlook and make sure that Instant Search is enabled. You must have completed the previous exercises in this lesson.

1. In your account, click the Tasks button in the Navigation Pane to display the Tasks folder if necessary.
2. Click the More button in the Current View group to open the Current View gallery of the Ribbon and select To-Do List from the dropdown menu.
3. Click the Search All Task Items box. The Search Tools tab is displayed.
4. Verify that Search All Task Items is selected. Key brochure. As you key the search text, Outlook displays the matching task items in any folder, as shown in Figure 11-17.

Figure 11-17

Task items that meet search criteria

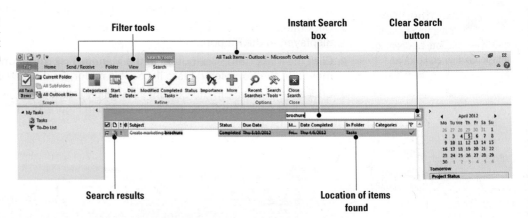

PAUSE. LEAVE the Instant Search results open to use in the next exercise.

Moving or Copying a Task to Another Folder

Even with the variety of views available in the Task module and the efficiency of the Instant Search feature, as with other Outlook modules, you can create custom folders in which to store related tasks. You may choose to create a folder for each project, for a specific time frame, or for each customer. The key is to choose an organization system that works for you. Once you have decided on a system, you can easily move items into their new location. In this exercise, you will create a folder for the Big Blue product line and move the related tasks into it.

STEP BY STEP   **Move or Copy a Task to Another Folder**

GET READY. LAUNCH Microsoft Outlook and ensure that Instant Search is enabled. Complete the previous exercises in this lesson.

1. Right-click on the Tasks folder in the Navigation Pane.
2. Select New Folder from the shortcut menu. The Create New Folder window opens, as shown in Figure 11-18.

Figure 11-18

Create New Folder window

3. In the *Name* field, key Big Blue.

4. Click the Tasks folder in the *Select where to place the folder* pane.

5. Click OK to create a new folder, as shown in Figure 11-19.

Figure 11-19

Big Blue folder added
under Tasks folder

New Task folder ——

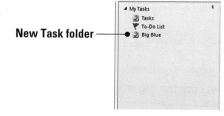

Another Way
To copy a task,
drag the item while holding
the right-click button on your
mouse. Select Copy Here from
the shortcut menu.

6. In the Instant Search results, select the Create marketing brochure task. If you have a copy of the Travel Itinerary task on your account, select it too.

7. Drag the items over the new Big Blue folder to move them.

PAUSE. LEAVE Outlook open to use in the next exercise.

CERTIFICATION
R E A D Y   **6.1.5**

How do you move or copy a
task to another folder?

Printing Tasks

As in other Outlook modules, tasks can be printed quickly from the Backstage area. In this exercise, you will print two tasks, one active and one completed. Table 11-4 describes the available task print styles.

Table 11-4

Task Printing Options

Print Styles	Description
Table Style	This style prints your tasks in a list, one after the other.
Memo Style	This style prints the contents of each task, including attachements.

STEP BY STEP   **Print Tasks**

GET READY. LAUNCH Microsoft Outlook if it is not already running.

1. In your account, click the Tasks button in the Navigation Pane to display the To-Do List. Click the Tasks folder if necessary.

2. Click the File tab and select Print.

3. Select Table Style from the Settings pane to see a preview of your printout, as shown in Figure 11-20. Click Print.

Figure 11-20

Printing tasks in List view (Table Style)

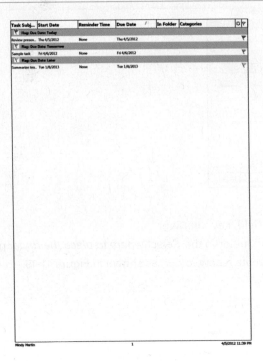

4. In the Navigation Pane, click the Big Blue folder to display the completed Create Marketing Brochure task.

5. Double-click the Create marketing brochure task to open it. Click the File tab and select Print.

6. Select Memo Style from the Settings Pane to see a preview of your printout, as shown in Figure 11-21. Click Print.

Figure 11-21

Printing Task details (Memo Style)

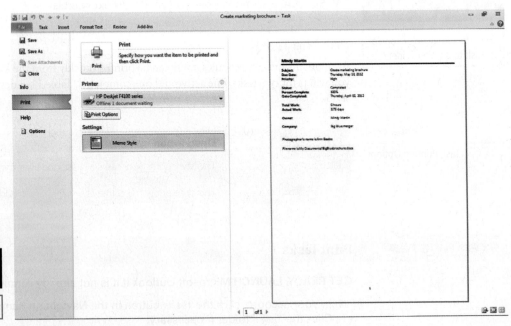

CERTIFICATION
READY   **1.5.5**

How do you print tasks?

PAUSE. LEAVE Outlook open to use in the next exercise.

WORKING WITH ASSIGNED TASKS

The Bottom Line

In the previous sections, you have created, modified, and completed tasks. In this section, you will assign tasks to other Outlook users and respond to tasks assigned to you.

Assigning a Task to Another Outlook User

The task **owner** is the only Outlook user who can modify a task. The creator of a task is automatically the task owner. To transfer ownership of a task, you can **assign** the task to another Outlook user with a **task request**. By default, Outlook will keep a copy of any task you assign to someone else in your task list. If you are using a Microsoft Exchange network, your task list will be updated when the new owner updates the task on their task list.

In this exercise, you will send two task requests to your partner. When you send a task request, the recipient becomes the task owner when you click the Send button. You can recover ownership of the task only if the recipient declines the task and you return the task to your task list.

STEP BY STEP   **Assign a Task to Another Outlook User**

GET READY. LAUNCH Microsoft Outlook if it is not already running.

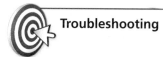

Troubleshooting You cannot assign a task to yourself; therefore, this series of exercises requires exchanging messages with a partner using Outlook 2010. If you do not have a partner, you can use a different Outlook profile tied to a separate e-mail account. If you need to create a profile, see Outlook's Help topics for more information.

WileyPLUS Extra! features an online tutorial of this task.

1. If necessary, click the Tasks button in the Navigation Pane to display the Tasks folder.
2. Click the New Items dropdown arrow and select More Items from the dropdown menu.
3. Click Task Request. The Task request window containing elements of a Task window and a Message window is displayed, as shown in Figure 11-22.

Figure 11-22

Task Request window

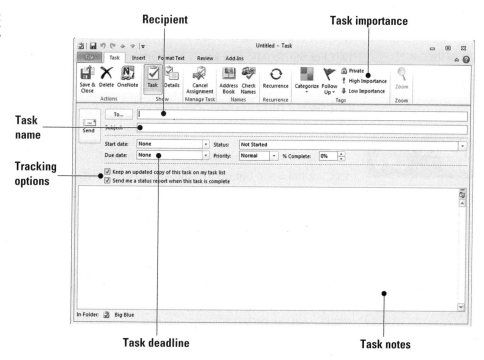

4. Click the *To* field and key [your partner's e-mail address]. Your partner is the Outlook user who will own this task.

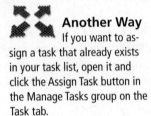

Another Way
If you want to assign a task that already exists in your task list, open it and click the Assign Task button in the Manage Tasks group on the Task tab.

5. Click the *Subject* field and key Prepare training materials for new employees.

6. Click the *Due date* field. Key or select [next Friday's date].

7. In the message area, key the following message: Hi, [Press Enter.] Please prepare training materials and a schedule for the one-day training seminar next week. [Press Enter twice.] Thanks, [Press Enter twice.] Key [your name].

8. Click the Send button to send the task request. If you kept a copy of the task, it is displayed on your To-Do List.

9. Click the Prepare training materials for new employees task on your To-Do List to verify that your partner is identified as the task owner, as shown in Figure 11-23.

Figure 11-23

Assigned task displayed after task request sent

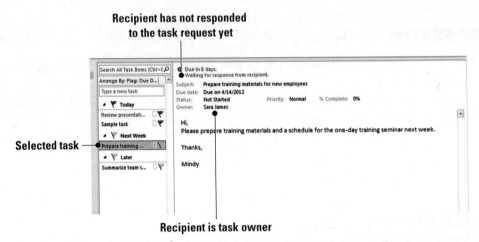

Recipient has not responded to the task request yet

Selected task

Recipient is task owner

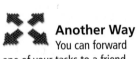

Another Way
You can forward one of your tasks to a friend or colleague. Select the task you want to forward and click Forward on the Home tab. The task is sent as an attachment to a Mail message. Your friend can drag the attachment to their own Task list.

10. If necessary, click the Tasks button in the Navigation Pane to display the Tasks folder.

11. Click the New Items dropdown list arrow and select More Items from the dropdown list.

12. Click Task Request.

13. Click the *To* field and key [your partner's e-mail address]. Your partner is the Outlook user who will own this task.

14. Click the *Subject* field and key Greet new employees.

15. Click the *Due date* field. Key or select [next Friday's date].

16. In the message area, key the following message: Hi, [Press Enter] It's a good idea to introduce ourselves to the new employees before the training session starts next Friday. [Press Enter twice] Key [your name].

17. Click the Send button to send the task request.

PAUSE. CLOSE Outlook to access your partner's account, if necessary. Otherwise, leave Outlook open to use in the next exercise.

CERTIFICATION READY 6.1.6

How do you assign tasks to others?

Accepting or Declining a Task Assignment

A task request is received in your mailbox like any other message. When you receive a task request, you can accept the task, decline the task, or assign the task to another Outlook user. Once a task is assigned to you, you become the owner. Even if you decline a task request, you are the owner until the person who sent the original task request returns the declined task to his or her task list. When a task you assigned to another user is declined, you will receive a Task Declined: Task Name message. Double-click the message to open it. Click the Return to Task List button in the Manage Task group on the Ribbon and then click Save & Close to return to your task list.

In this exercise, you have received two task requests. You will accept one task and decline the second.

STEP BY STEP   **Accept or Decline a Task Assignment**

GET READY. LAUNCH Outlook if it is not already running. Complete the previous exercise.

Take Note   This exercise is performed in your partner's account.

1. In your partner's account, click the Mail button in the Navigation Pane to display the Mail folder, if necessary. If the task requests sent in the previous exercise have not arrived, click the Send/Receive button.

2. In the Inbox, click the Task Request: Prepare training materials for new employees message. The task request is previewed in the Reading Pane, as shown in Figure 11-24.

Figure 11-24

Task request received

Respond to a task request

Task name

Meeting request icon

Task deadline

Person who assigned task to you

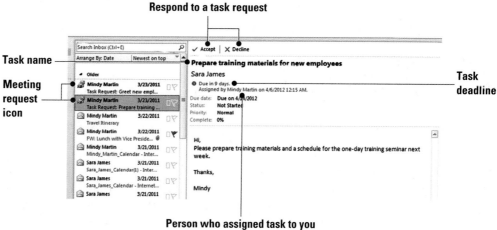

3. In the Task window, click the Accept button in the Respond group on the Ribbon. As shown in Figure 11-25, a small dialog box is displayed asking if you want to edit the message sent with the response.

Figure 11-25

Accepting Task dialog box

4. Click OK to send the response now. The task acceptance is sent and the task is added to your task list.

5. In the Inbox, click the Task Request: Greet new employees message to preview it.

6. In the Reading Pane, click the Decline button at the top of the message. The small Declining Task dialog box is displayed, asking if you want to edit the message sent with the response.

7. In the Declining Task dialog box, click the Edit the response before sending option and click OK.

8. In the Task window, key I will be out of town next Friday.

9. Compare your Task Request response to that shown in Figure 11-26.

Figure 11-26

Task Request response form

Figure 11-26

Task Request response form

Task name

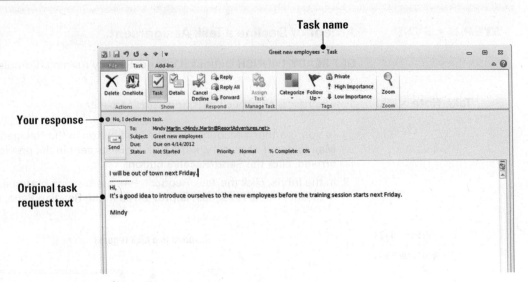

Your response

Original task request text

---

10. Click the Send button. Your partner has declined this task, so it is not added to his task list. However, until you—the person who originally assigned it to your partner—reclaims ownership of the task, he is still the owner.

PAUSE. LEAVE Outlook open to use in the next exercise.

Sending a Status Report

When you update a task assigned to you, the task copy kept on any previous owner's task list is automatically updated if the previous owner chose the tracking options when assigning the task. You can also choose to send a status report to previous task owners or other interested individuals.

In this exercise, you will update the *Prepare training materials for new employees* task and send a status report to the person who assigned the task to you.

STEP BY STEP   **Send a Status Report**

GET READY. LAUNCH Outlook if it is not already running. Make sure you've completed the previous exercises.

Take Note   This exercise begins in your partner's account.

1. In your partner's account, click the Tasks button in the Navigation Pane to display the Tasks folder if necessary.
2. Double-click the Prepare training materials for new employees task. The Task window is displayed.
3. Click the *% Complete* field. Key or select 50%.
4. Click the Save & Close button to update the task.
5. Double-click the Prepare training materials for new employees task. The Task window is displayed.
6. Click the Send Status Report button in the Manage Task group on the Ribbon. A Message window is displayed. The person who assigned the task to you is displayed in the *To* field.

Take Note   The *To* field is filled in automatically by Outlook. To see any individuals who will be automatically updated, open the task to display the Task window and click the Details button in the Show group on the Ribbon. The *Update list* field identifies individuals who are automatically updated in the status report.

7. The message content details the task's current status, as shown in Figure 11-27.

8. Click the Send button.

Take Note   Switch to your e-mail account.

9. In your e-mail account, click the Task Status Report: Prepare training materials for new employees message in your message list. The status report is previewed in the Reading Pane, as shown in Figure 11-27.

Troubleshooting If you haven't received the status report, press F9 to send and receive all messages.

Figure 11-27

Task Status Report

Task owner   Task name

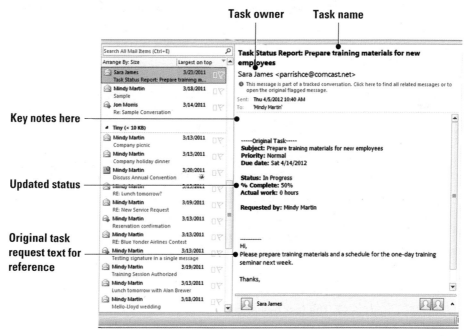

Key notes here

Updated status

Original task
request text for
reference

How do you send a status
report on an assigned task?

PAUSE. CLOSE Outlook.

When the status report is received, the task status report includes the original task text, the updated progress information, and any notes the task owner might want to include, as shown in Figure 11-27.

SKILL SUMMARY

In This Lesson You Learned How To:	Exam Objective	Objective Number
Create new tasks	Create a task.	6.1.1
Work with task options	Set Tasks options.	1.1.4
	Use Current view.	6.1.9
Manage and complete a task	Update an assigned task.	6.1.8
	Manage task details.	6.1.2
	Mark a task as complete.	6.1.4
	Move or copy a task to another folder.	6.1.5
	Print tasks.	1.5.5
Work with assigned tasks	Assign a task to another Outlook user.	6.1.6
	Send a status report.	6.1.3

Knowledge Assessment

Fill in the Blanks

Complete the following sentences by writing the correct word or words in the blanks provided.

1. Only the task _____ can modify a task.
2. A(n) _____ task occurs at regular intervals.
3. After you start a task, the task's status is _____.
4. Click the Tasks button to view the _____.
5. Use a(n) _____ to assign a task to another user.
6. The To-Do List displays tasks and _____.
7. The task owner can _____ the task to another Outlook user.
8. A(n) _____ task is not displayed on your To-Do List.
9. You can track a(n) _____ from creation to completion.
10. A(n) _____ task is postponed.

Multiple Choice

Select the best response for the following statements.

1. Which of the following can be a to-do item?
   a. Task
   b. Message
   c. Flagged contact
   d. All of the above
2. Who owns a task when you assign the task to another user and the task is declined?
   a. You
   b. You and the other Outlook user
   c. The other Outlook user
   d. No one owns the task

3. What is the difference between a task and a to-do item?
    a. A task takes longer to complete.
    b. To-do items are displayed on the To-Do List.
    c. Tasks can be tracked.
    d. There is no difference between a task and a to-do item.

4. How do you protect the details of a task from casual observers on your network?
    a. Complete the task.
    b. Make the task private.
    c. Assign the task to another Outlook user.
    d. Hide the task.

5. What is automatically created when you create a task?
    a. To-do item
    b. Deadline
    c. Task request
    d. Message

6. Who owns a task you assign to another Outlook user?
    a. You
    b. You and the other Outlook user
    c. The other Outlook user
    d. No one owns the task

7. What happens when you complete a recurring task?
    a. The task is deleted.
    b. The task is assigned to another Outlook user.
    c. An entry is made in your calendar.
    d. The task is automatically re-created with the next due date displayed.

8. Where does a task request arrive?
    a. Tasks folder
    b. Mail folder
    c. To-Do List
    d. Task Requests folder

9. What feature finds tasks quickly?
    a. Instant Search
    b. Search folder
    c. Sort tasks
    d. All of the above

10. What folder must be active to create a task?
    a. Task folder
    b. Mail folder
    c. Contacts folder
    d. Any Outlook folder

Project 11-1: Create a One-Time Task

Eugene Kogan is setting up a small business to bake and sell cupcakes. He believes that "personal cakes" will be popular at children's parties, open houses, and office events. Before he can get started, Eugene needs to create a list of tasks. He is a procrastinator, so he knows that deadlines are needed to keep him focused on the business. Since he already has a full-time job, he will only be able to work a few hours a week on this new venture and he wants to update his task settings accordingly.

GET READY. LAUNCH Outlook if it is not already running.

1. On the File tab, click Options.
2. Click Tasks. The Outlook Options window is displayed.
3. In the Work hours group, key or select 4 in the *Task working hours per day* field to indicate that you work only 4 hours a day on tasks.
4. In the *Task working hours per week* field, key or select 24 because Eugene plans to work on Saturdays as well.
5. Click OK.
6. If necessary, click the Tasks button in the Navigation Pane to display the Tasks folder.
7. Click New Task on the Home tab.
8. In the *Subject* field, key Cupcakes—Identify potential clients. In the *Due date* field, key or select [the date two weeks from today]. Click the Save & Close button in the Actions group on the Ribbon.
9. Click New Task on the Home tab.
10. In the *Subject* field, key Cupcakes—Identify competitors. In the *Due date* field, key or select [the date two weeks from today]. Click the Save & Close button in the Actions group on the Ribbon.
11. Click New Task on the Home tab.
12. In the *Subject* field, key Cupcakes—Research prices and recurring expenses. In the *Due date* field, key or select [the date two weeks from today]. Click the Save & Close button in the Actions group on the Ribbon.
13. Click New Task on the Home tab.
14. In the *Subject* field, key Cupcakes—Identify initial equipment and financial investment needed. In the *Due date* field, key or select [the date four weeks from today]. Click the Save & Close button in the Actions group on the Ribbon.
15. Click New Task on the Home tab.
16. In the *Subject* field, key Cupcakes—Identify time investment required. In the *Due date* field, key or select [the date four weeks from today]. Click the Save & Close button in the Actions group on the Ribbon.
17. Click New Task on the Home tab.
18. In the *Subject* field, key Cupcakes—Research and select marketing methods. In the *Due date* field, key or select [the date four weeks from today]. Click the Save & Close button in the Actions group on the Ribbon.
19. Click New Task on the Home tab.
20. In the *Subject* field, key Cupcakes—Write a business plan. In the Due date field, key or select [the date six weeks from today]. Click the Save & Close button in the Actions group on the Ribbon.

PAUSE. LEAVE Outlook open for the next project.

Project 11-2: Modify Tasks

Eugene has made progress on making his cupcake dream come true. Update his progress on each of the tasks.

GET READY. LAUNCH Outlook if it is not already running.

1. If necessary, click the Tasks button in the Navigation Pane to display the Tasks folder.
2. Double-click the Cupcakes—Identify potential clients task. The task is opened in a Task window.
3. Click the *Status* field. Select In Progress.
4. Click the *% Complete* field and key or select 50%.
5. Click the Save & Close button in the Actions group on the Ribbon.
6. Double-click the Cupcakes—Identify competitors task. The task is opened in a Task window.
7. Click the *Status* field. Select In Progress.
8. Click the *% Complete* field and key or select 25%.
9. Click the Save & Close button in the Actions group on the Ribbon.
10. Double-click the Cupcakes—Research prices and recurring expenses task. The task is opened in a Task window.
11. Click the *Status* field. Select In Progress.
12. Click the *% Complete* field and key or select 75%.
13. Click the Save & Close button in the Actions group on the Ribbon.

PAUSE. LEAVE Outlook open for the next project.

Proficiency Assessment

Project 11-3: Assign a Task to Another Outlook User

Eugene has been researching his business prospects for several weeks now. He is ready to pull the information together in a business plan. However, Eugene knows that a business plan is a critical document. For example, the business plan is necessary for obtaining funds from a bank. Although Eugene has many important business skills, he decided to ask his cousin, a technical writer at Litware, Inc., to write the business plan.

 **Troubleshooting** You cannot assign a task to yourself; therefore, Projects 11-3 and 11-4 require exchanging messages with a partner using Outlook 2010. If you do not have a partner, you can use a different Outlook profile tied to a separate e-mail account. If you need to create a profile, see Outlook's Help topics for more information.

GET READY. LAUNCH Outlook if it is not already running.

Take Note   This exercise is performed in your account.

1. If necessary, click the Tasks button in the Navigation Pane.
2. Double-click the Cupcakes—Write a business plan task.
3. Click Assign Task in the Manage Task group on the Ribbon. In the *To* field, key [the recipient's e-mail address].
4. In the *Priority* field, select High.
5. In the *Due date* field, key or select [the date four weeks from today].
6. In the message area, key the following message: Hi, Press Enter. Please let me know if you need any additional information. [Press Enter.] Thanks!
7. Click the Send button to send the task request.

PAUSE. CLOSE to access your partner's account if necessary. Otherwise, leave Outlook open to use in the next exercise.

Project 11-4: Accept an Assigned Task

Eugene's cousin is helping Eugene by sorting through all of the information necessary to create a business plan. His cousin understands the importance of creating a professional document that will give Eugene the best chance of obtaining financing from the bank. Eugene's cousin is just as excited about the new business as he is; he completes the business plan in record time and marks the task as complete, which automatically updates Eugene's task list too.

GET READY. LAUNCH Outlook if it is not already running.

Take Note   This exercise is performed in your partner's account.

1. In your partner's account, view the mailbox. If the task request sent in the previous project has not arrived, click the Send/Receive All Folders button.
2. Click the Task Request: Cupcakes—Write a business plan message to preview it.
3. In the Reading Pane, click the Accept button at the top of the message.
4. Click OK to send the acceptance without editing it.
5. In the Inbox, double-click the Task Request: Cupcakes—Write a business plan message to open it. Mark the task as complete.

PAUSE. CLOSE Outlook to access your account if necessary. Otherwise, leave Outlook open to use in the next project.

Mastery Assessment

Project 11-5: Complete Tasks

At the end of two weeks, Eugene has completed several tasks on time. He marks these tasks as complete. He checks the Completed view to see his progress on this new venture.

GET READY. LAUNCH Outlook if it is not already running.

1. If necessary, display the Tasks folder.
2. Open the Cupcakes—Identify potential clients task.
3. Mark the task as completed using the tools on the Ribbon.
4. Open the Cupcakes—Identify competitors task.
5. Mark the task as completed using the tools on the Ribbon.
6. Open the Cupcakes—Research prices and recurring expenses task and mark the task as complete.
7. Change the Task view to Completed. These tasks, as well as the Cupcakes—Write a business plan task completed by Eugene's cousin, appear on this view.

PAUSE. LEAVE Outlook open for the next project.

Project 11-6: Search for Tasks

Eugene has been operating his cupcake business on the side for the last six months and wants to better organize his Tasks folder by creating a Cupcakes subfolder. He moves his cupcake tasks into the new folder. Seeing his progress so far helps make up Eugene's mind. It's time to take the cupcakes business full time. Afterwards, you will clean up your folders after completing all of these projects.

GET READY. LAUNCH Outlook if it is not already running.

1. In your account, right-click the Tasks button in the Navigation Pane and create a new folder named Cupcakes.
2. Click the Tasks folder in the Select where to place the folder pane.
3. If necessary, display the Tasks folder.

4. Use Outlook's search tools to locate all tasks containing the key word Cupcakes. Make sure that all task items are searched.

5. Move the found tasks to the new *Cupcakes* subfolder to move them.

6. Click the Clear Search button to clear the search criteria.

7. To clean up Outlook after completing these projects, restore your working hours options and delete the new Cupcakes folder.

CLOSE Outlook.

INTERNET READY

Have you thought of starting a business? Create a task list to research your business idea. Use the Internet to research your business idea and the tasks involved.

Workplace *Ready*

BREAK IT DOWN

Earning a degree, managing a project, and training new workers seem like unrelated activities. What do they have in common? All three activities are complicated processes that seem daunting when you look at the whole. However, each activity is made up of smaller steps.

Break down a large goal into smaller tasks that you can perform yourself or assign to others for completion. In each case, start with the ultimate goal and break it down into a list of steps to be completed. Next, convert the steps into tasks, then match the tasks with the people available to perform the tasks.

When you assign tasks to other people, make sure that the task owner has all the tools needed to complete the task. The task owner needs the ability and authority to perform the task. Ability includes skill and equipment. Authority ensures that the task owner can obtain any necessary information or assistance from other workers.

When you create tasks, remember these important tips.

- Break down large jobs into manageable tasks.
- Match tasks to people.
- Ensure that the task owner has the ability and authority to succeed.

12 Categories and Outlook Data Files

LESSON SKILL MATRIX

Skills	Exam Objective	Objective Number
Working with Categories	Categorize Outlook items.	1.2.1
Working with Data Files		

KEY TERMS

- color category
- compacting
- data file

Bart Duncan is a sales representative for Contoso, Ltd. He sells insurance policies to businesses. He works with large corporations, small businesses, and new businesses that are struggling to grow. Because the size of the company dictates the level of service that his company offers its clients, he chooses to categorize clients based on their employee headcount. To make the client's status easily visible, Bart uses five color categories based on size. His two most important clients have separate color categories to indicate their importance in his sales activities. In this lesson, you'll use categories to color code your Outlook items. You'll also learn to create, open, and close Outlook data files to help you manage your Outlook items.

SOFTWARE ORIENTATION

Microsoft Outlook's Color Categories Window

The Color Categories window displayed in Figure 12-1 enables you to create, modify, and delete color categories.

Figure 12-1

Outlook Color
Categories window

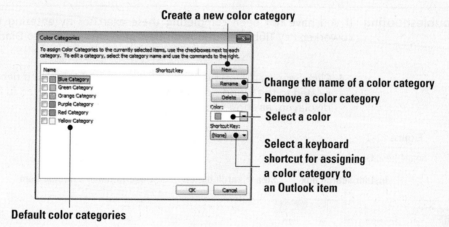

Use the Color Categories window to customize the new color categories for your use. Refer to Figure 12-1 as you complete the following exercises.

WORKING WITH CATEGORIES

The Bottom Line

A **color category** assigns a color to an Outlook item, providing a new way to visually indicate relationships among Outlook items. For example, you might assign the red category to all Outlook items related to your supervisor. In that instance, all items related to your supervisor, including her contact record, messages you exchange with her, and meetings scheduled with her, would be marked with the red color category. You can use color categories to sort or quickly find your Outlook items.

Categorizing Outlook Items

In this exercise, you will find all the Outlook items related to a specific contact and assign them to a category. Every Outlook item can be assigned to one or more color categories without opening the item. You can also create rules to assign a color category automatically to messages you send and receive.

Ref You can find more information on creating rules in Lesson 5.

Take Note Throughout this chapter you will see information that appears in black text within brackets, such as [Press Enter], or [next Friday's date]. The information contained in the brackets is intended to be directions for you rather than something you actually type word for word. It will instruct you to perform an action or substitute text. Do **not** type the actual text that appears within brackets.

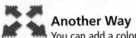 **STEP BY STEP** **Categorize Outlook Items**

GET READY. LAUNCH Microsoft Outlook if it is not already running.

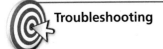 **Another Way**
You can add a color category before you send a new e-mail. Click the Options tab, click the dialog launcher in the More Options group, and select Categories.

1. Click the Folder List button in the Navigation Pane to display the Folder List.
2. Click the Instant Search box. The Search Tools tab appears in the Ribbon.
3. In the Instant Search box, key [the name of a friend or coworker you've been sending items during previous lessons]. Outlook displays a list of items related to your friend or coworker. If necessary, click the All Outlook Items button in the scope group of the Search Tools tab to display items from every folder in the search results list, as shown in Figure 12-2.

Troubleshooting If you have not been completing these exercises by entering the name of a friend or coworker, key Tibbott. Outlook displays any items related to Diane Tibbott.

4. Click Search All Outlook Items on the Search Tools tab, if necessary. All Outlook items related to the friend or coworker whose name you keyed in Instant Search box are displayed, as shown in Figure 12-2.

Figure 12-2

Search results

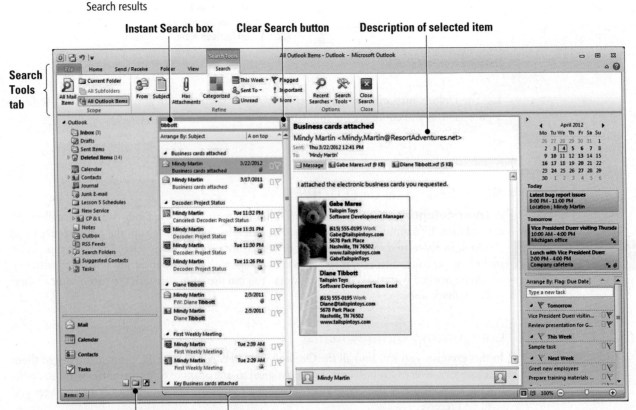

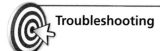

Troubleshooting The Outlook items in the search results depend on the exercises and projects you completed in previous lessons. They may differ from the results shown here.

5. Click the first item on the list. Scroll to the end of the list. Press **Shift** and click the last item on the list. All the search results are selected.

6. Right-click over the highlighted list of items. On the shortcut menu, point to Categorize and click the Red Category option. If you have not used Red Category before, a dialog box allowing you to rename the category is displayed, as shown in Figure 12-3.

Figure 12-3

Rename Category dialog box

7. Click No in the Rename Category dialog box. You will rename the category in the next exercise. All the items are assigned to the Red Category, as shown in Figure 12-4.

Figure 12-4

Categorizing Outlook items

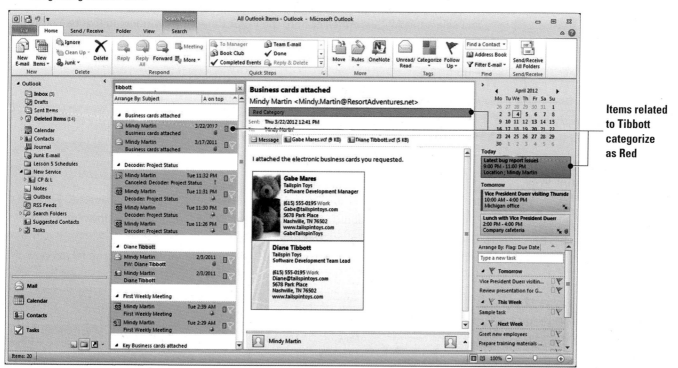

8. Click the Close Search button to clear the search criteria, which in this case is the name of your friend or coworker.

PAUSE. LEAVE Outlook open to use in the next exercise.

CERTIFICATION READY? 1.2.1

How do you categorize messages, appointments, meetings, contacts, and tasks by color?

Modifying and Creating Color Categories

If you, like most people, find that a category named Red Category is a little vague, you will be glad to know that color categories can be renamed to meet your needs. Use names that identify the Outlook items assigned to the color category. Using an individual's or a project's name more clearly identifies a color category. Outlook comes with six color categories, but you can add more as you need them.

In this exercise, you will rename an existing color category and create a new one.

STEP BY STEP   **Modify and Create Color Categories**

GET READY. LAUNCH Microsoft Outlook if it is not already running.

Another Way
You can also access the Color Categories window by right-clicking a message, pointing to Categorize, and then clicking All Categories from the list.

1. Click the Mail button in the Navigation Pane to display the Mail folder. Click the Inbox, if necessary.

2. Click any message in the message list. A preview of the message appears in the Reading Pane. Though you don't have to open it, an Outlook item must be selected to activate the Categorize button.

3. On the Home tab, click the Categorize button in the Tags group and click the All Categories option from the dropdown list. The Color Categories window in Figure 12-1 is displayed.

4. Click Red Category in the list of categories and click the Rename button on the right side of the window. The Red Category text becomes active.

5. Key Partner Exercises in the activated space and press Enter.

6. Click OK to rename the category and close the Color Categories window.

Take Note   If you want to rename multiple color categories at the same time, click OK after all of your changes have been made.

7. To create a new category, select any message in the message list and click Categorize and select the All Categories option. The Color Categories window in Figure 12-1 is displayed.

8. Click the New button. The Add New Category window is displayed, as shown in Figure 12-5.

Figure 12-5

Add New Category window

Key a name for a new category

Select a shortcut key

Select a color

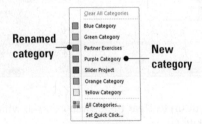

Another Way
You can also create categories that don't use a color. To create a colorless category, select None in the Color field in the Add New Category window.

9. In the *Name* field, key Slider Project. In the *Color* field, select Dark Olive.

10. Click OK. The new category is displayed in the Color Categories window.

11. Click OK to close the Color Categories window.

12. With an Outlook item selected, click the Categorize button on the Home tab to view the modified list of categories, as shown in Figure 12-6.

Figure 12-6

Modified list of available categories

Renamed category

New category

13. Because a message was selected when you created the new color category, that message is assigned to the new category. Select the message again, then click Categorize and select Clear All Categories to remove the category from this message.

PAUSE. LEAVE Outlook open to use in the next exercise.

Sorting Items by Color Category

To sort items, you arrange the items in a sequence based on specific criteria. After assigning Outlook items to a color category, you can use the color category as a sort criterion in each of the Outlook modules. Once sorted, Outlook items are placed in groups based on the color categories. The order of the groups is determined alphabetically by the names of the categories. For example, the category "Apple" will be placed before the category "Banana," regardless of the color assigned to the categories. In the Contacts, Tasks, and Notes folders, you can click the By Category radio button in the Navigation pane to sort contacts by category.

In the Calendar folder, click the View menu, point to Current View, and click By Category. Calendar items without a category are displayed before those assigned to a color category. If you added holidays to your calendar in Lesson 10, the holidays are displayed in the Holiday category.

In this exercise, you will sort your Mail messages by color category.

STEP BY STEP   **Sort Items by Color Category**

GET READY. LAUNCH Microsoft Outlook if it is not already running and be sure to complete the previous exercises.

Another Way
To sort items, you can click the *Arranged By: Date* text below the Instant Search box. Click *Categories* in the dropdown menu.

1. If necessary, click the Mail button in the Navigation Pane to display the mailbox.

2. On the View tab, click Categories in the Arrangement group. The messages in the message list are rearranged by category. Messages without an assigned category appear at the top of the list. Scroll down to the bottom of the message list to view the categorized messages if necessary, as shown in Figure 12-7.

3. On the View tab, click Date in the Arrangement group. The messages are resorted to the default order.

Figure 12-7

Sorting items by category

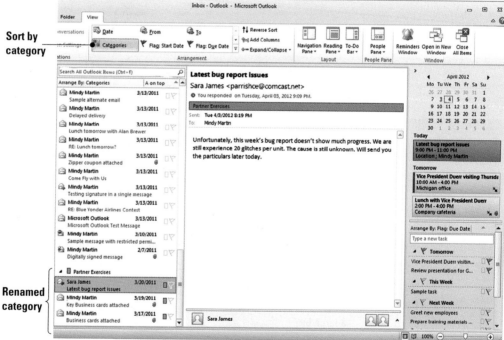

Sort by category

Renamed category

PAUSE. LEAVE Outlook open to use in the next exercise.

Searching for Items by Category

Outlook's Instant Search feature allows you to search for Outlook items that meet a variety of search criteria. In previous lessons, you keyed text to use as the search criterion. You can use the Advanced Find feature to search by category or other characteristics, such as the Importance flag and sensitivity assignment. In addition, you can use Outlook's predefined Categorized Mail Search Folder to quickly search for text within categorized messages without having to specify advanced search criteria. In this exercise, you will add a selection criterion using Advanced Find.

STEP BY STEP   **Search for Items by Category**

GET READY. Before you begin these steps, complete the previous exercises in this lesson.

1. Click the Mail button in the Navigation Pane to display the Calendar folder. Click the Folder List button to display the complete list of Outlook folders.

2. Click in the Instant Search box to activate the Search Tools tab and click Has Attachments in the Refine group. The Instant Search box is updated to include the attachments criterion, as shown in Figure 12-8.

Figure 12-8

Instant Search box

3. On the Search Tools tab, click the Search Tools button in the Options groups and click Advanced Find from the dropdown list that appears. The Advanced Find window is displayed.

4. Click the More Choices tab. The *Only items with* field displays the attachment requirement you specified in step 2, as shown in Figure 12-9.

Figure 12-9

Advanced Find window

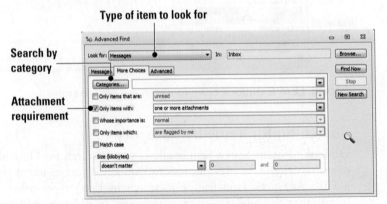

 Ref   You can find more information on Search Folders in Lesson 7.

5. Click the Categories button and select Partner Exercises. Click OK to close the Color Categories dialog box.

6. Click Find Now. Search results are displayed below the Advanced Find window as they are located, as shown in Figure 12-10.

Figure 12-10

Results of searching by category

Search category

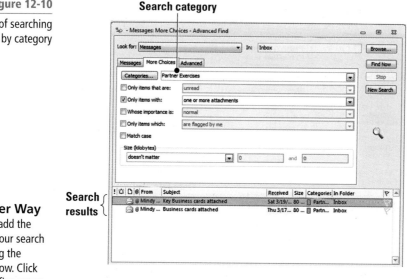

Another Way
You can add the category option to your search criteria without using the Advanced Find window. Click Categories in the Refine group on the Search Tools tab and select Partner Exercises.

Search results

7. Click the Close button in the upper-right corner of the Advanced Find window.

PAUSE. LEAVE Outlook open to use in the next exercise.

WORKING WITH DATA FILES

The Bottom Line

When you create an Outlook account, Outlook creates a **data file** to store all of your Outlook data. That data file is visible inside Outlook at the top-level folder in your Navigation Pane. Depending on your settings, this data file might be called Outlook Data Files or Personal Folders, or could have the same name as your e-mail address. Microsoft Exchange Server accounts usually don't use individual Outlook Data Files. However, when you use the AutoArchive feature, Outlook stores the archived data on your computer as an Outlook Data File with a .pst extension.

X Ref

For more information about the AutoArchive feature, see Lesson 4.

Creating a Data File

You can create your own data files by manually archiving items related to a specific project, client, or time frame and store the information in a separate .pst file. An Outlook Data File is a convenient way to transfer Outlook data from one computer to another computer. In this exercise, you will create a new top-level Outlook Data File and protect the new folder with a password.

Create a Data File

Another Way
You can access the New Items button on the Home tab in every feature in Outlook.

GET READY. LAUNCH Microsoft Outlook if it is not already running.

1. Click the Mail button in the Navigation Pane to display the mailbox. Click the Folder List button in the Navigation Pane to display the Folder List.

2. On the Home tab, click New Items in the New group. A dropdown list of items that you can create is displayed.

3. Click the More Items option to display the dropdown list of new items you can create, as shown in Figure 12-11.

Figure 12-11

Creating a new Outlook Data File

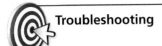

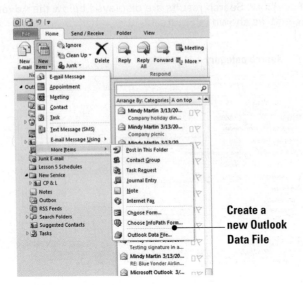

Create a
new Outlook
Data File

Troubleshooting For this exercise, you want to select the top-level folder. It might be called Outlook Data Files or Personal Folders, or simply state your e-mail address.

4. Click Outlook Data File. The Create or Open Outlook Data File window is displayed, as shown in Figure 12-12.

Figure 12-12

Create or Open Outlook Data File window

Default Outlook Data File location

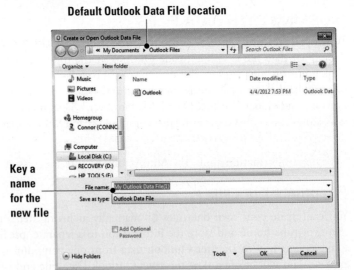

Key a
name
for the
new file

Troubleshooting If you're working on an account that is part of Exchange Server, check with your administrator for the correct location to store your new data file.

5. In the *File name* field, key Slider Project and click OK. A new Slider Project.pst file is created on your computer and the new Slider data file appears in the Navigation Pane.

Take Note You can see where Outlook created this file in the Account Settings. Click the File tab, then click Account Settings. On the Data Files tab, click Slider project.pst to see the path and file name.

6. Click the expand arrow next to the Slider Project folder to display its contents, as shown in Figure 12-13.

Figure 12-13

New Outlook Data File in the Navigation Pane

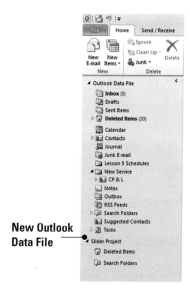

New Outlook Data File

PAUSE. LEAVE Outlook open to use in the next exercise.

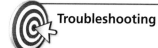
Troubleshooting Depending on the exercises and projects you completed in previous lessons, the Outlook folders displayed in your Folder List could differ from the folders in Figure 12-9.

Selecting a Data File for a Mail Account

When messages are received, they are delivered to the Inbox, which is part of your default Outlook data file. If you create a new data file, you can choose to direct messages into the Inbox of the new data file. Normally, users will use this feature only if they send and receive messages in two or more e-mail accounts. In this exercise, you will select a new data file for your e-mail account so that all incoming messages will be delivered to the new data file. You will also restore the original location so that your incoming messages will continue to be received in your original Inbox.

Take Note   Refer to the Outlook Help to find more information about configuring Outlook to send and receive messages through a second e-mail account.

STEP BY STEP   **Select a Data File for a Mail Account**

GET READY. Before you begin these steps, complete the previous exercise.

Troubleshooting If you are operating on a Microsoft Exchange Network, these options may be disabled. Contact your network administrator with any questions.

1. Click the Mail button in the Navigation Pane to display the mailbox.

2. Click the File tab to open Backstage view, and click the Account Settings option and select Account Settings from the dropdown menu. The Account Settings window is displayed. Your e-mail account is listed on the E-mail tab. If you already receive messages from more than one e-mail account, the additional accounts will also be displayed, as shown in Figure 12-14.

Figure 12-14

Account Settings window

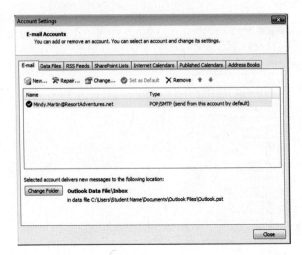

3. Click your main e-mail account to select it and click the Change Folder button near the bottom of the window. The New E-mail Delivery Location window is displayed, as shown in Figure 12-15.

Figure 12-15

New E-mail Delivery Location window

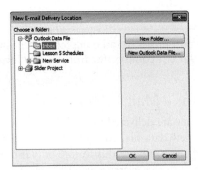

4. In the New E-mail Delivery Location window, click the Slider Project folder. Click the New Folder button. The Create Folder dialog box is displayed, as shown in Figure 12-16.

Figure 12-16

Create Folder window

5. In the Create Folder dialog box, key Inbox in the *Name* field and click OK.

6. In the New E-mail Delivery Location window, click the Inbox folder you just created in the Slider Project folder. Click OK. In the Account Settings window, you can see that mail will be delivered to Slider Project.pst.

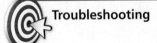

Troubleshooting Changing the location of your e-mail delivery settings may affect any rules you have created or Internet calendars that you have subscribed to.

7. Click the Change Folder button near the bottom of the window. The New E-mail Delivery Location window is displayed.

8. In the New E-mail Delivery Location window, click the plus sign (+) next to the Outlook Data File folder and then click the Inbox folder in the Outlook Data File folder. Click OK. This returns Outlook to your original data file settings. In the Account Settings window, you can see that mail will be delivered to the original location.

9. Click the Close button to close the Account Settings window.

PAUSE. LEAVE Outlook open to use in the next exercise.

Changing Data File Settings

After creating a data file, you can use the Account Settings to modify some of its characteristics, as shown in Table 12-1. In this exercise, you will rename and compact the Slider Project data file.

Table 12-1

Data File Properties

Properties	Description
Name	In general, it is never a good idea to change the name of your original data file; however, you can change the name of any data files that you have created.
Change Password	A password can be used to protect the information stored in the data file. However, you are solely responsible for remembering your password. Neither Microsoft nor your network administrator will be able to help you access the data file if your password is lost or forgotten.
Compact Now	Outlook data files get very large very quickly. **Compacting** a file is a process that reduces the size of the data file.

STEP BY STEP **Change Data File Settings**

GET READY. Before you begin these steps, complete the previous exercise.

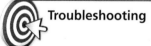

Troubleshooting If you are operating on a Microsoft Exchange Network, these options may be disabled. Contact your network administrator with any questions.

1. If necessary, click the Mail button in the Navigation Pane to display the Mail folder.

2. Right-click on the Slider Project folder and click Data File Properties in the shortcut menu.

Another Way
You can also access a data file's properties from the navigation pane.

3. Click the Advanced button. The Outlook Data File window is displayed, as shown in Figure 12-17.

4. Click the Compact Now button. A small window shows you the progress.

5. Click the Name field and key New Slider Project. Click OK.

6. Click the OK button to close the Outlook Data File window.

CLOSE Outlook.

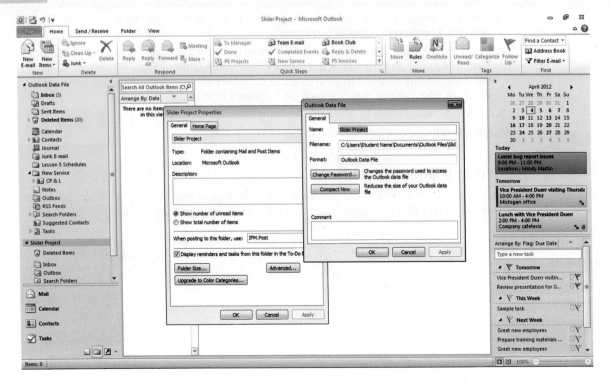

Figure 12-17

Outlook Data File window

SKILL SUMMARY

In This Lesson You Learned How to:	Exam Objective	Objective Number
Work with categories.	Categorize Outlook items.	1.2.1
Work with data files.		

Knowledge Assessment

Matching

Match the term with its definition.

a. archive

b. color category

c. compacting

d. criteria

e. compacting

f. Outlook Personal Folders

g. rule

h. Instant Search

i. search folder

j. sort

1. Color assigned to an Outlook item, providing a way to visually indicate relationships among Outlook items

2. Defines an action that happens automatically when messages are received or sent

3. A good way to save space in your data file

4. A virtual folder that searches your e-mail folders to locate items that meet the saved search criteria

5. A feature used to find items that meet specific criteria

6. Store messages in a separate folder to reduce the number of messages in the folders you use most often

7. Characteristics used to select items

8. Process that reduces the size of a data file

9. Arrange items in a sequence based on specific criteria

10. File containing stored Outlook data

True/False

Circle T if the statement is true or F if the statement is false.

T F 1. You can create new color categories.

T F 2. A color category indicates a relationship among Outlook items.

T F 3. Rules can't be used to assign color categories.

T F 4. Archived Outlook items are stored in data files.

T F 5. A color category must use a color.

T F 6. You can use color categories to sort Outlook items.

T F 7. Outlook data files can be protected by a password.

T F 8. When sorted, items without a color category are displayed below items with a color category.

T F 9. You can use the Category Search feature when searching for categorized messages.

T F 10. Outlook automatically creates data files the first time it is launched.

Competency Assessment

Project 12-1: Assign an Outlook Item to a Color Category

Terry Crayton at Trey Research is starting a new project. After sending an e-mail to welcome Charles Fitzgerald, she realizes that it would be convenient to assign a color category to all of their correspondence.

GET READY. LAUNCH Outlook if it is not already running.

1. Click the Mail button in the Navigation Pane to display the Mail folder, if necessary.

2. Click New E-mail. The Message window is displayed.

3. In the *To* field, key Charles@treyresearch.net.

 **Troubleshooting** The e-mail addresses provided in these exercises belong to unused domains owned by Microsoft. When you send a message to these addresses, you will receive an error message stating that the message could not be delivered. Delete the error messages when they arrive.

4. In the *Subject* field, key Project Team.

5. In the message area, key the following message: Hi Charles, [Press Enter twice.] I look forward to working with you on the new project. The product sounds like an interesting challenge. [Press Enter twice.] Terry.

6. Click the Send button.

7. Click the Sent Items folder in the Navigation Pane.

8. Double-click the Project Team message in the message list.

9. Click Categorize in the Tags group. Click Green Category in the dropdown list. If you have not used Green Category before, a dialog box allowing you to rename the category is displayed.

10. Click No in the Rename Category dialog box.

LEAVE Outlook open for the next project.

Project 12-2: Modify a Color Category

The new project that Terry Crayton and Charles Fitzgerald are leading has been named. Change the name of Green Category to POD Project.

GET READY. Before you begin these steps, complete the previous exercise.

1. Click the Mail button in the Navigation Pane to display the Mail folder, if necessary.
2. Click the Sent Items folder in the Navigation Pane.
3. Click the Project Team message in the message list.
4. On the Home tab, click Categorize and click the All Categories option. The Color Categories window is displayed.
5. Click Green Category in the list of categories. Click the Rename button. The Green Category text becomes active.
6. Key POD Project and press Enter.
7. Click OK to rename the category and close the Color Categories window.

LEAVE Outlook open for the next project.

Proficiency Assessment

Project 12-3: Sort Items by Color Category

A week later, Terry Crayton needs to find the message she sent to Charles. Because only one message has been sent, sorting the sent messages is the simplest way to find the message.

GET READY. Before you begin these steps, complete the previous exercise.

1. Click the Mail button in the Navigation Pane to display the Mail folder if necessary.
2. Click the Sent Items folder in the Navigation Pane.
3. On the View tab, click Categories in the Arrangement group. The messages in the message list are rearranged.
4. Messages without an assigned category appear at the top of the list. Scroll down to the bottom of the message list to view the message in the POD Project category.
5. On the View tab, click Date in the Arrangement group. The messages are resorted to the default date sort.

LEAVE Outlook open for the next project.

Project 12-4: Search Items by Category

Several weeks later, the POD project is in full swing. Terry has added new contacts, and dozens of messages have been exchanged with POD Project team members. Searching is the easiest way to view all Outlook items associated with the project.

GET READY. Before you begin these steps, complete the previous exercise.

1. Click the Mail button in the Navigation Pane to display the Calendar folder. Click the Folder List button to display the complete list of Outlook folders.
2. Click in the Instant Search box to activate the Search Tools tab.
3. Click Search Tools in the Options groups and click Advanced Find. The Advanced Find window is displayed.
4. Click the More Choices tab.
5. Click the Categories arrow and select POD Project.
6. Click Find Now.
7. The search results are displayed below the Advanced Find window as they are located.
8. Click the Close button in the upper-right corner of the Advanced Find window.

LEAVE Outlook open for the next project.

Project 12-5: Create a Data File

Terry has been assigned to the POD project exclusively. She creates a new data file that she will use until the project is complete.

GET READY. Before you begin these steps, complete the previous exercise.

1. Click the Folder List button in the Navigation Pane to display the Folder List, if necessary.
2. Right-click Outlook Data Files and click the New arrow to display the dropdown list of new items you can create. Click Outlook Data File. The New Outlook Data File window is displayed.
3. In the New Outlook Data File window, click OK. The Create or Open Outlook Data File window is displayed.
4. In the *File name* field, key POD to create a new POD.pst file. Click OK. The Create Microsoft Personal Folders window is displayed.
5. In the Create Microsoft Personal Folders window, key POD Project in the *Name* field to identify the name of the folder that will be displayed in Outlook's folder list in the Navigation Pane. Click OK. The POD Project folder is displayed in the Navigation Pane.

LEAVE Outlook open for the next project.

Project 12-6: Select a Data File for a Mail Account

After creating the new data file, Terry wants to add the data file to her mail account. After making the change, you will restore your original settings.

GET READY. Before you begin these steps, complete the previous exercise.

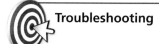 **Troubleshooting** If you are operating on a Microsoft Exchange Network, these options may be disabled. Contact your network administrator with any questions.

1. Click the Mail button in the Navigation Pane to display the Mail folder. Click the Folder List button in the Navigation Pane to display the Folder List.
2. Click the File tab to open Backstage view, and click the Account Settings option. The Account Settings window is displayed. Your e-mail account is listed on the E-mail tab.
3. Click [your main e-mail account] to select it and click the Change Folder button near the bottom of the window. The New E-mail Delivery Location window is displayed.
4. In the New E-mail Delivery Location window, click the POD Project folder. Click the New Folder button. The Create Folder dialog box is displayed.
5. In the Create Folder dialog box, key Inbox in the *Folder Name* field and click OK.
6. In the New E-mail Delivery Location window, click the Inbox folder you just created in the POD folder. Click OK. In the Account Settings window, you can see that mail will be delivered to POD.pst.
7. Before finishing these projects, you will change the data file to your default data file. Click the Change Folder button near the bottom of the window. The New E-mail Delivery Location window is displayed.

8. In the New E-mail Delivery Location window, expand the top-level data file folder and click the Inbox folder. Click OK. This returns your original data file settings. In the Account Settings window, you can see that mail will be delivered to the original location.

9. Click the Close button to close the Account Settings window.

CLOSE Outlook.

 **INTERNET READY**

If you subscribe to an e-mail provider such as Earthlink or RoadRunner, your account comes with several mailboxes. Many people use one mailbox for business correspondence, one mailbox for personal correspondence, and one mailbox for shopping or other activities. Access your account on the Internet to configure a mailbox, add a data file in Outlook, and associate the mailbox with the data file in Outlook.

LESSON SKILL MATRIX

Skills	Exam Objective	Objective Number
Working with Notes	Set Notes and Journals options.	1.1.5
	Create a note.	6.2.1
	Categorize notes.	6.2.3
	Print multiple notes.	1.5.6
	Exploring the Notes views.	6.2.2
Working with the Journal	Set Notes and Journal Options.	1.1.5
	Automatically record Outlook items.	6.3.1
	Automatically record files.	6.3.2
	Edit a Journal entry.	6.3.3

KEY TERMS

- Journal
- notes

Mindy Martin and Jon Morris own and operate Resort Adventures, a luxury resort. As part of their business, they run custom tours for private parties. In order to provide the best experience for their guests, they make several phone calls before the guest's visit to find out the guest's preferences and expectations. They record details of those conversations in Outlook's Journal module. In addition, as part of Mindy's job, she researches local sites even before a guest has requested a tour. She records that research in Outlook's Notes module so that she has access to them at a later date. In this lesson, you'll learn how to record journal entries both automatically and manually. You will also learn how to create and categorize notes.

SOFTWARE ORIENTATION

Microsoft Outlook's Notes Options

Before you begin working with Outlook's Notes module, you need to be familiar with the primary user interface. Outlook's Notes feature, displayed in Figure 13-1, enables you to create, modify, and delete notes.

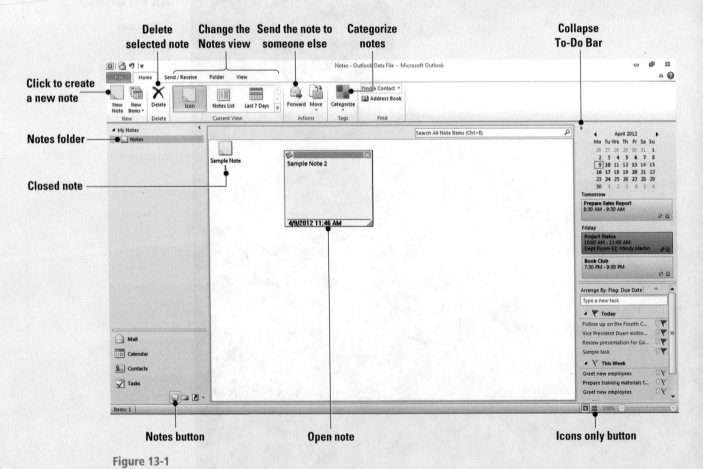

Figure 13-1

Outlook's Notes feature

Think of Outlook notes as sticky notes that you can use to jot down quick notes and stick them on your desktop or your Notes window. You can also use the Notes feature to record detailed notes on a specific meeting or event.

WORKING WITH NOTES

The Bottom Line

Just like the repositionable sticky notes you probably have on your desk, the **Notes** module enables you to keep important information that may not be related to a particular contact or project. And, just like those sticky notes, Notes come in a variety of colors and sizes.

Setting Notes Options

Outlook's notes appear in the Notes module as yellow sticky notes. You can change the default color, font, and size of new notes in Outlook's Backstage. In this exercise, you will change your default color for Notes and ensure that Outlook is tracking the date and time that the note was last modified.

STEP BY STEP   **Set Notes Options**

GET READY. LAUNCH Outlook if it is not already running.

1. Click the File tab and click Options to open Backstage view.
2. Click Notes and Journal from the list. The Outlook Options window opens, as shown in Figure 13-2.

Figure 13-2

Notes and Journal Options

Set the default color

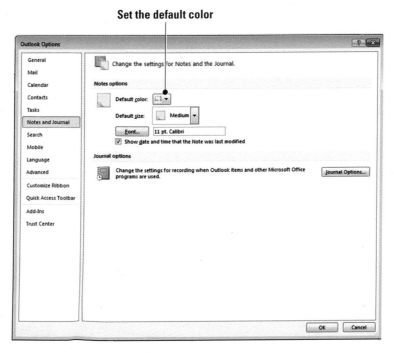

3. In the Notes options section, select Blue in the *Default color* field.
4. If necessary, click the Show date and time that the Note was last notified check box.
5. Click OK to close the window.

PAUSE. LEAVE Outlook open to use in the next exercise.

CERTIFICATION
READY   **1.1.5**

How do you set Notes options?

Creating a New Note

Unlike tasks, notes do not have a due date. In this exercise, you will create a new note.

STEP BY STEP | Create a New Note

GET READY. LAUNCH Outlook if it is not already running.

1. Click Notes in the Navigation Pane to open the Notes feature. Click Icons Only in the status bar.

2. Click the New button on the Ribbon. A blank blue sticky note appears in the Reading Pane. Below the sticky note is the current date and time, as shown in Figure 13-3.

Figure 13-3

New blank note

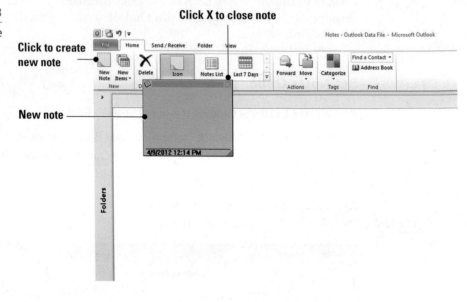

Troubleshooting If you did not complete the previous exercise, the default color for the sticky note is yellow.

3. Key Just heard that the Big Red River has class 4 rapids. Maybe we could hold whitewater rafting tours there.

4. Click the Close button (the X at the top-right corner of the note) to close the note. Your note appears as a sticky note with the note's text below it.

5. Click the New button on the Ribbon.

6. Key Should we offer pizza if our fishing tours don't catch their dinner?

7. Click the Close button (the X at the top-right corner of the note) to close the note. Notice that only the first two lines of text are displayed for the non-selected note. Your Notes folder should appear as shown in Figure 13-4.

Figure 13-4

Notes in the Notes window

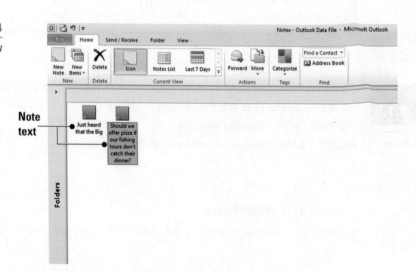

CERTIFICATION READY 6.2.1

How do you create a new note?

Take Note

PAUSE. LEAVE Outlook open to use in the next exercise.

Right-click on a note and click Forward on the shortcut menu to forward a note as an Outlook attachment.

Categorizing and Printing Notes

Once a note has been created, you can quickly make necessary changes to it. Notes can be printed individually or as a set. In this exercise, you will open an existing note, add a category, and print it.

 Ref

For more information about categories, see Lesson 12.

STEP BY STEP | **Categorize and Print Notes**

GET READY. LAUNCH Outlook if it is not already running and be sure to complete the previous exercise.

1. If necessary, click Notes in the Navigation Pane to open the Notes window and click Icons Only in the status bar.
2. Click the Big Red River note to select it.
3. On the Home tab, click Categorize.

Troubleshooting If your note disappeared when you clicked the Categorize button, then you probably opened the note. Because notes are created in a separate window, clicking a button on the Outlook application window makes it the active window and places it on top of an open note. If this happens, just minimize Outlook and close your open note.

4. Select the All Categories option to create a new category. The Color Categories window is displayed.
5. Click the New button. The Add New Category window is displayed.
6. In the *Name* field, key Resort Tours.
7. Click OK to accept Outlook's suggested color and apply the color category to the Big Red River note. The note's icon changes color to match the category, as shown in Figure 13-5.

Figure 13-5

Categorized Note icon

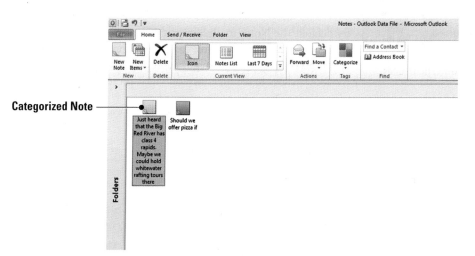

Categorized Note —

**CERTIFICATION
READY   6.2.3**

How do you categorize notes?

8. Select the Big Red River and the Pizza notes. Click File and click Print, as shown in Figure 13-6.

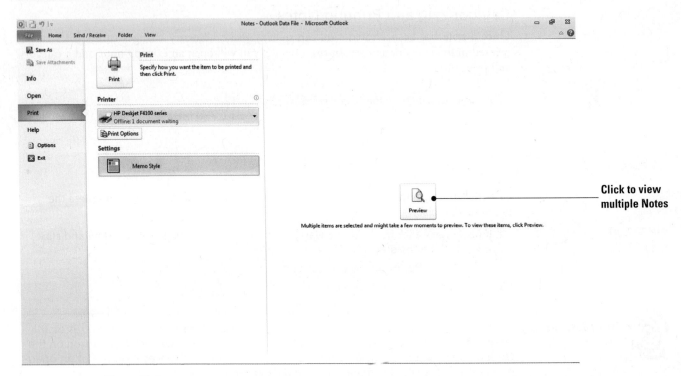

Click to view
multiple Notes

Figure 13-6

Printing multiple notes

Another Way
To print a single note, right-click and choose Quick Print on the shortcut menu.

9. In the Preview pane, click the Preview button. When the Preview becomes available, click the Next Page button to view both notes.

10. Click Print.

PAUSE. LEAVE Outlook open to use in the next exercise.

Exploring Notes Views

**CERTIFICATION
READY   1.5.6**

How do you print notes?

By default, the Notes module organizes your Notes as sticky note icons in neat rows across the Reading pane of Outlook. You can change that view in several ways, as shown in Table 13-1. All notes can be arranged by category and date from the View tab. In this exercise, you will explore the Notes views to see how the content is presented in each.

Table 13-1

Notes Views

View Name	Description
Icon	The default Notes view shows each note as a colored icon arranged in the order they were created.
Notes List	The notes are presented in a vertical list as a tiny colored sticky note icon followed by the note's text.
Last 7 Days	This view is presented vertically, like the Notes List, but shows only the items added in the last week.

| STEP BY STEP | Explore Notes Views |

GET READY. LAUNCH Outlook if it is not already running.

1. Click Notes in the Navigation Pane. The notes are presented in the Icon view.
2. In the Current View group, click Last 7 Days.
3. In the Current View group, click Notes List. The notes are now presented as a vertical list.
4. On the View tab, click Categories in the Arrangement group. The journal entries are now grouped by category. The uncategorized notes appear at the top of the list, as shown in Figure 13-7.

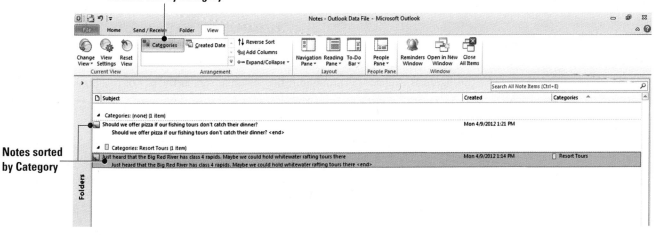

Figure 13-7

Exploring the Outlook Notes view

PAUSE. LEAVE Outlook open to use in the next exercise.

<table>
<tr><td>CERTIFICATION
READY</td><td>6.2.2</td></tr>
</table>

How do you change the Notes view?

The Bottom Line

WORKING WITH THE JOURNAL

Certain professionals, attorneys for instance, are required to keep track of the amount of time they have spent working on a particular client's case. They have to record the time spent on phone calls, e-mails, preparing documents, and holding meetings on behalf of the client. This can be done manually in an appointment book, or by using Outlook's Journal features. Think of the **Journal** as an online diary of all activities associated with one of your contacts. You also can add categories to your Journal entries as with any other Outlook item.

SOFTWARE ORIENTATION

Microsoft Outlook's Journal Options

Before you begin working with Outlook's Journal module, you need to be familiar with the variety of options available. From the Backstage, click Notes and Journal and then click the Journal button to see a screen similar to that shown in Figure 13-8.

Figure 13-8

Outlook's Journal Options window

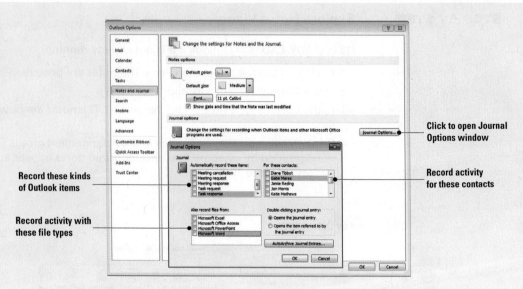

Use this figure as a reference throughout this lesson as well as the rest of this book.

Setting Journal Options

The People pane already does the job of keeping track of all of your e-mails, meetings, and task status reports that you have received from a contact, but the Journal goes one step further: it also can track any Office documents that you have prepared for this contact. In this exercise, you will set the Journal options for Outlook and see how that option appears within the Journal.

STEP BY STEP **Set Journal Options**

GET READY. LAUNCH Outlook if it is not already running.

1. Click the File tab and click Options to open Backstage view.
2. Click Notes and Journal from the list.
3. Click the Journal Options button in the bottom half of the screen. The Journal Options window is displayed, as shown in Figure 13-8.
4. In the *Automatically record these items* field, click the check box in front of E-mail Message.
5. In the *Also record files from* field, click the check box in front of Microsoft Word.

Take Note   The automatic Journal options create a Journal entry every time you open, close, or save a Microsoft Word document associated with a contact. Instead of making it easy to find information about a contact, however, you could instead end up with a lot more data to sort through. Choose automatic Journal options with care.

6. In the *For these contacts* field, click the check box in front of the friend or coworker for whom you have created a contact record.

Take Note   Every time you add a new contact record, you will need to select that new contact in the Journal options.

7. In the *Double-clicking a journal entry* field, click the radio-button in front of the Opens the Journal entry, if necessary.

Troubleshooting The Journal records e-mail messages as they come into the Inbox and the original location of documents added to the Journal. It cannot track when a document or message has been moved or deleted.

<table>
<tr><td>

CERTIFICATION READY   **1.1.5**

How do you set Journal options?

</td></tr>
</table>

<table>
<tr><td>

CERTIFICATION READY   **6.3.1**

How do you automatically record Outlook items in the Journal?

</td></tr>
</table>

@ The *Promotional Flyer* file for this lesson is available on the book companion website or in WileyPLUS.

8. Click OK to close the Journal Options window.

9. Click OK to close the Outlook Options window.

10. Click New Items in the New group and select E-mail message.

11. In the *To* field, key the e-mail address of the friend or coworker that you listed in the Journal Options window. In the *Subject* field, key Sample Journal Message.

12. Click Send.

13. In Microsoft Word, open the *Promotional Flyer* document in the data files for this lesson and save the file with the new name, *Journal Document*. Close the Word documents.

14. Click Normal in the status bar. Click Folder List in the Navigation Pane to open the Folder List.

15. Click Journal in the Folder List. Click the View tab, and click Change View in the Current Views group. Select Timeline from the Current Views gallery. Icons for the Promotional Flyer and Journal Document Word files appear in the Journal Timeline, as shown in Figure 13-9.

Figure 13-9

Outlook's Journal Timeline

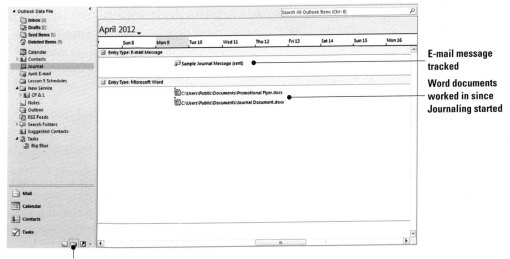

Folder List button

Troubleshooting If your document is not visible on the Journal Timeline, wait. Automatic Journal entries are added to the journal at regular intervals. Your Word document will arrive in the journal within a couple of minutes of your saving the file.

16. Right-click the Journal Document icon. A shortcut menu is displayed, as shown in Figure 13-10.

Figure 13-10

Journal shortcut menu

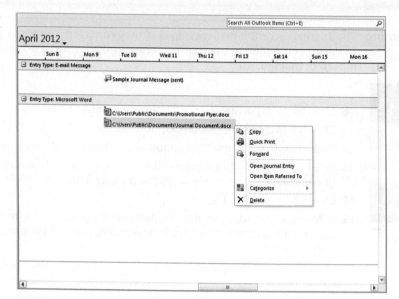

CERTIFICATION
R E A D Y   **6.3.2**

How do you automatically
record files in the Journal?

17. Click Open Item Referred To on the shortcut menu. The Journal Document file opens in Microsoft Word. Close the file and return to Outlook.

PAUSE. LEAVE Outlook open to use in the next exercise.

Connecting Automatic Journal Entries with a Contact

In the previous exercise, you added an automatic Journal entry by saving a Microsoft Word file. The document is present in your Journal, but it is not associated with any particular contact. To take full advantage of the Journal, your documents and Outlook items need to be tied to your contacts. In this exercise, you will connect an automatic Journal entry to an existing contact.

 Ref   For more information about contacts, see Lesson 2.

STEP BY STEP   **Connect Automatic Journal Entries with a Contact**

GET READY. LAUNCH Outlook if it is not already running and complete the previous exercise.

1. If necessary, click Folder List in the Navigation Pane. Click Journal in the Folder list.

2. Double-click on the Journal Document icon to open the journal entry associated with the file. The Subject field is already populated with the file path for the document on your computer.

3. In the Names group, click Address Book and select the contact record for the friend or coworker you identified in the Journal Options window (see Figure 13-11). The contact name appears in the *Filed as* field.

 Troubleshooting   If you have not been working with a friend or coworker for these exercises, choose your own contact record from the Address Book.

Figure 13-11

Associating a Journal entry
with a contact

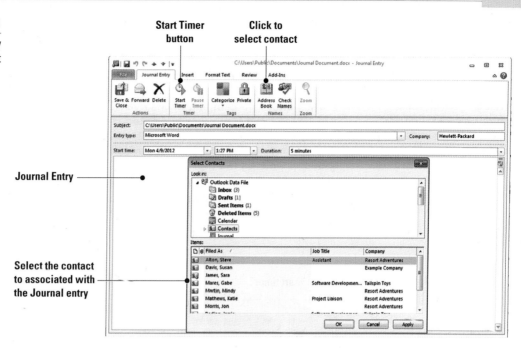

Start Timer
button

Click to
select contact

Journal Entry

Select the contact
to associated with
the Journal entry

How do you edit a Journal
entry?

4. Click Save & Close to close the Journal entry.

PAUSE. LEAVE Outlook open to use in the next exercise.

Creating a Manual Journal Entry

If you are attending a meeting with a client, you will want to record decisions that are made and any actions that you are responsible for completing. Without a computer in the meeting, these records are typically made on paper; then you can add these notes to your meeting notice when you return to your desk. These same actions occur if you are talking to someone over the telephone, but you can record these notes in a Journal entry during the conversation. In addition, Outlook's Journal entries include a timer that can record the amount of time spent on the phone call. In this exercise, you will create a manual Journal entry for a timed phone call and create a second entry to attach a document file.

Take Note   Throughout this chapter you will see information that appears in black text within brackets, such as [Press Enter] or [next Friday's date]. The information contained in the brackets is intended to be directions for you rather than something you actually type word for word. It will instruct you to perform an action or substitute text. Do **not** type the actual text that appears within brackets.

STEP BY STEP   **Create a Manual Journal Entry**

GET READY. LAUNCH Outlook if it is not already running.

1. If necessary, click Folder List in the Navigation Pane. Click Journal in the Folder list.
2. Click Journal Entry on the Ribbon. A blank Journal Entry window is displayed.
3. Click Start Timer in the Timer group on the Ribbon. Outlook starts a timer that will continue recording time until you stop the timer later in this exercise.

Take Note   The Journal timer records time in minutes. If you complete the call in less than 1 minute, the timer will record 0 minutes spent in the phone call.

4. In the Names group, click Address Book and select [the contact record for the friend or coworker you identified in the Journal Options window].

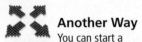

Another Way
You can start a Journal entry by selecting a Contact first. In the Communicate group on the Contact tab, click More and then click Journal Entry. The Journal Entry window will open with the contact already associated.

5. If necessary, in the *Entry type* field, select Phone call from the list. Because other Outlook modules already record tasks, e-mails, and meetings, the Phone call option is the default entry type.

6. In the *Subject* field, key Custom Tour Expectations.

7. In the message area, key: Wants to take a whitewater rafting trip. [Press Enter.] Wants at least one night camping by the river. [Press Enter.] There will be 13 people on the trip. [Press Enter.] Only 2 skilled rafters; the rest have never rafted before. [Press Enter.] They don't like fish. We'll need to bring in other food for dinner. [Press Enter.] They want us to include their logo which we have on file on T-shirts for the whole group to wear on the trip. He will e-mail T-shirt sizes following the call.

8. Click Pause Timer in the Timer group on the Ribbon. Outlook records the amount of time you spent on the phone creating this entry. Compare your Journal Entry window to the one shown in Figure 13-12.

Figure 13-12

Manual Journal Entry for a phone call

Start timer

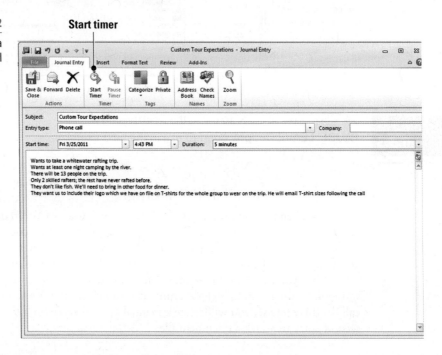

9. Click Save & Close.

10. Click Journal Entry on the Ribbon.

11. In the Subject field, key T-shirt logo for Whitewater Tour.

The *Logo* file for this lesson is available on the book companion website or in WileyPLUS.

12. In the memo area, click the Insert tab and select the Picture button. Navigate to your data files for this lesson and click the *Logo* file and click Insert.

13. On the Journal Entry tab, click Address Book in the Names group and select [the contact record for the friend or coworker you identified in the Journal Options window].

14. In the *Entry type* field, select Document from the list, as shown in Figure 13-13. Document is one the most common entry types typically used for manual entries.

Figure 13-13

Creating Journal entries

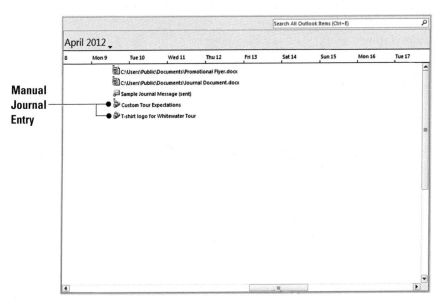

15. Click Save & Close.

PAUSE. LEAVE Outlook open to use in the next exercise.

Changing Journal Views

By default, the Journal folder organizes the contacts activities horizontally in a timeline fashion so that you can see how you spend time during each day. All views can be arranged by date or contacts. You can change that view in several ways, as shown in Table 13-2. In this exercise, you will explore the Journal views to see how the content is presented in each.

Table 13-2

Journal Views

View Name	Description
Timeline	The default view of the Journal, this view shows each entry by date and time it was created.
Entry List	The same entries are presented in a vertical list, grouped by entry time and sorted by time.
Phone Calls	This view shows only the phone call Journal entries.
Last 7 Days	Presented vertically, like the Entry List, this view only shows only items added in the last week.

STEP BY STEP   Changing Journal Views

GET READY. LAUNCH Outlook if it is not already running.

1. If necessary, click Folder List in the Navigation Pane to display the list. Click Journal in the Folder List. The Journal entries are presented in the Timeline view.

2. In the Current View group, click Entry List. The Journal entries are now presented as a vertical list.

3. In the Current View group, click Phone Calls. Only the Custom Tour Expectations Journal entry is visible.

4. In the Current View group, click Last 7 Days. This view looks very much like the Entry List view, but includes only the entries that were recorded over the last week.

5. Click the Arrange By field and select Contact from the dropdown list. The Journal entries are now grouped by contact name, as shown in Figure 13-14.

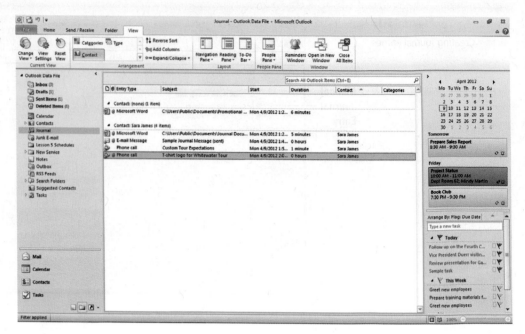

Figure 13-14

Changing the Journal view

CLOSE Outlook.

SKILL SUMMARY

In This Lesson You Learned How To:	Exam Objective	Objective Number
Work with Notes.	Set Notes and Journals options.	1.1.5
	Create a note.	6.2.1
	Categorize notes.	6.2.3
	Print multiple notes.	1.5.6
	Exploring the Notes views.	6.2.2
Work with the Journal.	Set Notes and Journal options.	1.1.5
	Automatically record Outlook items.	6.3.1
	Automatically record files.	6.3.2
	Edit a Journal entry.	6.3.3

Knowledge Assessment

True/False

Circle T if the statement is true or F if the statement is false.

T   F   **1.** Journal entries must be created from the Journal folder.

T   F   **2.** Once you turn on automatic journaling, the selected records are created for all contacts.

T   F   **3.** The Timer function can be used in all Journal entries.

T   F   **4.** Notes cannot be forwarded.

T   F   **5.** The Journal is like an online diary.

T   F   **6.** The default Journal view is called Entry List.

T   F   **7.** Notes must include a due date.

T F **8.** The automatic journaling feature records an entry each time a Word document is moved or deleted.

T F **9.** Notes are created in a separate window.

T F **10.** By default, Outlook's notes appear in the Notes module as yellow sticky notes.

Multiple Choice

Select the best response for the following statements.

1. All Journal views can be arranged by _____.
   a. By Contact
   b. By Date
   c. Both A and B
   d. None of the above

2. To print a single note, _____.
   a. Right-click and choose Quick Print on the shortcut menu.
   b. Right-click and choose Print on the shortcut menu.
   c. Click File and Print.
   d. Open the Backstage and click Print.

3. What kind of information should be stored as a note?
   a. client's e-mail address
   b. project number
   c. weekly status report
   d. ideas for a future project

4. Which of the following cannot be recorded with the automatic journaling options?
   a. E-mails
   b. Task requests
   c. Microsoft Word files
   d. Outlook data file

5. The Journal records e-mail messages in the _____.
   a. Sent Mail
   b. Draft
   c. Inbox
   d. All of the above

6. Double-clicking an automatic Journal entry _____.
   a. opens the related file
   b. opens the related Contact record
   c. opens the Journal entry
   d. starts the timer

7. To take full advantage of the Journal, _____.
   a. the Journal must be visible at all times
   b. automatic journaling must be turned on
   c. the Subject field must be modified
   d. Journal entries must be tied to your contacts

8. The Subject field of a document recorded by the automatic journaling feature is populated with the _____.
   a. file type
   b. document's title
   c. file path
   d. project number

9. The default color for the notes is _____.
   a. Blue
   b. Red
   c. Yellow
   d. Green
10. Which Journal view is the default view?
   a. Timeline
   b. Entry List
   c. Phone Calls
   d. Last 7 Days

Competency Assessment

Project 13-1: Set Notes Options

Clive Gilford just started a new job as a producer for a TV talk show about pets. His job involves thinking up show ideas, making sure experts are available to talk about the topics, and making sure the set and crew are ready for show time. He likes Outlook's Notes feature since he loses those little sticky notes all the time, but he decides to increase the default icon size in the Notes options.

GET READY. LAUNCH Outlook if it is not already running.

1. Click the File tab and click Options to open Backstage view.
2. Click Notes and Journal from the list. The Outlook Options window opens.
3. In the Notes options section, select Large in the *Default size* field.
4. Click OK to close the window.

PAUSE. LEAVE Outlook open for the next project.

Project 13-2: Create a New Note

Since he is always thinking of ideas for future shows, Clive uses Notes to record his ideas.

GET READY. LAUNCH Outlook if it is not already running and be sure to complete the previous exercise.

1. If necessary, click Notes in the Navigation Pane to open the Notes window.
2. Click the New button on the Ribbon. A new blank sticky note appears in the Reading Pane. Below the sticky note is the current date and time.
3. Key Hair loss. [Press Enter.] Do pets experience hair loss? Click the Close button (the small X in the top-right corner of the note).
4. Click New. Key Training. [Press Enter.] Is clicker training better than time-outs? Click the Close button.
5. Click New. Key Celebrities. [Press Enter.] Celebrity pets. Click the Close button.
6. Click New. Key Anxiety. [Press Enter.] Do pets have anxiety? Click the Close.

PAUSE. LEAVE Outlook open for the next project.

Project 13-3: Categorize a Note

Clive decides to categorize the Notes for programs that will require an expert to appear. That will make it easier to find when an expert is booked.

GET READY. LAUNCH Outlook if it is not already running and be sure to complete the previous exercise.

1. If necessary, click Notes in the Navigation Pane to open the Folder List.
2. Click the Hair loss, Training, and Anxiety notes to select them.
3. On the Home tab, click Categorize.
4. Select the All Categories option to create a new category. The Color Categories window is displayed.
5. Click the New button. The Add New Category window is displayed.
6. In the Name field, key Need experts.
7. Click OK to accept Outlook's suggested color and apply the color category to the notes. The notes' icon changes color to match the category.

PAUSE. LEAVE Outlook open for the next project.

Project 13-4: Print a Note

The show's executive producer has a famous veterinarian available to come on the show next month and has asked Clive to bring a list of show ideas that need a veterinarian to appear on camera. Clive prints those notes in Memo Style.

GET READY. LAUNCH Outlook if it is not already running and be sure to complete the previous exercise.

1. Click the Hair loss, Training, and Anxiety notes to select them.
2. Click File and click Print.
3. In the *Settings* field, select Memo Style to print each note on a separate page.
4. Click Print.

PAUSE. LEAVE Outlook open for the next project.

Project 13-5: Create a Manual Journal Entry

It looks like the show on hair loss will be moving forward. Clive will place a phone call to the veterinarian, Dr. Keeler, to find out more about this tragic condition.

GET READY. LAUNCH Outlook if it is not already running and complete the previous exercises.

1. Click Folder List in the Navigation Pane. Click Journal in the Folder List.
2. Create a new Journal Entry.
3. Use the Timer in the Timer group on the Ribbon to record the time spent on this project.
4. Set the Entry type as Phone call. Set the Subject as Hair loss research.

5. In the message area, key:

Dr. Keeler is very emotional.

Has 2 patients (1 dog and 1 cat) currently losing their fur.

Condition affects unknown numbers of animals in the wild.

Only 1 patient's family will agree to be on camera. The other will write a letter, but they are too embarrassed to be on TV.

6. Pause the Timer and save the Journal Entry.

PAUSE. LEAVE Outlook open for the next project.

Project 13-6: Connect a Journal Entry to a Contact

After hanging up the phone, Clive realized that he forgot to associate the Journal entry with Dr. Keeler's Contact record. He needs to fix that right away.

GET READY. LAUNCH Outlook if it is not already running and complete the previous exercises.

1. If necessary, click Folder List in the Navigation Pane. Click Journal in the Folder List.

2. Open the Hair loss research Journal entry.

3. Associate the Journal entry with two friends or coworkers. If you have not been working with a partner, select your own Contact record and one that you created in this course.

4. Click Save & Close to close the Journal entry.

CLOSE Outlook.

INTERNET READY

Outlook's Notes module is designed for those who need to who make occasional unrelated notes. The notes icons look like sticky notes because they act like sticky notes. If you are a student or work in a position that requires you to keep track of more copious notes, you might find that Microsoft OneNote 2010 is better suited to your needs. Research information about Microsoft OneNote 2010 and make a list of 10 ways you can use OneNote.

Benjamin Martin is a corporate travel agent with Margie's Travel. Next month, the executives at Fourth Coffee are meeting in Orlando for a workshop. Ben must arrange travel for 15 executives from three different locations, make hotel reservations, and reserve vehicles for the 15 workshop participants.

Project 1: Organizing a Project with Data Files, Notes and Tasks

Benjamin has just received the Fourth Coffee data file for this project. To make the project more manageable, Ben creates tasks. He plans to pass on part of the work to his assistant Tonya. To track their progress, he is going to use Outlook.

GET READY. LAUNCH Outlook if it is not already running.

@ The *Fourth Coffee. pst* file for this lesson is available on the book companion website or in WileyPLUS.

1. Click the File tab to open the Backstage, click Account Settings and select the Account Settings option. The Account Settings window is displayed.
2. Click the Data Files tab, and click Add. The Create or Open Outlook Data File dialog box is displayed. Navigate to the data files for this lesson and select *Fourth Coffee. pst*.
3. Click OK to return to the Account Settings dialog box and click the Close button to close the Account Settings dialog box as well.
4. If necessary, click the Folder List button to show your folders in the Navigation Pane. Click the expand arrow next to the *Fourth Coffee* data file. Click Project Inbox.
5. Click the Fourth Coffee Meeting message in the message list. You need to create task items to ensure that you don't forget anything.
6. Click New Items in the New group on the Home tab. Select Task from the list.
7. In the *Subject* field, key Fourth Coffee—Hotel Arrangements for 15.
8. In the *Due date* field, key or select the date for next Thursday.
9. In the *Priority* field, select High.
10. Click the Save & Close button in the Actions group on the Ribbon.

Subject	Due Date	Priority
Fourth Coffee—Car Rentals for 15	next Thursday	Normal
Fourth Coffee—Flight Arrangements for 15	next Wednesday	High

11. Repeat the same process to create the following two tasks.
12. Maggie wants you to follow up with her when the arrangements are made, so you decide to create a task from the message. Click Move in the Move group and select Other Folder from the dropdown list. Select the Tasks folder in the *Fourth Coffee* data file. Click OK.
13. In the *Subject* field, select the text and key Follow up with Maggie on the Fourth Coffee arrangements. In the *Due Date* field, select next Friday's date. Click Save & Close.
14. In the Fourth Coffee Meeting e-mail message, Maggie said that she included some notes. So click the Orlando Meeting Notes folder to take a look.
15. Click the Julie is free to work on the Fourth Coffee arrangements note and drag it to the task folder. The task window opens.
16. In the *Subject* field, change the text to read Assign Julie some of the Fourth Coffee Arrangements. Click Save & Close.

LEAVE Outlook open for the next project.

Project 2: Manage a Project with Data Files, Notes, and Tasks

Julie Valdez has offered to help make the arrangements. Assign Julie the task of making reservations from Seattle to Orlando. Record your time spent on the phone call with the car rental agency in a manual Journal entry and mark that task as complete.

GET READY. LAUNCH Outlook if it is not already running.

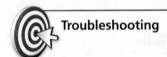 **Troubleshooting** The e-mail addresses provided in these exercises belong to unused domains owned by Microsoft. When you send a message to these addresses, you will receive an error message stating that the message could not be delivered. Delete the error messages when they arrive.

1. If necessary, click the Tasks button in the Navigation Pane to display the Tasks folder.
2. Click the New arrow and click the Task Request option.
3. Click the *To* field and key Rachel@margiestravel.com.
4. In the *Subject* field, key Fourth Coffee - Make five reservations to Orlando from Seattle.
5. In the *Due date* field, key or select [the date for next Friday].
6. In the *Priority* field, select High.
7. In the task note area, key the following list of names. These executives are travelling from Seattle to Orlando.

   Terry Adams

   Kari Hension

   Tamara Johnston

   Paula Nartker

   Benjamin C. Willett

8. Click the Send button to send the task request. Click Yes to add the task to your Tasks folder.
9. Click the Fourth Coffee Journal folder in the Folder list.
10. Click New Journal Entry on the Ribbon.
11. Click Start Timer in the Timer group on the Ribbon.
12. If necessary, in the *Entry type* field, select Phone call from the list.
13. In the *Subject* field, key Fourth Coffee Car Rental.
14. In the message area, key: Rental agent's name is Enrique. [Press Enter.] He only has 12 cars available for the date of the meeting. [Press Enter.] He is calling another agency while I'm on hold. [Press Enter.] The other agency has agreed to provide the remaining 3 cars for the days required. Enrique will handle the rental agreement with the other agency so that Fourth Coffee personnel will all pick up their cars at the same location. [Press Enter.] The confirmation number for all 15 cars is XUT2975K-34.
15. Click Pause Timer in the Timer group on the Ribbon.
16. Click Save & Close.
17. If necessary, click the Tasks button in the Navigation Pane to display the Tasks folder.
18. Double-click the Fourth Coffee—Car Rentals for 15 task and mark it as complete.

LEAVE Outlook open for the next project.

Project 3: Assign Fourth Coffee Items to a Color Category

Ben frequently handles large travel projects for Fourth Coffee. He decided to create a color category that matches the color category used for Fourth Coffee in his physical file cabinets. Ben searches for all Fourth Coffee tasks and prints his status in a Table Style.

GET READY. LAUNCH Outlook if it is not already running.

1. If necessary, click the Tasks button in the Navigation Pane to display the Tasks folder.
2. Click the Change View in the Current View group of the Ribbon and select To-Do List from the dropdown menu.
3. Click one of the Fourth Coffee tasks.
4. Click the Categorize button and click the All Categories option. The Color Categories window is displayed.
5. Click Orange Category in the list of categories. Click the Rename button. The Orange Category text becomes active.
6. Key Fourth Coffee and press Enter.
7. Click OK to rename the category. Close the Color Categories window.
8. Select the remaining Fourth Coffee tasks. Click the Categorize button on the Standard toolbar. Click the Fourth Coffee category in the dropdown list.
9. Click the Orlando Meeting Notes folder and select all of the notes.
10. Click the Categorize button and click the Fourth Coffee category. Close the Color Categories window.
11. Display the Tasks folder.
12. In the Instant Search box, verify that Search All Task Items is selected.
13. In the Instant Search box, key Fourth Coffee.
14. Click the File tab and select Print.
15. Select Table Style and click Print.
16. Make sure that all the Fourth Coffee items are in the Fourth Coffee.pst and close the data file.

CLOSE Outlook.

Microsoft Office Specialist (MOS) Skills for Outlook 2010: Exam 77-884

Matrix Skill	Objective Number	Lesson Number
Managing the Outlook Environment	1	
Apply and manipulate Outlook program options.	1.1	
Set General options.	1.1.1	1
Set Mail options.	1.1.2	3
Set Calendar options.	1.1.3	10
Set Tasks options.	1.1.4	11
Set Notes and Journal options.	1.1.5	13
Set Advanced options.	1.1.6	1
Set Language options.	1.1.7	1
Manipulate item tags.	1.2	
Categorize items.	1.2.1	12
Set flags.	1.2.2	4
Set sensitivity level.	1.2.3	3
Mark items as read or unread.	1.2.4	4
View message properties.	1.2.5	4
Arrange the Content Pane.	1.3	
Show or hide fields in a list view.	1.3.1	1
Change the reading view.	1.3.2	1
Use the Reminders Window.	1.3.3	4
Use the People Pane.	1.3.4	1, 3, 7
Apply search and filter tools.	1.4	
Use built-in Search folders.	1.4.1	3
Print an Outlook item.	1.5	
Print attachments.	1.5.1	2
Print calendars.	1.5.2	10
Print multiple messages.	1.5.3	3
Print multiple contact records.	1.5.4	7
Print tasks.	1.5.5	11
Print multiple notes.	1.5.6	13

Appendix A Microsoft Office Specialist (MOS) Skills for Outlook 2010: Exam 77-884 continued

Matrix Skill	Objective Number	Lesson Number
Creating and Formatting Item Content	2	
Create and send email messages.	2.1	
Specify a message theme.	2.1.1	2
Specify message content format.	2.1.2	2
Show or hide the From and Bcc fields.	2.1.3	2
Set a reminder for message recipients.	2.1.4	3
Specify the sending account.	2.1.5	3
Specify the sent item folder.	2.1.6	3
Configure message delivery options.	2.1.7	3
Configure voting options.	2.1.8	3
Configure tracking options.	2.1.9	3
Send a message to a contact group.	2.1.10	6
Create and manage Quick Steps.	2.2	
Perform Quick Steps.	2.2.1	5
Create Quick Steps.	2.2.2	5
Edit Quick Steps.	2.2.3	5
Delete Quick Steps.	2.2.4	5
Duplicate Quick Steps.	2.2.5	5
Reset Quick Steps to default settings.	2.2.6	5
Create item content.	2.3	
Insert graphical elements.	2.3.1	2
Insert a hyperlink.	2.3.2	2
Format item content.	2.4	
Use formatting tools.	2.4.1	2
Apply styles.	2.4.2	2
Create styles.	2.4.3	2
Create themes.	2.4.4	2
Use Paste Special.	2.4.5	2
Format graphical elements.	2.4.6	2
Attach content to email messages.	2.5	
Attach an Outlook item.	2.5.1	2
Attach external files.	2.5.2	2

Matrix Skill	Objective Number	Lesson Number
Managing Email Messages	3	
Clean up the mailbox.	3.1	
View mailbox size.	3.1.1	4
Save message attachments.	3.1.2	2
Save a message in an external format.	3.1.3	2
Ignore a conversation.	3.1.4	4
Use clean-up tools.	3.1.5	4
Create and manage rules.	3.2	
Create rules.	3.2.1	5
Modify rules.	3.2.2	5
Delete rules.	3.2.3	5
Manage junk mail.	3.3	
Allow a specific message (Not junk).	3.3.1	4
Filter junk mail.	3.3.2	4
Manage automatic message content.	3.4	
Manage signatures.	3.4.1	2, 3, 7
Specify the font.	3.4.2	3
Specify option for replies.	3.4.3	3, 5
Specify options for forwards.	3.4.4	3
Set a default theme for all HTML.	3.4.5	3
Managing Contacts	4	
Create and manipulate contacts.	4.1	
Modify a default business card.	4.1.1	7
Forward a contact.	4.1.2	6, 7
Update a contact in the address book.	4.1.3	6
Create and manipulate contact groups.	4.2	
Create a contact group.	4.2.1	6
Manage contact group membership.	4.2.2	6
Show notes about a contact group.	4.2.3	6
Forward a contact group.	4.2.4	6
Delete a contact group.	4.2.5	6
Send a meeting to a contact group.	4.2.6	9

Matrix Skill	Objective Number	Lesson Number
Managing Calendar Objects	5	
Create and manipulate appointments and events.	5.1	
Set appointment options.	5.1.1	8
Print appointment details.	5.1.2	8
Forward an appointment.	5.1.3	8
Schedule a meeting with a message sender.	5.1.4	9
Create and manipulate meeting requests.	5.2	
Set response options.	5.2.1	9
Update a meeting request.	5.2.2	9
Cancel a meeting or invitation.	5.2.3	9
Propose a new time for a meeting.	5.2.4	9
Manipulate the Calendar pane.	5.3	
Arrange the calendar view.	5.3.1	10
Change the calendar color.	5.3.2	10
Display or hide calendars.	5.3.3	10
Create a calendar group.	5.3.4	10
Working with Tasks, Notes, and Journal Entries	6	
Create and manipulate tasks.	6.1	
Create a task.	6.1.1	11
Manage task details.	6.1.2	11
Send a status report.	6.1.3	11
Mark a task as complete.	6.1.4	11
Move or copy a task to another folder.	6.1.5	11
Assign a task to another Outlook user.	6.1.6	11
Accept or decline a task assignment.	6.1.7	11
Update an assigned task.	6.1.8	11
Use Current view.	6.1.9	11
Create and manipulate notes.	6.2	
Create a note.	6.2.1	13
Change the current view.	6.2.2	13
Categorize notes.	6.2.3	13
Create and manipulate Journal entries.	6.3	
Automatically record Outlook items.	6.3.1	13
Automatically record files.	6.3.2	13
Edit a Journal entry.	6.3.3	13

Component	Requirement
Computer and processor	500 MHz or faster processor.
Memory	256 MB RAM; 512 MB recommended for graphics features, Outlook Instant Search, and certain advanced functionality.[1,2]
Hard disk	3.0 GB available disk space
Display	1024x576 or higher resolution monitor
Operating system	Windows XP (must have SP3) (32-bit), Windows 7, Windows Vista with Service Pack (SP) 1, Windows Server 2003 R2 with MSXML 6.0 (32-bit Office only), Windows Server 2008, or later 32- or 64-bit OS.
Graphics	Graphics hardware acceleration requires a DirectX 9.0c graphics card with 64 MB or more video memory.
Additional Requirements	Certain Microsoft® OneNote® features require Windows® Desktop Search 3.0, Windows Media® Player 9.0, Microsoft® ActiveSync® 4.1, microphone, audio output device, video recording device, TWAIN-compatible digital camera, or scanner; sharing notebooks requires users to be on the same network.
	Certain advanced functionality requires connectivity to Microsoft Exchange Server 2003, Microsoft SharePoint Server 2010, and/or Microsoft SharePoint Foundation 2010.
	Certain features require Windows Search 4.0.
	Send to OneNote Print Driver and Integration with Business Connectivity Services require Microsoft.NET Framework 3.5 and/or Windows XPS features.
	Internet Explorer (IE) 6 or later, 32-bit browser only. IE7 or later required to receive broadcast presentations. Internet functionality requires an Internet connection.
	Multi-Touch features require Windows 7 and a touch-enabled device.
	Certain inking features require Windows XP Tablet PC Edition or later.
	Speech recognition functionality requires a close-talk microphone and audio output device.
	Internet Fax not available on Windows Vista Starter, Windows Vista Home Basic, or Windows Vista Home Premium.
	Information Rights Management features require access to a Windows 2003 Server with SP1 or later running Windows Rights Management Services.
	Certain online functionality requires a Windows LiveTM ID.
Other	Product functionality and graphics may vary based on your system configuration. Some features may require additional or advanced hardware or server connectivity; **www.office.com/products.**

[1] 512 MB of RAM recommended for accessing Outlook data files larger than 1 GB.

[2] GHz processor or faster and 1 GB of RAM or more recommended for OneNote Audio Search. Close-talking microphone required. Audio Search is not available in all languages.

Outlook 2010 Glossary

A

action Determines what happens when a message meets the conditions defined in the Outlook message handling rule.

address book Stores names and e-mail addresses.

appointment A scheduled activity that does not require sending invitations to other people or resources.

archive Store messages in a separate PST file to reduce the number of messages in the folders you use most often.

assign Transfer ownership of a task to another Outlook user.

attachment File sent as part of an e-mail message.

attribute File characteristic such as size, subject, or sender.

AutoArchive Automatic function that archives messages.

AutoComplete Automatically completes the names of the months and days of the week.

AutoPreview Displays the first three lines of every message in the message list.

B

Backstage view The view that opens when you click the File tab; it contains commands for managing files, setting program options, and printing.

banner Text displayed at the top of a day to indicate an event.

busy An activity is scheduled for this time period. You are not available for other activities.

C

Calendar group A group of related calendars that are grouped together for easy viewing.

Calendar Snapshot A picture of your calendar at a specific moment.

Cancel (a meeting) Delete a meeting.

Categorized Mail Standard Search Folder Displays messages with an assigned color category.

character A letter, number, punctuation mark, or symbol.

clip art A single piece of ready-made art, often appearing as a bitmap or a combination of drawn shapes.

color category Color assigned to an Outlook item, providing a way to visually indicate relationships among Outlook items.

compact Process that reduces the size of a data file.

complete Designates that a task is 100 percent finished.

condition Identifies the characteristics used to determine the messages affected by a rule.

contact Collection of information about a person or company.

Contacts folder Electronic organizer that enables you to create, view, and edit contact information.

Contact Group Group of individual contacts saved together as a single contact.

Conversation view A view that enables you to organize every e-mail message you send or receive about the same subject together in one conversation group.

Coordinated Universal Time (UTC) The time standard used by Outlook, which is based on International Atomic Time.

crop To remove a portion of a picture or shape that is not needed. The cropped portion is hidden until you compress the picture.

Custom Search Folder A virtual folder that searches your e-mail folders to locate items that meet the custom search criteria.

D

Deferred Status indicating that a task has been postponed without changing the deadline or the percentage complete.

Deleted Items folder Deleted items are held in this folder until the folder is emptied. Emptying this folder removes the items from your computer.

delivery receipt Tells you that the message has arrived in the recipient's mailbox.

desktop shortcut An icon placed on the Windows desktop that launches an application, opens a folder, or opens a file.

digital ID Contains a private key that remains on your computer and a public key you give to your correspondents to verify that you are the message sender.

distribution list *see Contact Group.*

Drafts folder Outlook messages you write but haven't sent are stored in this folder.

duplicate contact Contact records containing the same information.

E

electronic business card Digital version of paper business cards. They can be sent as attachments, used as signatures, and used to create a contact record.

encryption Scrambles the text so that only the recipient with a key can decipher the message.

event An activity that lasts one or more days.

exception Identifies the characteristics used to exclude messages from being affected by a rule.

F

feature The different components that make up Outlook: Calendar, Contacts, Journal, Mail, Notes, Tasks.

fields Specific bits of information that Outlook stores about an item.

fly-out A menu or pane that opens floating above the main window instead of docked to a fixed place on the screen and which changes the way every other pane appears.

folder Common name for Outlook components.

fonts Typefaces used to display characters, numbers, and symbols in your PowerPoint presentations.

Format Painter A tool to copy character and paragraph formatting.

free No activities are scheduled for this time period. You are available.

G

gallery A dropdown window containing multiple options within a group.

group Ribbon segment containing related commands.

group schedule Displays scheduling information for several people. Requires Microsoft Exchange 2000 or a more recent version of Microsoft Exchange.

H

hyperlink An address that refers to another location, such as a website, a different slide, or an external file.

Hypertext Markup Language (HTML) Formatting language that enables you to format text and insert items such as horizontal lines, pictures, and animated graphics for viewing on the World Wide Web (web).

I

iCalendar (.ics) An updatable calendar format that is interchangeable between most calendar and e-mail applications, making it a versatile tool.

Internet Calendar Subscription A calendar format that can be downloaded and updated.

import Bring information into a file from an external source.

In Progress Status indicating that work on the task has started.

Inbox folder By default, new messages are placed in this folder when they arrive.

InfoBar Banner containing information added automatically at the top of a message.

Information Rights Management (IRM) An Outlook feature that allows you to control how the recipient can use a message.

Instant Search Outlook's enhanced search tool that includes two features that you can use to filter through the results: Search Suggestions List and the Search Contextual tab.

item A record stored in Outlook.

J

Journal An online diary of all activities associated with one of your Contacts.

Junk E-Mail folder Messages identified as spam are placed in this folder when they arrive.

L

Large Mail A standard Search Folder that displays messages larger than 100 kilobytes.

M

MailTips Messages that Outlook provides you in the InfoBar to alert you when you might be in danger of making an e-mail mistake.

mandatory attendee A person who must attend a meeting.

meeting A scheduled activity that requires sending invitations to other people or resources.

meeting organizer The person who creates the meeting and sends meeting invitations.

meeting request Outlook item that creates a meeting and invites attendees.

message header Text automatically added at the top of a message. The message header contains the sender's e-mail address, the names of the servers used to send and transfer the message, the subject, the date, and other basic information about the message.

Microsoft Office Button Accesses the commands to open, save, print, and finish a document.

Microsoft Outlook Calendar Sharing Service A service set up by Microsoft that allows you to share calendars with other Outlook users.

N

Navigation Pane Provides access to Outlook components such as Contacts and the Calendar folder.

Notes An Outlook feature that enables you to keep important information that may not be related to a particular contact or project.

O

occurrence A single meeting in a series of recurring meetings.

optional attendee A person who should attend the meeting but whose presence is not required.

out of office An automatic reply notification that you are not in the office during this time period.

Outbox folder Outgoing messages are held in this folder until you are connected to the Internet. When an Internet connection is detected, the message is sent.

Outlook Data file File containing stored Outlook data. It is identified by the .pst extension.

overlay mode Displays calendars on top of each other.

overlay stack Several calendars are displayed on top of each other.

owner The only Outlook user who can modify a task.

P

People Pane Displays all the e-mails, meetings, and attachments related to the selected person.

plain text Text without any formatting.

private Feature that protects the details of an activity from a casual observer, but does not ensure privacy.

Q

Quick Access Toolbar Toolbar that can be customized to contain commands from any tab.

Quick Steps Customizable shortcuts that you can use to perform several functions at the same time.

Quick Style Built-in formatting for text, graphics, SmartArt diagrams, charts, WordArt, pictures, tables, and shapes.

R

read receipt Tells you that the message has been opened in the recipient's mailbox.

Reading Pane Displays the text of a selected e-mail message.

Really Simple Syndication (RSS) A method that allows you to subscribe to content from a variety of websites offering the service.

recurring appointment An appointment that occurs at regular intervals.

recurring meeting A meeting that occurs at regular intervals.

recurring task A task that must be completed at regular intervals.

resource An item or a location that can be invited to a meeting.

restore Make an item available for use. For example, moving an item out of the Deleted Items folder restores it for use.

retention rules Guidelines that determine the length of time correspondence must be kept.

Ribbon Contains commands organized into groups that are located on tabs.

Rich Text Format (RTF) Formatting system that uses tags to format text.

rule Defines an action that happens automatically when messages are received or sent.

S

ScreenTip Brief description of an item's purpose displayed when the mouse hovers on the item.

Search Folder A virtual folder that searches your e-mail folders to locate items meeting the saved search criteria.

secondary address book The address book for an additional Contacts folder.

sensitivity Suggests how the recipient should treat the message and the type of information in the message. Sensitivity settings include normal, personal, private, and confidential.

Sent Items folder Items are automatically moved to this folder after they have been sent.

side-by-side mode Displays two or more calendars next to each other in the Calendar folder.

signature Text or images that may be automatically placed at the end of outgoing messages.

SmartArt graphic A visual representation of information and ideas that can be used with other images and decorative text.

sort Arrange items in a sequence based on specific criteria.

spam Unsolicited e-mail sent to many e-mail accounts.

split A split occurs when more than one person responds to a message.

spoofing Providing false information in a message header.

style A set of formatting attributes that users can apply to a cell or range of cells more easily than setting each attribute individually.

subject Topic of a message.

T

task An Outlook item that can be tracked from creation to completion.

task request Assigns a task to another user.

Tasks folder Store tasks in this folder.

template An existing rule provided by Outlook that contains specific pieces that can be customized to create new rules.

tentative An activity is scheduled for this time period, but the activity might not occur. You might be available for other activities.

theme A set of formatting choices that include colors, fonts (including heading and body text fonts), and theme effects (including lines and fill effects).

time zone A geographic area using the same standard time.

To Do Bar New feature that summarizes information about appointments and tasks.

to-do item Any Outlook item flagged for follow-up.

U

Unread Mail Standard Search Folder that displays unread messages.

V

view A specific layout for viewing details about the items in an Outlook feature.

virtual folder A folder that does not contain the actual items it displays.

W

Wizard A feature that guides you through steps for completing a process in Microsoft Office applications.

work week The hours or days you work in a calendar week.

Credits

Index